GREAT POWERS, GRAND STRATEGIES

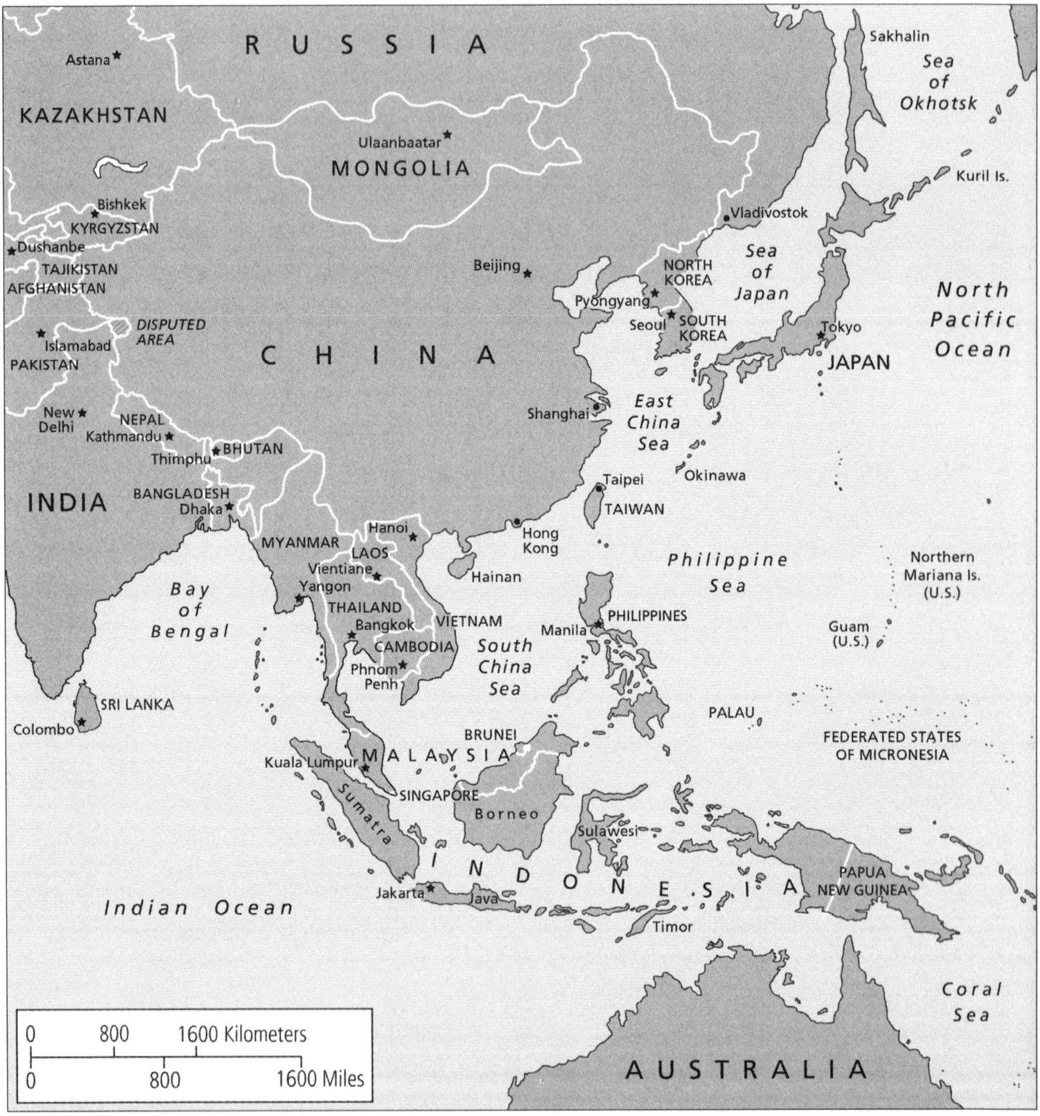
RUSSIA
Astana
KAZAKHSTAN
Ulaanbaatar
MONGOLIA
Sakhalin
Sea of Okhotsk
Kuril Is.
Bishkek
KYRGYZSTAN
Dushanbe
TAJIKISTAN
AFGHANISTAN
Vladivostok
Sea of Japan
Beijing
NORTH KOREA
Pyongyang
SOUTH KOREA
Seoul
Tokyo
JAPAN
North Pacific Ocean
DISPUTED AREA
Islamabad
PAKISTAN
CHINA
New Delhi
NEPAL
Kathmandu
Thimphu
BHUTAN
Shanghai
East China Sea
Okinawa
Taipei
TAIWAN
INDIA
BANGLADESH
Dhaka
MYANMAR
Hanoi
LAOS
Vientiane
Yangon
Hong Kong
Hainan
Philippine Sea
Northern Mariana Is. (U.S.)
Bay of Bengal
THAILAND
Bangkok
VIETNAM
CAMBODIA
Phnom Penh
South China Sea
Manila
PHILIPPINES
Guam (U.S.)
SRI LANKA
Colombo
PALAU
BRUNEI
MALAYSIA
Kuala Lumpur
SINGAPORE
Borneo
Sumatra
Sulawesi
FEDERATED STATES OF MICRONESIA
INDONESIA
Jakarta
Java
Timor
PAPUA NEW GUINEA
Indian Ocean
Coral Sea
AUSTRALIA
0 800 1600 Kilometers
0 800 1600 Miles

GREAT POWERS, GRAND STRATEGIES

The New Game in the South China Sea

Edited by **ANDERS CORR**

NAVAL INSTITUTE PRESS
Annapolis, Maryland

This book was made possible through the dedication of the U.S. Naval Academy Class of 1945.

Naval Institute Press
291 Wood Road
Annapolis, MD 21402

© 2018 by Anders Corr
All rights reserved. No part of this book may be reproduced or utilized in any form or by any means, electronic or mechanical, including photocopying and recording, or by any information storage and retrieval system, without permission in writing from the publisher.

Library of Congress Cataloging-in-Publication Data
Names: Corr, Anders, editor of compilation.
Title: Great powers, grand strategies : the new game in the South China Sea / edited by Anders Corr.
Other titles: New game in the South China Sea
Description: Annapolis, Maryland : Naval Institute Press, 2018. | Includes bibliographical references and index. |
Identifiers: LCCN 2017038147 (print) | LCCN 2017051635 (ebook) | ISBN 9781682472361 (epub) | ISBN 9781682472361 (epdf) | ISBN 9781682472361 (mobi) | ISBN 9781682472354 (hardback) | ISBN 9781682472361 (ebook)
Subjects: LCSH: South China Sea—Strategic aspects. | South China Sea Region—History—21st century. | Sea-power—China. | Great powers—History—21st century. | Geopolitics. | Strategy. | BISAC: HISTORY / Military / Naval. | POLITICAL SCIENCE / International Relations / General.
Classification: LCC VA630 (ebook) | LCC VA630 .G74 2018 (print) | DDC 355/.033059—dc23
LC record available at https://lccn.loc.gov/2017038147

♾ Print editions meet the requirements of ANSI/NISO z39.48-1992 (Permanence of Paper). Printed in the United States of America.

26 25 24 23 22 21 20 19 18   9 8 7 6 5 4 3 2 1
First printing

Contents

List of Illustrations ... vii

Introduction ... 1
Anders Corr

1 Why China Built Its New Islands:
From Abstract Claim to Concrete Assets ... 41
Bill Hayton

2 Old Game Plan, New Game: China's Grand
Strategy in the South China Sea ... 74
Ian Forsyth

3 China's Maritime Sovereignty Campaign: Scarborough Shoal,
the "New Spratly Islands," and Beyond ... 106
James E. Fanell

4 ASEAN, Grand Strategy, and the South China Sea:
Between China and the United States ... 122
Leszek Buszynski

5 The Evolution of U.S. Strategy in the South China Sea:
Tacking with Regional Strategic Winds ... 147
Sean R. Liedman

6	U.S. Rebalancing Strategy and Disputes in the South China Sea: A Legacy for America's Pacific Century	174
	Tongfi Kim	
7	Japan's Grand Strategy in the South China Sea: Principled Pragmatism	199
	Takashi Inoguchi and Ankit Panda	
8	India's "Grand Strategy" and the South China Sea: New Delhi's Evolving Response to Chinese Expansionism	224
	Gordon G. Chang	
9	Paradoxes Abounding: Russia and the South China Sea Issue	248
	Stephen Blank	
10	The European Union: Setting a New Course for the South China Sea	273
	Peter M. Solomon	
	Conclusion	289
	Bernard D. Cole	
	Contributor Biographies	307
	Index	313

Illustrations

TABLE I-1	Military Expenditures and Gross Domestic Product	7
TABLE 1-1	Chinese-Occupied Features in the Spratly Islands	51
TABLE 10-1	The European Union's Trade with Its Top Ten East Asian and Southeast Asian Trade Partners by Imports and Exports (2016)	275

Introduction

Anders Corr[1]

The South China Sea is disputed through international law by seven claimant countries: the People's Republic of China (China), the Republic of China (Taiwan), Vietnam, the Philippines, Malaysia, Brunei, and Indonesia.[2] These countries watch each other's tactical and strategic choices, especially in the military, economic, diplomatic, and legal realms. Alliance decisions with great powers that operate in Southeast Asia often have more effect on the political dynamics of the South China Sea conflict than a country's own military and economic capacity. For this reason, major powers globally take on great significance for what appears at first glance to be a purely local conflict. The nexus of major power grand strategies in the South China Sea is of interest to readers globally, especially among claimant countries. All interested parties try to assess and predict major power strategies and choices so as to optimize their own strategic choices in turn.

The South China Sea is simultaneously symbolic to broad segments of each claimant country's citizens; home to potentially vast supplies of critical energy, fishing, and other natural resources; strategically sensitive for military forces, intelligence gathering, and coastal defense; a major transit area for international trade and communications; and a source of developing international case law. However, facts on the ground in the South China Sea are a function not just or even primarily of law, but rather of power. This volume distinguishes itself from the many books that primarily examine regional country legal claims and actions in the South China Sea. We examine the impact and grand strategies of major global powers in the conflict. For the purposes of this study, we define grand strategy as *a set of plans to achieve a set of important state goals through the utilization of all its resources, including economic, diplomatic, and military means and interactions.*[3]

Major powers with influence on the South China Sea dispute, for the purposes of this volume, are the top five military spenders that operate significant military forces in the region. The European Union, which is one of the top two global economies and some of whose member states operate militarily in the South China Sea, and the Association of Southeast Asian Nations (ASEAN), which is diplomatically influential in Asia, are also included. The grand strategies of major powers and international organizations included in this volume have as much, or more, joint impact on the evolution of the South China Sea conflict than does any other factor. Yet no single volume to date has viewed the South China Sea conflict through this optic. In this volume, the authors demonstrate how major power struggle is the crux of the conflict and how claimant country interests are subordinated to the grand strategies of great powers, including China. We use the phrase South China Sea *conflict* rather than *dispute* because it is highly militarized and has already resulted in scores if not hundreds of deaths. A widening of the conflict, which all parties hope to avoid, could lead to war.

As much as we would like to see the Philippines' United Nations Convention on the Law of the Sea (UNCLOS) arbitration award more thoroughly determine the outcome of the conflict, China simply ignored the 2016 decision and is relying instead on its own military maneuvers, economic influence, and threatening diplomacy. China's grand strategy in the South China Sea is redolent of what former U.S. secretary of defense Ashton Carter called a "return to great power . . . competition . . . in the Asia-Pacific."[4] China's coordinated, measured, and highly strategic belligerency at the expense of international law forces the Philippines—and the rest of the world—to look first to China and the United States, but also to other major powers and their strategies in the South China Sea, to navigate the likely evolution of the conflict. By ignoring international law, China has raised the stakes above what any single claimant country can afford and has thrown the dispute into the ring of major power diplomacy, economic statecraft, and military brinkmanship. While international law is critical to the outcome of the South China Sea conflict, other authors have written much on the subject. Beijing's refusal to abide by the law requires a volume that focuses on China's choice of strategic endeavors in the South China Sea conflict (its military, diplomatic, and economic actions and influence) and how those tools interact with like endeavors by other major powers.

That the volume focuses on major powers does not mean that claimant countries such as Vietnam and the Philippines are left out. The Philippines is central to the conflict but is woven into the chapters, rather than having a chapter of its own. The same goes for Vietnam, Taiwan, and other claimant states. Given that South China Sea claimant countries that are members of ASEAN make efforts to resolve the conflict through changing major power grand strategies, we expect readers from those countries to welcome the focus of this volume.

This book is the first to focus on major power grand strategies, including economic, diplomatic, and military strategies, and their international interrelationships. The purpose of this focus is to explore the global nature of the South China Sea conflict and how global actors are interacting, contributing to the solution, and generating conflict. It draws on experts with regional knowledge of the major powers, as well as substantive and international experts to explicate interactions. Not all authors agree on all points, but all are eminently qualified and afforded the space to make their case.

THE SOUTH CHINA SEA IN GLOBAL PERSPECTIVE

China's dramatic economic growth over the last three decades was not followed by political liberalization, as some theories from the late 1950s had predicted.[5] Rather, realist scholarship better explains Chinese leadership's turn toward deepening control internally, expansion of the scope of that control externally, territorial expansion in Asia, overt criticism of democratic forms of government, use of its economic influence to deepen and widen its alliances, and attempts to revise institutions of global governance to reflect its growing power.

While China's increased military spending is largely consistent with a rise in its gross domestic product (GDP), in the context of its diplomatic, economic, and military coordination against the United States and attempts to revise post–World War II international organizations, China's aggression in the South China Sea is consistent with its global activity and that of its allies Russia, Iran, and North Korea. As a percentage of GDP, China's military spending has hovered around 2 percent, a global norm and the minimum for North Atlantic Treaty Organization members. As a point of comparison, U.S. military spending, both as a percentage of GDP and in total, far outstrips that of China. But the United States spends much more on personnel and benefits, and it is expected by allies and its own electorate to simultaneously provide security from Russia in Europe, China in Asia, and terrorists worldwide. This stretches U.S. defense dollars globally such that those dollars devoted to Asia are outstripped by China, especially when considering differences in purchasing power.

Unlike China, the United States and allies seek to support democratization and human rights globally. Granted, the United States sometimes fails spectacularly in the attempt (for example, in Vietnam, Afghanistan, and Iraq). At other times, though, the United States succeeded in democratizing autocratic regimes, such as in post–World War II Germany and Japan.

U.S. defense spending is further stretched by Asian and European allies that only occasionally meet the 2 percent defense spending threshold. Through free-riding and by taking advantage of moral hazard, European and Asian allies can effectively shunt the majority of the necessary defense spending to the United States. Consider worst-case scenarios. Were Russia to capture Europe or China to capture Japan, for example, it would be a disaster for these regions. Their economies and intellectual capital could then be used against the United States, making China and Russia much stronger adversaries than they are today. China and Russia are essentially competing for the human, intellectual, and financial capital of more peaceful countries worldwide. I am not being polemical or nationalist when I say that while China and Russia seek to exploit these countries through neomercantilist trade and resource extraction with the aid of economic influence and corruption, the United States seeks to remake the world in its liberal democratic image and extend the influence of liberal international law. The facts bear me out.

U.S. defense dollars are also stretched by asymmetric threats that could some day be enabled by Russia, China, or other U.S. adversaries. Were just three major U.S. cities, and thereby the nation's economy, to be decimated by multiple nuclear terror events, for example, the United States would have to pull back from its globally forward-deployed position. China and Russia would have much greater operational latitude in Asia and Europe respectively, which they could ultimately use against the U.S. homeland. Thus, an effective U.S. defense of its own territory requires deterrence on three fronts: Asia, Europe, and globally against terrorism. Meanwhile, China, Russia, Iran, and North Korea have reason to support each other's military development, territorial expansion, and endeavors in Asia and Europe. Their territorial goals are largely mutually exclusive and symbiotic. Indeed, there is extensive evidence of economic, diplomatic, and military cooperation between these autocratic regimes.

The United States is disadvantaged on multiple fronts when facing China and Russia. It must divide its forces for effective defense, contend with a public that is war weary after more than a quarter-century of conflict in Iraq and Afghanistan, and spend on costly asymmetric defense of the homeland against terrorists.

Thus, the forward-deployment advantage and the U.S. spending premia against China, Russia, and terrorists severally, and thought of in isolation as offensive, are illusory given the global and interlinked nature of U.S. security provision, alliance commitments, and territorial defense. What appears to some analysts as an offensive and large U.S. military force forward deployed to the South and East China Seas against China is in fact part of a global system of defense of not only the United States but also its allies and values, including international law, democracy, and human rights. To criticize the United States as offensive without this geographic and normative context is to ignore the global picture of which principles the United States is defending and where it is doing so.

Likewise, to view China's actions in the South China Sea as defensive against U.S. forward deployment is to ignore China's similar offensive territorial actions in the East China Sea and Himalayan region of India, its suppression of democracy, human rights, and international law in Asia and abroad (including within China, Hong Kong, and Taiwan), and its campaign to remake global governance to its own advantage rather than on principles of democracy. China's South China Sea acts are most recognizable as offensive when viewed in this global context.

While China has offensive push factors that lead it to grow its military, it also has defensive and opportunistic pull factors. Three historic events preceded China's increases in military expenditure starting in the 1990s and likely contributed to the decision to do so. First, the 1989 Tiananmen Square massacre led to a U.S. arms embargo that convinced many in China of the need for improved indigenous design, development, and production capabilities for military equipment.

Second, the Philippine senate voted to evict the United States from military bases adjacent to the South China Sea in 1991. Military, oil, fishing, and other interest groups in China likely saw this as an opportunity to extend their own roles in promoting Chinese influence and control over South China Sea resources. This strategy has largely failed to extract resources from Vietnamese claims in the South China Sea. However, it may have intimidated the Philippines, Malaysia, and Brunei into offering below-market rates on oil and gas to China in exchange for China allowing oil and gas development within those countries' respective parts of the "U-shaped line."

China reportedly has demanded joint development and sovereignty agreements, or what Xi Jinping calls a "win-win solution," from claimant countries in the South China Sea region prior to allowing oil and gas development. For example, if development by Vietnam is being interfered with but development by Malaysia and Brunei is not, it stands to reason that the latter countries may have agreed to such deals, as was implied by two well-placed sources. Malaysia and

Brunei may have done this privately to maintain the outward unity of ASEAN on the South China Sea issue. China's demand in such joint development could be as much as 50 percent or more of resource royalties from petroleum output.[6]

Third, the ease with which the U.S. military deposed the Saddam Hussein regime in Iraq in 1991 alarmed the Chinese military. China needed a bigger and more modern military force, some military interests argued, to defend against a potential invasion by the United States and its allies in Asia.

It is clear that China started to substantially expand its previously flat defense budget in the early 1990s. As the United States mired itself in wars in the Middle East and Central Asia in the mid-1990s and after the September 11, 2001, attacks, China doubled down. Since the late 1990s, China has increased its real military expenditure by more than 10 percent every year except one.[7] Overall since 1997, China's defense budget has grown by more than 600 percent, positioning the country as the world's second-largest defense spender in 2016, trailing only the United States.[8] China vastly exceeds the military spending of its neighbors, as table 1 shows. The Chinese military budget has steadily outstripped those of other countries in the region over the last two decades and is likely to continue increasing until China's leadership takes a less expansionist view of international relations. Between 2007 and 2016, China's inflation-adjusted military budget increased by an annual average of 8.5 percent.[9]

Chinese military spending and activity are driving the region's arms race. Together with spending and actions by Russia, the two countries are sustaining if not escalating military spending globally, to the detriment of development funding and innovation in peaceful technologies and with great potential risk of widening and deepening military conflict.

Note that accurate statistics on Chinese defense spending are difficult to find and vary greatly. China's self-reported military budget for 2015 was $144 billion, the U.S. Department of Defense estimated it to exceed $180 billion, and the Stockholm International Peace Research Institute (SIPRI) estimated it at $215 billion.[10] The Department of Defense report notes that lack of transparency makes judging the actual military expenditure difficult, and the official numbers do not include important categories such as purchases of foreign weapons[11] and equipment.[12] Given differences in relative purchasing power, even the SIPRI figure could understate Chinese defense spending, which, when adjusted for purchasing power, could be as high as $374 billion. One billion dollars goes about 1.74 times further in China than in the United States. China's lack of transparency also applies to the technological quality of China's weaponry, which experts expect is less than what China projects in the media.[13]

TABLE I-1. MILITARY EXPENDITURES AND GROSS DOMESTIC PRODUCT

Country	Total Military Spending 2016 ($ millions)	Gross Domestic Product 2015 ($ billions)	Military Spending as Percent of Gross Domestic Product 2016
United States	611,186	17,947	3.3
China	215,176	10,866	1.9
Russia	69,245	1,326	5.3
India	55,923	2,073	2.5
Japan	46,126	4,123	1
South Korea	36,777	1,378	2.7
Australia	24,617	1,340	2.0
Taiwan	9,924	524	1.9
Indonesia	8,183	862	0.9
Vietnam	5,017	194	2.4
The Philippines	3,899	292	1.3
Brunei	403	15	3.8

Notes: Spending is a Stockholm International Peace Research Institute (SIPRI) estimate in 2016 U.S. dollars. Gross domestic product (GDP) is sourced from the World Bank. Chinese and Russian relative defense spending is significantly higher than these figures imply, given differences in purchasing power.

Source: Data for total military spending and military spending as a percent of GDP is from the SIPRI Military Expenditure Database, http://www.sipri.org/research/armaments/milex/milex_database. Data for each country's GDP came from the World Bank, "GDP (current US$)," http://data.worldbank.org/indicator/NY.GDP.MKTP.CD, with the exception of Taiwan, which came from the Central Intelligence Agency, "The World Factbook: East & Southeast Asia: Taiwan," https://www.cia.gov/library/publications/the-world-factbook/geos/tw.html.

Increased defense spending and military modernization fuel a number of Chinese goals, including to 1) increase China's hard power to complement its growing economic and diplomatic influence and thereby solidify its standing as a global power and its ability to reform institutions of global governance; 2) maintain pressure on Taiwan to not declare independence and eventually rejoin the mainland; 3) develop expeditionary military capabilities (for example, anti-piracy operations in Africa) to support China's growing global trade, investment, and security interests; 4) expand control of sea lines of communication (SLOCs), hydrocarbon resources, and fishing in the South and East China Seas; 5) increase naval power projection, littoral security, and territorial claims; and 6) pressure U.S. military forces in the region to withdraw.[14]

By 2025, China's rapidly developing military will make a preemptive but limited war by the United States against China prohibitively costly. This will decrease U.S. capacity to protect friends and allies in Asia and wherever else China might decide to intervene abroad.[15] China will at that point be on a military par with the United States and could use its forces with impunity against relatively weak militaries or those with weak alliances, such as the Philippines and Vietnam.

CONFLICTED ALLIANCES: THE UNITED STATES IN ASIA, 1954 TO PRESENT

In 1954, the United States and allied nations in Asia formed the multilateral Southeast Asia Treaty Organization. However, it failed, in part due to lack of regional support for the United States and France in the Vietnam War. The lack of such an organization is one reason why China is as successful as it is in influencing and threatening its neighbors. Asian countries are insufficiently assured of U.S. defense and thereby are incentivized to pursue hedging strategies with China.

As an alternative, the United States formed a network of bilateral alliances in East Asia. One purpose of this "hub-and-spoke" approach was to restrain the more belligerent anticommunist allies and prevent them from dragging the United States into another war.[16] The United States directed this policy toward Japan, South Korea, and Taiwan, where bilateral alliances allowed the United States to more directly discourage partners from using military action to domestically justify their regimes.[17]

Japan is one of the United States' closest allies in the region. The two countries have regularly cooperated in a number of economic and security areas, which has important ramifications for the South China Sea conflict. The United States maintains a forward-deployed force of nearly 50,000 troops in Japan.[18] Although

Japan shelters under the U.S. nuclear umbrella that contributes to Japan's security through extended deterrence, the alliance has transformed as Japan takes more military initiative abroad.[19]

The Japan Self-Defense Forces carried out their first mission abroad by providing noncombat support to U.S.-led efforts in Iraq and Afghanistan.[20] In July 2014, the Japanese government announced a new interpretation of its constitution to allow active contribution of forces to collective self-defense under certain conditions, which the parliament's vote in September 2015 legalized.[21] The two countries announced the revision of the Mutual Defense Guidelines in April 2015, which seek to provide a framework for continued cooperation in new areas of cybersecurity, ballistic missile defense, and the protection of Japan's outlying islands and sea lanes.[22]

The U.S.-Japan alliance has found a new importance in countering China's actions in the South China Sea. Although U.S. policy historically had been not to take positions on territorial disputes, the 1960 U.S.-Japan Security Treaty states in Article 5 that the United States must protect the territories controlled by Japan. China, which also claims the Senkaku Islands, has attempted to test this alliance by increasing naval patrols nearby to discredit Japan's administrative control over them. In response, the U.S. Congress added a resolution to the Fiscal Year 2013 National Defense Authorization Act that clarified that a third party's unilateral action would not change the U.S. recognition of Japan's control over the Senkakus.[23]

South Korea is a major regional power that could have been included in this volume had there been space. Although it does not have any territorial claims in the South China Sea, its close security partnership with the United States, significant military, and oscillating security competition with China could lead it to have some influence on the outcome of the South China Sea dispute. Because China is its largest trade partner and leverages that trade for diplomatic purposes, South Korea will try to avoid tensions over the South China Sea, which concerns it less than the outcome of the North Korea dispute.[24] China also seeks to emphasize tensions between South Korea and Japan over historical grievances and competing claims to the Liancourt rocks (Dokdo or Takeshima Islands).[25] This complicates the U.S. position as an ally to both countries. The more South Korea integrates into the global security provided by the United States, the more it will weigh on the South China Sea issue, even indirectly in favor of claimants. At the very least, increased South Korean integration and defense spending could free U.S. troops for deployment to the South China Sea and environs.

Taiwan's claim in the South China Sea is identical to that of China and is based on the same U-shaped line published in 1936 by the nationalist cartographer Bai Meichu.[26] Yet Taiwan's relatively small military, hedging between China and the United States, and prioritization of at least de facto independence from China have led it to take a relatively quiescent approach to its claim. Arguably more important to Taiwan is freedom of navigation (FoN) in the South China Sea. FoN is critical to Taiwan's navy, merchant marine, and allied navies, all of which need SLOCs to access the island.

Since the Mutual Defense Treaty between the United States and Taiwan ended in 1979, the United States has maintained what it calls an unofficial relationship with Taiwan, as enshrined in the Taiwan Relations Act of 1979. This act calls for the peaceful settlement of the Taiwan issue and explains that nonpeaceful means are considered "of grave concern" and "a threat" to peace and security.[27] The Taiwan Relations Act also allows the United States to sell arms to Taiwan to ensure a "sufficient self-defense capability."[28] Since signing the act, the United States has continued to take a special interest in Taiwan's security vis-à-vis Beijing, such as deploying two aircraft carrier battle groups from 1995 to 1996 during the Taiwan Strait crisis.[29] Access to the Taiwan Strait depends upon FoN in the South China Sea—one key reason the United States refuses to recognize the sovereignty claims of China's U-shaped line.[30]

Taiwan's territorial claims have put the United States in an awkward position in relation to its other allies in the region. Taiwan has competing claims with Japan over the Senkaku Islands, which the U.S. Congress has stated are under the administration of Japan.[31] Provocations by Taiwan concerning these islands, including a 2013 incident where Taiwan sent four coast guard ships to escort a ship in the area, have not helped. This dispute is particularly troubling to the United States, since the Treaty of Mutual Cooperation with Japan obligates the United States to protect land under Japanese administration.[32] Taiwan has also had diplomatic issues and heightened military tensions with another U.S. regional ally, the Philippines, over an incident related to the death of two Taiwanese fishermen in the Luzon Strait.[33] In 2015, Taiwan's president began using language redolent of China's Xi Jinping—demanding joint development, win-win solutions, and an end to sovereignty disputes. Xi Jinping rejected the proposal, likely because it was not his own lead. Tension remains between China and Taiwan over their identical claim and verbiage, but Taiwan's legal and public relations efforts do sometimes tangentially support the identical claims of China.[34]

The United States also has a long-standing alliance with the Philippines.[35] Lawyers can argue over whether the 1951 Mutual Defense Treaty technically requires the United States to defend features such as Mischief Reef or Scarborough Shoal, occupied by China in 1995 and 2012 respectively, and within the Philippines' exclusive economic zone (EEZ) but outside the territorial sea. What is certain is that if any of the Philippines' main islands or its forces at sea are attacked, the treaty requires the United States to come to the defense of its ally. Regardless of the technicalities, though, it is in U.S. interests to take an expansive view of the treaty language in order to strengthen its reputation as a strong and resolute ally.[36]

The Philippines, perhaps due to Chinese economic influence, has wavered over welcoming U.S. troops on its territory.[37] In 1991, the Philippines initiated the closure of U.S. military bases in its territories, including the Subic Naval Base and Clark Air Force Base. After China's Mischief Reef occupation in 1995, however, the United States and the Philippines signed a number of agreements that reintroduced and increased the U.S. military presence there, including using Philippine ports and airports as a supply base for other military operations and hosting U.S. Marines to provide support to counterterrorism activities.[38] The Philippines again sought an increased U.S. military presence starting around 2005. In 2014, the two countries signed the Enhanced Defense Cooperation Agreement. Although not a formal treaty, this framework allows U.S. forces to utilize five bases in the Philippines on a more permanent but "rotating" basis.[39]

The Philippines sought to increase the U.S. military presence due to China's increasingly hostile activities in the South China Sea. This includes the Chinese-Philippines disagreement over control of the Spratly Islands and Scarborough Shoal.[40] Although relations between China and the Philippines started to improve under President Gloria Macapagal-Arroyo due to new economic agreements and China's alleged corruption of the president's family, disputes in the South China Sea, such as the Scarborough Shoal standoff and then occupation by China in 2012, significantly increased the importance of the U.S.-Philippine alliance.[41] Although the formal U.S. policy is to remain neutral in this territorial dispute, the Barack Obama administration did highlight its commitment to its resolution through international law, the importance of land features to claims of maritime sovereignty, and its "ironclad" commitment to the Mutual Defense Treaty to assist the Philippines in case its armed forces are attacked.[42] As a result, the United States and Japan are providing military assistance and training to help the Philippines create a stronger external military capacity. The Philippines has also purchased decommissioned U.S. ships, many of them Coast Guard vessels, to strengthen its navy.[43]

Rodrigo Duterte was elected president of the Philippines in 2016. He has implied, in words and actions, that he is considering the option of not challenging Chinese military control of Scarborough Shoal and features in the Spratly Islands, at least for a time, in exchange for joint development of maritime oil fields such as Reed Bank, Philippine fishing access to Scarborough Shoal, and infrastructure development assistance, including light rail. If China continues to partially block Philippine fishermen's access to the shoal and does not provide infrastructure assistance, it is unclear what the Philippines could do about China's occupation, especially since Duterte does not trust the United States to go to war against China to defend the Philippines, and Duterte has made public statements that at least charred, if not burned, Obama-era diplomatic bridges to the United States.[44]

President Donald Trump has tried to improve his personal relationship with Duterte, but the Philippine president will pay close attention to U.S. actions as well. In 2015, the United States provided $225 million in development and military aid to the Philippines. In 2016, China roundly beat that figure by pledging $24 billion in development aid, though much if not most of that would likely be in loans at undetermined interest rates and for work done by Chinese companies. Japan pledged almost $9 billion in early 2017.[45]

China's development funding is not free and often comes with political conditionality. China provided $600 million to Cambodia in 2016 in exchange for diplomatic support in international fora, including on ASEAN decisions regarding the South China Sea.[46] Such competing China-Japan-U.S. development funding for political influence would not necessarily be in the interest of the United States. While the United States engaged in foreign aid competitions with the Soviet Union in the 1950s and 1960s, this frequently resulted in nonaligned countries playing the superpowers against each other for extended periods. Both China and the United States have been accused of direct payments to heads of state, their offices, or their families to influence policy.[47]

The bilateral relationship between the United States and China—the two largest powers in the Asia-Pacific region—has the strongest effect on international crises in the area, including the South China Sea. Since the normalization of relations and the formal U.S. recognition of China in 1979, the two countries have had a complicated relationship, oscillating between periods of tension, including the Tiananmen Square massacre in 1989 and the accidental bombing of China's Belgrade embassy in 1999, and increasingly strong economic relations. In 2016, U.S.-China trade amounted to $578 billion, and China held more than $1 trillion in U.S. debt.[48]

Such economic links make the United States wary of deteriorating relations with China because of potentially deleterious effects on U.S. business interests exporting to China and on the U.S. interest rate in case China were to unload debt. But the opposite is even more true. China exports about four times more to the United States than the United States exports to China, and in the event of heightened hostilities, the United States could selectively default on Chinese debt for national security reasons. China's exports to the United States are far greater as a percentage of its economy than vice versa.

In 2011, the United States announced its "Pivot to Asia" aimed at curtailing the growing political and military influence of China within the region.[49] This policy, which included promotion of the Trans-Pacific Partnership trade alliance in Asia that excludes China, bolster of U.S. alliances, and unilateral military patrols of the South China Sea, led to increasing tensions between the two major players in recent years. The United States has been very clear that it desires the best for China's economy. It simply wants China to stop breaking international law, especially against U.S. allies. That message grew louder with the advent of the Trump administration. But the scuttling of the Trans-Pacific Partnership and the administration's attempt to enlist Chinese assistance on North Korean denuclearization took priority and thus weakened the U.S. bargaining position on the South China Sea.[50]

CHINA'S INTERESTS IN THE SOUTH CHINA SEA: NATIONALISM, OIL, GAS, SHIPPING, AND FISHING

China's interests in the South China Sea stem from a set of interacting factors. First, a sense of nationalism among its population is produced, mirrored, and remanufactured by the leadership. This is done through historical arguments, maintenance of local and regional animosities against major democratic powers, and hyper-nationalism that promotes the Communist Party and its increasingly authoritarian leader, Xi Jinping. Once nationalist momentum starts, party leadership can keep the ball rolling relatively easily through occasional conflicts with military forces operational in the region, especially the United States and Japan.

National pride, fully stoked by the government, drives the South China Sea dispute. In China, government leaders and the media purposely exploit the country's "Century of Humiliation" as a rallying cry to support the ends of particular interest groups such as the military, oil industry, and large fishing operations.[51] Creating this nationalistic sentiment by playing the victim emboldens and enables bureaucratic and industrial elites to use government resources to make aggressive gains in the South China Sea. Nationalism leads regular Chinese citizens to demand the territory claimed by the U-shaped line and "teach the Vietnamese, the Filipinos and the Malaysians a good lesson."[52] It increases support for centralization of power under Xi and the government's expanding budget, since Chinese citizens perceive such centralization and power to be necessary to achieve something as significant as overcoming U.S. efforts in Asia.[53]

Based on an imagined history of sovereignty over the South China Sea, China argues that a Western reading of modern international law, in particular compulsory arbitration under UNCLOS, should not determine China's ostensibly ancient historical claims in the region.[54] The counterargument is ably made by a contributor to this book, Bill Hayton. In *The South China Sea: The Struggle for Power in Asia*, Hayton notes that the Chinese name for the Paracel Island group in the South China Sea, the Xisha Islands, is derivative of the English given name of one of the islands, West Sand. In Chinese, West Sand translates as 西沙洲, or in the pinyin, *Xīshā-zhōu*. These translations resulted from Chinese duplication of earlier British maps of the region.[55]

In more recent times, China has laid claim to the vast majority of the South China Sea through its U-shaped line. In 2009, it circulated a map in the United Nations that used nine dashes to outline the part of the South China Sea that it claimed as sovereign territory.[56] This map is based on one that China's Nationalist government created in 1947, which used eleven dashes to outline the claimed territory.[57] On these maps, China claims the Paracel Islands in the west, Scarborough Shoal in the east, and the Spratlys in the south—along with part of the exclusive economic zone drawn from Indonesia's Natuna Islands in the southwest. The claimed area within China's U-shaped line is larger in square hectares than the entirety of India and has created an immense territorial dispute truly unequaled in the modern era.[58]

China has a number of economic interests in the South China Sea, the most important being access to potentially vast supplies of oil and natural gas. A May 2015 article by the China Institute of International Studies cited remarkably high hydrocarbon reserves in the South China Sea, including 70.78 billion tons of reserves, of which 29.19 billion tons are petroleum deposits and 58 trillion cubic meters are natural gas deposits.[59] The quantity of 29.19 billion tons of oil, multiplied by 7.32 barrels per ton, is equal to 213.67 billion barrels of oil.[60] This would make the South China Sea the third largest reserve in the world after Venezuela and Saudi Arabia. This quantity of oil and gas could supply China for sixty years.

Separately, the Chinese Ministry of Land and Resources estimates that the area China claims in the South China Sea has 23 to 30 billion tons (89 to 115 trillion cubic feet) of natural gas. The study claims that the South China Sea has about one-third of China's total petroleum and natural gas resources and 12 percent of the world's total.[61]

The United States Energy Information Administration (EIA) also estimates large quantities of oil and gas in the South China Sea, including approximately 28 to 213 billion barrels of oil (the larger figure is from the Chinese estimate), plus 190 trillion cubic feet of proved and probable natural gas (which is greater than the Chinese estimate). The EIA estimate of natural gas in the South China Sea is approximately 3 percent of proved global natural gas reserves.[62]

South China Sea hydrocarbon resource valuation varies over two main metrics: the estimated number of barrels of oil, which ranges from 28 to 213 billion barrels, and the price of oil, which since 2005 has mostly ranged between $50 and $100 per barrel. Thus, the lower-bound value of oil is 28 billion barrels at $50 per barrel, or $1.4 trillion. The upper bound is 213 billion barrels at $100 per barrel, or $21.3 trillion.

The range of the gas estimates is between 58 and 190 trillion cubic feet, or about $580 billion to $2 trillion more at $10 per thousand cubic feet of natural gas. The total value of oil and gas in the South China Sea, therefore, could be anywhere between $2 trillion and $23 trillion, depending on the price and quantity of hydrocarbons ultimately extracted.

The perceived tangible value of the oil and gas to China, however, probably tended toward the upper range of these dollar figures, in addition to its unquantifiable strategic value. First, China likely more heavily weights its own higher estimate of oil reserves, rather than the lower estimate from the United States, in its calculations.

Second, China made key decisions about occupying and defending remote points of the South China Sea between 2009 and 2014 when oil was trending toward $100 per barrel, meaning that at the time the dollar value of its own estimate was closer to $23 trillion, or more than double China's GDP in 2015. Once China's leadership made the decision to very publicly assert sovereignty, including with its population—by printing the claim on all Chinese passports, for example—it was harder for them to back away from the claim without loss of reputation. Xi Jinping does not seem to have taken the face-saving opportunity to relinquish claims to the U-shaped line provided by the 2016 Permanent Court of Arbitration award; rather, he doubled down through various People's Liberation Army (PLA) naval and air force actions in the South China Sea that militarily underlined China's refusal to recognize the court's jurisdiction. Perhaps China's strong diplomatic voice on the South China Sea is meant more for domestic audiences than for the concerned global public.

Third, China seeks to defend the South China Sea, within the First Island Chain formed by the Philippines, to ensure ingress and egress of naval ships and the Chinese merchant marine and to forestall naval blockade during wartime. In the event of such a blockade, China could require a strategic reserve of oil and gas to maintain its economy and war production. Just as the United States has a strategic petroleum reserve of up to 727 million barrels of oil in case of extreme circumstances, China seeks to claim what could be a strategic reserve of hydrocarbons in the South China Sea.

This gives a hint as to why China's regional claims are so persistent. The loss in reputation and soft power from threatening naval and air activity in the South China Sea may be worth the economic gain from oil alone, especially since it is a relative gain at the loss of strategic competitors. Yielding control of this strategic resource to the Philippines or Vietnam, for example, could strengthen them militarily and economically, to the point where dominating Asia would simply be too costly for China to consider. China would thereby be relegated to a medium-power status in perpetuity, and Communist Party control could be threatened by the more successful democratic economies, especially if the United States, European Union, India, and Japan were to more thoroughly join forces based on a commonality of democratic values. By this logic, the Chinese Communist Party must grow its territorial control and thereby its own domestic support or risk its own existence. As noted elsewhere in this volume by Gordon Chang, "In a world of depredation by authoritarian states, people in democracies are beginning to understand the importance of supporting other free societies."[63] China understands the flip side of this coin, which is that nearby democracies and competitors must therefore be divided and weakened.

Beyond energy resources, the South China Sea accounts for nearly 10 percent of the world's annual fish catch.[64] The region contains 30 percent of the world's coral reefs, which provide a habitat for thousands of marine species.[65] Fishing is an important source of employment and protein for millions of people who live in the region.[66] Due to overfishing and pollution in littoral areas of China, the Chinese fishing industry is increasingly interested in large-scale deep-sea fishing in disputed areas of the South China Sea.[67] Other important natural resources in the region include the phosphoric acid and lime mines on the islands and the metallic ores on the sea floor.[68]

The South China Sea, one of the busiest maritime trade routes in the world, supports three times more tanker traffic than the Suez Canal. It has five times more traffic than the Panama Canal.[69] Economists estimate that more than 50 percent of the world's oil tanker shipments and merchant fleet (by tonnage) pass through the region, and more than half of the world's ten busiest shipping ports are located in the area.[70] The transportation-related value of the South China Sea stems from its strategic location, since it provides a maritime link between the Indian and Pacific Oceans. But for the South China Sea, transport would be forced south of Indonesia, which would add billions of dollars per year to global maritime shipping costs. Thus, navigation through this region is of vital importance for the continuing economic growth of not only China but also all of Asia. Were China to militarily control the South China Sea and continue to successfully challenge international law on the matter, it could potentially capture these increased shipping costs through transit taxes or constrict the economies of Taiwan, Japan, and South Korea through naval blockade of the merchant marine.[71]

China also cites the stability of the South China Sea as a necessary component for its national security, from the perspective of both littoral defense and power projection. As mentioned above regarding oil and gas, China seeks to control the region as an access point to its coastal cities and for strategic access to the Indian and Pacific Oceans.[72] Considered the "south gate of China's national defense and security," the South China Sea is vital to the economy and SLOCs on which China's military depends.[73]

However, Chinese control of the South China Sea would threaten or even tax freedom of navigation, an existential threat to some Southeast and East Asian countries. If the South China Sea were made into a "Chinese lake," as Japanese prime minister Shinzo Abe warned in 2012, Malaysia and Vietnam would be relegated to land-bound status.[74] Their access to international trade would only be through the tax authorities of another country. Were China to gain sovereignty over the East China Sea as well, Taiwan would essentially be an island surrounded by Chinese lakes. Such actions are existential threats to these countries.

The result of China's attempt to enforce its East and South China Sea claims leads to a dangerous security dilemma in which its growing military strength in the region and provocative changes to the status quo induce other regional and international powers to increase their own military capabilities, form closer alliances and security partnerships, and engage in counter-brinkmanship with their naval and air forces.[75]

Backing down for any country's leaders is more difficult with domestic political audiences watching every move via globalized and instantaneous media. Given its censorship of domestic media, social control of protests, and blocking of international online media, China could have an easier time discreetly backing down than could Indonesia, the Philippines, Malaysia, Brunei, or Vietnam, all of which have less social control and a free press (or at least citizens with ready access to most news on the Internet). As previously noted, China could have gradually and quietly withdrawn its claim after the 2016 Permanent Court of Arbitration ruling and could have pacified domestic audiences with reference to the ruling. But it did not do so.

CHINA'S ACTIONS IN THE SOUTH CHINA SEA AND THE U.S. RESPONSE

The perception of a China threat among Asian countries is based on the diminishing relative military advantage of the United States, especially when limiting the geographic scope of analysis to Asia. The U.S. military advantage is eroding on multiple metrics: absolute military spending, military spending when corrected for purchasing power parity, and absolute volume of military hardware, including surface ships, ballistic missile submarines, attack submarines, tanks, fighter aircraft, bombers, cruise missiles, ballistic missiles, and electronic warfare.[76] The public perception in Asia and among some defense analysts is that Chinese hardware may not be as technologically sophisticated as U.S. equipment, but it does have sufficient sophistication to destroy U.S. military targets, especially when coordinated and launched en masse. And its sophistication is rapidly increasing. In the realms of artificial intelligence and super-computing, both of which have military applications, China even claims to have surpassed the United States.

The key question for U.S. allies in Asia is the extent to which the United States is willing to use its diminishing relative force to defend its allies in the region, with all the accompanying risks of major power war. The United States has indicated, at least in speech, that it is indeed ready to defend the territory of its Asian partners from China. In action, however, the United States is focused on freedom of navigation, counterproliferation, and counterterrorism operations, none of which contradict core security goals of China.

Some analysts think that the United States decided not to defend the South China Sea decades ago and has repeatedly signaled as much through a persistent lack of significant response to, for example, China's 1992 law unilaterally annexing Taiwan, Japan's Senkaku Islands, the Spratly Islands within the Philippines' EEZ, and the Paracel Islands within Vietnam's EEZ; Indonesia's 1993 discovery of a map that included a depiction of the Natuna Islands within China's EEZ; the

1995 Mischief Reef occupation within the Philippines' EEZ and subsequent militarized artificial island building; and China's increasing assertiveness starting in 2010, including the Scarborough Shoal occupation in 2012, just 123 miles west of the strategic ports of Manila and Subic Bay, the Philippines.

China's expansionist territorial claims can also be tracked by its use of the symbolic term "core interest" over time. The term in the past signaled the territory for which China claimed to be willing to go to war; this was previously limited to Taiwan. But China perceived weakness in the Obama administration starting with the financial crisis of 2008. It wasted no time in claiming slices of territory in Asia and asserting that the U.S. military should stay out of Asia altogether. China applied the term "core interest" to Tibet and Xinjiang in 2008, to the South China Sea in 2010, and to the East China Sea in 2013.[77] These are surprisingly bold actions against a wide range of countries and populations, three of which are party to a U.S. defense treaty. When viewed together, the moves are militarily astonishing and diplomatically tone-deaf.

The United States failed to respond with sufficient force to China's actions and claims from 1992 to 2013 to maintain a peaceful equilibrium and stop further transgressions. "The Obama administration has not wanted to respond to the Chinese assertion of control and establishment of regional hegemony," according to political scientist June Teufel Dreyer. "I don't think the Bush administration would have behaved differently."[78] So given this history in the region, Asian allies can reasonably question U.S. resolve against China's claims in the South China Sea.

The South and East China Seas are within the First Island Chain. But China's ambitions do not stop there. China is increasing its operations and economic and political influence in Melanesia, Polynesia, and Micronesia, considered the Second and Third Island Chains, as well as in ASEAN states as a whole. China has turned the nineteenth-century observation that trade follows the flag on its head. For Chinese trade partners in the twenty-first century, the flag is following trade. If current trends continue, all three island chains and the ASEAN states could be claimed as core interests by China in the next twenty to thirty years. In doing so, China would be imposing a sphere of influence in Southeast Asia and the Pacific islands, similar to the U.S. Monroe Doctrine applied to Latin America in 1823 and the Japanese Greater East Asia Co-Prosperity Sphere applied in 1938.

As China gradually claims more territory and rights, it watches the reaction of the United States, Japan, Australia, and South Korea very carefully. Rather than a strong military or diplomatic reaction, however, the opposite seems to have happened. The early Obama administration, prioritizing health care reform and disengagement from the Middle East between 2008 and 2013, continued or increased trade, friendly diplomacy, and military-to-military engagement such as joint military exercises.

Only after China's 2013 air defense identification zone (ADIZ) declaration over the East China Sea did the United States match Chinese actions with a deterrent show of force. The U.S. Air Force flew two unarmed nuclear-capable bombers through China's ADIZ on November 27, 2013, and has flown regular missions since.[79] In 2016, the United States put new forces into South Korea, including nuclear-capable bombers and submarines, in response to North Korean nuclear tests.[80]

But in the South China Sea, the U.S. response to China's militarization has been more muted. The United States only flew an A-10 conventional ground attack plane over Scarborough Shoal in April 2016. However, the flight of a Chinese nuclear-capable bomber over the feature the following July elicited no public response by the Obama administration. This sent yet another message to the Philippines and China of a lack of U.S. resolve in defending the Philippines.

The United States need not fear China at this point in history, because China is bluffing in the South China Sea. The last thing China wants is a shooting war with the United States.[81] In interviews in 2015, Chinese foreign ministry officials stated very clearly that they did not want any war with regional countries and "definitely" not with the United States. One even said that if the Philippines and United States jointly retook Scarborough Shoal, China would protest but not fight back.[82] The slow acquisition of maritime territory in the South China Sea, always waiting to see the reaction before taking more, should be a signal of China's underlying caution. This should embolden the United States and its allies to take much tougher military stands against China at Scarborough Shoal, Mischief Reef, and elsewhere in the South China Sea. That the United States and Philippines do not even have military forces permanently patrolling these locations is surprising to many defense analysts. The Trump administration has made no major change to South China Sea operations.

Starting in 2014, the United States made increasingly high-level protests regarding the South China Sea. In testimony before the House Committee on Foreign Affairs Subcommittee on Asia and the Pacific on February 5, 2014, Assistant Secretary of State for East Asian and Pacific Affairs Daniel R. Russel cited a list of concerns, including restrictions on access to Scarborough Reef;[83] pressure on the long-standing Philippine presence at the Second Thomas Shoal; putting hydrocarbon blocks up for bid in an area close to another country's mainland and far away even from the islands that China is claiming; announcing administrative and even military districts in contested areas in the South China Sea; an unprecedented spike in risky activity by China's maritime agencies near the Senkaku Islands; the sudden, uncoordinated and unilateral imposition of regulations over contested airspace in the case of the East China Sea Air Defense Identification Zone; and the recent updating of fishing regulations covering disputed areas in the South China Sea.[84]

Russel followed that by questioning China's objectives in the area and then noting China's lack of transparency and adherence to international law. He blamed China's lack of clarity for creating insecurity and instability in the region. He also took a stand on territorial issues: "I want to reinforce the point that under international law, maritime claims in the South China Sea must be derived from land features. . . . Any use of the 'nine-dash line' by China to claim maritime rights not based on claimed land features would be inconsistent with international law."[85]

The next major statement from the United States turned up the volume. Secretary of Defense Ashton Carter spoke at the 2015 International Institute for Strategic Studies Shangri-La Dialogue in Singapore. He began addressing the South China Sea issue by asserting that all Asian countries and the United States have a stake in the outcome of the dispute. This was in direct response to China's claim that the U.S. military should stay out of the neighborhood: "We've all benefitted from free and open access to the South China Sea and the Strait of Malacca. We all have a fundamental stake in the security of the South China Sea. And that's why we all have deep concerns about any party that attempts to undermine the [status] quo and generate instability there, whether by force, coercion, or simply by creating irreversible facts on the ground, in the air, or in the water."[86]

Carter continued by ascribing blame for the dispute to China. He contradicted China's claim that instability in the region originates from U.S. military pressure and influence:

> Now, it's true that almost all the nations that claim parts of the South China Sea have developed outposts over the years . . . of differing scope and degree. In the Spratly Islands, Vietnam has 48 [outposts]; the Philippines, eight; Malaysia, five; and Taiwan, one.

Yet, one country has gone much further and much faster than any other. And that's China.

China has reclaimed over 2,000 acres, more than all other claimants combined . . . and more than in the entire history of the region. And China did so in only the last 18 months. It is unclear how much farther China will go. That is why this stretch of water has become the source of tension in the region and front-page news around the world.

The United States is deeply concerned about the pace and scope of land reclamation in the South China Sea, the prospect of further militarization, as well as the potential for these activities . . . to increase the risk of miscalculation or conflict among claimant states. As a Pacific nation, a trading nation, and a member of the international community, the United States has every right to be involved and concerned. But these are not just American concerns. Nations across the region and the world, many of you here in the room today, have also voiced the same concerns and raised questions about China's intentions in constructing these massive outposts.[87]

Finally, Carter explicated the position of the United States, which included a focus on diplomacy over military conflict, a commitment to freedom of navigation (including for the U.S. military), and finally a veiled warning to China: the United States would continue to work with its allies to uphold international law. Together, and in the context of speaking publicly to an assembly of Asian defense ministers, these statements amounted to a warning shot across the bow:

> [T]here should be an immediate and lasting halt to land reclamation by all claimants. We also oppose any further militarization of disputed features. . . . As it is central to the regional security architecture, ASEAN must be a part of this effort: the United States encourages ASEAN and China to conclude a Code of Conduct this year. And America will support the right of claimants to pursue international legal arbitration and other peaceful means to resolve these disputes, just as we will oppose coercive tactics. . . . With its actions in the South China Sea, China is out of step with both the international rules and norms that underscore the Asia-Pacific's security architecture, and the regional consensus that favors diplomacy and opposes coercion. These actions are spurring nations to respond together in new ways.[88]

Carter made clear that he was critical of China's actions in the South China Sea, that the United States was committed to a military presence in the region, and that the United States would stand with its allies and partners to uphold international law.

But despite these strong words, there were no specifics on support to the Philippines or Japan in their near-daily military encounters with China. There was no promise to defend, for example, Mischief Reef or Scarborough Shoal. China's occupations, and the lack of a strong response from the United States, have Asian and defense analysts particularly worried. Compounding their concern was the lack of a strong U.S. response to Russia's annexation of Crimea in 2014. In 2016, President Duterte of the Philippines even belittled the United States publicly, saying that when Russia occupied Crimea, "America wasn't able to do anything." He used this as part of a justification for downgrading the Philippines' alliance with the United States in favor of stronger ties with China.[89]

CHINA'S MILITARY STRATEGIES IN THE SOUTH CHINA SEA

In May 2015, the Chinese government issued its first-ever military strategy white paper.[90] The document focuses on the broad topics of upholding China's supposed policy of "active defense" (not to strike first but to respond strongly), modernizing its military to become a first-class naval power, and having a larger global military presence.[91] All of these topics relate to the South China Sea. It is disingenuous to claim not to take preemptive action, but to occupy shoals and reefs that belong to other nations, and to intimidate, with militarized coast guard and a fishing militia, the commercial boats of other countries in their own EEZs. Likewise, it is telling that China focuses on the naval power that is specifically needed to support its expansive claims in the South China Sea, East China Sea, and beyond.

Other sections of China's 2015 military strategy specifically refer to the South China Sea. China claims that the growing U.S. presence in the region and Japan's efforts to increase its military are "grave concerns" and that China must also safeguard "its maritime rights and interests" against other countries that "take provocative actions and reinforce their military presence on China's reefs and islands that they have illegally occupied."[92]

This is a warning to all other claimants in the region, which have smaller militaries than China, to vacate disputed areas or face the consequences. In addition, China mentions its top interests in the South China Sea in order—energy, fishing, and SLOCs—by calling them "overseas interests" and stating the importance of protecting them.[93]

Incrementalism

To increase its control of territory within the U-shaped line, China has implemented the military strategies of incrementalism and brinkmanship. Assistant Secretary Russel, in his speech before Congress on July 9, 2015, highlighted multiple instances of China's attempts to change the status quo and then noted China's strategy of incrementalism: "There is a growing concern that this pattern of behavior in the South China Sea reflects an incremental effort by China to assert control over the area contained in the so-called 'nine-dash line,' despite the objections of its neighbors."[94]

The international community has charged China with incrementalism, also known as what theorist Thomas Schelling identified in 1966 as "salami-slicing" or, as Philippine and Chinese theorists call it, "peeling the cabbage."[95] These phrases describe how China has slowly accumulated de facto slices of territory through multiple relatively small aggressive actions rather than a large effort that could provoke retaliation.[96] China's aim is to gradually gain control of the islands and regions it claims within the U-shaped line, so that de facto control will lead to de jure sovereignty, despite competing claims of other countries under UNCLOS.[97]

After occupying new territory, China typically attempts to legitimize its action by establishing both a civilian and military presence. In June 2012, China created Sansha City on Woody Island, part of the Paracel Islands chain that China took in 1974 from Vietnam. China claimed Sansha as the seat of a new prefecture in control of about 2 million square kilometers of sea, including the Paracel and Spratly Islands.[98] China reinforced this settlement by sending a military garrison and building a runway, coastal defense positions, harbor, and four large aircraft hangars.[99]

Through land reclamation projects on Woody Island and elsewhere, China pumps sand onto coral reefs and then covers the artificial islands with concrete. The purpose of this "land reclamation" is to turn reefs, which international law does not consider territory, into land that China can claim under UNCLOS.[100] As of June 2017, China had created about 13 square kilometers of artificial islands in the Spratly Islands, not including the Paracels.[101] None of them were recognized as legitimate in the 2016 ruling by the Permanent Court of Arbitration in The Hague. China militarily reinforced many of these man-made islands with airstrips capable of supporting PLA Air Force fighters and bombers, as well as hangars, artillery, and antiaircraft missiles. They dredged deep channels and harbors for submarines and large warships and built logistics, communications, and intelligence-gathering facilities.[102]

Brinkmanship

Artificial island-building is an integral part of the brinkmanship strategy that China uses in the South China Sea, East China Sea, and Himalayan region of India. This method pushes a conflict to the brink of military action, an outcome no party wants, to make small gains in territory and operational latitude. Brinkmanship works well for larger competitors against smaller, more vulnerable adversaries, and when the aggressor can present itself as committed to military conflict at any cost if it does not obtain its goal. Brinkmanship works best if the pain inflicted on the defending party by military conflict would be greater than the pain imposed on the aggressor, whether that be in aggregate or scaled, for example, by population or GDP. Brinkmanship is a form of intimidation.

China normally uses brinkmanship against smaller Pacific powers, but it also uses it regularly against Japan and the United States. In 2016, a military helicopter lifted off from a People's Liberation Army Navy frigate in the South China Sea and advanced toward a U.S. Navy cruiser. It was most likely a Z-9 helicopter, armed with torpedoes that could destroy the cruiser.[103] China regularly challenges U.S. Navy surveillance planes flying through the South China Sea, including over China's artificial islands. The buffer maintained by the two military forces in what is essentially a large no-man's land of the South China Sea is a multi-layered and contested border of sorts. While China uses brinkmanship against its smaller neighbors and the United States in the South China Sea quite effectively, it complains loudly when the United States uses the same tactic against China.[104]

The strategy of brinkmanship loses effectiveness when procedures are put into place that decrease the likelihood of disaster from one party using the method. Thus, it is almost always in the interests of the weaker party to a dispute to implement such steps, and not in the interests of the stronger party to do so, even if such procedures appear prima facie to be a logical means of avoiding military conflict. This is demonstrated in the South China Sea case by ASEAN's attempts, agreed to in principle but still blocked by China, to create a more stringent code of conduct for the region.[105] Such a code would put in place rules and mechanisms such as hotlines and procedures to prevent disputes from escalating. ASEAN, the weaker party, seeks such a code while China, the stronger actor, wants to parry that restraint using its strategy of brinkmanship. Assistant Secretary Russel supported ASEAN's code of conduct and has called on China to accelerate negotiations, which have been ongoing since 2002.[106] As an ally of ASEAN against China's expansionism and as a supporter of international law, it makes sense for the United States to support this agreement. As the stronger party in the dispute with ASEAN countries, China follows a realist rationality in resisting the code of conduct.

The relationship is reversed in the case of the United States and China. The United States, as the stronger side (for at least a few more years), has in the past sought to preserve its option of brinkmanship. China, as the weaker party, sought to regulate encounters so that the U.S. tactical option of brinkmanship was constrained. China does indeed want to implement procedures for military-to-military encounters with the United States and, after several years of negotiation starting in 2011, agreed to a Memorandum of Understanding (MOU) with the United States in 2013 and the Code for Unplanned Encounters at Sea in 2015.[107] If its military advantage continues to decline, the United States will become increasingly willing to sign such agreements with China in coming years, increasing U.S. predictability and therefore the operational space of China. In other words, with more agreements, China will be less constrained by the current opportunity of the United States to use brinkmanship.[108]

Therefore, such forms of cooperation and engagement at a time when China is newly occupying Philippine territory and Japanese airspace and is in a border dispute with India seem dangerously naive to some defense analysts. If the United States signs an MOU with China regulating military-to-military encounters, it should have conditionality attached. First, China should agree to similar codes with the smaller nations adjacent to the South China Sea. Second, China should cease to occupy territory, whether islands or airspace (for example, the ADIZ over Japan) in or over the territory or EEZs of U.S. allies. Not requiring such concessions from China sends the message that China's military actions in the South China Sea are becoming business as usual.

While the United States is signing cooperation and rules of engagement agreements with the PLA, enduring North Korea's regional destabilization, and doing joint military exercises with the Chinese military such as the annual Rim of the Pacific off Hawaii,[109] the Chinese leadership can rest easy knowing that their ambitions in the South China Sea are not yet being militarily opposed. As long as the United States does not seek, even through the relatively costless tactic of brinkmanship, to militarily oppose Chinese expansionism in the South China Sea, China can continue to expand its de facto occupation of territory with confidence and a sense of security.

U.S. secretary of state Rex Tillerson has recognized that the United States may be required to accept more risk in the South China Sea. "If a contingency occurs, the United States and its allies and partners must be capable of limiting

China's access to and use of its artificial islands to pose a threat to the United States or its allies and partners," Tillerson wrote in answer to questions from Senator Ben Cardin. "The United States must be willing to accept risk if it is to deter further destabilizing actions and reassure allies and partners that the United States will stand with them in upholding international rules and norms."[110]

CHINA'S DIPLOMATIC STRATEGIES IN THE SOUTH CHINA SEA

The Take and Talk Strategy

While building artificial islands and otherwise advancing its territorial expansion, China has simultaneously and aggressively used diplomacy to advance its interests in the South China Sea and maintain the hope of peaceful dispute resolution for Southeast Asian claimants. This is China's "Take and Talk" strategy. While China's foreign ministry and business interests are busy making friends and talking about peace, the PLA is expanding its land, sea, and air claims and attempting to intimidate military forces of any other country operating in the region.[111]

China publicly claims commitment to rising peacefully and creating harmonious relations with its neighbors.[112] It seeks joint talks, operations, and exercises to ensure that neither military conflict nor economic sanctions impede its rise. Its agreements on other issues, including the environment, piracy, and terrorism, normalize its diplomacy.[113] While the talks do not lead to multilateral negotiations with China on one side and the Southeast Asian claimants on the other, China sees them as an opportunity in which its relative power gives it a bargaining advantage. Such bilateral negotiations, along with a tendency of the hopeful and biased to focus on China's words rather than its actions, are a major strategic mistake that most nations doing business with China make.

Win-Win Solutions

The other diplomatic strategy China has extensively used in the South China Sea is what Xi Jinping has called a "Win-Win" solution. Starting in the 1990s, Beijing proposed to establish a method of "shelving disputes and carrying out joint development," where China and its neighbors would agree to focus on common interests to jointly develop the region instead of continuing disputes that stalemate development. Such development could significantly increase the GDP for participating nations and the bank accounts of well-connected politicians and businessmen involved in the deals.[114] Thus, a significant portion of the ruling elites in the Philippines, Vietnam, Malaysia, Brunei, and Taiwan are in favor of

China's "joint development" approach. Others—typically nationalists, patriots, and those politicians, businessmen, and other interested parties unlikely to profit from joint development—are against it.

The most important form of joint development in the South China Sea is oil and gas extraction, which yields multiple revenue streams. Typically, the government or owner of the land or ocean from which oil and gas are extracted obtains a mineral royalty fee akin to rent. This royalty is often a percentage of the total dollar value of the extracted resources. The other revenue stream goes to the company doing the technical work to extract and transport the oil and gas, such as Exxon or Standard Oil. As points of comparison, the U.S. government typically gets 12.5 percent of oil revenues from oil extracted from federal lands.[115] Internationally, royalty rates are typically 10 to 20 percent but can go as high as 30 percent in places like Venezuela.[116] Taxes are additional and can be greater than royalties.

In China's vision of joint development, oil and gas development within the EEZ of Southeast Asian claimant countries must be approved by not only the country with the resource within its EEZ and the oil company but also China if the development is within the U-shaped line. China is demanding approximately 50 percent, and in some cases more, of the royalties and taxes in non-Chinese EEZs according to my diplomatic sources. Some diplomats and countries within Southeast Asian claimant countries are willing to agree to this.[117] Businessmen are biased in favor of any royalty-sharing agreement, no matter how contrary to international law, so they can start extraction. China leaves whatever remains after its royalty to the Southeast Asian claimant country. The extracting company gets close to the normal rate of return, plus any risk premium that the company perceives from the contract.

In 2004 and 2005, oil companies from China, the Philippines, and Vietnam signed the Tripartite Agreement for Joint Marine Seismic Undertaking, whereby they agreed to jointly explore the South China Sea for hydrocarbons.[118] This was a victory for China, as it broke ASEAN unity and took a step toward joint development within the Philippines' EEZ. The deal may have resulted from alleged Chinese corruption of Philippine president Arroyo-Macapagal.[119] However, it went sour after Philippine congressional and media scrutiny of these and other allegedly corrupt Chinese deals at the time. Subsequent legislation made such nontransparent deals more difficult. Arroyo-Macapagal was exonerated during the presidency of Rodrigo Duterte, who reopened the possibility of joint development with China in 2016.[120]

Sovereignty has been a key sticking point for some Southeast Asian countries, including the Philippines and Vietnam. Two unnamed sources indicated that China refused to even discuss joint development with Vietnam without it first agreeing to relinquish sovereignty of the overlap of that country's EEZ beyond its twelve-nautical-mile territorial zone and the U-shaped line.[121]

Because of the Vietnamese and Philippine experience in negotiations with China, it logically follows that Malaysia and Brunei might have given substantial concessions to China in exchange for China's acquiescence to their oil and gas development. They may have compromised, at least in private communications with China, their sovereign rights to their EEZs beyond the twelve-mile territorial limit. If royalty-sharing deals were made between China, Malaysia, and Brunei, they likely occurred sometime between 2009, when China famously submitted the U-shaped line to the United Nations, and 2012, when Chinese ships interfered with hydrocarbon exploration by Vietnam and India by cutting seismic cables towed behind boats for oil exploration.[122]

In 2011, Chinese patrol boats interfered with Philippine oil exploration activities near Reed Bank.[123] Malaysia and Brunei were spared such confrontations, possibly because of their agreements with China, which allowed their oil extraction activities within the U-shaped line to continue during this period and afterward. China-Malaysia and China-Brunei agreements probably predate 2014.[124]

Despite China's activities in multilateral forums to address its South China Sea disputes, it has reiterated its preference to resolve issues through bilateral negotiations, stating that multilateral efforts can only play a supporting role.[125] China's preference for bilateral negotiations stems from its ability to corrupt or intimidate weaker neighbors in one-on-one settings and thereby dominate the result.[126] Others believe that China is using diplomatic talks as a delaying strategy so it can wait to resolve the conflict until after it solidifies control of more territory.[127] This delaying strategy seems to be particularly targeted to rebuff other countries' claims under UNCLOS.[128]

THE U.S. AND ALLIED STRATEGY IN THE SOUTH CHINA SEA

U.S. actions in the South China Sea are an integral part of Washington's "Pivot to Asia," which will likely be strengthened under a different name by the Trump administration. Under the Obama administration, the pivot discursively enabled the drawing down of forces in Iraq and Afghanistan and the rebalance of the U.S. budget not to Asia but to domestic funding.[129] It might have more accurately been called "the pivot back to America."

Many aspects of the pivot, including improving economic ties through a free trade agreement with South Korea and the Trans-Pacific Partnership free trade agreement, are relatively inexpensive.[130] Military aspects of the pivot include small U.S. Marine deployments in Australia on a rotational basis, a U.S. naval presence in Singapore, and more military cooperation with the Philippines, including rotating U.S. troops and more frequent joint exercises.[131] An additional 75 U.S. Navy ships to make a 350-ship Navy, as Trump called for during his campaign, will be more substantial.

China took a vocal stand against the pivot, claiming that it increased tensions in the region. The Philippines, historically one of the staunchest U.S. allies in Southeast Asia, is now balancing between the United States and China. U.S. efforts to rebalance to Asia were not only targeted to curb China's rise. Former secretary of defense Carter called Chinese military challenges to the United States part of a new "great power competition."[132] However, President Obama's military operations and economic aid were too weak to accomplish the task.

Military Alliances and Defending the Status Quo

Many existing U.S. alliances in Asia have strengthened in response to China's increasingly militaristic activities.[133] Japan, for example, plans on conducting joint patrols with the United States in the South China Sea.[134] In 2011, the United States and Australia signed an agreement to enhance defense cooperation.[135] The United States and Thailand signed the Joint Vision Statement for the Thai-U.S. Defense Alliance in 2012. But since U.S. criticism of Thailand's coup in 2014, Thailand has gravitated toward closer diplomatic relations with China. Australia in 2016 declined to take part with the United States in joint naval patrols in the South China Sea.

In May 2015, U.S. Navy ships passed through the Spratly Islands to prove they are legally international waters, in direct opposition to China's claims that the island chain is its sovereign territory.[136] While important, freedom of navigation patrols do not address allied territorial issues. They can be ignored by Chinese forces that build, occupy, and rapidly militarize islands in the south China Sea.

U.S. Public Diplomacy

One of the most effective U.S. strategies on the South China Sea is public diplomacy that raises global awareness of China's activities. This includes disseminating intelligence that provides proof of what China has done in the region. In addition to releasing satellite imagery that confirms the presence of artillery vehicles on China's artificial islands, for example, in May 2015, the Department of Defense released videos and audio recordings of a U.S. surveillance aircraft that flew in international airspace near Fiery Cross Reef, a part of the Spratly Islands where China has undertaken expansive island building.[137] During the mission, the plane received eight warnings from the Chinese navy to leave the airspace.[138]

The United States has complemented the release of evidence with analysis by high-ranking representatives of the U.S. military. The commander of the U.S. Pacific Fleet, Adm. Harry Harris Jr., publicly discussed how China's efforts to build artificial islands increased tension in the region, and Secretary Carter called on China to halt militarization of the islands.[139] The U.S. public diplomacy campaign not only raises awareness of China's actions but also alerts China that the United States is willing to challenge it and signals solidarity with U.S. allies in the region.

To specifically address recent events in the South China Sea, the U.S. approach includes FoN transits, upholding its military alliances, public statements in defense of the status quo, and publicly exposing China's expansionary efforts. James Fanell, a contributor to this volume, elsewhere argues that the U.S. military should dramatically increase disclosure of information about China's illegal actions in the South China Sea, including its frequent mistreatment of the maritime assets of other countries. This is a low-risk strategy that erodes China's soft power. But the lack of a stronger military response in places such as Mischief Reef and Scarborough Shoal, and elsewhere in the world such as Ukraine, risks making the United States appear weak in the eyes of global public opinion. Such a perception could invite more aggressive actions—for example, by China, Russia, North Korea, and Iran. The perception of U.S. weakness decreases U.S. global influence and furthers a perceived abandonment of alliances, especially in countries that see themselves as becoming buffer states. These include the Philippines, Taiwan, and Ukraine.

Buffer states do not consider themselves sufficiently important in the eyes of superpowers such as the United States to warrant a U.S.-China or U.S.-Russia war. They consequently cannot rely on the United States for defense and think they must make peace with adversaries such as China and Russia on the adversary's terms. These terms often include announcement of a nonaligned status and economic concessions, thereby opening themselves to additional influence and concessions in the future.

During World War II, the alternate strategy to the creation of buffer states was U.S. action in Europe. The U.S. military moved east as quickly as possible until they met Russian forces. Where they met, the iron curtain descended. Today, the United States has a perhaps fleeting opportunity to help democracies in Asia secure their territory. But it would take political will, including in the South China Sea.

Notes

1. Thanks to Samantha Gay, Matthew Michaelides, Christine Nelson, Lauren Weiss, and Rachel Wunder for research, editorial, and writing assistance with this introduction and on the administration of the series. My deep appreciation goes to Emily Bakely, Elena Bernini, Erin Brown, James Fanell, Glenn Griffith, Meagan Szekely, Lisa Yambrick, anonymous peer reviewers, and friends who made this volume possible.
2. I use the term "countries" advisedly, knowing it is controversial when applied to Taiwan. I take the position that Taiwan, as a sovereign democracy, should be treated as a country. A 2016 poll in Taiwan found that 75.8 percent of respondents believe the country is a sovereign and independent nation ("Majority Says Taiwan Is Independent," *Taipei Times,* October 29, 2016, http://www.taipeitimes.com/News/front/archives/2016/10/29/2003658136).
3. This definition of grand strategy is derived from definitions by B. H. Liddell-Hart, Paul Kennedy, John Lewis Gaddis, and Edward Luttwak. Gaddis defines grand strategy as "the calculated relationship of means to large ends. It's about how one uses whatever one has to get to wherever it is one wants to go." See John Lewis Gaddis, "What Is Grand Strategy?" Yale University, February 26, 2009, http://tiss-nc.org/wp-content/uploads/2015/01/KEYNOTE.Gaddis50thAniv2009.pdf. See also B. H. Liddell-Hart, *Strategy: The Indirect Approach,* (London: Faber and Faber Ltd., 1954): 335–36; Paul Kennedy, *Grand Strategies in War and Peace* (New Haven: Yale University Press, 1992); and Edward Luttwak, *The Grand Strategy of the Byzantine Empire* (Cambridge: Harvard University Press, 2009).
4. Ashton Carter, "Remarks by Secretary Carter on the Budget at the Economic Club of Washington, D.C.," February 2, 2016, http://www.defense.gov/News/Transcripts/Transcript-View/Article/648901/remarks-by-secretary-carter-on-the-budget-at-the-economic-club-of-washington-dc.
5. This argument stems from Modernization Theory, which posited that economic growth would lead to democracy. One of the fundamental texts of this theory was Seymour Martin Lipset, "Some Social Requisites of Democracy," *American Political Science Review* 53, no. 1 (1959): pp. 69–105.
6. Sources for this information include two not-for-attribution interviews conducted by the author. When cornered at a conference, Dr. Wu Shicun, president of China's National Institute for South China Sea Studies, declined to comment. The theory that Malaysia and Brunei are somehow compensating China for the right to develop oil and gas resources within the disputed areas of the South China Sea near their own coasts is published for the first time here and contradicts the current

prevailing theory that all South China Sea claimant countries have refused China's joint development proposals (see Bill Hayton, *The South China Sea: The Struggle for Power in Asia* [New Haven: Yale University Press, 2014], 253). If true, it helps explain the persistence of China's claims in the South China Sea, especially after the 2011 oil and gas development cable-cutting incidents. In October 2013, Chinese media proclaimed a joint development deal with Brunei, but this was later reinterpreted by Carlyle Thayer in his article "China-ASEAN Joint Development Overshadowed by South China Sea," *The Diplomat,* October 25, 2013, http://thediplomat.com/2013/10/china-asean-joint-development-overshadowed-by-south-china-sea/.
7. Richard Bitzinger, "Modernising China's Military, 1997–2012," *China Perspectives* 4 (2011): pp. 7–15.
8. Ibid., 9.
9. U.S. Department of Defense, *Annual Report to Congress: Military and Security Developments Involving the People's Republic of China 2017* (Washington, D.C.: Department of Defense, May 15, 2017), https://www.defense.gov/Portals/1/Documents/pubs/2017_China_Military_Power_Report.PDF.
10. Ibid.*,* 49.
11. Ibid.
12. Other scholars, however, have cited China's white papers as showing that one-third of the budget is allocated to equipment purchases. See Bitzinger, "Modernising China's Military," 9.
13. Kyle Mizokami, "Why the Chinese Military Is Only a Paper Dragon," *The Week*, September 24, 2014, http://theweek.com/articles/445300/why-chinese-military-only-paper-dragon.
14. Bitzinger, "Modernising China's Military," 7. For more information on the motivations, see Yves-Heng Lim, "The Driving Forces Behind China's Naval Modernization," *Comparative Strategy* 30, no. 2 (2011): pp. 105–20. Despite China's defense modernization efforts, there are still a number of weaknesses, including with the navy's capabilities for sustained operations by larger formations in distant waters, joint operations with other parts of its military, dependency on foreign suppliers for certain ship components, and lack of experience in combat operations. Ronald O'Rourke, *China Naval Modernization: Implications for U.S. Navy Capabilities—Background and Issues for Congress,* RL33153 (Washington, D.C.: Congressional Research Service, 2015), 3, https://www.fas.org/sgp/crs/row/RL33153.pdf.
15. David C. Gompert, Astrid Stuth Cevallos, and Cristina L. Garafola, *War with China: Thinking Through the Unthinkable* (Santa Monica, Calif.: RAND Corporation, 2016), http://www.rand.org/content/dam/rand/pubs/research_reports/RR1100/RR1140/RAND_RR1140.pdf.
16. Victor D. Cha, "Powerplay: Origins of the U.S. Alliance System in Asia," *International Security* 34, no. 3 (2009–2010): pp. 158–96.
17. Ibid., 159.
18. Emma Chanlett-Avery et al., *Japan-U.S. Relations: Issues for Congress,* RL33436 (Washington, D.C.: Congressional Research Service, 2015), 18, https://www.fas.org/sgp/crs/row/RL33436.pdf.

19. Ibid.
20. Lee Hudson Teslik, "Japan and Its Military," Council on Foreign Relations Backgrounder, April 13, 2006, http://www.cfr.org/japan/japan-its-military/p10439; Ministry of Foreign Affairs of Japan, "Japan's Contribution to Afghanistan—Working on the Frontline in the War on Terrorism," March 2007, http://www.mofa.go.jp/region/middle_e/afghanistan/pamph0703.pdf.
21. Chanlett-Avery et al., *Japan-U.S. Relations*, 21; "Japan to Allow Military Role Overseas in Historic Move," BBC, September 18, 2015, http://www.bbc.com/news/world-asia-34287362.
22. Chanlett-Avery et al., *Japan-U.S. Relations*, 20.
23. Ibid., 9.
24. Lee Jong-wha, "The China-South Korea Trade War Must End," *Japan Times*, March 26, 2017, http://www.japantimes.co.jp/opinion/2017/03/26/commentary/world-commentary/china-south-korea-trade-war-must-end/.
25. Ibid., 21.
26. Hayton, *The South China Sea*, 56.
27. Shirley A. Kan and Wayne M. Morrison, *U.S.-Taiwan Relationship: Overview of Policy Issues*, R41952 (Washington, D.C.: Congressional Research Service, December 11, 2014), 4.
28. Ibid.
29. Ibid., 5.
30. Ibid., 14–15.
31. Ibid., 20.
32. Ibid., 20–21.
33. Ibid., 21.
34. Ma Ying-Jeou, "A Plan for Peace in the South China Sea," *Wall Street Journal*, June 11, 2015, http://www.wsj.com/articles/a-plan-for-peace-in-the-south-china-sea-1434040267; J. R. Wu, "Taiwan Offers South China Sea Peace Plan," Reuters, May 26, 2015, http://www.reuters.com/article/2015/05/26/us-taiwan-south-china-sea-idUSKBN0OA16420150526.
35. Thomas Lum, *The Republic of the Philippines and U.S. Interests*, RL33233 (Washington, D.C.: Congressional Research Service, 2012), 14, https://www.fas.org/sgp/crs/row/RL33233.pdf.
36. Manuel Mogato et al., "Philippines Says U.S. Obligated to Help in Case of Attack," Reuters, April 30, 2014, http://www.reuters.com/article/2014/04/30/us-philippines-usa-idUSBREA3T02U20140430; Toby Sterling, "Court Begins Hearing Philippines, China Dispute over South China Sea," Reuters, July 8, 2015, http://www.reuters.com/article/2015/07/08/us-southchinasea-arbitration-idUSKCN0PH1KH20150708. Note that China refused to participate in the Permanent Court of Arbitration case brought by the Philippines, claiming that the court lacks jurisdiction. This has been a successful strategy in some cases before international courts. Iran successfully argued lack of jurisdiction in the United Kingdom vs. Iran (1952) case before the International Court of Justice. "Anglo-Iranian Oil Co. (United Kingdom v. Iran)," International Court of Justice, http://www.icj-cij.org/docket/index.php?sum=82&p1=3&p2=3&case=16&p3=5. China's case turns on Article 298 of UNCLOS, which provides for exceptions to sea boundary delimitations,

historic bays, and titles. "In 1996, China made a formal declaration under Article 298 stating that it does not accept the system of compulsory procedures entailing binding decisions in Section 2 of Part XV of UNCLOS for any of the categories of disputes listed in Article 298" (Robert C. Beckman, "The Philippines v. China Case and the South China Sea Disputes," in *Territorial Disputes in the South China Sea: Navigating Rough Waters,* ed. Jing Huang and Andrew Billo [New York: Palgrave Macmillan, 2015], 56). Nevertheless, the court found that it does have jurisdiction and ruled broadly against China in 2016.

37. Anders S. Corr and Priscilla A. Tacujan, "Chinese Political and Economic Influence in the Philippines: Implications for Alliances and the South China Sea Dispute," *Journal of Political Risk* 1, no. 3 (2013), http://www.jpolrisk.com/chinese-political-and-economic-influence-in-the-philippines-implications-for-alliances-and-the-south-china-sea-dispute/#more-480.
38. Lum, *The Republic of the Philippines and U.S. Interests,* 14.
39. Armando J. Heredia, "New Defense Agreement Between the Philippines and U.S.: The Basics," USNI News, April 29, 2014, http://news.usni.org/2014/04/29/new-defense-agreement-philippines-u-s-basics.
40. Lum, *The Republic of the Philippines and U.S. Interests,* 14.
41. Ibid., 22, 24; Corr and Tacujan, "Chinese Political and Economic Influence in the Philippines."
42. Lum, *The Republic of the Philippines and U.S. Interests,* summary; Daniel Russel, keynote address, Fifth Annual Center for Strategic and International Studies South China Sea Conference, Washington, D.C., July 21, 2015.
43. Lum, *The Republic of the Philippines and U.S. Interests,* 27–28.
44. Richard C. Paddock, "Behind Duterte's Bluster, a Philippine Shift Away from the U.S.," *New York Times,* October 9, 2016, http://www.nytimes.com/2016/10/10/world/asia/philippines-rodrigo-duterte-obama.html.
45. Associated Press, "U.S. Mood Against Ally Hardens as Philippines President Rodrigo Duterte Stokes Outrage," *Los Angeles Times,* October 1, 2016, http://www.latimes.com/world/la-fg-us-philippines-mood-20161001-snap-story.html; Associated Press, "A Look at the First 100 Days of Duterte's Turbulent Rule," *New York Times,* October 8, 2016, http://www.nytimes.com/aponline/2016/10/08/world/asia/ap-as-philippines-duterte-100-days.html.
46. Associated Press, "China Gives $600 Million Aid to Ally Cambodia," *Jakarta Post,* July 15, 2016, http://www.thejakartapost.com/seasia/2016/07/15/china-gives-600-million-aid-to-ally-cambodia.html.
47. Matthew Rosenberg, "With Bags of Cash, C.I.A. Seeks Influence in Afghanistan," *New York Times,* April 28, 2013, http://www.nytimes.com/2013/04/29/world/asia/cia-delivers-cash-to-afghan-leaders-office.html.
48. United States Census Bureau, "Foreign Trade: Trade in Goods with China," https://www.census.gov/foreign-trade/balance/c5700.html; U.S. Treasury, "Major Foreign Holders of Treasury Securities," http://www.treasury.gov/ticdata/Publish/mfh.txt.
49. "U.S. Relations with China."
50. Anthony Kuhn, "Tensions Continue Over Disputed Islands in South China Sea," National Public Radio, May 31, 2015, http://www.npr.org/2015/05/31/410958263/tensions-continue-over-disputed-islands-in-south-china-sea.

51. Matt Schiavenza, "How Humiliation Drove Modern Chinese History," *The Atlantic*, October 25, 2013, http://www.theatlantic.com/china/archive/2013/10/how-humiliation-drove-modern-chinese-history/280878/; International Crisis Group, "Stirring Up the South China Sea (I)," Asia Report 223, April 23, 2012, 27, http://www.crisisgroup.org/~/media/Files/asia/north-east-asia/223-stirring-up-the-south-china-sea-i.pdf.
52. International Crisis Group, "Stirring Up the South China Sea (I)," 27.
53. Ibid., 28.
54. Government of the People's Republic of China, "Position Paper of the Government of the People's Republic of China on the Matter of Jurisdiction in the South China Sea Arbitration Initiated by the Republic of the Philippines," December 7, 2014, http://www.fmprc.gov.cn/mfa_eng/zxxx_662805/t1217147.shtml; Su Hao, *China's Positions and Interests in the South China Sea: A Rational Choices* [sic] *in its Cooperative Policies* (Washington, D.C.: Center for Strategic and International Studies, September 2011), 2. Note that Republican senators have blocked U.S. ratification of UNCLOS, a position that is highly unpopular among Democrats. The convention was negotiated at a time when the United States had better bargaining leverage relative to China and so is likely the best agreement we could get that might help resolve the South and East China Sea conflicts. China frequently uses the failure of the United States to ratify UNCLOS to parry UNCLOS-related arguments wielded against China.
55. Hayton, *The South China Sea*, 55.
56. Kevin Baumert and Brian Melchior, "China: Maritime Claims in the South China Sea," *Limits in the Seas* no. 143 (Washington, D.C.: U.S. Department of State, 2014), 1, http://www.state.gov/documents/organization/234936.pdf.
57. Ibid., 2.
58. Ibid., 4.
59. Li Guoqiang, "China Sea Oil and Gas Resources," *China Institute of International Studies* 1, May 11, 2015, http://www.ciis.org.cn/english/2015-05/11/content_7894391.htm.
60. U.S. Energy Information Administration, "International Energy Statistics," http://www.eia.gov/cfapps/ipdbproject/IEDIndex3.cfm?tid=94&pid=57&aid=32.
61. Guoqiang, "China Sea Oil and Gas Resources," 1.
62. U.S. Energy Information Administration, "South China Sea," http://www.eia.gov/beta/international/analysis_includes/regions_of_interest/South_China_Sea/south_china_sea.pdf.
63. Gordon Chang, "Say Hello to Taiwan," *National Interest*, October 18, 2016, http://nationalinterest.org/feature/say-hello-taiwan-18092.
64. International Crisis Group, "Stirring Up the South China Sea (I)," 1, 22.
65. David Rosenberg, "Governing the South China Sea: From Freedom of the Seas to Ocean Enclosure Movements," *Harvard Asia Quarterly* 12, no. 3 (2010): pp. 4–12.
66. Ibid., 4.
67. International Crisis Group, "Stirring Up the South China Sea (I)," 22–23.
68. Hao, *China's Positions and Interests in the South China Sea*, 7–8.
69. Beina Xu, "South China Sea Tensions," Council on Foreign Relations Backgrounder, May 14, 2014, http://www.cfr.org/china/south-china-sea-tensions/p29790.

70. Rosenberg, "Governing the South China Sea," 7.
71. Hao, *China's Positions and Interests in the South China Sea*, 8.
72. Hayton, *The South China Sea*, 252.
73. Hao, *China's Positions and Interests in the South China Sea*, 7.
74. Shinzo Abe, "Asia Democratic Security Diamond," Project Syndicate, December 27, 2012, http://www.project-syndicate.org/print/a-strategic-alliance-for-japan-and-india-by-shinzo-abe.
75. Jim Sciutto, "Behind the Scenes: A Secret Navy Flight over China's Military Buildup," CNN, http://www.cnn.com/2015/05/26/politics/south-china-sea-navy-surveillance-plane-jim-sciutto/.
76. Peter E. Robertson and Adrian Sin, "Measuring Hard Power: China's Economic Growth and Military Capacity," *Defence and Peace Economics,* April 20, 2015, 1–21.
77. Editorial Board, "China's Evolving 'Core Interests,'" *New York Times*, May 11, 2013, http://www.nytimes.com/2013/05/12/opinion/sunday/chinas-evolving-core-interests.html; John Pomfret, "Beijing Claims 'Indisputable Sovereignty' over South China Sea," *Washington Post*, July 31, 2010, http://www.washingtonpost.com/wp-dyn/content/article/2010/07/30/AR2010073005664.html.
78. June Teufel Dreyer, e-mail to the author, October 20, 2016.
79. Tim Kelly and Phil Stewart, "Defying China, U.S. Bombers and Japanese Planes Fly Through New Air Zone," Reuters, November 27, 2013, http://www.reuters.com/article/2013/11/27/us-china-defense-usa-idUSBRE9AP0X320131127.
80. Chang Jae-soon and Choi Kyong-ae, "S. Korea, U.S. to Consider Deploying U.S. Strategic Assets to Deter N. Korea," Yonhap News, October 20, 2016, http://english.yonhapnews.co.kr/news/2016/10/20/34/0200000000AEN20161020011851315F.html.
81. Hayton, *The South China Sea*, 268.
82. Author interview with three Chinese Ministry of Foreign Affairs officials on two occasions in 2015, New York.
83. The U.S. government changed the name Scarborough Shoal to Scarborough Reef in its documents and statements starting in 2012. One knowledgeable source said that this could have been part of a U.S.-brokered deal with China that coincided with the 2012 standoff at Scarborough Shoal. Assistant Secretary of State for East Asian and Pacific Affairs Kurt Campbell negotiated the deal between China and the Philippines that led to resolution of the standoff and that was shortly thereafter abrogated by China when it reoccupied Scarborough Shoal. China might have perceived the new name as beneficial to its claims at the time.
84. "Maritime Disputes in East Asia: Testimony," U.S. Department of State, February 22, 2014, http://www.state.gov/p/eap/rls/rm/2014/02/221293.htm.
85. Ibid.
86. "Secretary of Defense Speech," U.S. Department of Defense, May 30, 2015, http://www.defense.gov/Speeches/Speech.aspx?SpeechID=1945.
87. Ibid.
88. Ibid.
89. Jim Gomez, "Duterte on U.S. Alliance: 'Do You Really Think We Need It?'," ABC News, October 11, 2016, http://abcnews.go.com/International/wireStory/duterte-us-alliance-42719852.

90. Keith Johnson, "China's Military Blueprint: Bigger Navy, Bigger Global Role," *Foreign Policy*, May 26, 2015, http://foreignpolicy.com/2015/05/26/chinas-military-blueprint-bigger-navy-bigger-global-role/.
91. Ibid.
92. "Full Text: China's Military Strategy," Xinhua, May 26, 2015, http://www.china.org.cn/china/2015-05/26/content_35661433.htm.
93. Ibid.; Hayton, *The South China Sea*, 252.
94. "Maritime Disputes in East Asia: Testimony."
95. Thomas Schelling, *Arms and Influence* (New Haven: Yale University Press, 1966), 66; Howard W. French, "China's Dangerous Game," *The Atlantic*, November 2014, http://www.theatlantic.com/magazine/archive/2014/11/chinas-dangerous-game/380789/; Pia Lee Brago and Aurea Calica, "China's Salami Slicing, Cabbage Strategy Hit," *Philippine Star*, July 9, 2015, http://www.philstar.com/headlines/2015/07/09/1474877/chinas-salami-slicing-cabbage-strategy-hit.
96. Robert Haddick, "Salami Slicing in the South China Sea," *Foreign Policy*, August 3, 2012, http://foreignpolicy.com/2012/08/03/salami-slicing-in-the-south-china-sea/?wp_login_redirect=0.
97. Ibid.; Jane Perlez, "Philippines and China Ease Tensions in Rift at Sea," *New York Times*, June 18, 2012, http://www.nytimes.com/2012/06/19/world/asia/beijing-and-manila-ease-tensions-in-south-china-sea.html?_r=0.
98. Haddick, "Salami Slicing in the South China Sea."
99. James Hardy, "China Expands Runway, Harbour at Woody Island," *IHS Jane's Defence Weekly*, August 29, 2014, http://www.janes.com/article/42538/china-expands-runway-harbour-at-woody-island.
100. Emma Graham-Harrison, "South China Sea Islands Are Chinese Plan to Militarise Zone, Claims U.S.," *The Guardian*, May 30, 2015, http://www.theguardian.com/world/2015/may/30/us-claims-south-china-sea-islands-are-beijing-plot.
101. Asia Maritime Transparency Initiative, "Country: China," 2017, https://amti.csis.org/island-tracker/chinese-occupied-features/; Associated Press in Canberra, "U.S. Navy: Beijing Creating a 'Great Wall of Sand' in South China Sea," *The Guardian*, March 31, 2015, http://www.theguardian.com/world/2015/mar/31/china-great-wall-sand-spratlys-us-navy.
102. Graham-Harrison, "South China Sea Islands Are Chinese Plan to Militarise Zone, Claims U.S."; Associated Press in Singapore, "China Has Artillery Vehicles on Artificial Island in South China Sea, U.S. Said," *The Guardian*, May 29, 2015, http://www.theguardian.com/world/2015/may/29/us-says-china-had-artillery-vehicles-on-artificial-island-in-south-china-sea.
103. Helene Cooper, "Patrolling Disputed Waters, U.S. and China Jockey for Dominance," *New York Times*, March 31, 2016, http://www.nytimes.com/2016/03/31/world/asia/south-china-sea-us-navy.html.
104. Jim Sciutto, "Exclusive: China Warns U.S. Surveillance Plane," CNN, September 15, 2015, http://edition.cnn.com/2015/05/20/politics/south-china-sea-navy-flight/.
105. Association of Southeast Asian Nations, "Declaration on the Conduct of Parties in the South China Sea," http://www.asean.org/asean/external-relations/china/item/declaration-on-the-conduct-of-parties-in-the-south-china-sea.
106. "Maritime Disputes in East Asia: Testimony."

107. U.S. Department of Defense, "Memorandum of Understanding Between the Department of Defense of the United States of America and the Ministry of National Defense of the People's Republic of China Regarding the Rules of Behavior for Safety of Air and Maritime Encounters," November 9, 2014, http://archive.defense.gov/pubs/141112_MemorandumOfUnderstandingRegardingRules.pdf.
108. Li Bao, "U.S., China to Establish Military Dialogue," Voice of America News, June 13, 2015, http://www.voanews.com/content/united-states-china-sign-deal-on-military-dialogue/2820468.html.
109. William Wan, "Chinese Spy Ship Lurks around U.S.-led Pacific Naval Drills," Washington Post, July 21, 2014, https://www.washingtonpost.com/blogs/worldviews/wp/2014/07/21/chinese-spy-ship-lurks-around-u-s-led-pacific-naval-drills/.
110. Jesse Johnson, "Behind the Scenes, Tillerson Tones Down Rhetoric on South China Sea," Japan Times, February 7, 2017, http://www.japantimes.co.jp/news/2017/02/07/asia-pacific/behind-scenes-tillerson-tones-rhetoric-south-china-sea/.
111. Sciutto, "Behind the Scenes: A Secret Navy Flight over China's Military Buildup."
112. Hao, China's Positions and Interests in the South China Sea, 9.
113. Ibid., 10.
114. Ibid., 9.
115. Stuart Iler and David Rosner, "Revenue Sharing 101," Bipartisan Policy Center, August 16, 2013, http://bipartisanpolicy.org/blog/revenue-sharing-101/.
116. Library of Congress, "Crude Oil Royalty Rates," June 9, 2015, http://www.loc.gov/law/help/crude-oil-royalty-rates/index.php.
117. Note that the sources who have contributed to this section have requested or implied that they wish to remain anonymous. No identifying details, such as date of meeting or nationality of the source, are given to protect their identities. All sources are well positioned to have access to the data they have communicated.
118. Hao, China's Positions and Interests in the South China Sea, 10.
119. Corr and Tacujan, "Chinese Political and Economic Influence in the Philippines."
120. Ernest Z. Bower, "The JMSU: A Tale of Bilateralism and Secrecy in the South China Sea," Center for Strategic and International Studies, July 27, 2010, http://csis.org/publication/jmsu-tale-bilateralism-and-secrecy-south-china-sea. The Philippines may not even have data from the Joint Marine Seismic Undertaking. One source indicated to me in 2015 that members of the Philippine government who should have access to the results of the survey cannot now locate them.
121. Anonymous interviews with the author.
122. Baumert and Melchior, "China: Maritime Claims in the South China Sea," 1; Jane Perlez, "Dispute Flares Over Energy in South China Sea," New York Times, December 4, 2012, http://www.nytimes.com/2012/12/05/world/asia/china-vietnam-and-india-fight-over-energy-exploration-in-south-china-sea.html.
123. James Hookway, "Philippine Oil Vessel Confronted by China, Spurring New Dispute," Wall Street Journal, March 4, 2011, http://www.wsj.com/articles/SB10001424052748703300904576178161531819874.
124. Anonymous interviews with the author.
125. Hao, China's Positions and Interests in the South China Sea, 10–11.
126. Haddick, "Salami Slicing in the South China Sea."

127. M. Taylor Fravel, "China's Strategy in the South China Sea," *Contemporary Southeast Asia* 33, no. 3 (2011): p. 297.
128. Ibid., 299.
129. Mark E. Manyin et al., *Pivot to the Pacific? The Obama Administration's "Rebalancing" Toward Asia*, R42448 (Washington, D.C.: Congressional Research Service, 2012), summary, https://www.fas.org/sgp/crs/natsec/R42448.pdf.
130. Ibid.
131. Ibid., 5.
132. Natalie Liu, "China Sees Threat in U.S. Pivot to Asia," Voice of America News, June 7, 2013, http://www.voanews.com/content/china-sees-threat-in-us-pivot-to-asia/1677768.html.
133. See previous section on U.S. alliances.
134. Nobuhiro Kubo, Tim Kelly, and David Brunnstrom, "Exclusive: Japan Considering Joint U.S. Air Patrols in South China Sea—Sources," Reuters, April 29, 2015, http://www.reuters.com/article/2015/04/29/us-usa-japan-southchinasea-idUSKBN0NK15M20150429.
135. White House, Office of the Press Secretary, "Fact Sheet: The U.S.-Australia Alliance," November 10, 2014, https://www.whitehouse.gov/the-press-office/2014/11/10/fact-sheet-us-australia-alliance.
136. David S. Cloud, "U.S. Publicly Challenges China's Moves in Disputed Islands," *Los Angeles Times*, May 21, 2015, http://www.latimes.com/world/asia/la-fg-us-china-20150522-story.html#page=1.
137. Graham-Harrison, "South China Sea Islands Are Chinese Plan to Militarise Zone, Claims U.S."
138. Cloud, "U.S. Publicly Challenges China's Moves in Disputed Islands."
139. Associated Press in Canberra, "U.S. Navy: Beijing Creating a 'Great Wall of Sand' in South China Sea"; "U.S. Calls for Land Reclamation 'Halt' in South China Sea," BBC News, May 30, 2015, http://www.bbc.com/news/world-asia-32941829.

1

Why China Built Its New Islands

From Abstract Claim to Concrete Assets

Bill Hayton

In June 2015, the Chinese government announced that it had, in effect, completed the construction of seven artificial islands within the Spratly archipelago in the southern part of the South China Sea.[1] The islands were built on top of coral reefs that China had occupied for at least two decades. These were not the first examples of "terraforming" in the archipelago, but the construction program, which had begun less than two years earlier, was unlike anything previously seen in the region.[2] Satellite photographs revealed the presence, at each of the seven installations, of harbors capable of hosting large naval warships. By 2016, three of the new islands accommodated three-thousand-meter runways—long enough to accommodate all the aircraft in service with the People's Liberation Army (PLA).[3]

This massive civil engineering project has changed the balance of power among the disputing states that claim ownership of features in the Spratlys. The new runways and harbors will allow China to reduce some of the "home advantage" available to the other main claimants (Vietnam, the Philippines, and Malaysia) whose mainlands are much closer to their bases in the Spratlys. They are likely to significantly enhance China's ability to project and sustain force in the area and beyond.

Over the past half century, the islands' remoteness and the desire of the various claimants to keep their activities secret have kept developments in the Spratlys largely hidden from international view. The advent of commercially available satellite imagery has pulled back the curtain. Pictures of China's activities, gathered by two organizations in particular—the commercial information service IHS Jane's and the Washington, D.C.–based think tank Center for Strategic and International Studies (CSIS)—prompted much greater discussion of the island-building than would have been possible previously. The images these organizations disseminated were sufficiently dramatic to appear on the front pages of newspapers and websites around the world.

Most of the ensuing international media coverage contained an element of panic about China's apparent "swallowing" of the South China Sea. The scale of the construction tended to obscure the fact that China had not occupied any new territory; it had built on reefs it had occupied for two decades. The coverage also tended to conflate two separate sets of disputes in the region—the regional and the global—and to mischaracterize the motivations behind China's actions as expansionism when, from a Chinese perspective, the impetus was to protect the country's inherent territory. This chapter will argue that underlying the island-building and China's wider actions is a sense of national entitlement to the islands, reefs, and—most controversially—waters of the South China Sea based upon nationalist readings of regional history.[4] This sense of entitlement is likely to lead China to make even more assertive moves in the region over the coming years—a creeping annexation of strategic and resource-rich areas. The result will be further confrontations.

CHINA'S SENSE OF ENTITLEMENT

How does China view its strategic aims in the South China Sea? This crucial question is surprisingly understudied compared to other aspects of the disputes. Given the opacity of China's political process, it is difficult to reach definitive conclusions about how the country's policymaking elite really regard the South China Sea, but official documents and statements do give us some insights. In June 2014, at the Fifth National Border and Coast Defense Work Meeting in Beijing, President Xi Jinping asserted that China must place the highest priority on building "an impregnable wall [literally, 'a wall of copper and iron'] for border and ocean defense." As Ryan Martinson noted, "Ocean defense (海防) . . . refers to actions to defend all 'Chinese' space from encroachment, including offshore islands and remote waters under Chinese jurisdiction." Xi's starting point in his remarks was China's "national humiliation" at the hands of foreigners (between the First Opium War of 1840 and the Communist revolution of 1949), and his conclusion was that the country's priority is to "resolutely safeguard territorial sovereignty and maritime rights and interests."[5]

Five months later, in November 2014, Xi addressed the entire senior leadership of the Communist Party of China and the foreign policy establishment at the Central Conference on Work Relating to Foreign Affairs. It was the country's highest level foreign policy event since the 1949 revolution. Michael Swaine noted that Xi singled out as a national priority "the need to firmly uphold China's territorial sovereignty, maritime rights and interests and national unity, and properly handle territorial and island disputes." Swaine argues that "given its repeated use in various other Xi speeches and official People's Republic of China (PRC) statements, [a] dual stress on development and the protection of national interests has become a hallmark of the Xi Jinping regime."[6]

China's 2015 Defense White Paper identified the major threats facing the country as "hegemonism, power politics, and neo-interventionism" and prioritized one task for the military above all: "to safeguard [China's] national unification, territorial integrity and development interests."[7] According to Ryan Martinson, it is likely that when Chinese officials talk about territorial integrity as a core interest (核心利益), they include both offshore land features and zones emanating from them within their understanding of China's "territory."[8] Elsewhere in the document we can see clear perceptions of threat: from the U.S. military presence in the Asia-Pacific, from Japan's growing assertiveness, from the loss of territory and maritime rights, and from China's growing dependence on international trade. While the United States, Japan, and the Southeast Asian states are all concerned about China's growing assertiveness, the opposite is also true. The region is locked in a cycle of action and reaction.

Speeches and official documents make clear that the Chinese leadership is confident of the correctness of the country's territorial claims and of the actions it takes to assert them. This assumption is so deeply embedded in Chinese policy-making that it is barely mentioned at all, yet it is always there. In March 2009, for example, Rear Admiral Yang Yi of China's National Defense University argued that any discussions with countries with claims in the South China Sea that overlapped China's "must be based on the premise that sovereignty [over disputed areas] belongs to China."[9] What has changed since then is the degree of assertiveness China has been prepared to exhibit. In the opinion of Zhou Fangyin, director of the department of China's regional strategy in the National Institute of International Strategy at the Chinese Academy of Social Sciences, the attitude toward the territorial claim began to shift in 2011: "A general consensus was reached that China should not allow its essential sovereign rights to be compromised for the sake of maintaining regional stability."[10]

Non-Chinese observers tend to underestimate the degree to which China views the South China Sea through a particular historical lens that lends an air of "righteousness" to its actions. This is a mistake. Singapore-based analyst Li Minjiang, having interviewed more than fifty Chinese foreign policy thinkers between 2009 and 2012, noted that "although unclear about the exact terms of entitlement, the general Chinese public seems to believe that China enjoys some exclusive entitlement in the South China Sea."[11]

HISTORICAL NARRATIVE

This attitude toward the sea dates back to the birth of the Republic of China (ROC) in the early twentieth century. A claim to the Spratlys was first articulated by the ROC in 1947, when an official map including a "U-shaped line" around the different archipelagos in the South China Sea was first drawn, and has been reiterated many times since—notably in the 1958 Declaration of the Government of the People's Republic of China on China's Territorial Sea and the 1992 Law of the People's Republic of China on the Territorial Sea and the Contiguous Zone. It is simply taken for granted among the Chinese leadership that all the features within the U-shaped line are rightfully China's. Therefore, actions to assert a Chinese claim to these features are regarded not as expansionist but as a defense against foreign incursions.

I have previously described this sense of entitlement as a case of "false memory syndrome" because of its reliance upon nationalistic misreadings of regional history.[12] The problem for the region is that, during the twentieth century, this unevidenced belief became intimately bound with China's national search for respect after what its ideologues have called the "Century of National Humiliation," the period of imperial domination after the 1840 Opium War with Britain.[13]

The "imagined history," frequently restated by Chinese officials, that the South China Sea has been Chinese territory "since ancient times" is underpinned by claims that owe more to myth than history. A notable one is that the Spratly Islands rightfully belong to China because the Ming-era admiral Zheng He sailed past them in the early fifteenth century—six hundred years ago. There is no evidence that the Ming court ever regarded the islands as more than a navigation hazard. Nor is there any to suggest that Chinese officials landed on them before 1946. Nonetheless, Chinese schools continue to teach these myths as fact, and Chinese officials continue to repeat them. In late June 2015, for example, China's foreign minister, Wang Yi, told an audience of academics and former officials at the Fourth World Peace Forum at Tsinghua University in Beijing that "China was the first country to discover, use and administer the Nansha Islands."[14] Ironically, this imagined history has been accepted by some key Western writers on regional security. Both Bernard Cole (in his *Great Wall at Sea*) and Greg Austin (in his *China's Ocean Frontier: International Law, Military Force, and National Development*) accept it uncritically, for example.[15]

This narrative of South China Sea history has been demolished in recent years by the work of independent historians. Accounts by scholars such as Derek Heng, Roderick Ptak, Angela Schottenhammer, Li Tana, and Geoff Wade describe a much more heterogeneous history.[16] The evidence we have suggests the South China Sea was an ungoverned space, a realm of semi-nomadic fisherfolk, sea gypsies, and pirates, until the beginning of the twentieth century. In the words of one particularly eminent scholar of the region, Leonard Blussé, during most of recorded history Chinese rulers could barely control their own coast, let alone the islands offshore.[17]

ORIGINS OF CHINA'S CLAIM

China's sense of ownership toward the South China Sea only emerged among nationalist intellectuals in the twentieth century.[18] In the dying decade of the Qing Dynasty, questions of where China's rightful borders lay became highly politicized. For the most part, the boundaries of the imperial realm had not been formally defined, except in certain places where other powers had forced boundaries upon the Qing through a series of "unequal treaties." The "borders question" became more acute with the collapse of the Qing Dynasty and the birth of the Republic of China, but internal disputes, civil war, and then Japanese invasion delayed its resolution until after World War II. The question then became part of the Communist Party of China's "victory narrative"—the notion that the party's revolution in 1949 had ended the "Century of National Humiliation."

Most of the initial focus of the border question was directed toward the colonial settlements imposed on China's trading ports, including Hong Kong, Shanghai, and Tsingtao. However, in early 1909, public opinion became sensitized to Japanese guano mining activities on Pratas Island, between Hong Kong and Taiwan. This prompted the viceroy of the "two Guangs" (Guangdong and Guangxi) to dispatch an expedition to the Paracel Islands in May 1909—the first time that China had made any gesture of sovereignty there. Chinese attention remained focused on the Paracels, not the Spratlys, for decades. Even when France (then the colonial power in Indochina) annexed several of the Spratly Islands in

1933, the Chinese central government in Nanjing chose not to issue a diplomatic protest.[19] At a meeting in September 1933, the Republic of China's military committee decided to regard the Paracels as China's "southernmost territory."[20] It was not until thirteen years later that official Chinese attention moved southward toward the Spratlys.

In an effort to formally define its borders, the ROC convened an "Inspection Committee for Land and Water Maps" in June 1933. The first volume of the committee's journal, published in January 1935, included Chinese names for 132 islands and islets in the South China Sea. Twenty-eight were in the Paracels and 96 in the Spratlys. However, the committee did not base its work on Chinese surveys but rather on copying foreign maps, thus demonstrating how little knowledge the Chinese government had of the islands. The committee's list was not a collection of traditional Chinese names for the features but rather transliterations and translations of the Western names printed on navigation charts. A few of those appear to have had Chinese or Malay roots, but most had been conferred by Europeans. For example, North Danger Reef became *běi xiǎn* (Chinese for "north danger"), Antelope Reef (named after a British surveying vessel) became *líng yang* (the Chinese word for "antelope"), and Spratly Island became *si-ba-la-tuo* (the Chinese transliteration of the English name). The Macclesfield Bank in the center of the sea was named *Nansha* (southern sand) and the Spratlys named *Tuansha* (area of sand).[21] It is significant, of course, that at this juncture the Macclesfield Bank was regarded as "southern."

The committee simply translated the names of the features on the British maps into Chinese, including many of the existing errors, and added some of its own. The James Shoal seems to be a case in point. The committee gave it the Chinese name of *Zeng-mu* (the transliteration of James) *Tan* (the Chinese word for a beach or sandbank—something that sticks out of the water). In English nautical terminology, however, a shoal is an underwater feature—an area of shallow sea. James Shoal is in fact twenty-two meters below the surface. But because of the committee's unfamiliarity with the area, they declared it to be a land feature. After World War II, Chinese officials declared the James Shoal to be the "southernmost point of Chinese territory." Thus, it would seem that China's claim in the South China Sea is, to some extent, based on a translation error. The "southernmost point of Chinese territory" does not actually exist. Nonetheless, a typical exercise for an eighth-grade geography student in China, even today, is to use a ruler to measure the distance on a map from the northern border with Mongolia to the James Shoal, one hundred kilometers (km) from the coast of Borneo, to calculate the dimensions of the national territory.[22]

The First Island Occupations

France and Japan had occupied some of the Spratly Islands during the late 1930s and World War II. In July 1946, a newly independent Philippines made a verbal claim to the archipelago, and in October of that year, France "reclaimed" Itu Aba with a voyage there. It was only in December 1946, having recently received second-hand warships and training from the United States, that China first had the ability to send officials as far south as the Spratly Islands. Two Chinese ships dropped a landing party on Itu Aba on December 12, 1946. It was after this voyage that the ROC formally claimed sovereignty over the islands. When the first official Chinese government map of the South China Sea was drawn up in 1947 and then published in early 1948, it also included a revised list of Chinese names for the reefs and islands. Spratly Island became *Nanwei* ("Noble South"), for example. James Shoal became *Zengmu Ansha* (*Ansha* appears to have been a newly coined word for "shoal"), and the *Nansha* moved south from the Macclesfield Bank to the Spratlys. The *Tuansha* disappeared from the map.

The 1948 map also contained a U-shaped line running parallel with the coasts of Vietnam, Borneo, and the Philippines and encompassing almost all the reefs and islands within the main body of the South China Sea. The exact meaning of the line was not made explicitly clear at the time. However, recent research in the ROC archives by Canadian scholar Christopher Chung seems to confirm that the cartographers' original intention was only to indicate which islands the country was claiming.[23] This contrasts with the position sometimes asserted today in which China appears to be claiming "historic rights" over resources and navigation within the entirety of the U-shaped line.

Available records show that the ROC only ever occupied one feature in the Spratlys: Itu Aba (known in Chinese as *Taiping Dao*). The ROC garrisoned it between December 1946 and May 1950, when it withdrew following the loss of Hainan to the Communists. In 1956, a Philippine entrepreneur, Tomas Cloma, attempted to claim most of the Spratly Islands as his own personal independent country under the name of Freedomland. This prompted Taiwan to reoccupy Itu Aba and the newly independent Republic of Vietnam (South Vietnam) to also stake its claim with a voyage to the islands.

Interest in the islands had initially been limited to gestures of nationalist flag-waving and the collection of guano. However, after United Nations–sponsored surveys in the late 1960s suggested the possible presence of oil reserves in the sea, Southeast Asian countries began to take a more serious view and permanently occupy some of the islands and reefs. At the same time, negotiations for a new

Law of the Sea, which lasted from 1973 until 1982, gave rise to the concept of the exclusive economic zone (EEZ) and greatly increased the value of remote islands. Whichever country owned a habitable island would gain the rights to all the fish and mineral resources within a radius of up to two hundred nautical miles around it.

In 1970, President Ferdinand Marcos ordered the Philippine military to occupy seven features in the Spratlys in preparation for oil prospecting. In 1974, after the People's Republic of China had evicted Republic of Vietnam forces from the western half of the Paracel Islands, the Saigon government ordered its troops to occupy several of the Spratlys. Shortly afterward, China built a naval base and runway on Woody Island in the eastern half of the Paracel archipelago, allowing it to project power farther south. In 1983, Malaysian forces established a base on Swallow Reef. They occupied two other features in 1986 (and would occupy two more in 1999).[24] By the end of the 1980s, everything that could be called an island—and most of the reefs—was firmly occupied. There was almost nothing else left. Around this time, the PLA Navy (PLAN) began making voyages and surveys in and around the Spratlys.

China Enters the Spratlys

In early 1987, the Beijing leadership decided to occupy territory in the Spratlys.[25] In March 1987, a United Nations Educational, Scientific, and Cultural Organization meeting mandated countries to establish monitoring stations as part of a survey of the world's oceans. None of the rival claimants appeared to notice that one of the sites China proposed was in the Spratlys. On November 6, 1987, the Beijing leadership gave the green light to construct an observation post on Fiery Cross Reef. On January 21, 1988, engineers began building a two-story barracks, a wharf, a helicopter hangar, and a landing pad. On February 18, the Chinese landed sailors on the only feature on London Reefs that the Vietnamese did not occupy: Cuarteron Reef (*Huayang* in Chinese), a rocky outcrop just 19 km from the nearest Vietnamese outpost.

On March 14, 1988, Chinese forces grabbed Johnson Reef from under the noses of the Vietnamese. Units from both countries landed on the feature at the same time, and a verbal dispute between them escalated into a fight. The Chinese then machine-gunned the Vietnamese on the reef and shelled the Vietnamese ships, killing sixty-four marines and sailors in the process. By April 8, the PRC had occupied three more features: Hughes Reef, a part of Union Banks, nineteen kilometers east of Vietnamese-occupied Sin Cowe island; Gaven Reef, part of Tizard Bank on which sit both Itu Aba, the largest of the Spratlys and still the only one occupied by Taiwan, and Namyit Island, occupied by Vietnam; and Subi Reef, an isolated feature fifteen kilometers from the Philippines-occupied Thitu Island (*Pagasa* in Tagalog).

In February 1992, the Chinese National People's Congress passed a new Law on the Territorial Sea.[26] Shortly afterward, China issued a license to a tiny American company, Crestone, to explore for oil in an area of sea southeast of Vietnam and immediately adjacent to the EEZ claims of Malaysia and Indonesia. In July 1992, in an effort to try to calm the situation, the six members of the Association of Southeast Asian Nations (ASEAN) issued their Manila Declaration calling on "all parties" to "exercise restraint" in their actions in the South China Sea.

However, in May 1994, the Philippine government under President Fidel Ramos secretly approved an application from a Philippine company, Alcorn Petroleum (a subsidiary of an American company, Vaalco Energy), to conduct a paper assessment of the oil and gas potential in an area off the coast of Palawan. News of the Alcorn survey leaked, and Beijing issued a protest on the grounds that it was an infringement of Chinese sovereignty and a violation of the principle of joint development that the two countries had agreed in 1988.[27] This seems to have been the trigger for Chinese action to, in its view, defend its resource claims in the area. Sometime toward the end of the year, Chinese forces occupied Mischief Reef right inside the survey area and just 209 km from the Philippine island of Palawan. They constructed what they referred to as fishermen's shelters on the reef, but aerial photographs revealed they were also equipped with heavy machine guns.

Developing Islands

All the Chinese occupations began with very basic facilities—usually huts on stilts. Over time, these were developed into more substantial blockhouses, sometimes with helipads and jetties. Only the outpost at Fiery Cross Reef was of any significant size, and it was the only facility with a wharf for large vessels.

The other claimant countries, having begun their occupations earlier, controlled a mixture of reefs and larger natural islands. On top of the reefs they built lighthouses and small defensive fortifications, and they constructed more sophisticated facilities on the islands. Both Spratly Island, occupied by Vietnam, and Thitu, occupied by the Philippines, are large enough to have had runways since the mid-1970s (although the one on Thitu projects from each side of the island). The most significant example of terraforming in the Spratlys before China's 2013–15 spree was Malaysia's construction of a runway, naval base, and civilian diving resort on Swallow Reef in 1986.

It was developments such as these, but particularly China's occupation of Mischief Reef, that led to ASEAN persuading China to sign up to the "Declaration on the Conduct of Parties in the South China Sea" in 2002. Under Article 5, "the Parties undertake to exercise self-restraint in the conduct of activities that would complicate or escalate disputes and affect peace and stability including, among others, refraining from action of inhabiting on the presently uninhabited islands, reefs, shoals, cays, and other features and to handle their differences in a constructive manner."

While this does not explicitly prevent the signatories from enlarging their existing island bases, the parties had, since 2002, generally avoided any major developments. The Philippines has not engaged in any land reclamation; indeed, the runway on Thitu/Pagasa has been significantly eroded by wave action and not repaired. Manila has both lacked the financial resources to do so and been reluctant to incur Beijing's displeasure.

Vietnam, however, has had both the resources and the political will. According to satellite imagery analyzed by CSIS, Vietnam doubled the size of its (natural) island base at Sand Cay between 2010 and 2014 and, between August 2012 and 2014, created 65,000 square meters of artificial land at West London Reef.[28] Taiwan, which is not a signatory to the Declaration on the Conduct, finished building a runway on Itu Aba in 2008, although this did not involve any land reclamation. These were all relatively small developments compared to China's recent island-building and did not dramatically change the strategic situation in the South China Sea. Nonetheless, they were probably regarded as provocations by the Beijing leadership.

Island-building

None of the seven features the PRC physically occupies in the Spratlys is large enough to host a runway—or even support human habitation—in its natural state (see table 1-1). Before Chinese engineers added steel and concrete to them, Cuarteron, Fiery Cross, Gaven, and Johnson Reefs each boasted a few jagged rocks that remained above the surface at high tide. Surveys carried out before the Chinese occupations indicate that the three other features, Hughes, Subi, and Mischief Reefs, would naturally be under water at high tide.[29]

Like the other claimants, China had periodically upgraded the facilities on these reefs over the years. Fiery Cross Reef, in particular, had become a substantial base. However, in September 2013, China initiated dramatic developments at all seven features. The commercial information service IHS Jane's used data

TABLE 1-1. **CHINESE-OCCUPIED FEATURES IN THE SPRATLY ISLANDS**

Feature	Occupied	Part of	Named after	Natural State[†]	Definition of Feature by 2016 Arbitral Tribunal Ruling[*]
Fiery Cross	January 1988	Solo	Tea Clipper *Fiery Cross* wrecked 1860	"covered except for a prominent rock" (13)	Rock
Cuarteron	February 1988	London Reefs	Spanish mariner/priest Carlos Cuarteron (1816–1880)	"on the north side of the reef there are some rocks standing 1.6 m[etres] high that do not cover" (14)	Rock
Johnson South	March 1988	Union Bank	Officer on HMS *Herald* survey expedition 1831	"a number of large rocks show above high water in the southeast of the reef; the largest stands 1.2 metres" (10)	Rock
Hughes	April 1988	Union Bank	Officer on HMS *Herald*, survey expedition 1831	"coral patch" (11)	Low tide elevation (but within 12 nautical miles [nm] of the rock at McKennan Reef)
Gaven (North and South)	April 1988	Tizard Bank	Not known	North Reef: "dries in part to 1.2 metres and has one large rock that stands 1.9 metres above high water" (8) South Reef: "dries to 1 metre" (9)	Gaven North: low tide elevation Gaven South: rock
Subi	April 1988	Solo	Not known	"drying reef" (6)	Low tide elevation (but within 12 nm of the rock at Sandy Cay)
Mischief	1994	Solo	British ship *Mischief* under Captain Walsh[**]	"the reef is awash and dries in patches to 0.6 metres" (29)	Low tide elevation

[*] Award in the Matter of the South China Sea Arbitration, PCA case no. 2013-19, p.174.
[**] U.S. Navy Hydrographic Office, *Reported Dangers to Navigation in the Pacific Ocean* (Washington, D.C.: U.S. Government Printing Office, 1871).
[†] D. J. Hancox and John Robert Victor Prescott, "A Geographical Description of the Spratly Islands and an Account of Hydrographic Surveys Amongst Those Islands," *Maritime Briefing* 1, no. 6 (1995). Numbers in parentheses refer to page number.

from the maritime Automatic Identification System to track the movements of a six-thousand-ton German-designed dredging vessel, the *Tian Jing Hao*.[30] It began operations at Cuarteron Reef in September 2013 before moving on to Fiery Cross Reef and Johnson Reef in December and finally to Gaven Reef in May 2014. This dredger was only the largest of several dozen vessels that the Chinese authorities used in the operation. This April 2015 description of the activity on Mischief Reef demonstrates the scale of the undertaking: "Satellite imagery shows a minimum of 23 dredgers operating at Mischief on April 13, along with at least two dozen other large construction-related vessels within the lagoon formed by the circular reef. In that day's satellite image, 28 concrete transport/mixing trucks can be seen, in addition to dozens of other large trucks and dozens of backhoes."[31]

Fiery Cross Reef, Mischief Reef, and Subi Reef were sufficiently enlarged to create space for three-thousand-meter runways usable by every type of combat and transport aircraft in China's navy and air force. The ports at all three are able to accommodate and resupply large naval vessels. The other reefs (Cuarteron, Gaven, Hughes, and Johnson) now also have port facilities, albeit smaller ones.[32]

The scale of the construction and the amount of resources deployed would have required considerable planning and preparation. According to IHS Jane's, "Since the images of reclamation at the reef were published in May 2014, plans showing a runway, hangars for fast jets, a port, wind turbines, and greenhouses have been widely circulated online. The plans were first announced in 2012 and then published by the No. 9 Design and Research Institute of China State Shipbuilding Corporation, although they were later taken down from the institute's website."[33]

If plans were announced in 2012, it seems reasonable to assume that the political decision to build the islands would have been taken even earlier. There had been suggestions of construction plans about three years previously, according to Singapore analyst Li Minjiang:

> In 2009, General Zhang Li, the former Deputy Chief of the General Staff of the PLA, declared that China should build an airport and seaport on Mischief Reef so that Chinese aircraft could patrol the area to protect Chinese fishing activities and declare Chinese sovereignty over the islands of the Spratlys.[34] In the same year, in July, a senior official at the Administration of Fishery and Fishing Harbor Supervision of the South China Sea proposed that China build fishery administration bases on features under Chinese occupation to better protect China's fishery resources in the South China Sea.[35]

This would suggest that a number of Chinese officials had plans to build the islands at least as early as 2009. The degree of planning reflects China's long-term approach to the South China Sea. Since the early 1970s, it has sought to bring islands, reefs, and the areas of sea in between under its control as and when its capabilities and resources allowed. Initially its ability to project naval power more than a few miles off its coast was highly limited, but during the 1970s and 1980s, it improved considerably.[36] Having occupied the reefs in 1988, it consolidated its presence there incrementally until it had the necessary resources, technology, and political consensus to build the new islands in 2013–15.

WHY DID CHINA BUILD THE ISLANDS?

Chinese officials are rarely explicit about China's aims in the South China Sea. However, in his memoirs, the man regarded as the father of the modern Chinese navy, Admiral Liu Huaqing, enumerated six maritime objectives that formed the core of his strategy of "near-seas active defense": reunify Taiwan with the mainland, enable the return of lost and disputed maritime territory in the First Island Chain, defend national maritime resources, secure China's strategic lines of communication, preclude preferably but if necessary defeat decisively any seaborne attack by foreigners, and build sufficient strategic nuclear deterrence.[37]

What seems most significant is that the first three objectives involve questions of "returning" territory and resources to national control. This is testament to the Chinese leadership's enduring obsession with ending the country's national humiliation. These issues may have been less of a priority in earlier eras, when the country and communist regime faced existential threats, but the situation clearly changed in the 1980s. Admiral Liu formulated his strategy of near-seas active defense in late 1985, writing, "Our military had to switch from wartime condition to concepts for times of peace."[38] It prompted a complete change in China's actions in the South China Sea.

A particular weakness of much international analysis of Chinese actions in the South China Sea has been that it concentrates too much on the second half of Admiral Liu's list—the classic subjects of traditional naval studies and international relations—and not enough on the first half. By downplaying the Chinese leadership's own priorities, such analysis fails to understand the key motivations driving Chinese policy. A typical example might be a 2015 paper by Christopher H. Sharman for the Center for the Study of Chinese Military Affairs at the Institute for National Strategic Studies. Sharman notes that "China's primary interests that drive PLAN missions are national security and economic stability. Its maritime security concern is homeland defense, which includes Taiwan, its territorial claims within the "nine-dash line" in the South China Sea, and the Diaoyu (called Senkaku by Japan) Islands in the East China Sea. Threats to its security interests come from any military that can prevent China from asserting its claims. China's maritime strategy must anticipate these threats, which may require the PLAN to be defensively postured in the far seas."[39] However, he practically ignores the issues of homeland defense and territorial sovereignty throughout the remainder of the paper. Naval analysts need to take China's historical narrative much more seriously.

China's emphasis on its territorial narrative is a particular problem because China's neighbors strongly reject it. This is the origin of all the current disputes. If analysts discount the territorial elements and focus only on questions of grand strategy, they will end up answering the wrong question, leaving the problem of the South China Sea to fester. To take but one example, Chinese officials regarded fish around the James Shoal as "Chinese" even though they are hundreds of miles from the mainland. When they send vessels to protect fishermen catching these fish, they do not see themselves as encroaching on others' territory. Rather, they see themselves defending Chinese entitlements from the encroachments of others. The end result, as the region has repeatedly seen, is conflict. This conflict cannot be resolved by confidence-building measures alone. The root cause, China's sense of entitlement, needs to be addressed.

That said, the second half of Admiral Liu's list is clearly important. For a country dependent on trade, access to the open ocean through the South China Sea is a matter of national survival. Linda Jakobson of Australia's Lowy Institute argues that "China's realistic strategic maritime objective . . . is to ensure that it is not denied access to its near seas and what it perceives as its sovereign maritime rights."[40] Andrew Chubb has pointed out that Chinese discussions often describe the region as China's "lifeline" and as a site of strategic struggle. Admiral Liu also regarded the sea as a buffer against foreign attacks, describing it as China's "protective screen."[41] Finally, many observers, particularly in Japan, believe that China is attempting to turn the deep water in the center of the South China Sea into a "bastion" in which to hide its ballistic missile submarines. I briefly examine each of these motivations below.

Global Motivations

On a global scale, it can easily be argued that China's island-building is a defensive response to a possible future U.S. warfighting strategy. China's leadership perceives that the country is acutely vulnerable to the interdiction of its maritime trade routes. Some vocal American strategic thinkers have openly advocated a strategy of "offshore control" in the event of a future war with China.[42] T. X. Hammes of the Institute for National Strategic Studies, for example, argued that in an "unlikely conflict," the United States should aim to strangle China's supply lines by closing the straits of "Malacca, Lombok, Sunda, and the routes north and south of Australia."[43] A more recent study by the RAND Corporation noted that "even a brief, severe war would produce a shock to Chinese global trade."[44] These are highly alarming notions to a country dependent upon imports and exports of oil, other commodities, and consumer goods.

Ever since Deng Xiaoping ordered the creation of China's first special economic zone in Shenzhen in 1980, national prosperity has depended upon an arc of cities around the coast and the movements of imports and exports that sustain them. China has been a net importer of food since 2007, and in September 2013, China surpassed the United States to become the world's largest net oil importer, just as the shale-fracking boom was starting to lead the United States in the direction of energy self-sufficiency.[45] Foreign trade makes up around 40 percent of Chinese gross domestic product (compared to less than a third in the United States), yet the country has no clear access to the open sea. The forces of geophysics have thrown up islands all around its coast, and the forces of geopolitics have turned them all into potentially hostile neighbors. In the view of Wu Shicun, president of China's National Institute for South China Sea Studies, the number-one reason for China's stance on the South China Sea is to ensure strategic access through it to the world's oceans.[46] A country serious about maintaining that access—and fearful of the intentions of the United States—must necessarily develop the capabilities to protect it. A key driver motivating the island-building therefore appears to be a means to complicate a hostile strategy of "offshore control." By creating runways, naval bases, and logistics depots on the reefs, China is creating the capacity to project power closer to all three of the main Southeast Asian straits.

A possible second element to this defensive agenda is to add to China's options in some kind of anti-access/area denial strategy against efforts (particularly by the United States) to support Taiwan in the event of a conflict there. Since Chinese leaders regard Taiwan as a part of the motherland, they would regard intervention as a defense of China's territorial integrity, not an offensive act against an independent state. This is obviously not a view shared by Taiwan's leadership or the United States and its allies. China's new island bases greatly increase the space monitored by its early warning systems, facilitate easier tracking of potential targets, and offer dispersed havens for warships and planes. Any future deployment of China's emerging supersonic antiship missile capability would be a complicating factor for any U.S. or other fleet attempting to traverse the sea in support of Taiwan or another state.

A third element is that China is expecting to use the deep-water areas of the sea as maneuvering space for its new Type 094 (*Jin*-class) ballistic missile submarines. At least three of these boats are now based at the recently expanded and partly underground Yulin naval base just outside the resort city of Sanya on Hainan Island. There has been speculation that China might try to use the sea as a defended bastion—a semi-enclosed area in which it would have a better chance of protecting the submarines than if they tried to exit the sea through narrow, U.S.-monitored chokepoints and head into the more open waters of the Pacific or Indian Ocean.[47] Since the purpose of the submarines is to defend the country, and Communist Party rule, against the threat of nuclear attack or coercion, it follows that the party leadership regards the construction of such a bastion as a defensive action.

It would be considerably easier for the PLAN to achieve this bastion if it were able to control Scarborough Shoal. It would form the third point of a triangle with existing bases in the Paracels and Spratlys. At the time of writing, it has not built upon the feature. However, a Chinese government statement in July 2016 asserted a continuing territorial claim to the shoal.[48] Chinese coast guard vessels have not withdrawn from it, and it appears that China retains the ambition to use it as a strategic asset in the future.

The installation of large "aerial farms" and radar towers on the new islands implies they are intended to be bases for air, surface, and undersea surveillance operations, tracking vessels and other assets from the United States and other states. The islands could also offer basing for the antisubmarine warfare aircraft and other assets necessary for an integrated defense of the submarines within the bastion. The U.S. Navy no longer has permanent bases within the South China Sea region, but it does have good access to harbors and prepositioned supplies in Singapore, the Philippines, and elsewhere. If China does move ahead with a bastion strategy, there is likely to be considerable jostling between the two navies in the foreseeable future.

Regional Motivations

The other main set of motivations for China's island-building is regionally focused, and its purpose is to dominate the southern part of the South China Sea and to deter Southeast Asian claimants from any action that might prevent China from exploiting the resources there. For some time, there has been a symbiotic relationship in China between nationalist voices arguing that the country must exploit the resources of the sea because they belong to China and state agencies arguing that China must control the sea because of all the resources it is supposed to contain. Again, this is predicated upon a sense of right. A century of nationalist education has convinced the Chinese population and its government that they have the moral right to do whatever they choose in the South China Sea and that other claimants are illegitimate interlopers.

In recent years, various lobbies within China have promoted an interpretation of the meaning of the U-shaped line that goes well beyond both what was originally intended by the ROC cartographers in the 1940s and mainstream interpretations of the United Nations Convention on the Law of the Sea (UNCLOS). In the words of Wu Shicun, the U-shaped line is "based on the theory of 'sovereignty + UNCLOS + historic rights.' According to this theory China enjoys sovereignty over all the features within this line, and enjoys sovereign right and jurisdiction, defined by the LOS Convention. . . . In addition to that, China enjoys certain historic rights within this line, such as fishing rights, navigation rights and priority rights of resource development."[49] This interpretation would be compatible with the ambiguous formulation used by President Xi in a November 2015 speech in Singapore: "The South China Sea islands have been China's territory since ancient times. It is the bounden duty of the Chinese government to uphold China's territorial sovereignty and legitimate maritime rights and interests.[50]

The third part of Wu's formulation, the idea of "historic rights," seems to have emerged in Taiwan rather than on the mainland, and only in the early 1990s.[51] Nonetheless, the statements and actions of agencies including the Chinese coast guard, the PLAN, oil corporations, and southern provinces suggest they subscribe to this three-part interpretation: they regard the line as a claim not just to the land features but also to rights across all the waters within it. There are three areas of shallow sea with potential hydrocarbon resources that appear to be of particular interest to China: the Vanguard Bank off the Vietnamese coast, the Reed Bank off the Philippines coast, and the James Shoal/Luconia Shoals area off the Malaysian coast.

In 1992, China issued a lease to Crestone, an American company with just three employees, for the development of suspected oil deposits around the Vanguard Bank. Vietnam deployed ships to prevent the development going ahead, and the Chinese rights have remained unexploited. In the interim, Vietnam has leased the same patch of seabed to other companies; Talisman of Canada (now owned by Repsol of Spain) drilled there in late 2014 and June–July 2017. However, in July 2014, the Chinese rights were sold to Brightoil, a Hong Kong–based company with connections to the Chinese political establishment.[52] This could be a prelude to renewed efforts by China to drill on the Vanguard Bank once the supporting military and coast guard infrastructure is in place in the Spratlys.

Equally, the Philippine-controlled company Forum Energy demonstrated the existence of large gas reserves on the Reed Bank but was unable to develop them because of diplomatic objections and the implied threat of military force from China. This obstruction was sufficient for Forum to delist its shares from the London Stock Exchange in mid-2015. The tripartite China-Philippines-Vietnam Joint Marine Seismic Undertaking also surveyed the Reed Bank between 2005 and 2008. Since the findings were shared between the three countries' national oil companies at the time, the Beijing authorities have a good idea of where any potential resources might be located.

Malaysia already has active oil production operations around the Luconia Shoals off the coast of Borneo. However, in June 2015, the Malaysian government revealed that a Chinese coast guard vessel had been anchored near the shoals for two years.[53] China is also thought to regard the James Shoal area, farther to the northeast but still within Malaysia's claimed EEZ, as oil-rich.[54]

Chinese estimates of the sea's oil wealth are vastly greater than those of every other informed source. In December 1989, following the first Chinese surveys of the area, the *China Daily* reported official calculations that the Spratly Islands contained 25 billion cubic meters of natural gas and 105 billion barrels of oil and the James Shoal area a further 91 billion barrels.[55] Deng Xiaoping and other political leaders began talking about the sea as the answer to China's looming crisis. That theme was amplified by key voices in the energy sector (particularly the state-owned offshore oil company CNOOC) and the military. The PLA newspaper *Jiefangjun bao* published a series of articles between 1987 and 1990 linking the "sacred" importance of defending national territory with pragmatic arguments in favor of harvesting the sea's resources.[56] Since then, it has been too politically difficult to roll back the numbers.

The most authoritative and transparent recent estimates of the hydrocarbon potential of the sea have come from the U.S. Geological Survey (USGS) in June 2010 and the U.S. Energy Information Administration (EIA) in February 2013. The EIA estimated that the sea contained just 11 billion barrels of oil and 190 trillion cubic feet of gas as commercially viable reserves. Those figures approximate to the oil reserves of Mexico and the gas reserves of Europe (excluding Russia).[57] Based on what is known about the region's geology, the USGS estimated undiscovered resources at around 11 billion barrels of oil (with low and high estimates of 5 and 22 billion barrels) and 4 billion barrels of natural gas liquids, making a combined total of 15 billion barrels. The survey further estimated that undiscovered gas resources could be more significant, at somewhere between 70 and 290 trillion cubic feet. In other words, undiscovered resources could be about the same as the current level of reserves.[58]

These figures, however, refer to the whole sea region, including areas outside the U-shaped line. Only a fraction of the headline figures lie in the disputed territory, and only one-tenth of that fraction is likely to be commercially recoverable. These prospects could make a sizeable impact in the economies of smaller, poorer countries such as the Philippines or Vietnam. But given that China consumes about three billion barrels of oil and about five trillion cubic feet of natural gas each year, the reserves and resources of the South China Sea are hardly worth all the current effort expended on them. Even if every drop and bubble were sent to China, they would power the country's economy for a few years at best. Furthermore, the geology is difficult, the region is prone to typhoons, and the supporting infrastructure is poorly developed.

Bureaucratic Interests

The prominent American analyst Bonnie Glaser of CSIS has argued that China's actions in the South China Sea are the fruit of a grand strategy authorized from the very top of its political system.[59] After Xi Jinping was formally appointed general secretary of the Communist Party of China in late 2012, there were indeed major changes in South China Sea policy. Wayne Hugar has traced some of the institutional changes that took place around this time. He notes that China's twelfth Five-Year Plan for Comprehensive Overall Socio-Economic Development was published in 2011. It included language supporting "the development of remote sea islands" and strengthening "reclamation management." In 2012, the China State Council promulgated "a major planning and policy implementation document entitled 'Island Protection and Exploration for the Period 2012–2020 and Vision to 2020'." Hugar suggests that this indicates that central approval for the island-building had been given by this point. Subsequent to this, the twelfth Five-Year Plan for National Marine Development was published in September 2014 to provide detailed guidance to state agencies.[60]

It is clear that after 2012 the overall number of clashes with neighboring countries (between Chinese state agencies and foreign oil survey vessels, for example) fell. Moreover, those incidents that did occur—such as the 2014 oil rig confrontation with Vietnam and the 2013–15 island-building—involved much greater central planning, many more resources, and multiple state agencies acting in concert. But whether it was Xi's appointment that was significant or an overall change in outlook, as argued by Zhou Fangyin, cannot be discerned from open sources. As noted, plans for island construction were being drawn up before Xi took office.

Linda Jakobson has argued that what appears to be a coordinated Chinese strategy can be explained by the competition between the many agencies that stand to benefit from an assertive South China Sea policy.[61] Xue Gong, senior analyst with the China program at the Rajaratnam School of International Studies, has drawn attention to the role of state-owned enterprises in Chinese policymaking.[62] The South China Sea may also be a place for political faction-fighting. In 1995, for example, some analysts attributed the occupation of Mischief Reef to future leader Jiang Zemin's need to win support from the military in order to succeed Deng Xiaoping.[63] There is explanatory power in both the Glaser and Jakobson arguments.[64] State agencies lobby for policies that benefit their own bureaucratic interests using language and arguments that appear to advance national interests. At the same time, the Communist Party leadership sets national priorities. Once policy is agreed at the top, the party-state can bring the agencies into line with coordinated power and large amounts of resources.

Two decades ago, historian John W. Garver argued that the Chinese navy's push into the South China Sea represented "the interaction of national and bureaucratic interests."[65] The interests are still interacting. The PLAN is getting bigger (as are its budgets) and more capable. Prestige, promotion, and pecuniary rewards are following. The same is true of the new Chinese coast guard, particularly following the merging of several smaller maritime authorities into one. Both the coast guard and the navy are looking for missions to demonstrate their usefulness and justify their funding.

What is true of the maritime agencies is true of other bureaucracies. Hainan is China's smallest province and is relatively poor, with an economy dominated by agriculture. In recent years, it has put great effort into developing its fishing industries and has become expert at harvesting state subsidies to equip new boats. Hundreds, perhaps thousands, of fishing boats receive between $300 and $500 per day to go fishing in disputed waters. One captain told the Reuters news agency that "the authorities support fishing in the South China Sea to protect China's sovereignty." It might be just as accurate to say the provincial authorities make use of the sovereignty claim to justify central government support for fishing. Reuters discovered that eight trawlers being launched in the port of Dongfang on Hainan would each qualify for $322,500 in "renovation" grants.[66]

Oil companies are also able to play the sovereignty card in support of their semi-commercial ventures in the South China Sea. In May 2012, when CNOOC launched HS-981, the heavily subsidized deep-water rig at the center of the Paracels standoff, its chairman famously described it as "mobile national territory and a strategic weapon."[67]

Sometimes these lobbies fight among themselves, but when they work together, their power is immense. One thing they can all agree on—whether for reasons of nationalism, security, profit, or jobs—is that China must have access to the space and resources of the South China Sea. This dovetails with arguments for expanding Chinese-controlled "security space" around the coast and offshore as far as what Chinese strategists call the First Island Chain running from Japan through Taiwan and the Philippines to Singapore.[68]

TIMING

There were probably three main reasons why China chose 2013 to begin constructing the island bases:

- First, because it could. Its maritime agencies had the capacity, budget, and political support to expend vast amounts of money on "territorial protection."
- Second, Chinese leadership felt it had nothing to lose diplomatically from pursuing the construction—or at least that the gains would outweigh any potential losses.
- Third, as a response to the Philippines launching a case against China in an UNCLOS-based arbitration tribunal.

The third point requires some elaboration. In January 2013, the Philippines brought a case against China under the arbitration provisions of UNCLOS. The case was not about which country was the rightful owner of each feature. Instead, Manila asked the tribunal to rule on the kind of maritime zones that China could rightfully claim from the seven features it occupies in the Spratlys (plus Scarborough Shoal). Its main argument was that none of the features in the

Spratlys generate an EEZ. The tribunal judges agreed, and this was, indeed, the outcome of the case.

At least as significant, the tribunal ruled that China's U-shaped line—which stretches far beyond the outer limit of any claim conceived of by UNCLOS—is incompatible with international law insofar as it represents a claim on resources. As a result, in the eyes of international law, China's maximum potential maritime claim in the Spratlys is now limited to circles with a radius of twelve nautical miles drawn around each feature that remains above water at high tide. The ruling is only binding on the Philippines and China, but if the logic were applied to all the disputing states, everywhere outside these circles would be part of the EEZ of the coastal state. They—and only they—would have the right to develop the oil and gas resources and protect the fishing interests therein.

China did not participate in the case and continues to argue that the tribunal lacked the jurisdiction to hear it.[69] Its main argument against the case, as developed in its December 2014 position paper, is that its "historic claim" to the waters inside the U-shaped line supersedes any UNCLOS-based claim.[70] This argument was dismissed by the tribunal judges. However, while the world waited for the verdict, China set about creating "facts on the ground." Its actions in the South China Sea might be considered analogous to Israel's settlement-building in the West Bank. Regardless of their status in international law, they represent a political reality that the Southeast Asian claimants will have to deal with, as China seems highly unlikely to abandon them. Then the simple presence of Chinese coast guard and PLAN vessels in the area may be sufficient to force other claimants to share the resources, regardless of the legal judgement.

STRATEGIC IMPLICATIONS

The contradiction that will shape the future of the South China Sea is this: as China develops the capacity to protect its coastal cities and lengthy supply lines through military means, it will inevitably develop the capacity to confront the U.S. Navy. But Washington fears that this policy is motivated not by self-defense but by a determination to obstruct U.S. freedom of navigation and then to achieve regional hegemony and will therefore oppose it. For the United States, freedom of navigation through the sea underpins its economic success and strategic supremacy. This is why it is now working to ensure continued U.S. access to every part of the ocean—but particularly the South China Sea.

On a regional scale, China's new islands will undoubtedly be significant military assets, enabling Beijing to project power over the sea, neighboring countries, and toward the Strait of Malacca. Shorter supply lines and reliable bases will enable more vessels and aircraft to be on station. China has already deployed its second-largest warship, the amphibious transport dock *Kunlun Shan*, to Fiery Cross Reef, and frigates and destroyers have visited the other main bases.[71] Satellite imagery analyzed by the Asia Maritime Transparency Initiative of CSIS suggests that the bases at Fiery Cross, Mischief, and Subi Reefs have hangars for twenty-four fighter jets and three larger aircraft. They would neatly house one naval aviation regiment.[72] The regular deployment of, for example, the maritime patrol and antisubmarine warfare variant of the Y-8 transport aircraft would facilitate greater domain awareness.[73] Air tankers could increase the ranges of all aircraft operating in the vicinity. Combined with the existing bases in the Paracel Islands and on the mainland, they will give China the capacity to provide air cover over the entire U-shaped line claim—and beyond.[74] In all scenarios short of a shooting war with a major power, they have the potential to give China key leverage. With sufficient assets in place, and with rivals unwilling to escalate to overt military confrontation, China could assert effective sea control over areas around the Spratlys.

This is likely to lead to more incidents of physical coercion, along lines similar to China's deployment of the oil rig HS-981 near the Paracel Islands in 2014. Large numbers of ships from the Chinese coast guard accompanied by fishing flotillas and maritime militia boats could be swarmed into contested areas. By using ostensibly civilian vessels, China will be able to push out weaker claimants but claim that it is not using military force. As Huang Jing, director of the Center on Asia and Globalization of Public Policy, said in 2013, "What China is doing is putting both hands behind its back and using its big belly to push you out, to dare you to hit first."[75] Other claimants will be faced with the choice of either escalating the disputes in a military direction or conceding to China's creeping annexation of the sea.

That said, China's regional rivals are playing with home advantage. Vietnam, the Philippines, and Malaysia have bases on their mainland territory that are much closer to the disputed features and waters. Vietnam has air and naval bases along its southwestern coast, Malaysia has bases in Borneo, and the Philippines has bases in Palawan and Luzon. However, only Vietnam and, to some extent, Malaysia and Indonesia have credible military deterrent capabilities vis-à-vis the PLA.

The Royal Malaysian Navy is relatively small for a country with a coastline of 4,600 kilometers. In September 2015, it comprised a total of 44 vessels, with the most potent being 2 frigates (6 more are on order), 6 corvettes, 8 missile attack boats, and 2 small multipurpose support ships.[76] It now possesses 2 French-built submarines based at Kota Kinabalu on Borneo near its offshore oil fields. The navy has pressed for more ships and helicopters, but economic problems exacerbated by falling oil prices obliged the government to announce a 2 percent cut in military spending in 2016.[77] Plans announced in October 2013 to create a new marine corps seem to have come to nothing. The Malaysian Maritime Enforcement Agency (the coast guard) has four offshore patrol vessels and a larger number of smaller craft.

Vietnam has spent much less on its military than Malaysia historically but has ramped up purchasing in the past few years. The Stockholm International Peace Research Institute estimated its 2015 spending at $4.4 billion, more than four times greater than the figure in 2005.[78] Vietnamese spending is also concentrated on cheaper equipment with the potential to inflict damage on a much stronger opponent. In early 2017, Vietnam received the last of six new Russian submarines. It has also bought two batteries of Russian Bastion shore-based antiship missiles and Israeli-made ballistic missiles with a range of 150 kilometers, and it will locally produce the Russian Uran antiship missile. The submarines are reportedly being equipped with Klub land-attack missiles that could target Chinese naval bases on both the islands and the mainland.[79]

The Philippines' navy is old and underpowered, and its air force is almost nonexistent. Its two largest naval ships are both former U.S. Coast Guard cutters. It has agreed to buy twelve South Korean FA-50 light attack planes, but it will be years before its crews are trained and ready to fight. President Benigno Aquino left office in June 2016 without achieving the minimum credible defense he set out to achieve. Nonetheless, he did put the country's armed forces on a new path away from internal security and toward international engagement and the maritime arena. It remains to be seen whether the administration of his successor, Rodrigo Duterte, will continue the same policies. Early signals suggest that it will not.

Although Indonesia does not claim any of the islands within the U-shaped line, its navy and coast guard have found themselves in conflict with Chinese vessels on a few occasions since 2009. China claims fishing and resource rights in an area of sea east of the Natuna Islands where the U-shaped line overlaps with Indonesia's claimed exclusive economic zone. During 2015 and 2016, Indonesia moved to reinforce its garrison in Natuna and staged large-scale military exercises there in October 2016.[80]

There are differing views about whether the advantages that the islands give to China in peacetime would endure in a shooting conflict. Small island bases are vulnerable to a high-end opponent. Runways can be knocked out of action, harbors can be mined, and port facilities can be damaged. However, China has installed radar and presumably air defense systems intended to enhance their survivability. James E. Fanell, former director of intelligence and information operations for the U.S. Pacific Fleet, argues elsewhere in this volume that Chinese anti-access/area denial capabilities are a significant threat to the U.S. Navy and that the new islands will be the key determinant of the future balance of power in the region. China's new supersonic antiship cruise missiles (ASCMs), the YJ-12 and YJ-18, which have ranges of up to three hundred nautical miles, are currently only deployed on ships and submarines but could potentially be modified for a shore-based battery. The existing land-based ASCM, the YJ-62, is subsonic but still a potent threat. In February 2017, U.S. officials revealed the existence of what appeared to be buildings with retractable roofs intended to house surface-to-air missiles at the three islands with runways: Fiery Cross, Subi, and Mischief. Although no such missiles had been deployed to the Spratlys at the time of writing, it seems that China has made preparations to do so in the future.[81] The United States might regard the installation of any of these systems on the islands as a direct threat to its freedom of navigation.[82] On the other hand, in October 2016, U.S. Chief of Naval Operations Adm. John Richardson told an audience in Washington that "the threats are not insurmountable. . . . We can fight from within these defended areas and if needed, we will."[83]

Regardless of which of these views is correct, on a day-to-day basis the enhanced presence of the PLA's navy and air force around the Spratlys will complicate U.S. military movements through the region. Even without the threat of antiship cruise missiles, routine U.S. missions—such as the military exercises, patrols, and particularly the surveillance operations that ships such as the USNS *Impeccable* and USNS *Bowditch* and P-3 and P-8 aircraft carry out—could be harassed more easily from the new island bases and require greater levels of force protection. The United States would also be concerned about threats to its treaty ally, the Philippines, and other countries in the region with which it has security partnerships.

As a result of these potential threats, the United States may decide to increase its military presence in the region. This will increase budgetary costs and perhaps prompt renewed questions in Washington about how long the country can sustain its defense commitments in Southeast Asia. This is the long-term war of budgetary attrition for the region.

CONCLUSION: UNDERSTANDING CHINA'S MOTIVATIONS

Having constructed the physical foundations for a more assertive military and coast guard presence in the Spratlys, China's next move could focus on occupying empty spaces with resource potential. Vanguard Bank, Reed Bank, and James Shoal are all areas of shallow sea where an oil rig or its equivalent could be easily installed. Some reports have highlighted a possible Chinese initiative to build large floating bases that eventually could also be used to support this kind of activity.[84] Moves to "occupy" these areas of sea would be accompanied by nationalist language about China's historic rights superseding the language of UNCLOS.

China's island-building is a dramatic development, but it is far from being game-over in the South China Sea. China occupies only seven features in the Spratlys, slightly more than Malaysia but fewer than the Philippines and far fewer than Vietnam, which occupies more than all the other claimants put together. Although China's bases are much larger and more capable than the features occupied by the other claimants, they are far from home territory. Vietnam, Malaysia, and Indonesia are able to mobilize small but potent deterrent forces from their coasts, and all three have considerable land-based resources relatively close at hand. These countries are also discreetly working to persuade the United States to increase its presence in the South China Sea. In addition, they are building closer ties with Japan and India and other states, hedging their bets in case the United States should dial down its presence.

This chapter has argued that China, both the central state and the various interest groups within it, has many reasons to maximize its control of the South China Sea. These include its need to protect the ruling regime, the national territory, and its supply routes, along with a desire to control maritime resources. These imperatives, which are shared by all coastal states, have become sources of conflict in the region because of the historical narrative about the sea that developed in China during the twentieth century. This asserts a Chinese territorial claim to islands that had never previously been part of a Chinese realm and to rights over waters that go far beyond what China agreed to at the conclusion of the UNCLOS negotiations. This historical narrative has generated an emotional claim to the features and waters of the South China Sea and imbued Chinese policymaking with a sense of grievance that other players in the disputes usually fail to appreciate. In this narrative, contemporary China is righting wrongs that were committed against it in previous decades. From Beijing's point of view, its advances in the South China Sea are justified because they reclaim "lost" territory. Any action by a foreign power that tries to obstruct the reunification of the national territory, whether it be a naval patrol or an international arbitral tribunal, must be resisted because it is simply another episode in a long history of foreign plots to split the Chinese homeland. China's inability to recognize other points of view in these issues seems to be a prime case of Edward Luttwak's "great power autism."

This brief account of the development of the Chinese territorial claim in the South China Sea should demonstrate the obvious problems with the official Chinese historical narrative. It is not necessary to agree with this narrative to realize that the sense of righteousness that it generates, which underpins Chinese policymaking, will lead to further conflict. Since, in the Chinese narrative, every feature within the U-shaped line is China's rightful territory, the logical conclusion is that Beijing will eventually try to occupy every one of them and control the spaces in between. If policymakers in the United States and elsewhere fail to recognize the motivating power of China's historical narrative and territorial imperative, they will fail to understand Chinese objectives. Neither confidence-building measures nor physical confrontation will take away the driving force behind China's actions in the South China Sea. While the use of force may obstruct Chinese advances temporarily, it will also amplify feelings of frustration and provoke calls within China for an even more assertive response. The disputes can only be truly resolved by challenging the Chinese version of history and thereby undermining China's sense of righteousness.

China's strategic reasons for maintaining a strong presence in the South China Sea—the defense of its coast, sea lanes, and nuclear deterrent—will endure. However, its arguments for exclusive control of maritime resources and the right to regulate navigation are based upon flawed narratives. Since these are the two issues most likely to cause conflict, challenging them would be time well spent. All states with an interest in the peaceful settlement of the disputes will need to go beyond their stances of neutrality on the territorial questions. Instead, they need to assert that territorial claims without a foundation in verifiable evidence are not a viable basis for dialogue and conflict resolution. A critical engagement with Chinese experts and policymakers about the basis of their South China Sea narrative is an essential first step. Interlocutors with Chinese officials must arm themselves with the evidence to challenge bogus historical narratives and be prepared to deploy it in their discussions. Over the past twenty years, all this evidence has become easily available. It is time to use it.

Notes

1. People's Republic of China, "Foreign Ministry Spokesperson Lu Kang's Remarks on Issues Relating to China's Construction Activities on the Nansha Islands and Reefs," June 16, 2016, http://www.fmprc.gov.cn/mfa_eng/xwfw_665399/s2510_665401/t1273370.shtml.
2. Ian Storey, "China's Terraforming in the Spratlys: A Game Changer in the South China Sea?" Institute for Southeast Asian Studies, June 23, 2015, http://www.iseas.edu.sg/documents/publication/iseas_perspective_2015_29.pdf.
3. Ethan Meick, "China's First Airstrip in the Spratlys Likely at Fiery Cross Reef," U.S.-China Economic Security Review Commission Staff Report, December 18, 2014, 1–2.
4. Bill Hayton, "China's False Memory Syndrome," *Prospect*, July 10, 2014, www.prospectmagazine.co.uk.
5. Ryan D. Martinson, "Panning for Gold: Assessing Chinese Maritime Strategy from Primary Sources," *Naval War College Review* 69, no. 3 (Summer 2016): pp. 23–44.
6. Michael D. Swaine, "Xi Jinping's Address to the Central Conference on Work Relating to Foreign Affairs: Assessing and Advancing Major Power Diplomacy with Chinese Characteristics," *China Leadership Monitor*, March 2, 2015, http://carnegieendowment.org/files/Michael_Swaine_CLM_46.pdf.
7. People's Republic of China, *China's Military Strategy* (Beijing: State Council Information Office, May 26, 2015).
8. Martinson, "Panning for Gold," 28–29.
9. Sarah Raine, "Beijing's South China Sea Debate," *Survival* 53, no. 5 (2011): pp. 69–88.
10. Zhou Fangyin, "Between Assertiveness and Self-restraint: Understanding China's South China Sea Policy," *International Affairs* 92, no. 4 (2016).
11. Li Mingjiang, "Chinese Debates of South China Sea Policy: Implications for Future Developments," Working Paper 239, Rajaratnam School of International Studies, Singapore, May 17, 2012, 22.
12. See Hayton, "China's False Memory Syndrome," and Bill Hayton, "When Good Lawyers Write Bad History: Unreliable Evidence and the South China Sea Territorial Dispute," *Ocean Development and International Law* 48, no. 1 (2017): pp. 17–34.
13. For more on national humiliation, see Zheng Wang, *Never Forget National Humiliation: Historical Memory in Chinese Politics and Foreign Relations* (New York: Columbia University Press, 2014), and William A. Callahan, *China: The Pessoptimist Nation* (Oxford: Oxford University Press, 2012).
14. Ben Blanchard, "China Says Changing Position on Sea Dispute Would Shame Ancestors," Reuters, June 27, 2015.
15. Bernard Cole, *The Great Wall at Sea: China's Navy in the Twenty-First Century*, 2nd ed. (Annapolis, Md.: Naval Institute Press, 2012), chapter 2, and Greg Austin, *China's Ocean Frontier: International Law, Military Force, and National Development* (Sydney: Allen and Unwin, 1998).
16. See, for example, Leonard Blussé, "Chinese Century: The Eighteenth Century in the China Sea Region," *Archipel* 58 (1996): pp. 107–30; Derek Heng, "Trans-Regionalism and Economic Co-Dependency in the South China Sea: the Case

of China and the Malay Region (Tenth to Fourteenth Centuries AD)," *The International History Review* 35, no. 3 (2013): pp. 486–510; Pierre-Yves Manguin, "The Southeast Asian Ship: An Historical Approach," *Journal of Southeast Asian Studies* 11, no. 2 (September 1980): pp. 266–76; Roderich Ptak, "The Northern Trade Route to the Spice Islands: South China Sea–Sulu Zone–North Moluccas (Fourteenth to Early Sixteenth Century)," *Archipel* 43 (1992): pp. 27–56; and Angela Schottenhammer, "The 'China Seas' in World History: A General Outline of the Role of Chinese and East Asian Maritime Space from its Origins to c. 1800," *Journal of Marine and Island Cultures* 1 (2012): pp. 63–86.
17. Leonard Blussé, conference remarks, "Maritime Governance in 21st Century Asia," Centre for Rising Powers, University of Cambridge, September 10, 2014.
18. Bill Hayton, "The Modern Origins of China's South China Sea Claim," article forthcoming in *Modern China* (2017).
19. Hayton, "When Good Lawyers Write Bad History."
20. Francois-Xavier Bonnet, "Geopolitics of Scarborough Shoal," Research Institute on Contemporary Southeast Asia Discussion Paper 14 (2012).
21. Ibid.,18.
22. Hayton, "The Modern Origins of China's South China Sea Claim," 55–56.
23. Chris P. C. Chung, "Drawing the U-Shaped Line: China's Claim in the South China Sea, 1946–1974," *Modern China* 42, no. 1 (2015): pp. 1–35.
24. Dzirhan Mahadzir, "Malaysia's Maritime Claims in the South China Sea," in *Entering Uncharted Waters? ASEAN and the South China Sea*, ed. Pavin Chachavalpongpun (Singapore: ISEAS, 2014).
25. M. Taylor Fravel, *Strong Borders, Secure Nation: Cooperation and Conflict in China's Territorial Disputes* (Princeton: Princeton University Press, 2008), 292.
26. People's Republic of China, "Law on the Territorial Sea and the Contiguous Zone," February 25, 1992, http://www.un.org/depts/los/LEGISLATIONAND TREATIES/PDFFILES/CHN_1992_Law.pdf.
27. Ian Storey, "Creeping Assertiveness: China, the Philippines and the South China Sea Dispute," *Contemporary Southeast Asia* 21, no. 1 (April 1999): pp. 95–118.
28. Asia Maritime Transparency Initiative, "West Reef Tracker," Center for Strategic and International Studies, http://amti.csis.org/west-reef-tracker/.
29. David Hancox and Victor Prescott, "A Geographical Description of the Spratly Islands and an Account of Hydrographic Surveys Amongst Those Islands," *Maritime Briefing* 1, no 6. (1995); see also the Award of the Arbitral Tribunal, PCA Case No. 2013–19, 496, https://pca-cpa.org/wp-content/uploads/sites/175/2016/07/PH-CN-20160712-Award.pdf.
30. James Hardy et al., "China Goes All Out with Major Island Building Project in Spratlys," *IHS Maritime 360*, June 20, 2014, http://archive.is/GCwFr.
31. Victor Robert Lee, "South China Sea: China's Unprecedented Spratlys Building Program," *The Diplomat*, April 25, 2015, http://thediplomat.com/2015/04/south-china-sea-chinas-unprecedented-spratlys-building-program/.
32. U.S. Department of Defense, *Annual Report to Congress: Military and Security Developments Involving the People's Republic of China 2017* (Washington, D.C.:

Department of Defense, May 15, 2017), 12, https://www.defense.gov/Portals/1/Documents/pubs/2017_China_Military_Power_Report.PDF.
33. Hardy and et al., "China Goes All Out."
34. *Ming Pao* (Hong Kong), June 22, 2009.
35. Mingjiang, "China Debates South China Sea Policy: Implications for Future Developments of the Dispute."
36. John W. Garver, "China's Push Through the South China Sea: The Interaction of Bureaucratic and National Interests," *China Quarterly*, no. 132 (December 1992): pp. 999–1028.
37. Liu Huaqing, *Memoir of Liu Huaqing* [*Liu Huaqing Huiyilu*, 刘华清回忆录] (Beijing: Liberation Army Press, 2004), 437–38, quoted in C. J. Jenner & T.T. Thuy, *The South China Sea: A Crucible of Regional Cooperation or Conflict-making Sovereignty Claims?* (Cambridge University Press, 2016), 314.
38. Xinhua Wenzhai, excerpt from Admiral Liu's memoirs, July 2005, 95–97, translated at http://www.franzbleeker.de/liuhuaqing.html.
39. Christopher H. Sharman, "China Moves Out: Stepping Stones Toward a New Maritime Strategy," *China Strategic Perspectives* 9 (Washington, D.C.: National Defense University Press, April 2015), http://inss.ndu.edu/Portals/68/Documents/stratperspective/china/ChinaPerspectives-9.pdf.
40. Linda Jakobson and Rory Medcalf, *The Perception Gap: Reading China's Maritime Strategic Objectives in Indo-Pacific Asia* (Sydney: Lowy Institute for International Policy, June 2015).
41. Andrew Chubb, "Chinese Popular Nationalism and PRC Policy in the South China Sea," PhD dissertation, School of Social Sciences, University of Western Australia, 2016.
42. See, for example, T. X. Hammes, "Offshore Control Is the Answer," U.S. Naval Institute *Proceedings* (December 2012), http://www.usni.org/magazines/proceedings/2012-12/offshore-control-answer.
43. T. X. Hammes, "Great Power War: Historical Inevitability or Deterrable Choice?" *Asia-Pacific Review* 21, no. 1 (May 2014): p. 18.
44. David C. Gompert, Astrid Stuth Cevallos, and Cristina L. Garafola, *War with China: Thinking Through the Unthinkable* (Santa Monica, Calif.: RAND Corporation, 2016), xii.
45. U.S. Energy Information Administration, "Short Term Energy Outlook," October 8, 2013.
46. Wu Shicun, personal interview, Haikou, October 2013.
47. Stuart Leavenworth, "China May Be Trying to Hide its Submarines in the South China Sea," McClatchy DC, June 22, 2015, http://www.mcclatchydc.com/news/nation-world/world/article25186678.html.
48. State Council Information Office of the People's Republic of China, "China Adheres to the Position of Settling Through Negotiation the Relevant Disputes Between China and the Philippines in the South China Sea," white paper, July 13, 2016.
49. Wu Shicun and Keyuan Zou, *Arbitration Concerning the South China Sea: Philippines Versus China* (New York: Routledge, 2016), 132.

50. Xi Jinping, "Forging a Strong Partnership to Enhance Prosperity of Asia," speech at the National University of Singapore, November 7, 2015, https://www.iseas.edu.sg/images/Events/pdf/Forging_a_Strong_Partnership_to_Enhance_Prosperity_of_Asia_English_Translation.pdf.
51. Bill Hayton, "China's 'Historic Rights' in the South China Sea: Made in America?" *The Diplomat*, June 21, 2016, http://thediplomat.com/2016/06/chinas-historic-rights-in-the-south-china-sea-made-in-america/.
52. "Oil on Troubled Waters," *The Economist*, January 24, 2015, http://www.economist.com/news/asia/21640403-two-case-studies-disputed-sea-oil-troubled-waters.
53. Jenifer Laeng, "China Coast Guard Vessel Found at Luconia Shoals," *Borneo Post*, June 3, 2015, http://www.theborneopost.com/2015/06/03/china-coast-guard-vessel-found-at-luconia-shoals/.
54. "Oil Discovered on Nansha Islands," Xinhua, July 24, 1987.
55. *China Daily*, December 24, 1989.
56. Garver, "China's Push Through the South China Sea"; Knut Snildal, "Petroleum in the South China Sea—A Chinese National Interest?" (thesis, Department of Political Science, University of Oslo, 2000).
57. U.S. Energy Information Administration, "South China Sea Energy Brief," February 7, 2013, http://www.eia.gov/countries/regions-topics.cfm?fips=scs.
58. U.S. Geological Survey, "Assessment of Undiscovered Oil and Gas Resources of Southeast Asia," Fact Sheet 2010–3015, June 2010, http://pubs.usgs.gov/fs/2010/3015/pdf/FS10-3015.pdf.
59. Bonnie Glaser, "Beijing Determined to Advance Sovereignty Claims in South China Sea," *Lowy Interpreter*, December 16, 2014, http://www.lowyinterpreter.org/post/2014/12/16/Beijing-determined-advance-sovereignty-claims-South-China-Sea.aspx.
60. Wayne R. Hugar, "Surprise! What Caused China's Recent and Massive Land Reclamation in the South China Sea?" *Journal of Strategic Intelligence* (Summer 2016): pp. 4–36.
61. Linda Jakobson, *China's Unpredictable Maritime Security Actors* (Sydney: Lowy Institute for International Policy, December 11, 2014).
62. Xue Gong, "Chinese Corporate Players in the South China Sea: Complicating the Disputes?" *Commentary* 228, Rajaratnam School of International Studies, September 14, 2016.
63. Storey, "Creeping Assertiveness," 100.
64. Bill Hayton, "South China Sea: Jakobson and Glaser Are Both Right," *Lowy Interpreter*, January 5, 2015, http://www.lowyinterpreter.org/post/2015/01/15/South-China-Sea-Jakobson-and-Glaser-are-both-right.aspx.
65. Garver, "China's Push Through the South China Sea."
66. John Ruwitch, "Satellites and Seafood: China Keeps Fishing Fleet Connected in Disputed Waters," Reuters, July 28, 2014, http://uk.reuters.com/article/2014/07/27/uk-southchinasea-china-fishing-insight-idUKKBN0FW0QV20140727.
67. Brian Spegele and Wayne Ma, "For China Boss, Deep-Water Rigs Are a 'Strategic Weapon,'" *Wall Street Journal*, August 29, 2012, http://www.wsj.com/news/articles/SB10000872396390444233104577592890738740290.

68. See, for example, James R. Holmes, "Defend the First Island Chain," U.S. Naval Institute *Proceedings* (April 2014), http://www.usni.org/magazines/proceedings/2014-04/defend-first-island-chain.
69. Anthony Deutsch, "In Defeat for Beijing, Hague Court to Hear South China Sea Dispute," Reuters, October 30, 2015, http://www.reuters.com/article/us-philippines-china-arbitration-idUSKCN0SN26320151030.
70. Ministry of Foreign Affairs, People's Republic of China, "Position Paper of the Government of the People's Republic of China on the Matter of Jurisdiction in the South China Sea Arbitration Initiated by the Republic of the Philippines," December 7, 2014, http://www.fmprc.gov.cn/mfa_eng/zxxx_662805/t1217147.shtml.
71. Liu Zhen, "How One of the Mainland's Most Celebrated Military Folk Singers Is Taking the South China Sea by Storm," *South China Morning Post*, May 4, 2016; James Clapper, "Letter from Director of National Intelligence to Sen. John McCain, Chairman, Senate Committee on Armed Services," February 23, 2016, https://news.usni.org/2016/03/08/document-dni-assessment-of-chinese-militarization-reclamation-in-south-china-sea.
72. Asia Maritime Transparency Initiative, "Build It and They Will Come," August 1, 2016, http://amti.csis.org/build-it-and-they-will-come; Mike Yeo, "Can China Enforce a South China Sea ADIZ?" USNI News, July 18, 2016, https://news.usni.org/2016/07/18/analysis-can-china-enforce-south-china-sea-air-defense-identification-zone.
73. Gareth Jennings, "China Fields New Maritime Patrol and Anti-Submarine Y-8/Y-9 Variant," *IHS Jane's 360*, June 28, 2015, http://www.janes.com/article/52603/china-fields-new-maritime-patrol-and-anti-submarine-y-8-y-9-variant.
74. Anders Corr and Matthew Michaelides, "Effect of South China Sea Air Strips on the Range of Chinese Surface-to-Air Missiles and the J-10 Fighter," *Journal of Political Risk* 3, no. 5 (May 2015).
75. Jeff Himmelman, "A Game of Shark and Minnow," *New York Times Magazine*, October 27, 2013.
76. Dina Murad, "Malaysian Navy Needs More Ships to Improve Security," *The Nation*, September 22, 2015, http://www.thestar.com.my/News/Nation/2015/09/22/navy-more-ships/.
77. Dzirhan Mahadzir, "Malaysian Naval Chief Says Priority Is Upgrades, but ASW Helos, Corvettes on Shopping List," *Jane's Defence Weekly*, May 21, 2015; Prashanth Parameswaran, "Malaysia Cuts Military Budget for 2016 Amid Economic Woes," *The Diplomat*, October 27, 2015, http://thediplomat.com/2015/10/malaysia-cuts-military-budget-for-2016-amid-economic-woes/.
78. Sam Perlo-Freeman et al., *Trends in World Military Expenditure 2015* (Stockholm: Stockholm International Peace Research Institute, April 2016), https://www.sipri.org/publications/2016/sipri-fact-sheets/trends-world-military-expenditure-2015.
79. Greg Torode, "Vietnam Buys Submarine-Launched Land Attack Missiles to Deter China," Reuters, April 30, 2015, http://uk.reuters.com/article/2015/04/30/uk-vietnam-military-idUKKBN0NL0B220150430.

80. Agustinus Beo Da Costa, "Indonesia Air Force Holds its Largest Military Exercise in South China Sea," Reuters, October 4, 2016, http://www.reuters.com/article/us-southchinasea-indonesia-idUSKCN1240O9.
81. Idrees Ali, "Exclusive: China Finishing South China Sea Buildings that Could House Missiles—U.S. Officials," Reuters, February 23, 2017, http://www.reuters.com/article/us-china-usa-southchinasea-exclusive-idUSKBN161029.
82. Lyle Goldstein, "China's YJ-18 Supersonic Anti-Ship Cruise Missile: America's Nightmare?" NationalInterest.org, June 1, 2015, http://nationalinterest.org/feature/chinas-yj-18-supersonic-anti-ship-cruise-missile-americas-13010.
83. Adm. John Richardson, "Maintaining Maritime Superiority," speech to Center for Strategic and International Studies, Washington, D.C., October 3, 2016. Partial text available at http://nationalinterest.org/feature/chief-naval-operations-adm-john-richardson-deconstructing-17918.
84. Jeffrey Lin and P. W. Singer, "Chinese Shipyard Looks to Build Giant Floating Islands," *Popular Science,* April 20, 2015, http://www.popsci.com/chinese-shipyard-looks-build-giant-floating-islands.

2

Old Game Plan, New Game

China's Grand Strategy in the South China Sea

Ian Forsyth

For observers of international relations of East Asia, few dynamics have been as captivating as the People's Republic of China's activities in the South China Sea. Reclamation activity was first publicly observed in September 2013 and has been going on at a breakneck pace since 2014.[1] China has been rapidly piling sand onto reefs in the Spratly Islands, creating seven new islets in the region. Several reefs have been destroyed to serve as a foundation for new islands, resulting in extensive damage to the surrounding marine ecosystem. As of October 2016, at least seven maritime features had been expanded. Satellite images reveal China has been building military features on the reclaimed land, including possible antiaircraft towers on Hughes and Gaven Reefs, a lighthouse, helipad, and high-frequency radar on Cuarteron Reef, radar facilities on Gaven, Hughes, and Johnson South Reefs, and a three-thousand-meter airstrip on Fiery Cross Reef.[2] In June 2015, China declared that it would soon complete land reclamation and begin constructing facilities to house a range of military and civilian activities.

While the Spratly construction commands most of the attention, China is also constructing sites in the Amphitrite group of the Paracel Islands.[3] In February 2016, China deployed up to two batteries of Hongqi-9 (HQ-9) surface-to-air missiles (SAMs) with an accompanying high-frequency radar system, which can be used to detect stealth aircraft on Woody Island, the largest of the Paracels.[4] China had already landed J-11 fighters and JH-7 fighter-bombers on the island in November 2015. Beijing's South China Sea airstrips can support all types of aircraft in China's inventory.

When faced with criticism, Beijing accuses the media of unfairly targeting it while ignoring radars and weapons deployed by other claimants in the South China Sea.[5] Vietnam, Malaysia, the Philippines, and Taiwan have all expanded islands in the Spratlys as well, but on nowhere near the same scale as China. The total amount of land reclaimed by China since December 2013 is approximately 3,200 acres (1,295 hectares), accounting for roughly 95 percent of all reclaimed land in the South China Sea. Over the last forty years, Vietnam has claimed 80 acres, Malaysia 70 acres, the Philippines 14 acres, and the Republic of China (Taiwan) 8 acres, for a total of 172 acres.[6]

The speed and scale of this construction have caught much of the region by surprise and are spreading alarm about what China plans to do with its new infrastructure. Communist Vietnam is buying arms from the United States, its one-time enemy. The Philippines is inviting U.S. forces back twenty-five years after expelling them. Even Singapore and Malaysia are becoming more proactive by allowing U.S. Navy P-8 surveillance aircraft to use bases on their territory.[7] Alarmed at what they see as Beijing's bid to dominate the strategic waterway, regional nations are spending billions of dollars on ships, submarines, planes, and other military hardware and actively seeking closer defense ties with Washington and with each other.[8]

This construction is the culmination of a regional policy formulated in the 1990s based on economic, military, and diplomatic capabilities in the region, which China calls "comprehensive national power." China has increased its assertiveness over its South China Sea claims in gradual, punctuated steps, reflecting the growth of its comparative economic, military, and political power at the regional level. In the 1980s and early 1990s, China under Deng Xiaoping declared a "good neighbor policy." Beijing consistently proclaimed Deng's guidance of *taoguang yanghui*, literally "avoiding the [spot]light, nurturing obscurity," or more informally, biding one's time and lying low. The reformers in Beijing recognized the value of taking an accommodating stance toward their East Asian neighborhood, particularly for the economic rewards that resulted from a stable region. One side of accommodation was to execute skillful diplomacy designed to reduce tensions and avoid conflict unless Beijing's fundamental interests were threatened. Militarily, accommodation meant the exercise of restraint and delay of modernization.

During Hu Jintao's period of leadership from 2002 to 2012, foreign policy moved from "peaceful rise" to "peaceful development," which softened the tone somewhat. Beijing's South China Sea vision began to further crystalize in this period, when it assessed that it would only be secure if it expanded its eastern and southern strategic perimeters into the East and South China Seas. Strategic concerns started to meld with maritime energy and natural resource concerns. Thus began a program to build the capabilities to project power into the maritime domain and then use that power to press its claims. The increasing Chinese dependence on the maritime domain led Hu Jintao to enunciate the "new historic missions" for the Chinese People's Liberation Army (PLA) in 2004.[9] One of these new missions was to provide strategic support in maintaining national interests.

This is not to say that Beijing originally formulated a clear, unified, and comprehensive long-term strategy for the South China Sea. Since the 1940s, China has considered the sea to be one of the "lost territories" that would eventually return to the mainland, but that was a general, long-term interest. Having an overarching strategy surrounding regional interests does not necessarily entail a solidified script of how to obtain those interests by a certain time. In other words, one should not assume a strategic coherence regarding the South China Sea on the part of Beijing. It is reasonable to infer that not being a "core interest" would make it less likely that China would have a detailed, thought-out script of strategies and supporting tactics to achieve clear and settled goals regarding the South China Sea. Notably, unlike Taiwan, Tibet, and Xinjiang, Chinese policymakers did not start to label the South China Sea as a core interest (核心利益) until 2010,[10] and even then, it was not an agreed-upon designation until years later.[11] It was not until China's twelfth Five-Year Plan in 2011 that a chapter on maritime interests and development was included. Furthermore, unlike Taiwan, the South China Sea and maritime interests did not substantially appear in the Chinese Defense White Papers until the 2015 edition.[12] In other words, Beijing's final strategic end state for the South China Sea and how it is to be achieved have likely evolved over the years. Regardless, this evolutionary quality does not mean China has or will become less dogmatic and unilateral and more accepting of other countries' claims.

The rapid pace of land reclamation in 2014–15 and the increase in military capabilities and coercion of foreign fishing vessels all point to a strategy of some form of control of the South China Sea. Control in this case refers to the prevention of non-Chinese fishing, hydrocarbon extraction, and military activities from occurring in the region, except with China's consent. Perhaps most important, control means the protection of Chinese sea lines of communication in any and all circumstances.

The control China is solidifying serves not only its economic and security needs but also its national identity needs. By establishing control of the region,

China feeds its national need to redress past humiliations over lost territory. In other words, China has made controlling the South China Sea part of its national identity, with the current Chinese leadership being the implementers of the rebalancing of regional power back to China where it belongs, according to a commonly articulated Chinese narrative of history. China—due to the increase in its military and economic power—is now in a position to challenge a regional order from which it has benefited.[13] Interestingly, in many open forums, Chinese officials and scholars are declaring that China's tactics in the South China Sea are not so much a home-grown strategy as a reaction to the United States, whose strategy is to "contain" China.[14] Beijing frames its South China Sea actions as a defense against U.S.—and its allies'—regional militarization.[15]

The result is that the current end state strategy that Beijing holds for the South China Sea is one that has evolved over the last two decades in gradual yet incremental steps but that is resulting in a tactics-strategy mismatch. China's current actions are based on a strategic calculus that is predicated on its increasing power in these arenas. However, the flaw in this approach is that it does not account for its rival claimants' fluctuating views, strengths, reactions, or own tactics.

The one country that China has seemed to account for and factor into its grand strategy has been the United States. Given the United States' superior military capabilities, China has traditionally been wary about giving it reasons to increase its regional military presence. Consequently, China has carefully tested and measured Washington's reactions—and non-reactions—to its regional activities. China has a much clearer read on the reactions of the United States than those of any regional claimants. But by focusing primarily on the United States, China is suffering pushback from unexpected sources. It should have known better.

CHINA'S TACTICS IN THE 1990s AND THE CONDITIONS SURROUNDING THEM

Although juxtaposed against an interest in reclaiming the South China Sea as a "lost territory," China once saw the value in negotiation, particularly given its resource and economic needs; it became a net importer of oil in 1993 and needed to secure supplies to extract and transport in the South China Sea. China also recognized that it was outmatched by the U.S. military, so patience and compromise were necessary. Yet a hole in this tactic was that China was measuring itself against only the U.S. military, and it was ignoring the reactions and roles that its regional rival claimants might have had.

China's regional territorial claim tactics comprised several key elements. The first element was to limit any substantive negotiations on territorial sovereignty issues to the bilateral level. By excluding the United States and multilateral mechanisms, China ensured that it was always the strongest negotiator at the table.

The second element was to be active in multilateral fora for the purpose of increasing soft power and establishing trust and credibility, but to refrain from ratifying legally binding commitments. Although Beijing signed the 2002 Declaration on the Conduct of Parties in the South China Sea with the Association of Southeast Asian Nations (ASEAN) in 2002, it has not signed a binding version, and it has ensured that South China Sea sovereignty discussions are muffled in ASEAN and other multilateral venues. For example, China refused to submit its precise maritime claims to the United Nations Commission on the Limits of the Continental Shelf (CLCS), other than the "U-shaped line," which loops down from the Chinese coast to encompass most of the South China Sea. In 1996, China ratified the United Nations Convention on the Law of the Sea (UNCLOS). However, in an appended reservation, it excluded itself from mandatory compliance and mediation of disputes over sea boundaries and land territory.

The third element was to ensure that the problem was not internationalized and that it did not provoke the United States to deploy its military in the region. China came close on several occasions, but each act of encroachment and/or violence was just small enough not to warrant a U.S. military response. For example, in 1994 and 1995, China surreptitiously occupied the Philippine-claimed Mischief Reef, building an outpost that has since grown to a landing strip long enough to accommodate bomber aircraft. The United States, in the wake of the Taiwan Strait crisis of 1996, increased its naval operational presence in the region. The United States was the one country that China did factor into its calculus and, as such, now had incentive to be more accommodating.

The fourth element was for China to use its growing economic power to advance its political goals. The Asian financial crisis of 1997–98 hammered a number of economies in the region, notably Thailand and Indonesia. But China was spared, due primarily to its relatively closed financial system at the time. China could have devalued its currency during the crisis to maintain export competitiveness, but it chose not to, earning the goodwill of countries throughout the region.

The fifth element was to use domestic laws to help legitimize its territorial claims. This was first witnessed in February 1992, when China passed the Law on Maritime Boundaries, which essentially declared the entire South China Sea as its territory. China utilized this tactic again in 1996 when it drew its maritime baselines in contravention of customary international law. In 1997, China passed a law regarding its exclusive economic zones (EEZs), domestically codifying its South China Sea claims.

China linked its South China Sea tactics to its own power, but it discounted the reactions of its neighbors as a factor. In other words, it omitted—or at the very least misinterpreted—the crucial factor of other countries' military power, diplomatic maneuverings, and, most important, nationalistic fervor. These omissions rendered China's strategic calculus incomplete and therefore self-defeating. China now faces a new regional status quo, one in which its prior policies will not work as Beijing desires. As such, Beijing must adjust its tactics or risk alienating the region and jeopardizing its efforts over the past two decades. Meanwhile, Beijing's missteps are a historic opportunity for the United States to expand its role and alliances in Asia.

Military Strategy of the 1990s

In the era roughly encompassing the 1990s, China established a pattern of proportional coercion linked to maintaining its claims while not taking more military risk than was necessary.

In 1994, China occupied the Philippines-claimed Mischief Reef (Panganiban in Tagalog), which lies roughly 700 miles from Hainan but is only 130 miles off the Philippine coast and well within its EEZ. January 1996 witnessed the so-called Mischief Reef incident, whereby three Chinese naval vessels fought a ninety-minute battle with a Philippine navy gunboat near Capones Island at Mischief Reef, part of the Spratly chain of islands claimed by Manila. The clash, which triggered a crisis in Sino-Philippine relations, revived U.S.-Philippine military ties; soon after the incident, U.S. Navy SEALs conducted a joint exercise with their Philippine counterparts on Palawan Island, although then–Philippine president Fidel Ramos denied that it was connected to Manila's row with Beijing. Tensions over the occupation subsided by midyear, when the Philippines and China signed a nonbinding code of conduct that called for a peaceful resolution to the territorial dispute and the promotion of confidence-building measures.

In this era, the PLA was outclassed by the U.S. military in every arena. RAND research revealed that the PLA's conventionally armed ballistic missiles could not reach any of the relevant U.S. bases. The People's Liberation Army Air Force (PLAAF) had a total of twenty-four fighters (plus eighty bombers) that could reach the Spratly Islands in 1996.[16] RAND modeling concluded that roughly one-third of a U.S. air wing equivalent (supplied by either the Air Force or the

Navy) would have been sufficient to gain air superiority in a seven-day campaign over the Spratly Islands. U.S. maritime dominance was equally comprehensive. RAND concluded that Chinese surface ships, highly vulnerable in any scenario in the 1996 time frame, would have had to venture farther from ground-based air and SAM protection, making them exceedingly vulnerable. U.S. aircraft carriers and other surface ships could be positioned a safe distance from the Chinese coast and would therefore be only slightly vulnerable to Chinese submarine, air, and missile attack.[17]

Diplomatic Strategy of the 1990s

The Tiananmen Square massacre of June 1989 made China something of a global pariah, with many countries reducing their diplomatic contacts with, and their economic assistance programs to, China. In response, China made extensive efforts to reach out to its regional neighbors. Specifically, Beijing reestablished relations with Indonesia and normalized relations with Singapore in 1990 and with Brunei in 1991.

Beijing's tactic of denying multilateral negotiations was in full force at this time and was yielding positive results. Sino-Malaysian relations improved markedly after Malaysian prime minister Mahathir Mohamad visited Beijing in June 1993 and adopted more strident anti-U.S. rhetoric and policies. In May 1999, Malaysian foreign minister Hamid Albar visited Beijing and formally adopted the Chinese position of bilateral, rather than multilateral, negotiations in South China Sea disputes. This angered Manila, which wanted to have multilateral talks over the Mischief Reef seizure in venues such as the ASEAN Regional Forum, where the United States was present. Another tactic to exclude the United States was Beijing's articulation of its "New Security Concept" in the late 1990s. This policy advocated China and its neighbors disavowing a Cold War mentality (that is, relying on the United States for security) and instead increasing security through deeper regional diplomatic and economic integration. Security concerns were defined to be not just military, but economic, environmental, and public health as well.

China also utilized its domestic laws to advance its regional interests. In February 1992, China passed the Law on the Territorial Sea and the Contiguous Zone. This law employs more generous methods of territorial determination in contravention of UNCLOS. However, China reserved out of mandatory compliance and mediation of disputes. In 1997, the ASEAN member nations and China, South Korea, and Japan agreed to hold yearly talks to further strengthen regional cooperation via the ASEAN "Plus Three" meetings.

The turn of the century saw a slight uptick in maritime encounters, but again, they were not a principal issue in bilateral relations. From January to March 2000, the Philippine navy interdicted fourteen trawlers under the Chinese flag, confiscated their catch, and escorted the ships away from the sea area of the Spratly Islands claimed by the Philippines. In May 2000, Philippine soldiers seized Chinese fishing vessels at the Palawan Islands.

There were also positive signs. In November 2002, China and ASEAN drafted the 2002 Declaration on the Conduct of Parties in the South China Sea, but since then Beijing has continuously balked at signing a binding version. Though the declaration fell short of a binding code of conduct, as the Philippines had sought, it signaled China's recognition that such an agreement could work in its favor by limiting the risk of conflict in the area, which could involve the United States in the dispute. Yet to avoid commitment and to maximize the asymmetry of separate bilateral talks between China and each Southeast Asian claimant, Beijing calls the discussions with ASEAN "consultations," not "negotiations."

Economic Strategy of the 1990s

China's economy grew at an average rate of 10 percent per year during the period 1990–2004, the highest growth rate in the world. China's economic relationship with the region entered a new phase in 1997 as a result of the Asian financial crisis. Beijing found a regional leadership role for itself, garnering much regional goodwill in the process. Specifically, it provided Thailand and other Asian nations with more than $4 billion in aid. China also decided not to devalue its renminbi so as to maintain stability and development. In 1999, China commenced negotiations with the United States to permanently normalize its trade status in anticipation of joining the World Trade Organization, and it also adopted a new, more modern securities law that same year. China's economic gravity increased in 2001 when it joined the organization. To comply with membership requirements, China eliminated price controls to protect domestic industry and eliminated export subsidies on agricultural products. Subsequent to that, the economic reforms came at a furious pace. In 2004, China reached open-market agreement with ten Southeast Asian nations, and ASEAN reached a consensus on a "Plus Three" trade framework with China, Japan, and South Korea.

U.S. Role in the 1990s

From the mid to late 1990s, the Bill Clinton administration sought security engagements with Beijing as the People's Liberation Army Navy (PLAN) evolved from a predominantly coastal defense force to a blue-water fleet beyond Chinese territorial waters. In January 1998, China and the United States signed the Military Maritime Consultative Agreement (MMCA), the countries' first bilateral military agreement, which served as a confidence-building measure after a period of frigid relations following the 1989 Tiananmen Square massacre. The accord aimed to promote defense dialogue between naval forces to prevent misunderstandings. However, its efficacy was questioned in April 2001, when a Chinese J-8 interceptor and a U.S. Navy surveillance aircraft collided over the South China Sea, killing a Chinese pilot, and the MMCA process became dormant. Also in 1998, the United States and the Philippines signed the Visiting Forces Agreement, allowing renewed access of U.S. forces to the Philippines for training purposes.

CURRENT MILITARY DYNAMICS

The churn that took place in the 1990s made sense at the time, but international relations are not static. Other countries' capabilities have changed, and China's actions were increasingly based on outdated realities. China has made massive improvements in its military capabilities. While this is logical in terms of balancing the United States, it has also made many of China's neighbors nervous.

Asia is the only region in the word that saw increased defense spending in aggregate in 2015.[18] Military expenditures in Asia rose, led by an 11 percent rise in China's military budget. The Philippines also recorded a solid increase at 10 percent. Yet the region's military spending is dominated by China, with its roughly $356 billion budget accounting for some 40 percent of the total for Asia. In 2014, as global defense spending sank, Asian spending increased.[19] China's military expenditures are roughly five times the combined defense budgets of the major ASEAN powers.

RAND research highlighted how China's military improvements undermine U.S. advantage in the South China Sea.[20] With all of their regional main operating bases located in northeast Asia, U.S. forces face logistical and operational challenges for combat in the South China Sea. However, China faces similar challenges, primarily because of the position of Chinese bases relative to South China Sea combat. Power projection assets, such as aerial refueling tankers, satellite-based sensors and communications support, and long-range heavy bombers, will be important to the Chinese in a Taiwan conflict but will be critical in the South China Sea.

The PLA has made massive strides in the last two decades in terms of power projection capabilities. The PLAN possesses the longest range antiship cruise missiles of any country in the region. While the PLA's improved power projection capabilities are indeed formidable, it still has some progress to make when compared with the United States. RAND concludes that through 2017, the U.S. military will almost certainly continue to enjoy the upper hand in most areas, though the degree of advantage is rapidly eroding.

The United States will probably retain the ability to attack and close all Chinese air bases relevant to a Spratly Islands scenario in 2017. Yet assuming that the PLA deploys additional advanced SAMs in southern China by 2017, strikes by legacy aircraft may become risky, forcing the United States to rely, at least initially, on its much smaller force of stealthy aircraft and its limited supply of cruise missiles. In the maritime realm, both sides may be able to target the other's surface warfare assets in the confined spaces of the South China Sea, forming consequential areas that are high-risk for both sides.[21]

Although Taiwan remains the PLA's top-priority scenario, since 2004 it has also been preparing to execute "new historic missions."[22] This formulation, which calls on the PLA to protect China's national interests and play a role in supporting world peace and development, results in its supporting the acquisition of additional power projection capability.[23] Greater emphasis on the acquisition of support capabilities, such as tankers and airlift, could significantly improve the Chinese capability to conduct operations in the South China Sea in the years beyond 2017.[24]

As such, this new decade has seen an emphasis on maritime power. In 2013, Chinese officials laid out a timeline calling for China to become one of the top eight navies by 2020, one of the top five by 2030, and one of the top three by 2049 (the centennial of China's founding).[25] The Chinese Defense White Paper of May 2015 states: "It is necessary for China to develop a modern maritime force structure commensurate with its national security."[26]

In the national security law passed in 2015, one of the first tasks enumerated for the PLAN is to provide for maritime security.[27] The PLAN already outmatches every regional navy. Perhaps the most obvious manifestation of this is the commissioning of the *Liaoning*, China's first aircraft carrier. Complementing the *Liaoning* are several new classes of Chinese destroyers and frigates, all entering serial production. China is expected to add more than six *Luyang* II and a dozen *Luyang* III destroyers. Supplemented by twenty *Jiangkai* II frigates, China has clearly been addressing the long-standing problem of weak air defense. By 2018, the PLAN may field more ships equipped with phased array radar and may be able to concentrate more such vessels than the U.S. Navy. Moreover, all these ships are equipped with helicopter hangars, substantially improving their antisubmarine warfare capabilities. China is also reportedly working on a larger, cruiser-sized surface combatant. It plans to replace its *Houbei* missile-armed fast attack craft with *Jiangdao* corvettes.

China's submarine fleet has also benefited from two decades of double-digit defense budget growth. With its fleet of at least seventy diesel-electric, air-independent propulsion, and nuclear-powered submarines, the PLAN can interdict both commercial and military maritime traffic and potentially overwhelm any response. Currently, China's submarine fleet is able to keep the U.S. Navy at significant distances from the Chinese mainland. The consequence is approximate parity between U.S. and Chinese capabilities in terms of Chinese antisurface warfare in a Spratly Islands scenario.[28] By 2030, the PLAN probably will have more than eighty submarines, all likely armed with antiship cruise missiles.

Meanwhile, the PLAN Air Force (PLANAF) is also steadily modernizing. While the H-6 remains in service, it is backed by more than one hundred JH-7 strike aircraft. In addition, the PLANAF has been replacing many of its second-generation aircraft with modern, fourth-generation aircraft. The PLANAF inventory now includes 4th-generation and 4.5-generation fighters, such as the J-10, J-11, and Su-30. Consequently, China has closed the qualitative gap between the U.S. and Chinese air forces. In a Spratly Islands conflict, China would likely attempt to use its long-range aviation assets to strike targets and protect its ground and naval forces. China could base fighters and integrated air defense systems on the Spratly islets that it is building on, but such forces would be ripe targets and would not likely last beyond the first several hours of high-intensity conflict with the United States.[29]

In the South China Sea, the modernization of the PLAN, the PLAAF, and the PLA Rocket Force (PLARF) means that the PLAN can both seek to establish control of the waters out to the First Island Chain and engage in sea-denial operations. The combination of PLAAF, PLARF, and PLAN assets poses an existential threat to any surface forces that local navies could field. Meanwhile, China's air forces would likely overwhelm all regional air forces in the area between the Chinese coast and the First Island Chain, while China's array of short-, medium-, and intermediate-range ballistic missiles could hold targets on both land and sea at risk.

In March 2013, the Chinese government consolidated control over its various maritime law enforcement agencies, grouping them under the State Oceanic Administration and effectively creating a unified coast guard with more concentrated capabilities.[30] The Chinese coast guard serves a quasi-military purpose in that it uses coercion to enforce Chinese claims, notably fishing rights, against foreign states. In 2011 and 2012, China's fishing boats and law enforcement vessels intimidated Vietnam's survey ships, three times severing their seismic cables during those years.

China's military modernization has not gone unnoticed by its neighbors, and they have reacted to the extent they can. The Philippines is planning to purchase three ELM-2288 radar defense and air traffic control radars from Israel.[31] The radars will bolster the Philippines' surveillance capabilities of the South China Sea and will complement the capabilities of the recently acquired KAI FA-50PH light fighter. The Philippines is set to receive ten coast guard vessels from Japan.[32] In 2015, the Philippine supreme court approved the Enhanced Defense Cooperation Agreement (EDCA) with the United States that allows U.S. forces to deploy to a variety of bases throughout the country. The court ruled that the agreement did not amount to a treaty that would need approval from the country's senate and instead could stand as an "executive agreement" under the authority of the country's president. The agreement will grant the U.S. military access to eight bases, including two in the strategic South China Sea: Antonio Bautista Air Base and Naval Station Carlito Cunanan.[33] The EDCA is a direct result of China's assertive tactics in the South China Sea. One emerging complication is the change of leadership in Manila. In June 2016, the Philippines swore in Rodrigo Duterte as president. He did not win on a foreign policy mandate, nor has he any foreign policy experience. Duterte is an outspoken, erratic nationalist, but he has expressed a willingness to negotiate with Beijing on South China Sea issues and does not want to be tethered to the United States. However, despite his overtures to Beijing and vitriol directed at Washington, a firm nationalist Philippine public opinion makes it difficult for Duterte to compromise Philippine sovereignty claims and the legal victory his country won in The Hague.

Vietnam is another country that is improving combat readiness. Vietnam's generals are reaching out to a broad range of strategic partners. Hanoi is building ties with the United States and its Japanese, Australian, and Philippine allies. Since 2008, the Vietnamese navy has taken delivery of one BPS-500 corvette and two *Gepard 3.9*–class guided missile stealth frigates armed with 3M24 Uran antiship missiles. Hanoi's concerns about Chinese encroachment reached a new, pitched level in May 2014 when China placed the *Hai Yang Shi You* 981, an oil rig of the China National Offshore Oil Corporation (CNOOC), into waters disputed by China and Vietnam. China enforced its presence there by shouldering and ramming Vietnamese vessels. On February 2, 2016, the fifth of six *Kilo*-class submarines that Vietnam bought from Russia arrived at Cam Ranh Bay.

The *Kilo*-class conventional submarines are armed with antiship and land attack cruise missiles and are supported by four guided missile corvettes, five light frigates, and several *Molniya*-class missile corvettes. In recent years, the Vietnamese have acquired more than thirty Su-30MKK fighters. Vietnam has shipped a set of EXTRA mobile rocket launchers to its Spratly garrisons. The EXTRAs, with their 150-kilometer range, are capable of targeting runways on many China-held Spratly islets.[34] Also of note, Vietnam's naval infantry force has conducted an exercise simulating the recapture of an island.[35]

CURRENT DIPLOMATIC DYNAMICS

China's actions have fostered diplomatic countermoves as well. In May 2009, Malaysia and Vietnam filed a joint submission to the CLCS to extend their continental shelves beyond the standard two hundred nautical miles from their coastlines, renewing friction over maritime sovereignty in the South China Sea. China viewed this as a challenge to its territorial claims and objected to the submission, saying it had seriously infringed on China's indisputable sovereignty over the islands in the South China Sea.

Diplomacy has proven unable to prevent incidents that could spark confrontation. From May through July 2010, Indonesia and China each captured several of the other's fishing boats, accusing them of fishing illegally in foreign waters. In June of that year, an Indonesian patrol clashed with Chinese fishermen escorted by ships from the Chinese ministry of fisheries off Natuna Island in the southern part of the South China Sea.

In February 2011, a Chinese frigate fired warning shots at a Philippine boat near Jackson Atoll off the Spratly Islands. In May, Vietnamese authorities accused China of having severed the seismic survey cables of the oil exploration ship *Binh Minh 02*, operated by Vietnam's state-owned energy firm PetroVietnam. One month later, a Chinese ship was caught in the cables of a Vietnamese oil exploration ship one thousand kilometers from Hainan Island. In March 2011, Chinese surveillance ships forced a Philippine vessel conducting surveys in the Reed Bank to leave the area. Both parties declared the incident a violation of the 2002 ASEAN-China Declaration on the Conduct of Parties in the South China Sea, and the event set off a series of skirmishes in the region between the two countries.

In February 2012, Chinese authorities prevented the landing of eleven Vietnamese fishermen seeking refuge from a storm on one of the Paracel Islands. Vietnam lodged a protest, but China rejected the allegations. From April to June, after a Philippine reconnaissance plane identified Chinese fishing boats at Scarborough

Shoal, the Philippine navy deployed its largest warship, the BRP *Gregorio del Pilar* (former USCGC *Hamilton*), to investigate. Manila said the fishermen were fishing illegally there. China also deployed two maritime law enforcement vessels to block any enforcement, resulting in a stalemate. Manila claimed that under a 2012 deal mediated by the United States, Beijing and Manila agreed to withdraw their forces from the reef until a compromise over its ownership was reached. China has not complied with this agreement and has maintained its presence in the area ever since.[36]

In June 2012, Vietnam passed a maritime law asserting its jurisdiction over the disputed Spratly and Paracel Islands, demanding notification from any foreign naval ships passing through the area. China issued a strong response, announcing the establishment of a city, Sansha, on the Paracels that would administer the Paracels and Spratlys and the Macclesfield Bank. On July 13, for the first time in its history, ASEAN failed to issue a communiqué at the conclusion of its annual meeting in Cambodia. Its ten members hit an impasse over China's claims in the South China Sea, and member countries disagreed over whether to include the territorial issue in the joint statement. China's influence on Cambodia, the 2012 rotating chair of the conference, caused the exclusion of the Scarborough Shoal and EEZ issues from the text, resulting in the deadlock. Cambodia also excluded stronger language in the 2016 ASEAN statement. Both Manila and Hanoi wanted the communiqué issued by ASEAN foreign ministers after their meeting to refer to the ruling and the need to respect international law. Yet Phnom Penh opposed the proposed wording, creating an ASEAN impasse that had not been seen since 2012.[37]

In March 2013, a Chinese marine surveillance vessel confronted a Vietnamese fishing vessel near the Paracels. In March and April 2013, a four-ship PLAN flotilla deployed to James Shoal, eighty kilometers from the Malaysian coast, where the crew participated in a televised oath-taking ceremony, pledging to defend the South China Sea and maintain national sovereignty for China. In July, a Chinese coast guard crew boarded two Vietnamese fishing vessels near Woody Island and allegedly removed Vietnamese property. The year 2014 proved to be one of the tensest years in the region. China harassed Vietnamese fishing vessels near the Paracels in January, March, August, and November. China harassed Philippine vessels near Scarborough Shoal in January and near Second Thomas Shoal in March. Yet the high point of tension was in May through July, when China deployed CNOOC 981 to the disputed waters of Vietnam and China near the Paracels.

The following year, 2015, proved to be tense as well. China confronted Philippine vessels near Scarborough Shoal in January and April. China harassed Vietnamese vessels in June, July, and September near the Paracels and in November near Subi Reef. The trend continued in 2016, as China harassed Philippine vessels near Half Moon Shoal and Jackson Atoll, both in February and March, near Scarborough Shoal in March, and near Camiguin province in May. China frustrated Indonesia when it prevented Indonesian authorities from arresting a Chinese fishing vessel operating illegally near the Natuna Islands in March and in June. Chinese coast guard ships also rammed Vietnamese fishing vessels near Discovery Reef in the Paracels in July.

At the bilateral level, mutual concern with Beijing's attempts to solidify its claims in the disputed waters spurred Manila and Hanoi to pursue enhanced security cooperation, which culminated in the signing of a joint statement on the establishment of a strategic partnership on November 17, 2015. While encompassing multiple areas of cooperation, the joint statement has a notable focus on security and defense.

At the multilateral level, in August 2015, in the face of Beijing's objections, ASEAN called for all claimants to halt land reclamation activities in the South China Sea. The communiqué issued by ASEAN stated that land reclamations "have eroded trust and confidence, increased tensions and may undermine peace, security and stability in the South China Sea."[38] The Sunnylands Declaration released on February 16, 2016, at the end of the two-day U.S.-China presidential summit laid out seventeen principles to guide U.S.-ASEAN cooperation going forward.[39] The fifth of these reaffirms "respect and support for ASEAN Centrality and ASEAN-led mechanisms in the evolving regional architecture of the Asia-Pacific." The summit conveyed "shared commitment" to "freedom of navigation and overflight" in and above the South China Sea and twice endorsed UNCLOS. However, those phrases are not softening China's refusal to allow international rules to restrain its maritime ambitions.

CURRENT LEGAL DYNAMICS

China declares the right to exploit fishery resources in the South China Sea, but not only in the waters within two hundred nautical miles from its mainland coast and from the Paracel Islands.[40] By using the U-shaped line, China's claim extends beyond any possible EEZ limits that can be generated by its mainland and by any islands in the South China Sea over which it claims sovereignty. China's fishing rights claim appears to be based on both EEZ entitlement and historic claim.[41] Beijing argues that the features in the South China Sea are entitled to a full-fledged EEZ and continental shelf as a group, but it has yet to make any official declaration of the limit of its EEZ claim from the islands. Additionally, China argues that it has a form of exclusive historic rights within the waters inside the U-shaped line but beyond the maritime zones generated from the islands.[42] China officially used the U-shaped line for the first time in 2009 in its response to the joint submission to the CLCS made by Malaysia and Vietnam.[43] China, however, has not officially clarified the meaning of the U-shaped line map, nor the maritime zones generated by the islands in the South China Sea over which it claims sovereignty. Even though China has declared straight baselines around the Paracel Islands, it has yet to do the same for the rest of the Spratly Islands, over which it claims sovereignty.[44] When the People's Republic of China became the official government of China, it more or less adopted the U-shaped line map drawn by the government of the Republic of China.

China's fishing rights claim appears to be based on both EEZ entitlement and historic claim.[45] First, Beijing argues that the features in the South China Sea are entitled to a full-fledged EEZ and continental shelf as a group. Yet China has not made any official declaration of the limit of its EEZ claim from the islands. Second, it argues that it also has a form of exclusive historic rights within the area the U-shaped line encompasses but beyond the maritime zones generated from the islands. However, the view that the U-shaped line represents China's historic claim that is akin to an EEZ does not seem to be attainable. The EEZ concept is a fairly new one; thus, the international community would be unlikely to agree to China claiming "EEZ-like rights" under the historic title concept.[46]

The Philippines pursued legal recourse on January 22, 2013, when it initiated an international arbitration case at the Permanent Court of Arbitration (PCA) in The Hague under UNCLOS Annex VII.[47] The Philippines asked for a finding that "China has unlawfully interfered with" the Philippines' exercise of sovereign rights with respect to resources of its EEZ and continental shelf.[48] It also requested the tribunal to rule as illegal the U-shaped line as a violation of international law

China rejected the process, forcing the arbitration to continue without its participation.[49] China asserted that it has a form of exclusive historic rights within the waters inside the U-shaped line and beyond the maritime zones generated from the islands.[50] Instead of filing a formal legal response to the Philippines' case, China has sought to establish a de facto position, using its construction projects and marine law enforcement to convince others to recognize Chinese control practically if not legally.

On July 12, 2016, the PCA issued an ex parté award that surprised most legal and security scholars by how comprehensively it ruled in the Philippines' favor. The PCA upheld nearly all of the fifteen issues the Philippines submitted before it, most notably that none of the features in the South China Sea are "islands," that China's U-shaped line is invalid as a claim for maritime rights, and that China's activities in those waters are illegal.[51] Not surprisingly, Beijing continued to reject the PCA's jurisdiction, declaring that the award was invalid and had no binding force.[52] China reasserted its historic rights in the South China Sea, even though the PCA explicitly ruled that the historic rights arguments were invalid under UNCLOS. Chinese foreign ministry officials even chastised the judges' alleged lack of understanding of East Asian history and culture.[53]

China is trying to make itself an international maritime judicial center by promoting its maritime court system under the Supreme People's Court. This is not about replacing the International Tribunal for the Law of the Sea (ITLOS) but rather about providing a forum of adjudication for China's growing maritime commercial activities. The courts assert jurisdiction over all maritime zones claimed by China, to include the South China Sea. However, these courts have many reforms to undertake (notably regarding transparency and professionalism) before they can challenge London or Singapore as preferred maritime dispute settlement venues.

CURRENT ECONOMIC DYNAMICS

Economics has been China's trump card in regard to regional relations. Chinese trade in Asia is outpacing that of the United States. U.S. trade in goods and services with ASEAN more than doubled between 1996 and 2015, exceeding $260 billion per year to make ASEAN the fourth-largest trading partner of the United States.[54] This growth is impressive but is eclipsed by China's economic connections with the region since the 1990s—conditions that empower China. Prior to the 1997 Asian financial crisis, the United States and Japan were ASEAN's largest trading partners, between them accounting for more than 30 percent of the region's imports and exports, while China's share was less than 5 percent. By 2015, however, China's weight had grown and represented about 15 percent of ASEAN's total trade, with a value of trade more than twenty times what it was in 1996.

From the Chinese side, in some respects, ASEAN is negligible. In 2014, China's regional export destinations as a percentage of its overall exports were Singapore (1.9 percent), Thailand (1.6 percent), Vietnam (1.6 percent), Malaysia

(1.6 percent), and Indonesia (1.4 percent). In terms of shares of imports that regional partners compose, those numbers are Malaysia, 2.1 percent; Singapore, 2 percent; Thailand, 2 percent; Indonesia, 1.6 percent; the Philippines, 1 percent; and Vietnam, 0.92 percent.[55]

While none of these countries are in China's top-five export or import destinations, the same cannot be said for the reverse. China has embedded itself as a top-five trade partner for all members of ASEAN. The degree of dependence varies due largely to wealth: wealthier ASEAN countries have a diversified set of trading partners, but poorer ASEAN countries depend heavily on China, particularly as a source for imports. For example, Vietnam's dependence has grown, whereas Singapore's has waned. China is Brunei's third-largest source of imports (9.9 percent); Cambodia's second-largest import source (26.7 percent); Indonesia's second-largest export market (10 percent) and largest source of imports (17.2 percent); Laos' largest export market (34.9 percent) and second-largest import source (25.6 percent); Malaysia's second-largest export destination (10 percent) and its largest import supplier (16.9 percent); Myanmar's largest export market (63.1 percent) as well as its largest supplier (42.4 percent); the Philippines' third-largest export market (13 percent; second place with 22 percent if Hong Kong is included) and its largest supplier (15.8 percent); Singapore's largest export market (12.7 percent; 23.8 percent if Hong Kong is included) along with Singapore's largest supplier (12.1 percent); Thailand's largest market (12.1 percent) along with its second-largest supplier (15.6 percent); and Vietnam's second-largest market (10.4 percent) and its largest supplier (30.3 percent).[56] China is banking on this economic relationship as leverage over rival claimants' actions vis-à-vis China.

CURRENT U.S. ROLE

In 2009, the region saw China abandoning a certain principle that it had previously strongly followed: commit no action that would provide an excuse for the U.S. military to establish and maintain a frustrating presence. This most recent and most dramatic uptick in assertiveness has yielded results that China had not planned for but nonetheless should have foreseen. China now faces an irony of the highest order: its strategy to keep the United States out of the region is resulting in a more robust, militarized presence by Washington.[57]

On July 23, 2010, in a speech at an Asian regional security meeting in Hanoi, U.S. secretary of state Hillary Clinton reiterated Washington's neutrality on sovereignty in the South China Sea but affirmed American interests in the "open access to Asia's maritime commons."[58] Beijing was furious at this statement. In

June 2011, the U.S. Senate passed a resolution unanimously condemning China's use of force in the South China Sea and called for an international solution to the territorial disputes. The next month the United States and Vietnam conducted a series of naval drills in the South China Sea.[59]

On November 17, 2011, President Barack Obama delivered the "Pivot" (later called the "Rebalance") speech to the Australian parliament, announcing that the United States would pivot its strategic attention to the Asia-Pacific, particularly the southern part of the region.[60] The Obama administration announced new troop and equipment deployments to Australia and Singapore and pledged that reductions in defense spending would not come at the expense of commitments to the region. That same month, the United States and ASEAN pressed China at the Sixth East Asia Summit in Bali, Indonesia, over maritime security in the South China Sea, especially over China's claims of indisputable sovereignty over the area. As part of the rebalance, U.S. defense secretary Leon Panetta laid out the U.S. plan to alter its global naval deployment, shifting from a 50/50 split between the Atlantic and Pacific Oceans to 60 percent in the Pacific by 2020.

Manila improved its security relations with the United States as a response to China's activities. On April 28, 2014, President Obama, on the last leg of a four-nation Asia tour, signed a ten-year military pact with the Philippines. Under the EDCA, the U.S. military would gain increased rotational troop presence in the country, engage in more joint training, and have greater access to bases across the archipelago, including ports and airfields.[61] In the Philippines, proponents of the deal have described EDCA as an urgently needed initiative to upgrade the country's bilateral alliance with the United States.[62] The new pact, which builds on the 1998 Visiting Forces Agreement, facilitates the expansion of joint military exercises and enhances interoperability among their armed forces. The EDCA immediately faced a backlash in the Philippine senate, which insisted that the new pact was a treaty that demanded ratification. The case was eventually heard before the Philippine supreme court, which after almost a year of deliberations ruled that the EDCA was an executive agreement that fell within the prerogative of the Benigno Aquino administration.

To accommodate America's massive military platforms, Manila expected Washington to upgrade the facilities as well as the surrounding infrastructure of designated Philippine bases. The two allies were also contemplating the prospect of joint patrols close to South China Sea land features occupied by China. The deal was the centerpiece of Obama's first visit to the Philippines and underscored the administration's commitment to the Asia "pivot."

While President Obama expressed solidarity with Manila as it sought international arbitration over the disputed South China Sea islands, he insisted that the deal was not aimed at containing China. On October 2, 2014, China wasted no time in lashing out at the EDCA, accusing Manila of "turning to Uncle Sam to back its ambition to counter China" and warning that the Philippines would "bear the negative consequences of its stupid move in the future."[63] It prodded the Philippines to instead solve "disputes with China through negotiations without seeking help from a third party."[64]

Washington's solidarity with Manila has been facing serious challenges since Rodrigo Duterte became president of the Philippines on June 30, 2016. He has been arguably the most anti-U.S. president in modern Philippine history and has actively courted Beijing, though primarily in the economic sphere and less so the security sphere. However, the United States is still considered to be a vital security partner by much of the Philippine senate, general populace, and even Duterte's own cabinet. As such, there are limits as to how closely he can embrace Beijing and how far he can drift from the United States as an ally.

U.S. activities with Vietnam are increasing as well. Vietnam's purchase of maritime security weaponry is expected to bolster the defense of its territorial claims in the South China Sea and defend against China's expanding military capabilities. Hanoi and Washington in June 2015 signed a Joint Vision Statement outlining expanded defense cooperation in twelve areas.[65] The United States ended its arms embargo on Vietnam and announced $18 million worth of assistance to help the Vietnam coast guard acquire patrol boats, both modest but symbolically significant steps.[66]

In terms of doctrine, the U.S. Defense Department released the Asia-Pacific Maritime Security Strategy in 2015. The strategy essentially provided two services. First, it identified what the department felt were the most pressing regional challenges to the United States. Second, it consolidated the military initiatives the department was pursuing in the region. The strategy described China as the major source of regional instability and articulated U.S. efforts to stabilize the South China Sea.[67]

The year 2015 saw new levels of U.S. strategic messaging. On October 26, 2015, Washington deployed the USS *Lassen* to transit inside twelve nautical miles of five features, including Subi Reef, and flew B-52 bombers near a group of Chinese-built artificial islands in the Spratlys.[68] This transit was to assert "freedom of navigation" in disputed waters in the South China Sea. China's ambassador to the United States called the patrol a "serious provocation, politically and militarily."[69] The mission came after an August 2015 U.S. Department of Defense report stated that China had reclaimed nearly three thousand acres on the Spratlys. These transits were not meant to address the core territorial conflict over the land features among China and the other claimants, however. Nor will such operations address the territorial conflict unless and until the United States chooses a side in the conflict over who has sovereign title over each land feature

On January 30, 2016, the USS *Curtis D. Wilbur* conducted an innocent passage through the territorial seas of Triton Island of the Paracels, which is claimed by China, Taiwan, and Vietnam. This freedom of navigation operation (FONOP) again contested China's demand for prior notification, a demand that is issued by only a handful of other governments around the world, including Taiwan and Vietnam. The USS *Curtis D. Wilbur* operation was similar to the USS *Lassen* passage with respect to its legal assertion and insofar as it transited features claimed by multiple states. The destroyer USS *William P. Lawrence* passed within twelve nautical miles of Fiery Cross Reef on May 10, 2016.

FUTURE TRENDS

China's leaders—notably Xi Jinping—have called for a change in the global governance system to reflect China's growing power and what it perceives as diminishing U.S. power. In other words, Beijing wants to be an agenda setter and a rule-maker. This does not mean China can brazenly shatter the status quo to reflect this vision, however. It has pushed its agenda and pursued its interests via operating just below the threshold of U.S. military response. This is the "salami slicing" technique that is in full force in the South China Sea. In one regard, China's salami-slicing hybrid tactics have yielded success; witness how, by January 2016, China had landed civilian and military aircraft and passengers on the Fiery Cross Reef airstrip with no substantial pushback. In another regard, China's actions have made the region a theater of big-power competition, as the United States increases its presence near China's large-scale land reclamation and construction on several disputed reefs.[70] China's aggressive assertion of its territorial claims sets it on a collision course with several Southeast Asian nations with competing sovereignty claims in one of the world's busiest waterways, an area rich with fisheries and possible oil and gas reserves.[71] In 2015, U.S. defense secretary Ashton Carter called for an immediate and lasting halt to land reclamation in the disputed area and announced that the United States would fly, sail, and operate wherever international law allows.[72] Moreover, Beijing's response in the weeks subsequent to the PCA award—nationalist venting, a dismissive rejection of the ruling, a Supreme People's Court counter-Hague ruling, and threats to arrest any intruders into its claimed South China Sea territories—undermined China's claims about peaceful developments. Moreover, China's legal woes may not be over. If it persists in illegal island-building activities and interferes with lawful Philippine fishing in the vicinity of Second Thomas Shoal, Scarborough Shoal, or Mischief Reef, an international court such as the International Court of Justice or ITLOS could theoretically impose sanctions on China for flaunting a lawful UNCLOS decision. Such legal sanctions could entail having China's privileges essentially revoked in three UNCLOS institutions: ITLOS, the International Seabed Authority, and the CLCS.

Is China's late-twentieth-century strategy leading to conflict in the twenty-first century? China is attempting to create a situation in which the United States, to uphold international law, will either have to accede to China's territorial claims in the South China Sea or openly resort to the use of hostile force, allowing China to publicly portray the United States as an imperialist aggressor state.[73] Beijing is betting that the United States will not take this action and that power over the South China Sea and all the resources that lie beneath it will pass to China, breaking U.S. influence in the region. Beijing hopes to frame the United States as a fading Cold War power whose reluctance to accept its inevitable decline is causing regional instability. China puts forth the message that the United States is trying to unjustifiably retard China's fair and natural rise. Its strategic message in the region is that this U.S. stubbornness is a greater threat to regional stability than any Chinese land reclamation. Consequently, U.S. FONOPs are destabilizing in their effect, according to China.

The challenge for China is that under mounting nationalist pressure, there is no guarantee that Beijing will be able to maintain restraint in responding to future FONOPs.[74] If, as expected, the FONOP program continues in the South China Sea, U.S. officials should expect intercepts and the possibility of unsafe encounters. Still, the present situation is such that any miscalculation or any accident can easily erupt into a scenario that no one wants.[75]

Furthermore, this strategy becomes problematic at home to the degree that Chinese nationalists make the same (or greater) inference about the territorial claims and security postures that are intended for foreign audiences. China could face significant pressure from domestic forces that do not appreciate the careful nuance of its official positions. Chinese media have cried foul against other claimant countries, along with the United States and Japan, for causing problems in the South China Sea.

If push comes to shove, regional support for U.S. determination to preserve the status quo will be tested. The choice in Asia is not, as many assume, a simple one between the U.S.-led order many know and trust and a Chinese hegemony they understandably fear. Certainly no one in Asia wants to live under China's shadow, and everyone realizes that a strong U.S. strategic role in Asia is the best way to avoid that.

But regional powers also value their relationships with China enormously and fear the consequences of escalating U.S.-China rivalry. Bluntly put, these countries have become economically linked with China, and they are aware that, geographically speaking, China is literally not going anywhere. As a consequence, they are incurring increasing risks in the event of openly defying China. Despite—or perhaps because of—this, they still want the United States to remain in Asia on a basis that avoids escalating rivalry—which means on a basis that China is willing to accept. If China cannot be persuaded to accept U.S. primacy, China's neighbors would far prefer a compromise that preserves a U.S. role large enough to balance China's power and avoid Chinese hegemony but not so large that it inflames relations with China. That means there would be strong regional support for some kind of U.S. role, but not necessarily the role the United States has in mind. The reality is that Asian countries may support the United States against China to avoid Chinese hegemony, but not to the point that the United States is empowered to interfere in regional independent internal politics.

That being the case, regional countries have a range of positions when it comes to Sino-U.S. rivalry. These positions can be broadly placed into one of three groups. Most of the claimants, notably the Philippines and Vietnam, have been highly critical of China. The Philippines has elected to renew the EDCA with the United States, despite domestic criticism on the question of sovereignty and expanding content. However, Beijing is betting that the Duterte administration in Manila will prove amenable to Chinese influence and has evidence to believe so.[76] As for Vietnam, although an alliance remains out of reach given resistance from hardline elements, relations with the United States are increasingly warm, and China is the primary factor in this. These countries were, in response to China, employing soft-balancing (that is, hedging) techniques through defense build-ups and bandwagoning with the United States.[77] China's tactics, such as constructing military outposts on disputed features in the South China Sea, could intensify this group's alignment toward the United States, even in the face of improving Sino-Philippine relations.[78]

A second group of ASEAN members, notably Indonesia, Singapore, and Thailand, has been very keen to maintain strategic autonomy. Nevertheless, with a massive influx of Chinese investment, countries that are in need of infrastructure and engagement, such as Indonesia and even Thailand, will struggle to preserve their neutrality.[79] They value their relationship with both China and the United States and seek to reap maximum rewards from positive relations with both. For them, regional instability is the biggest enemy, though China is slowly eroding these countries' trust. Thailand is slowly moving towards the third group, however. It has contracted with China to buy three S26T diesel-electric attack submarines, 34 ZBL-O9 VN-1 armored personnel carriers (APCs), and 12,506 units of 30mm rounds from China North Industries Corporation (NORINCO). Though this speaks more to Thailand wanting to diversify its arms suppliers and adapt to post-coup sanctions by the United States, it still generally does not bode well for the United States and its regional interests.

The third group includes Cambodia, Brunei, Laos, and Myanmar (though Myanmar is moving toward the second group). These are all countries determined to avoid any position that puts them directly at odds with China. These countries are small and politically, militarily, and economically at risk from an angry, hegemonic China. China is also able at times to play off historical animosities among and between these countries. That still does not mean that China can never overplay its hand with them, however.

The gaps between these already divergent positions have been widening since the PCA delivered its strongly pro-claimant award. It is motivating claimants to step up their efforts to reassert their claims and to bolster security ties with external powers, especially the United States and Japan. As claimants such as Vietnam determine second- and third-order effects of the Philippines' case, they may initiate their own legal actions. The Philippines, Vietnam, Malaysia, and even nonclaimants such as Singapore and Indonesia will support the primacy of rules in managing disputes and regional affairs. ASEAN members will also pressure ASEAN meetings to address the challenges that China's claims present. This will put nonclaimants in the difficult position of having to choose between their fellow ASEAN members and China. These divisions make it unlikely that ASEAN, the most important regional grouping, will be able to reach consensus on any serious strategy for addressing disputed South China Sea claims or dealing with any other challenges from China.

How, then, will the United States and its allies respond? Many in the United States will no doubt demand that steps be taken to punish China for what they perceive to be Xi Jinping's duplicity—most likely in the form of economic sanctions. Sanctions, however, could potentially hurt the U.S. economy as well and will have little appeal for nations such as Vietnam, Malaysia, or Australia, all of which are deeply engaged with China economically. Even less appealing would be any attempt to respond militarily, given China's burgeoning anti-access/area denial capabilities, along with other levers of national power, most notably its economic influence. Thus, while economic sticks hold little appeal, military sticks hold even less. Washington cannot sit idly by as China effectively salami-slices the United States and its allies out of the South China Sea. Yet Washington must avoid taking a hard line that puts Beijing in a corner (one created by its own tactics) and forces it to lash out militarily to save face and appease domestic nationalism. No one wants a shooting war in a major global trade artery involving at least two of the world's largest powers.

CONCLUSION

The increased anti-China sentiment arising in the region begs the question of why China would risk its interests and not be more accommodating. The explanations lie in how it has plotted its regional strategy.

China holds a new position in the region and globally. In its own eyes, and in the eyes of others, China has achieved the status of a world power. After thirty years of following the famous maxim, attributed to Deng Xiaoping, to "hide your light and bide your time," China has adopted a foreign policy that seems to arise from the wish to act militarily and diplomatically in accordance with its increased economic power. Even if there is no enemy that wants to attack China, it may regard a strong military as something that a world power "needs." Ninety percent of global trade goes by sea, but under the current order, only the United States (with allies) has the means to police the sea lanes. Why, from the point of view of the newly arrived world power, should that remain the case close to China's coast? The fact that China profits from the status quo does not mean that it cannot perceive a need to improve it and extend its own maritime reach. From that perspective, the U.S. security guarantee and, since 2011, its "rebalance" that aims to bring 60 percent of the U.S. fleet to the Pacific by 2020 may look to China very much like "soft containment" at the least. It might seem only natural to seek an arrangement in the region that makes China less dependent on the United States and wins it access to the natural resources and the fish of the region in the process.

China's strategy has not been as iterative and adaptive as it needs to be to the changing region around it, and it is resulting in a tactics-strategy mismatch. Its strategy does not account for the national politics of its adversaries and only looks at its own strengths, current and projected, as guidelines for regional security policies. This mismatch guarantees increasing alienation against China from surrounding countries. China has been iterative vis-à-vis the United States, and China's military and economic power may secure the loyalty of Laos and Cambodia, but its strategy is a flawed one when applied uniformly to all countries in the region, notably Vietnam. For any future resistance it encounters from its neighbors, China will only have itself to blame.

Notes

1. Derek Watkins, "What China Has Been Building in the South China Sea," *New York Times*, July 30, 2015, http://www.nytimes.com/interactive/2015/07/30/world/asia/what-china-has-been-building-in-the-south-china-sea.html.
2. Simon Denyer, "Satellite Images Show China May Be Building Powerful Radar on Disputed Islands," *Washington Post*, February 22, 2016, https://www.washingtonpost.com/news/worldviews/wp/2016/02/22/satellite-images-show-china-may-be-building-powerful-radar-on-disputed-islands/.
3. Victor Robert Lee, "Satellite Images: China Manufactures Land at New Sites in the Paracel Islands," *The Diplomat*, February 13, 2016, http://thediplomat.com/2016/02/satellite-images-china-manufactures-land-at-new-sites-in-the-paracel-islands/.
4. Sam LaGrone, "New Possible Chinese Radar Installation on South China Sea Artificial Island Could Put U.S., Allied Stealth Aircraft at Risk," USNI News, February 23, 2016, http://news.usni.org/2016/02/22/new-possible-chinese-radar-installation-on-south-china-sea-artificial-island-could-put-u-s-allied-stealth-aircraft-at-risk; Richard D. Fisher Jr., "China Deploys HQ-9 Surface-to-Air Missiles to Woody Island," *IHS Jane's Defence Weekly*, February 17, 2016, http://www.janes.com/article/58071/china-deploys-hq-9-surface-to-air-missiles-to-woody-island; Denyer, "Satellite Images Show China May Be Building Powerful Radar on Disputed Islands."
5. Ben Blanchard, "China Says Media Ignores Other Claimants' Weaponry in South China Sea," Reuters, February 24, 2016, http://www.reuters.com/article/us-south chinasea-china-idUSKCN0VX0SZ.
6. Xiaodong Lang, "High Tensions Over Low-Tide Elevations in the South China Sea," National Bureau of Asian Research, January 2016, http://nbr.org/research/activity.aspx?id=644.
7. David Brunnstrom, "South China Sea: U.S. Agrees to Spy Plane Deployment in Singapore," *Sydney Morning Herald*, December 8, 2015, http://www.smh.com.au/world/south-china-sea-us-agrees-to-spy-plane-deployment-in-singapore-20151207-glhuke.html; "P 8-A Malaysia Deployment a 'Serious Threat to China's Security': PLA Admiral," IndianDefence.com, September 16, 2014, http://indiandefence.com/threads/p-8a-malaysia-deployment-a-serious-threat-to-chinas-security-pla-admiral.49404/.
8. Dan De Luce, C. K. Hickey, and Keith Johnson, "Why China's Land Grab Is Backfiring on Beijing," *Foreign Policy*, December 7, 2015, http://foreignpolicy.com/2015/12/18/maps-money-and-the-military-fps-most-read-china-stories-of-2015/.

9. James Mulvenon, "Chairman Hu and China's 'New Historic Missions,'" *China Leadership Monitor* 27 (Winter 2009), http://media.hoover.org/sites/default/files/documents/CLM27JM.pdf.
10. Edward Wong, "Chinese Military Seeks to Extend Its Naval Power," *New York Times*, April 23, 2010, http://www.nytimes.com/2010/04/24/world/asia/24navy.html. Wong cites "an American official involved in China policy" as follows: "In March, Chinese officials told two visiting senior Obama administration officials, Jeffrey A. Bader and James B. Steinberg, that China would not tolerate any interference in the South China Sea, now part of China's 'core interests' of sovereignty, said an American official involved in China policy. It was the first time the Chinese labeled the South China Sea a core interest, on par with Taiwan and Tibet, the official said." "China Tells U.S. that S. China Sea is 'Core Interest' in New Policy," *Kyodo News*, July 3, 2010; Hillary Rodham Clinton, interview with Greg Sheridan of *The Australian*, Melbourne, November 8, 2010, http://www.state.gov/secretary/rm/2010/11/150671.htm. Uncertainty remained about precisely what language Chinese officials used in their private discussions—namely, whether they referred to the contested islands as part of China's core interests or whether they referred to the waters of the South China Sea as a whole.
11. M. Taylor Fravel, "Maritime Security in the South China Sea and the Competition over Maritime Rights," in *Cooperation from Strength: The United States, China, and the South China Sea*, ed. Patrick Cronin (Washington, D.C.: Center for a New American Security, 2012), 42; Michael D. Swaine, "China's Assertive Behavior: Part One: On 'Core Interests,'" *China Leadership Monitor* 34 (Winter 2011): pp. 8–9; Ministry of Foreign Affairs of the People's Republic of China, "Foreign Ministry Spokesperson Jiang Yu's Regular Press Conference on September 21, 2010," September 21, 2010, http://www.fmprc.gov.cn/eng/xwfw/s2510/2511/t756092.htm. In response to a specific question ("U.S. officials said China once expressed that the South China Sea is its core interest. Please confirm."), Jiang replied: "Each country has its own core interests. Issues concerning state sovereignty, territorial integrity and major development interests are significant to all countries. China believes the South China Sea issue is only the dispute of territorial sovereignty and maritime rights and interests between relevant countries rather than an issue between China and ASEAN, let alone a regional or international issue. It can only and must be settled through friendly consultations between both parties in a peaceful manner. Adhering to 'putting aside disputes and seeking common development,' we are always committed to proper settlement through bilateral consultations with relevant countries. The channel of communication is smooth."
12. Government White Papers, http://www.china.org.cn/e-white/.
13. G. John Ikenberry, "The Future of the Liberal World Order: Internationalism after America," *Foreign Affairs* 90, no. 3 (2011): pp. 56–68.
14. Fu Ying and Wu Shicun, "South China Sea: How We Got to this Stage," *National Interest*, May 13, 2016, http://www.chinadaily.com.cn/world/2016-05/13/content_25254747.htm.
15. "Commentary: Harsh Talk from U.S. Military Only Undermines Peace in Asia-Pacific," Xinhua, May 30, 2016, http://news.xinhuanet.com/english/2016-05/30/c_135399678.htm.

16. The Taiwan numbers include roughly half of the total PLAAF fighter and bomber inventory, with the rest held for defensive missions or a reserve capability.
17. Eric Heginbotham et al., *The U.S.-China Military Scorecard: Forces, Geography, and the Evolving Balance of Power, 1996–2017* (Santa Monica, Calif.: RAND Corporation, 2017), 339–40.
18. Mariko Kodaki, "China's Territorial Ambitions Driving up Asia's Defense Spending," *Nikkei Asian Review*, February 10, 2016, http://asia.nikkei.com/Politics-Economy/International-Relations/China-s-territorial-ambitions-driving-up-Asia-s-defense-spending.
19. Ankit Panda, "Global Defense Spending Is Down, But Asia's Spending Is Up," *The Diplomat*, April 16, 2015, http://thediplomat.com/2015/04/global-defense-spending-is-down-but-asias-spending-is-up/.
20. Heginbotham et al., *The U.S.-China Military Scorecard*, 338–42.
21. Ibid.
22. James Mulvenon, "Chairman Hu and the PLA's 'New Historic Missions,'" *China Leadership Monitor* 27 (Winter 2009), http://www.hoover.org/research/chairman-hu-and-plas-new-historic-missions.
23. Previous mission guidance to the PLA varied over time but was more narrowly focused. For a discussion of the possible implications of China's "new historic missions" for the PLAN, see Cortez A. Cooper, *The PLA Navy's "New Historic Missions": Expanding Capabilities for a Re-Emergent Maritime Power*, testimony before the U.S.-China Economic and Security Review Commission, CT-332 (Santa Monica, Calif.: RAND Corporation, June 11, 2009).
24. Ibid.
25. Dean Cheng, *China's Pivot to the Sea: The Modernizing PLA Navy*, Backgrounder 3084 (Washington, D.C.: Heritage Foundation, December 17, 2015).
26. "China's Military Strategy," USNI News, May 26, 2016, http://news.usni.org/2015/05/26/document-chinas-military-strategy.
27. Ashwin Kaja, Yan Luo, and Timothy P. Stratford, "China's New National Security Law," Global Policy Watch, July 7, 2015, https://www.globalpolicywatch.com/2015/07/chinas-new-national-security-law/.
28. Heginbotham et al., *The U.S.-China Military Scorecard*, 199.
29. Ibid., 71.
30. China State Oceanic Administration, https://www.soa.gov.cn.
31. Jon Grevatt, "Philippines to Acquire Elta Systems Radars," *IHS Jane's Defence Industry*, February 7, 2016, http://www.janes.com/article/57802/philippines-to-acquire-elta-systems-radars.
32. Manuel Mogato, "Philippines Gets First Coastguard Boat from Japan to Boost Security," Reuters, August 18, 2016, http://www.reuters.com/article/us-southchinasea-philippines-japan-idUSKCN10T11V.
33. Dan De Luce, "China Fears Bring the U.S. Military Back to the Philippines," *Foreign Policy*, January 12, 2016, http://news.yahoo.com/china-fears-bring-u-military-215745691.html.
34. Greg Torode, "Exclusive: Vietnam Moves New Rocket Launchers into Disputed South China Sea—Sources," Reuters, August 10, 2016, http://www.reuters.com/article/us-southchinasea-vietnam-exclusive-idUSKCN10K2NE.

35. Richard D. Fisher, "Vietnamese Amphibious Force Trains 'Island Recapture,'" *IHS Jane's Defence Weekly*, August 3, 2016, http://www.janes.com/article/62752/vietnamese-amphibious-force-trains-island-recapture.
36. Joshua Keating, "China Has the Philippines on the Ropes," *Foreign Policy*, September 4, 2012, http://foreignpolicy.com/2012/09/04/china-has-the-philippines-on-the-ropes/.
37. Manuel Mogato, Michael Martina, and Ben Blanchard, "ASEAN Deadlocked on South China Sea, Cambodia Blocks Statement," Reuters, July 26, 2016, http://www.reuters.com/article/us-southchinasea-ruling-asean-idUSKCN1050F6.
38. Mong Palatino, "ASEAN's Joint Communique: It's Not Just About China or the South China Sea," *The Diplomat*, August 14, 2015, http://the diplomat.com/2015/08/aseans-joint-communique-its-not-just-about-china-or-the-south-china-sea/.
39. White House, Office of the Press Secretary, "Joint Statement of the U.S.-ASEAN Special Leaders' Summit: Sunnylands Declaration," February 16, 2016, https://www.whitehouse.gov/the-press-office/2016/02/16/joint-statement-us-asean-special-leaders-summit-sunnylands-declaration.
40. Li Xiaokun and Liu Xiaoli, "Ancient Book 'Provides Ironclad Proof of Chinese Ownership,'" *China Daily*, May 24, 2016, http://www.chinadaily.com.cn/china/2016-05/24/content_25433846.htm; "Backgrounder: Tomas Cloma's Once Daydream on South China Sea," Xinhua, May 4, 2016, http://news.xinhuanet.com/english/2016-05/04/c_135332976.htm.
41. See, generally, Zhiguo Gao and Bing Bing Jia, "The Nine-Dash Line in the South China Sea: History, Status, and Implications," *American Journal of International Law* 107, no. 95 (2013); "Backgrounder: China Has Indisputable Sovereignty over South China Sea Islands," Xinhua, April 29, 2016, http://news.xinhuanet.com/english/2016-04/29/c_135322815.htm; Zhang Tao, "Nansha Islands, Huangyan Island Have Never Been Philippine Territory," Xinhua, April 27, 2016, http://english.chinamil.com.cn/news-channels/today-headlines/2016-04/27/content_7026254.htm.
42. Amy He, "China's South China Sea Claims Are 'Legal, Justified': UN Rep," *China Daily*, June 13, 2016, http://www.chinadaily.com.cn/world/2015-06/13/content_20990569.htm.
43. In the communication to the Commission on the Limits of the Continental Shelf in response to the Joint Submission of Malaysia and Vietnam, China asserted that "China has indisputable sovereignty over the islands in the South China Sea and the adjacent waters, and enjoys sovereign rights and jurisdiction over the relevant waters as well as the seabed and subsoil (see attached map)," which referred to the U-shaped line map. See Commission on the Limits of the Continental Shelf (CLCS), "Communication Received from China with Regard to the Joint Submission by Malaysia and the Socialist Republic of Vietnam," May 7, 2009, http://www.un.org/depts/los/clcs_new/submissions_files/mysvnm33_09/chn_2009re_mys_vnm_e.pdf.
44. "Declaration of the Government of the People's Republic of China on the Baselines of the Territorial Sea of the People's Republic China (15 May 1996)," http://www

.legislation.gov.hk/blis_pdf.nsf/4f0db701c6c25d4a4825755c00352e35/56E183FB501638DF482575EF0028ECFA/$FILE/CAP_2205_e_b5.pdf. It is doubtful that such a straight baseline is consistent with international law, since only "archipelagic States" are allowed to draw straight baselines around mid-ocean archipelagos and China is not an "archipelagic State"; see United Nations Convention on the Law of the Sea, Arts. 46 and 47(1), http://www.un.org/depts/los/convention_agreements/texts/unclos/part4.htm.

45. CLCS, "Communications Received from China with Regard to Republic of the Philippines' Note Verbale No. 000228," April 14, 2011, http://www.un.org/depts/los/clcs_new/submissions_files/mysvnm33_09/chn_2011_re_phl_e.pdf; CLCS, "Communications Received from China with Regard to the Submission Made by Vietnam," May 1, 2011, http://www.un.org/depts/los/clcs_new/submissions_files/mysvnm33_09/vnm_2011_re_phlchn.pdf.

46. Melda Malek, "A Legal Assessment of China's Historic Claims in the South China Sea," *Australian Journal of Maritime and Ocean Affairs* 5, no. 1 (2013): p. 33.

47. "Philippines Halts Tests after China Patrol Challenge," BBC, March 8, 2011, http://www.bbc.co.uk/news/mobile/world-asia-pacific-12672889.

48. Permanent Court of Arbitration, "Arbitration between the Republic of the Philippines and the People's Republic of China," press release, October 29, 2015, http://www.pcacases.com/web/sendAttach/1521.

49. "The Tribunal's Award in the 'South China Sea Arbitration' is Null and Void, Says Chinese Think-tank in a Paper," *People's Daily Online*, June 11, 2016, http://en.people.cn/n3/2016/0612/c98649-9070632.html.

50. In the communication to the Commission on the Limits of the Continental Shelf (CLCS) in response to the Joint Submission of Malaysia and Vietnam, China asserted that "China has indisputable sovereignty over the islands in the South China Sea and the adjacent waters, and enjoys sovereign rights and jurisdiction over the relevant waters as well as the seabed and subsoil," which referred to the U-shaped line map. See CLCS, "Communication Received from China with Regard to the Joint Submission by Malaysia and the Socialist Republic of Vietnam," May 7, 2009.

51. Permanent Court of Arbitration, "Arbitration between the Philippines and the People's Republic of China," press release, June 3, 2014, https://www.pcacases.com/web/sendAttach/230; http://www.pca-cpa.org/showpage.asp?pag_id=1529.

52. Simon Denyer and Emily Rauhala, "Beijing's Claims to South China Sea Rejected by International Tribunal," *Washington Post*, July 12, 2016, https://www.washingtonpost.com/world/beijing-remains-angry-defiant-and-defensive-as-key-south-china-sea-tribunal-ruling-looms/2016/07/12/11100f48-4771-11e6-8dac-0c6e4accc5b1_story.html.

53. Chun Han Wong, "Beijing Lashes Out at South China Sea Tribunal—and the People on It," *Wall Street Journal*, July 13, 2016, http://blogs.wsj.com/chinarealtime/2016/07/13/beijing-lashes-out-at-south-china-sea-tribunal-and-the-people-on-it/.

54. U.S. Census Bureau, "U.S. International Trade Data," https://www.census.gov/foreign-trade/balance/index.html.

55. Observatory of Economic Complexity, "Where Does China Export To (2014)?" http://atlas.media.mit.edu/en/visualize/tree_map/hs92/export/chn/show/all/2014/.
56. Economist Intelligence Unit, Country Reports (2016): http://country.eiu.com/brunei; http://country.eiu.com/cambodia#; http://country.eiu.com/indonesia; http://country.eiu.com/laos; http://country.eiu.com/malaysia; http://country.eiu.com/myanmar; http://country.eiu.com/philippines; http://country.eiu.com/singapore; http://country.eiu.com/thailand; http://country.eiu.com/vietnam.
57. Zhang Tao, "Behind South China Sea Tensions, U.S. Tries to Maintain Domination over World Issues," Xinhua, May 26, 2016, http://english.chinamil.com.cn/news-channels/pla-daily-commentary/2016-05/26/content_7072754.htm.
58. Hillary Rodham Clinton, remarks at the Seventeenth ASEAN Regional Forum, Hanoi, July 23, 2010, http://iipdigital.usembassy.gov/st/english/texttrans/2010/07/20100723164658su0.4912989.html#axzz3bIuS19us.
59. Daniel S. Inhofe, "Inhofe Resolution on China Passes: U.S. Senate Unanimously 'Deplores' China's Use of Force in South China Sea," press release, June 28, 2011, http://www.inhofe.senate.gov/newsroom/press-releases/inhofe-resolution-on-china-passes.
60. White House, Office of the Press Secretary, "Remarks by President Obama to the Australian Parliament," November 17, 2011, https://www.whitehouse.gov/the-press-office/2011/11/17/remarks-president-obama-australian-parliament.
61. "Enhanced Defense Cooperation Agreement between the Philippines and the United States," April 29, 2014, http://www.gov.ph/2014/04/29/document-enhanced-defense-cooperation-agreement/.
62. Richard Javad Heydarian, "Will America Go to War for the Philippines?" *National Interest*, January 27, 2016, http://atimes.com/2016/01/will-america-go-to-war-for-the-philippines/.
63. Philippine Daily Inquirer, "China Slams PH-U.S. Base Deal," January 14, 2016, http://www.janes.com/article/58071/china-deploys-hq-9-surface-to-air-missiles-to-woody-island.
64. Ibid.
65. Gordon Lubold and Vu Trong Khanh, "U.S. Says Vietnam Weighing Ending Island Expansion in Disputed Waters," *Wall Street Journal*, June 1, 2015, http://www.wsj.com/articles/u-s-says-vietnam-weighing-ending-island-expansion-in-disputed-waters-1433162877.
66. Gardiner Harris, "Vietnam Arms Embargo to Be Fully Lifted, Obama Says in Hanoi," *New York Times*, May 23, 2016, http://www.nytimes.com/2016/05/24/world/asia/vietnam-us-arms-embargo-obama.html; Lesley Wroughton and Andrea Shalal, "U.S. Eases Arms Embargo against Vietnam for Maritime Security," Reuters, October 2, 2014, http://www.reuters.com/article/us-usa-vietnam-arms-idUSKCN0HR29V20141002.
67. Department of Defense, *Asia-Pacific Maritime Security Strategy* (Washington, D.C.: Department of Defense, 2015), http://www.defense.gov/Portals/1/Documents/pubs/NDAA%20A-P_Maritime_SecuritY_Strategy-08142015-1300-FINAL FORMAT.PDF.

68. "SECDEF Carter Letter to McCain on South China Sea Freedom of Navigation Operation," January 5, 2016, http://news.usni.org/2016/01/05/document-secdef-carter-letter-to-mccain-on-south-china-sea-freedom-of-navigation-operation.
69. Jim Sciutto and Katie Hunt, "China Says It Warned and Tracked U.S. Warship in South China Sea," CNN, October 27, 2015, http://www.cnn.com/2015/10/27/asia/us-china-south-china-sea/index.html.
70. Prashanth Parameswaran, "U.S. South China Sea FONOPs to Increase in Scope, Complexity: Commander," *The Diplomat*, January 28, 2016, http://thediplomat.com/2016/01/us-south-china-sea-fonops-to-increase-in-scope-complexity-commander/.
71. Liu Haiyang, "Time for U.S. to Stop Militarization of South China Sea," *China Daily*, June 2, 2016, http://www.chinadaily.com.cn/opinion/2016-06/02/content_25583869.htm; "Commentary: Harsh Talk from U.S. Military Only Undermines Peace in the Asia-Pacific," Xinhua, May 30, 2015, http://news.xinhuanet.com/english/2016-05/30/c_135399678.htm.
72. David Brunnstrom, "Carter Says U.S. Will Sail, Fly and Operate Wherever International Law Allows," Reuters, October 13, 2015, http://www.reuters.com/article/us-usa-australia-southchinasea-carter-idUSKCN0S72MG20151013.
73. Yuan Can, "China Sets Four Bottom Lines Regarding the South China Sea Disputes," *People's Daily Online*, May 27, 2016, http://en.people.cn/n3/2016/0527/c90000-9064485.html.
74. Zhang Yunbi, "Firm Line Taken on Sea Dispute," *China Daily*, June 6, 2016, http://www.chinadaily.com.cn/world/2016-06/06/content_25616771.htm; Wang Jian, "U.S. 'Charting Clear Course Aimed at Containing China,'" *China Daily*, May 24, 2016, http://www.chinadaily.com.cn/world/2016-05/24/content_25434017.htm.
75. See, generally, Tuosheng Zhang, "The Gap Between Threat and Threat Perception in the Asia-Pacific," in *The Stockholm China Forum Paper Series* (Washington, D.C.: German Marshall Fund of the United States, 2014).
76. "Duterte Could Help Heal Breach with China," *Global Times*, June 14, 2016, http://en.people.cn/n3/2016/0614/c90780-9071869.html; Zhang Yunbi, "Door Open to Bilateral Negotiations," *China Daily*, June 9, 2016, http://www.chinadaily.com.cn/world/2016-06/09/content_25656519.htm.
77. Yanmei Xie, "The Storm Beneath the Calm: China's Regional Relations in 2016," *China File*, January 8, 2016, http://www.chinafile.com/reporting-opinion/viewpoint/storm-beneath-calm-chinas-regional-relations-2016.
78. Darren J. Lim and Zack Cooper, "Are East Asian States Really Hedging between the U.S. and China?" *East Asia Forum*, January 30, 2016, http://www.eastasiaforum.org/2016/01/30/are-east-asian-states-really-hedging-between-the-us-and-china/.
79. Hua Yisheng, "Commentary: China Is Winning More Support over the South China Sea Issue," *People's Daily Online*, May 27, 2016, http://en.people.cn/n3/2016/0527/c98649-9064201.html.

3

China's Maritime Sovereignty Campaign

Scarborough Shoal, the "New Spratly Islands," and Beyond

James E. Fanell

In apparent disregard of international law, the People's Republic of China (PRC) is engaged in unilateral territorial expansion across the South China Sea, which over the past five years has dramatically altered the geo-military balance of power in the Indo-Asia Pacific region. PRC president Xi Jinping has justified these actions as a legitimate part of his effort to restore and rejuvenate the PRC under the rubric of the "China Dream," empowered by the financial incentives of Beijing's newly created Asia Infrastructure Investment Bank and the tendrils of the Belt and Road Initiative that rely upon a strong global navy.

Indicators of China's future actions on the global stage for the remainder of the first half of the twenty-first century include the creation of the "New Spratly Islands" in the South China Sea; declaration of an air defense identification zone in the East China Sea; assertions of sovereignty over the Senkaku Islands; and increasing naval operations in the Western Pacific, South Pacific, and Indian Oceans, as well as in the Gulf of Aden and the Mediterranean Sea. In response to this expansionism, the United States, other major powers, and regional nations are engaged in building and enhancing existing bilateral military cooperation, as well as expanding from bilateral to stronger and more expansive multilateral military alliances. China's actions, with respect to international norms, will also undoubtedly impact the rest of the world's security concerns in the coming years and decades.

This chapter was first published as an article in the May 2016 edition of Switzerland's *Military Power Review* under the title "The 'New Spratly Islands': China's Words and Actions in the South China Sea."

PEOPLE'S LIBERATION ARMY: "NEW HISTORIC MISSIONS"

In December 2004, PRC president Hu Jintao gave a speech that outlined the "new historic missions" for the People's Liberation Army (PLA). While his speech was not publicly advertised, experts have assessed that it reflected "a critically important change in the orientation" for the PRC and the PLA. It set in motion a new approach for China that sought to remove the shame and guilt of over one hundred years of foreign intervention and occupation.[1] While President Hu's speech was internally focused, the Indo-Asia Pacific region got its first glimpse of China's intentions in October 2007 when the Seventeenth National Congress of the Communist Party of China amended its constitution by adopting the directive to "earnestly ensure the PLA to accomplish its historic missions in the new era."[2]

Concurrent with these seemingly innocuous indications, China reemerged on the international stage with the hosting of the 2008 Olympics and thus began its current path of public pursuit of "a peaceful environment for the country's strategic development" and "the country's interests."[3] Since President Xi's rise to power in 2013, the PLA's "new historic missions" have been incorporated into his vision for the "restoration" and "rejuvenation" of the country, which are the key and essential elements of his widely proclaimed "China Dream."

What is unknown is the type of "peaceful environment" China's leaders believe is required to reach their goal of a restored China. While initial assessments from Western Sinologists and government officials asserted that Beijing's interests were simply limited to land territories, such as Xinjiang, Tibet, and the island of Taiwan, a series of incidents at sea from 2012 to the present have severely shaken this assumption.

Now, after nearly four years of activity in the maritime domain, it seems unmistakable that the PRC also seeks sovereignty over a large expanse of maritime territory within the First Island Chain, an area that Chinese government officials and academics routinely refer to as "China's three million square miles of maritime territory."[4] China's historically mistaken irredentist claims of sovereignty over this area, which includes the South and East China Seas, have spurred an effort of acquisition best characterized as China's "maritime sovereignty campaign." Japan and the majority of Association of Southeast Asian Nation (ASEAN) members view this campaign as the primary cause for discord and a new arms race in Asia.

While there were hints of this maritime sovereignty campaign as far back as the September 2010 ramming of a Japanese coast guard vessel by a Chinese fishing trawler in the East China Sea,[5] it was the tumultuous 2012 Scarborough Reef incident that stands out as the first tangible manifestation of Beijing's effort to take possession of maritime territory.[6]

The Scarborough Shoal "seizure" exemplifies the confrontational grand strategy China is imposing on its neighbors. It exhibited a set of common characteristics with incidents across China's maritime sovereignty campaign. First, incidents are initiated by the egregious conduct of the Chinese government or private Chinese entities. Second, Chinese official spokesmen issue fabricated stories to explain the incident. Third, China bullies its adversary, linking it to a variety of unconnected trade, economic, or political issues, while insisting that the negotiation remain bilateral. Fourth, China states a historical claim that is unsupported by documentation, omitting evidence and ignoring other narratives. Fifth, the PLA Navy (PLAN) is always present. As has been stated, "The PLA Navy is now active at sea throughout the South and East China Seas 365 days a year."[7] The PLA is increasingly postured for combat should any of China's adversaries dare provide opposition.[8]

This pattern of expansionism in the maritime domain has been repeated again and again. Following the seizure of Scarborough Shoal, China increased its pressure on the Republic of the Philippines. For instance, in 2013, after the Philippines submitted its legal case to the Permanent Court of Arbitration against the PRC, pursuant to Annex VII to the United Nations Convention on the Law of the Sea of January 2013, China turned its attention to Second Thomas Shoal (also known in the Philippines as Ayungin Shoal), located just 105 nautical miles west of the Philippine island of Palawan in the Spratly Island chain.[9] The escalation by China was made manifest when, in May 2013, the Philippines publicly démarched the PRC for dispatching more than thirty Chinese fishing vessels and patrol vessels to Second Thomas Shoal in an effort to intimidate the handful of Philippine navy sailors and marines residing on a grounded amphibious tank landing ship (LST), the *Sierra Madre*.[10] While this encounter did not directly threaten Philippine territory, it did demonstrate the PRC's complete disregard of the Philippines' claimed exclusive economic zone (EEZ) and further demonstrated Beijing's insincerity toward the 2002 Declaration on the Conduct of Parties in the South China Sea, which both Beijing and Manila signed.

The complex, dangerous, and rapidly changing strategic and legal environment of the South China Sea is in large part due to the unilateral actions of the PRC. Professionals in the field once again focused on Scarborough Shoal when U.S. Chief of Naval Operations Adm. John Richardson "expressed concern that an international court ruling expected in coming weeks on a case brought by the

Philippines against China over its South China Sea claims could be a trigger for Beijing to declare an exclusion zone in the busy trade route."[11]

Not satisfied with the tactic of swarming the fishing area around Second Thomas Shoal with Chinese fishermen, the PRC escalated tensions in 2014 by directly interfering with the resupply of food and water and the rotation of the Philippine sailors and marines living in austere conditions on the *Sierra Madre*. Chinese coast guard ships blocked Philippine civilian resupply vessels for these troops. Manila again démarched Beijing about their actions at Second Thomas Shoal in March 2014, but this time the stakes were much higher, as China's tactics threatened the lives of the sailors and marines on the grounded LST.[12] At least through 2015, China continued to repeat aggressive actions to disrupt and prevent the resupply efforts, demonstrating the PRC's ongoing flagrant disregard for the 2002 Declaration on the Conduct of Parties in the South China Sea and its call for peaceful resolution of maritime disputes.

China has not confined its escalation of tensions in the South China Sea to the Republic of the Philippines. On May 5, 2014, China dispatched the China National Offshore Oil Corporation (CNOOC) semisubmersible drilling rig *Hai Yang Shi You* (HYSY 981) to an area approximately 120 nautical miles east of Vietnam for three months through August 15, 2014.[13] In addition to announcing its three-month-long oil exploration operations, a proactive press announcement from the China Maritime Safety Administration also declared that all ships would be prohibited from entering a three-nautical-mile radius around HYSY 981.[14] As a direct result of China's unprecedented operations within Vietnam's EEZ, demonstrators (sometimes violent) in Vietnam demanded that China remove its vessel.[15]

But it was events at sea, not the protests ashore, that were the real worry for those who feared a confrontation between China and Vietnam.[16] Unlike its reaction to the Republic of the Philippines at Scarborough Shoal and Second Thomas Shoal, during the CNOOC HYSY 981 incident, China dispatched more than one hundred vessels from the Chinese coast guard and other maritime organizations, plus several combatants from the PLAN and fighter aircraft from both its naval and air forces.[17] While much of the world fixated on the anti-Chinese protests in Vietnam, daily confrontations between Chinese and Vietnamese vessels at sea generated deep concern that a military confrontation would occur.[18] Although HYSY 981 eventually departed the area after concluding its exploration activities, the message to Hanoi was loud and clear: the PRC has complete and utter disregard for Vietnam's EEZ.[19]

In response, Vietnam embarked on a military modernization program that has focused on increasing its maritime firepower at sea, as most recently exemplified with its acquisition of a fifth *Kilo*-class diesel-electric submarine from Russia with the potent supersonic sea-skimming SS-N-27/Sizzler antiship cruise missile (with a range of 220 kilometers).[20]

China's maritime forces have concurrently expanded their operations into waters as far south as Malaysia's coast in Borneo. While China and Malaysia are frequently described as having a "special relationship," it has not proven sufficiently special to deter Beijing from the pursuit of its maritime sovereignty campaign. As evidenced in 2013, China dispatched a four-ship flotilla headed by the amphibious dock landing ship *Jinggangshan* (LPD 981) to James Shoal, a submerged feature 60 meters below the waterline, just 80 kilometers off the coast of Malaysia and some 1,800 kilometers south of the Chinese mainland—what Beijing has declared is "China's southernmost point."[21] That event was marked by Chinese "naval officers and soldiers taking part in the mission" by holding "an oath-taking ceremony, pledging to safeguard China's territorial integrity and marine interests."[22]

While the ceremony was not the first conducted by PRC maritime forces at James Shoal, its wide publicity and concurrence with Malaysia's Langkawi International Maritime and Aerospace Exhibition 2013 disturbed the Malaysian government. The PRC was not content to conduct the ceremony in private; instead, it embarrassed the Malaysian government by piggybacking on Kuala Lumpur's premier defense exposition when all of Asia's officials were attending.

If this event did not cast enough doubt on what it means to have a "special relationship" with China, the PRC has further demonstrated its disrespect for Malaysia by dispatching patrol vessels to another area just off Malaysia's Borneo coast at Luconia Shoals, less than one hundred kilometers from shore. While Malaysia remained "largely silent on China's actions" at Luconia Shoals, by June 2015, a Malaysian government minister "posted aerial photos of a 1,000-ton-class Chinese Coast Guard vessel" located well within Malaysia's EEZ.[23] The PRC's presence at Luconia Shoals has continued for more than two years, and as recently as October 2015, Malaysian fishermen claimed that they "were chased from the shoals by the Chinese Navy boats, and now they dare not go near the place to fish."[24]

In 2016, China confronted Indonesia's maritime claims. Armed Chinese coast guard ships interfered with an Indonesian Maritime and Fisheries Monitoring Task Force patrol boat (KP *Hiu 11*). According reports, KP *Hiu 11* was attempting to tow a Chinese motor vessel (MV *Kway Fei)* that had been illegally fishing in Indonesia's EEZ near the Natuna Islands.[25] The PRC coast guard ship was reported to have rammed MV *Kway Fei* in order to prevent Indonesia from gaining control of the Chinese vessel and its illegal catch.[26] Not surprisingly, PRC state-sponsored media editorialized, "If China wants to safeguard its territorial sovereignty and maritime interests, it will be bound to face certain conflicts" and will not "make unprincipled concessions to please other nations."[27] Again, the message from Beijing was clear: the South China Sea is Chinese maritime territory.

While President Xi has solemnly promised to adhere to a path of "peaceful development," his other irredentist statements (such as "the South China Sea islands are China's territory since the ancient times") cast serious doubt on China's intentions.[28] Further, the United States and the nations of the Indo-Asia Pacific region view the PRC's past fifteen-year military modernization as the means for achieving China's strategic end state of rejuvenation and restoration.

What is most alarming are the pace and scale of this military modernization program, one that is empowering the pursuit of the "China Dream." From 2005 through 2014, China's defense expenditures increased at around 10 percent annually, outpacing those of Japan, Korea, Taiwan, and India combined.[29] Therefore, while Chinese officials and government press agencies have sought to downplay the focus and attention on China's military modernization as being nothing more than a Western ploy to contain China through a sophisticated "China Threat Theory," the reality remains that this dramatic military growth fuels the unease that has gripped the Indo-Asia Pacific region.

THE "NEW SPRATLY ISLANDS"

The most significant evidence of the PRC commitment to the "China Dream" via a maritime sovereignty campaign has been the construction of the "New Spratly Islands" in the South China Sea. Starting as far back as the summer of 2014, indications of the PRC's massive dredging and construction effort were visible via commercial satellite imagery. At seven of its existing outposts in the Spratly Islands, the PRC built artificial islands, including on Fiery Cross, Cuarteron, Gaven, Hughes, Johnson, Mischief, and Subi Reefs.

The timing of this unprecedented and massive effort now appears to have been coordinated with Beijing's attempt to preempt the United Nation's Permanent Court of Arbitration. The court's July 12, 2016, decision on the Philippines case now stands in direct contradiction to the PRC's assertion of sovereignty over the so-called nine-dash line, some 2 million square kilometers of the South

China Sea.[30] The PRC aggressively embarked upon the New Spratly Islands building program to usurp the court's decision, challenge the international legal perception, and give China's physical presence in the Spratly Islands a de facto legitimization. While most international legal scholars believe the PRC's construction of the New Spratly Islands will not change their legal status, Beijing's actions clearly demonstrate that China has chosen to rely on the old adage that possession is nine-tenths of the law, a trademark of the "China Dream."

Despite Beijing's assertions that the New Spratly Islands were built for civilian purposes and will not be "militarized,"[31] on February 23, 2016, U.S. director of national intelligence Gen. James Clapper stated in a letter to the U.S. Senate Armed Services Committee chair John McCain that PLAN surface combatants have used the three largest port facilities at Fiery Cross, Mischief, and Subi Reefs and that at least two military radar stations, most likely for air surveillance, early warning, and high-frequency direction finding, have been installed at Cuarteron and Fiery Cross Reefs.[32] The precise number of Chinese port calls has not been reported, but given the increased presence of the PLAN, it likely is now routinely using these deep water ports to sustain a continuous presence in the South China Sea. This is in addition to the fact that three of the New Spratly Islands are "naval air stations" that are capable of supporting the forward deployment of PRC reconnaissance, fighter, and bomber aircraft.[33]

The impact of the PRC's initial militarization of the New Spratly Islands has substantially altered the military operating environment. For instance, "Australian air force patrols flying over the South China Sea are now being routinely challenged by the Chinese military in a sign of the growing stranglehold Beijing has over the strategically vital waters."[34] This type of activity had previously not been the norm, and it is likely changing the level of comfort for allied forces, and therefore their operations in, the South China Sea. Australian chief of the air force Air Marshal Leo Davies indicated in an interview that the changes the PRC has made to the balance of military affairs in the South China Sea have altered the operational environment—"because the Chinese have done the reclamation, there is a greater Chinese presence"—and that "nearly all" flights were now challenged, something that had not happened prior to the New Spratly Islands construction.[35]

In addition to the increased airborne challenges noted by Australian and U.S. aircrews, the PRC reported it was on "high alert" because of the Republic of the Philippines' announcement that it was leasing five TC-90 twin-turboprop trainer aircraft from Japan.[36] While the Philippines maritime reconnaissance capabilities are known to be both old and limited, this lease was reason enough for PRC foreign ministry spokesman Hong Kei to warn on March 11, 2016: "If the Philippines meant to challenge China's sovereignty and security interests, it will be met with firm opposition from the Chinese side."[37] This rhetoric by Beijing suggests a new self-confidence that is reinforced by the creation of three naval air stations on the New Spratly Islands.

Challenges by the PRC have not been limited to the air. Since the creation of the islands, the PLAN has also increased its reactions on the surface of the sea. In response to the USS *John C. Stennis* carrier strike group's transit and operations in the South China Sea in March 2016, PLAN warships were reported to be operating around the U.S. group. The *Stennis*' commanding officer reported that he "noted an increase in Chinese activity near the ships in his strike group," stating that "we have Chinese ships around us that we normally didn't see in my past experience."[38]

While PLAN warships operating in the South China Sea is not unprecedented by any measure, what is now unusual is that PLAN warships appear to be shadowing all U.S. Seventh Fleet ships in the sea. This is a new phenomenon for Chinese naval operations and one that can be directly attributed to the PRC building the New Spratly Islands, which provide naval basing support that allows for more PLAN warships to operate on a sustained presence throughout the South China Sea. These new naval stations have not only increased the tonnage of Chinese warships in the region but also have provided Beijing with the confidence to challenge anyone who would dare sail in or fly over their so-called territorial waters.

China also uses its maritime sovereignty claims in the South China Sea to target fishing vessels. Fishermen and fishing boats from all the nations that border the Spratly Islands have long been earning their living from the sea, but since the creation of the islands, the PRC has increased its efforts to restrict these operations through the use of civilian proxies, supported by the PLAN warships that are now always in the area. Most recently, the PRC sent ships from its ministry of transportation, and most probably from the PLAN, to Jackson Atoll in the Spratly Islands, just sixty nautical miles from the Philippine island of Palawan, to drive off Philippine fishing boats. The PRC forcibly towed one boat that had been grounded near the atoll.[39] While the PRC foreign ministry sought to justify this aggressive action on the basis that the Philippine fishing vessel "hampered navigation safety and infringed upon the nation's sovereignty," the important lesson from this event is the increasing scope of when and where PRC maritime forces are conducting "sovereignty enforcement" operations. This is in violation of the spirit of the 2002 Declaration on the Conduct of Parties in the South China Sea that Beijing signed.

General Clapper also assessed "that China has established the necessary infrastructure to project military capabilities in the South China Sea beyond that which is required for point defense of its outposts," something much more important and alarming for the region.[40] Clapper's letter points toward a very near future when China will have capabilities that would "include the deployment of modern fighter aircraft, surface-to-air missiles, and coastal defense cruise missiles, as well as increased presence of People's Liberation Army Navy (PLAN) surface combatants and China Coast Guard (CCG) large patrol ships."[41] The question being asked today is not if but when the deployment of these offensive power projection military capabilities will occur in the South China Sea.

What seems clear is that the exact timing of the PRC introduction of offensive military capabilities into the deepest reaches of the South China Sea will be obscured by an information warfare strategy that seeks to justify China's actions as a defensive response to alleged U.S. provocation. For example, PLAN head Admiral Wu Shengli told his U.S. counterpart Admiral Richardson during a January 20, 2016, video teleconference that "the amount of defense facilities on islands and reefs of the Nansha Islands totally depends on the level of threat China faces," a clear portent that the PRC will militarize the New Spratly Islands in response to alleged U.S. provocations.[42]

Despite the PRC's assertions that the islands will not be militarized, the fact remains that it has built more than three thousand acres of naval port facilities and air stations in the South China Sea, which has de facto changed its military posture in the region. Given this trajectory, many ASEAN members see the militarization of the New Spratly Islands as being the cause for unrest and tensions in the area. Many members of ASEAN have expressed, publicly and in private, legitimate questions and concerns about the PRC's commitments to the 2002 Declaration on the Conduct of Parties in the South China Sea, which forbade all parties, including China, from unilateral actions that in the past have "escalated or complicated the disputes."[43]

It is because of China's unilateral actions in the New Spratly Islands that the region is witnessing the emergence of new forms of military alliance structures. Joint patrols with nations such as Australia, Japan, and India and the rotation of U.S. military forces in locations such as Singapore, the Philippines, Malaysia, Vietnam, and even Brunei—unthinkable just five to ten years ago—are being pursued.

PEACEFUL ASPIRATIONS?

By any measure, PRC leaders have sought to reassure the Indo-Asia Pacific region, if not the rest of the world, that their "peaceful development" in the South China Sea is intended to be mutually beneficial to all. For instance, in Xi Jinping's November 2015 speech at the National University of Singapore, he stated, "China sticks to the diplomatic notion featuring amity, sincerity, mutual benefits and inclusiveness, adheres to the security outlook of a common, comprehensive, cooperative and sustainable Asia, strives to construct a closer China-ASEAN community of common destiny and promotes the construction of Asian community of common destiny."[44] In his keynote opening speech at the 2016 Boao Forum, he reassuringly asserted that the future is "about a peaceful Asia of equals, where every country should be treated equally, and be respected to choose their own development path. . . . Development and progress were only possible in a stable and peaceful domestic and international environment."[45]

While these words sound reasonable, the reality of China's actual approach to conflict resolution does not always look so bright. For instance, China's leaders have been very vocal in stating that "only countries in this region . . . most impacted by events in the South China Sea . . . are capable of making decisions in the best interests of their 'neighborhood,' unlike countries far from the center of events."[46] Beijing has also made it clear that only China and those nations that have a physical connection to the South China Sea are entitled to be involved in negotiations over the disputed territories and the free flow of commerce, with the United States and Japan being specifically identified as "outsiders." Thus, it is more than ironic when *People's Daily* claims that "it is a legitimate action for China's nuclear submarine to enter the Indian Ocean since China has interests in the region" and that "China is a stakeholder in the Indian Ocean."[47] It is precisely this dualism in Beijing's statements and actions that causes such concern across the Indo-Pacific region.

PATTERN OF UNTRUSTWORTHINESS

What does this mean for Asia and the rest of the world? The "incidents" in the South China Sea over the past five years seem to demonstrate that Beijing's grand strategy incorporates all its instruments of comprehensive national power (economic incentive, political pressure, information warfare, the threat of military intimidation, and the actual use of force) to achieve its national goal of "rejuvenation." While PRC leaders proclaim China's global aspirations will follow a path of "peaceful development," its actions in the South China Sea demonstrate a single-minded commitment to "restore" the country to its rightful place in history, no matter the cost, no matter the location, and no matter the issue. This uncompromising pattern of behavior by China is at the heart of increased tensions across the Indo-Asia Pacific region. Beijing's actions vis-à-vis the Philippines, Vietnam, Malaysia, Brunei, and Indonesia call into question whether the PRC can be trusted.

The strongest counterargument against this thesis of "untrustworthiness" is that China's actions only extend to what the PRC believes is historically its sovereign territory and, as such, does not represent a threat to the rest of the globe. While PRC officials have been keen to calm these concerns by asserting that there is no risk of China acting in the same way in other parts of the globe, serious doubts grow as the "China Dream" expands outward under the rubric of a new "Beijing Consensus."[48]

For instance, as a counter to not only major powers but also the existing international order, China has developed competing international organizations, such as the Asia Infrastructure Investment Bank, which was established to challenge the Asia Development Bank and the World Bank. China has also created the Shanghai Cooperation Organization to challenge existing security alliances in the Indo-Pacific region, which is now extending its scope into Central Asia and Europe. This competing "Beijing Consensus" was reinforced at the 2016 Boao Forum on Hainan Island with the introduction of a "United Nations of Asia with its own Security Council of Asian members to decide the fate of the region's countries."[49]

Beijing is conducting ballistic missile submarine patrols in the Western Pacific and submarine operations in the Indian Ocean and Bay of Bengal, acquiring access to port facilities at Gwadar, Pakistan, and Piraeus, Greece,[50] building a naval base in a foreign port (as is currently under way in Djibouti), establishing air defense identification zones in the East China Sea (and likely in the South), and dispatching the PLAN into the "far seas" of the Mediterranean and Baltic Sea to support the Belt and Road Initiative. This flood of activity suggests that President Xi and the Communist Party of China are intent upon establishing China as a global power that seeks to control the international order for its advantage.

What should be most worrisome to global leaders is the extent to which Beijing is willing to respect and adhere to international agreements, laws, and customary norms. As the nations of Southeast Asia have witnessed, the PRC has essentially disregarded the spirit of cooperation that was so eagerly anticipated following the signing of the 2002 Declaration on the Conduct of Parties in the South China Sea. In 2003, China signed the Treaty of Amity and Cooperation, which, according to most experts, signaled Beijing's "nominal acceptance of ASEAN's security norm of peaceful settlement of disputes."[51] In the same year, China signed, along with ASEAN, a Joint Declaration on Strategic Partnership, which was again interpreted by regional actors and many leading Western Sinologists as evidence of Beijing's "commitment to long-term cooperation on regional security issues."[52] Indeed, Beijing's leaders have repeatedly told their counterparts in ASEAN that China would sincerely seek "to foster friendly relations, mutually beneficial cooperation and good neighborliness."[53] Unfortunately, what the world has witnessed are Chinese actions that are totally inconsistent with their stated goals. Beijing has instead obfuscated its real intentions while rapidly building up the New Spratly Islands for purposes of taking physical possession of these disputed territories and thus enabling it to control both military and even commercial shipping access.

Beijing has also demonstrated how quickly it will disregard international law when it does not benefit China's strategic ambitions. For instance, China's leaders have adamantly stated that they do not believe the United Nation's Permanent Court of Arbitration has any legal authority over the disputed maritime region of the Spratly Islands.[54] Not content with simply expressing this frustration, during the March 2016 National People's Congress, the PRC's "Supreme People's Court" announced that it would create its own "international maritime judicial center."[55] Within days of this pronouncement, Beijing sought to ease concerns by stating, "China is not aiming to build itself into a shaper of the international maritime order with such a center. Instead, it is realizing the natural evolution of the established order."[56] While these words may sound appealing to an optimist, one simply needs to review the difference between Beijing's previous statements and actions to conclude that evolutionary change may have revolutionary consequences.

In conclusion, as the world's leaders look to the future and contemplate the extent to which they want to negotiate and partner with a rising China, they would be wise to study China's creation of the New Spratly Islands and follow the age-old adage of "buyer beware." What seems clear from the foregoing is that the PRC adheres to a belief that "what is mine is mine, and what is yours can be negotiated."

Notes

1. James Mulvenon, "Chairman Hu and the PLA's 'New Historic Missions,'" *China Leadership Monitor,* January 9, 2009, 2, http://www.hoover.org/sites/default/files/uploads/documents/CLM27JM.pdf.

2. "Newly Revised Party Constitution Intensifies PLA's Missions," Xinhua, October 26, 2007, http://news.xinhuanet.com/english/2007-10/26/content_6951300.htm.
3. Ibid.
4. Amanda Conklin, "The Unnamed Protagonist in China's Maritime Objectives," Center for International Maritime Security, August 7, 2015, http://cimsec.org/chinese-military-strategy-week-unnamed-protagonist-chinas-maritime-objectives/17683.
5. Masami Ito and Mizuho Aoki, "Senkaku Collisions Video Leak Riles China," *Japan Times*, November 6, 2010, http://www.japantimes.co.jp/news/2010/11/06/news/senkaku-collisions-video-leak-riles-china/#.VquCQMcjGdB.
6. Prior to April 2012, the U.S. government referred to Scarborough as Scarborough Shoal; subsequent to this incident, it changed its reference to Scarborough Reef. Various opinions have been proffered for this name change, but this author assesses the change was a result of negotiations between U.S. and PRC authorities.
7. The author's remarks at the U.S. Naval Institute/Armed Forces Communications and Electronics Association Conference Panel, "Chinese Navy: Operational Challenge or Potential Partner?" January 31, 2013.
8. Ibid.
9. "Arbitrators Appointed in the Arbitral Proceedings Instituted by the Republic of the Philippines against the People's Republic of China," press release, April 25, 2013, https://www.itlos.org/fileadmin/itlos/documents/press_releases_english/PR_191_E.pdf.
10. Tarra Quismundo, "Withdraw Ships, Philippines Tells China," *Philippine Daily Inquirer*, May 28, 2013, http://globalnation.inquirer.net/75823/withdraw-ships-philippines-tells-china.
11. David Brunnstrom and Andrea Shalal, "Exclusive: U.S. Sees New Chinese Activity around South China Sea Shoal," Reuters, March 19, 2016, http://www.reuters.com/article/us-southchinasea-china-scarborough-exclu-idUSKCN0WK01B.
12. Department of Foreign Affairs, Republic of the Philippines, "DFA Statement on Ayungin Shoal Incident," March 11, 2014, http://www.dfa.gov.ph/index.php/newsroom/dfa-releases/2302-dfa-statement-on-ayungin-shoal-incident.
13. "Vietnam Protests Chinese Oil Rig in Disputed Sea," Associated Press, May 5, 2014, http://newsinfo.inquirer.net/599673/vietnam-protests-chinese-oil-rig-in-disputed-sea.
14. Ibid.
15. "Nation Protests Chinese Intrusion," *VietNam News*, May 13, 2014, http://vietnamnews.vn/politics-laws/254745/nation-protests-chinese-intrusion.html.
16. Hilary Whiteman, "How an Oil Rig Sparked Anti-China Riots in Vietnam," CNN, May 19, 2014, http://edition.cnn.com/2014/05/19/world/asia/china-vietnam-islands-oil-rig-explainer/.
17. Paul J. Leaf, "Learning from China's Oil Rig Standoff with Vietnam," *The Diplomat*, August 20, 2014, http://thediplomat.com/2014/08/learning-from-chinas-oil-rig-standoff-with-vietnam/.
18. Author's personal reflections as U.S. Pacific Fleet director of intelligence and information operations during the CNOOC HYSY 981 incident.

19. Some commentators suggest CNOOC HYSY 981 departed the controversial area because of pressure from Vietnam. This author assesses CNOOC HYSY 981 departed the area because they had concluded their oil exploration work and not for any other reason or acquiescence to the Vietnamese government.
20. "5th Russian-made Kilo Submarine Arrives in Vietnam," *PLA Daily*, February 3, 2016, http://english.chinamil.com.cn/news-channels/international-military-news/2016-02/03/content_6888399.htm.
21. Zhao Lei, "Combatant Ships Patrol China's Southernmost Point," *China Daily*, March 27, 2013, http://usa.chinadaily.com.cn/china/2013-03/27/content_16350400.htm.
22. Ibid.
23. Victor R. Lee, "South China Sea: Satellite Images Show Pace of China's Subi Reef Reclamation," *The Diplomat*, June 19, 2015, http://thediplomat.com/2015/06/south-china-sea-satellite-images-show-pace-of-chinas-subi-reef-reclamation/.
24. "Chinese Navy Bar Local Fishermen from Luconia Shoals," *Borneo Post*, October 31, 2015, http://www.theborneopost.com/2015/10/31/chinese-navy-bar-local-fishermen-from-luconia-shoals/.
25. Haeril Halim, Anggi M. Lubis, and Stefani Ribka, "RI Confronts China on Fishing," *Jakarta Post*, March 21, 2016, http://www.newsjs.com/url.php?p=http://www.thejakartapost.com/news/2016/03/21/ri-confronts-china-fishing.html.
26. "RI in Weak Position in Natuna Fishing Dispute," *Jakarta Post*, March 28, 2016, http://www.thejakartapost.com/news/2016/03/28/ri-weak-position-natuna-fishing-dispute-with-china.html.
27. "Jakarta, Beijing Should Cool Down on Sea Disputes," *Global Times*, March 23, 2016, http://www.globaltimes.cn/content/975399.shtml.
28. Ibid.
29. U.S. Department of Defense, *Annual Report to Congress: Military and Security Developments Involving the People's Republic of China 2015* (Washington, D.C.: Department of Defense, April 7, 2015), 49–50, http://www.defense.gov/Portals/1/Documents/pubs/2015_China_Military_Power_Report.pdf.
30. Kevin Baumert and Brian Melchior, "China: Maritime Claims in the South China Sea," *Limits in the Seas* no. 143 (Washington, D.C.: U.S. Department of State, 2014), 4, http://www.state.gov/documents/organization/234936.pdf.
31. David Brunnstrom and Michael Martina, "Xi Denies China Turning Artificial Islands into Military Bases," Reuters, September 25, 2015, http://www.reuters.com/article/us-usa-china-pacific-idUSKCN0RP1ZH20150925.
32. James Clapper, "Letter from Director of National Intelligence to Sen. John McCain, Chairman, Senate Committee on Armed Services," February 23, 2016, https://news.usni.org/2016/03/08/document-dni-assessment-of-chinese-militarization-reclamation-in-south-china-sea.
33. Sam LaGrone, "PACOM Harris: U.S. Would Ignore a 'Destabilizing' Chinese South China Sea Air Defense Identification Zone," *USNI News*, February 26, 2016, http://news.usni.org/2016/02/26/pacom-harris-u-s-would-ignore-a-destabilizing-chinese-south-china-sea-air-defense-identification-zone.

34. David Wroe, "RAAF Now Being Routinely Challenged by Beijing in South China Sea," *Sydney Morning Herald*, February 3, 2016, http://www.smh.com.au/federal-politics/political-news/raaf-now-being-routinely-challenged-by-beijing-in-south-china-sea-20160203-gmkvkb.html.
35. Ibid.
36. "China Expresses High Alert against the So-called 'Philippines-Japan Aircraft Deal,'" *People's Daily*, March 11, 2016, http://en.people.cn/n3/2016/0311/c90000-9028380.html.
37. Ibid.
38. Brad Lendon, "U.S. Aircraft Carrier Patrols South China Sea as Beijing Keeps Watch," CNN, March 4, 2016, http://edition.cnn.com/2016/03/04/politics/aircraft-carrier-patrols-south-china-sea/.
39. Li Xiaokun, "Foreign Boat Cleared from Chinese Reef," *China Daily*, March 3, 2016, http://www.chinadaily.com.cn/world/2016-03/03/content_23715904.htm.
40. Clapper, "Letter from Director of National Intelligence."
41. Ibid.
42. Yuan Can, "China Determined and Capable of Defending Islands and Reefs in South China Sea, Says PLA Navy Chief," People's Daily Online, January 21, 2016, http://en.people.cn/n3/2016/0121/c90000-9007471.html.
43. 2002 Declaration on the Conduct of Parties in the South China Sea as adopted by the foreign ministers of ASEAN and the People's Republic of China at the Eighth ASEAN Summit in Phnom Penh, Cambodia, November 4, 2002.
44. Ministry of Foreign Affairs of the People's Republic of China, "Xi Jinping Delivers Important Speech in National University of Singapore, Stressing to Jointly Open up New Dimension in All-round Cooperation and Build Beautiful Homeland of Asia," November 7, 2015, http://www.fmprc.gov.cn/mfa_eng/zxxx_662805/t1313709.shtml.
45. Ibid.
46. Tian Sulei, "Commentary: South China Sea Should Not Be Dominated by Outside Countries," Xinhua, March 10, 2016, http://news.xinhuanet.com/english/2016-03/10/c_135176156.htm.
47. Yuan Can, "China's Presence in Indian Ocean Legitimate, Military Expert Says," *People's Daily*, March 18, 2016, http://en.people.cn/n3/2016/0318/c90000-9032455.html.
48. Joshua Cooper Ramo, *The Beijing Consensus* (London: Foreign Policy Centre, 2004), http://fpc.org.uk/fsblob/244.pdf.
49. Chua Chin Leng, "Boao 2016, A New Asia for Asians," *China Daily*, March 22, 2016, http://www.chinadaily.com.cn/opinion/2016-03/22/content_24011580.htm.
50. Not to mention active efforts to sign leases for access to commercial port facilities in Sri Lanka, Bangladesh, and Australia.
51. Evan S. Medeiros, *China's International Behavior: Activism, Opportunism, and Diversification* (Santa Monica, Calif.: RAND Corporation, 2009), 131, http://www.rand.org/content/dam/rand/pubs/monographs/2009/RAND_MG850.pdf.
52. Ibid.

53. "China Joins Treaty of Amity, Cooperation in Southeast Asia," *People's Daily*, October 9, 2003, http://en.people.cn/200310/08/eng20031008_125556.shtml.
54. "Non-acceptance of S. China Sea Arbitration 'Observes the Law': Chinese FM," *People's Daily*, February 18, 2016, http://en.people.cn/n3/2016/0218/c90883-9018231.html.
55. "China to Build Int'l Maritime Judicial Center: Chief Justice," Xinhua, March 13, 2016, http://news.xinhuanet.com/english/2016-03/13/c_135183208.htm.
56. "Judicial Center Will Serve All," *China Daily*, March 16, 2016, http://www.chinadaily.com.cn/opinion/2016-03/16/content_23887219.htm.

4

ASEAN, Grand Strategy, and the South China Sea

Between China and the United States

Leszek Buszynski

The Association of Southeast Asian Nations (ASEAN) is caught between the grand strategies of the major powers that converge over the South China Sea. China's grand strategy is intended to elevate its position as leader of Asia and to reduce the role of Japan and the United States in the Western Pacific. It seeks deference from its Asian neighbors and the restoration of its status as the "middle kingdom," aspirations that demand the removal of the U.S. alliance system in the region and its replacement with a Chinese-centered regional order. The grand strategy of the United States is intended to retain its position in the Western Pacific, to defend freedom of navigation, and to prevent the dominance of a single country in the region in a way that would exclude it and restrict trade and commerce. For these reasons, the United States resists China's moves to dominate the South China Sea, which could undermine the U.S. presence in the Western Pacific and weaken its credibility with its allies Japan, the Philippines, and Australia.

As a regional organization, ASEAN struggles to maintain its identity and autonomy as the U.S.-China rivalry over the South China Sea deepens, but it can no longer contain its disunity and fragmentation over this issue. China has attempted to obtain ASEAN endorsement of its sovereignty over the sea and to bring the organization under its influence. The difficulty for China is that its local strategy in promoting its claims and physical presence in the South China Sea has conflicted with and undermined its grand strategy of pushing the U.S. military presence from the Western Pacific. Its assertive moves in the South China Sea and its harassment tactics against ASEAN claimants Vietnam and the Philippines have prompted those countries to seek U.S. support as a counterweight. The United States has developed security ties with Vietnam and has upgraded the alliance with the Philippines to ensure a rotational military presence there. In the past, Chinese leaders understood that ASEAN's unity and neutrality would serve their interests in keeping the United States at a distance. However, such considerations no longer restrain Chinese actions, with the result that the United States has become more deeply engaged in the South China Sea than ever.

ASEAN AND THE CODE OF CONDUCT

The ASEAN approach toward China was to engage it in multilateral dialogue in the expectation that this would wean the Chinese away from the use of force in the South China Sea and tie it to the existing status quo. ASEAN leaders sought to communicate to the Chinese that their interests would be best served in a stable regional framework that would act as a disincentive for the use of force in maritime disputes. ASEAN leaders were hopeful that China's good neighbor policy would predispose it to an eventual resolution of the South China Sea dispute and that Beijing would drop its claim to indisputable sovereignty over the area.[1] The major mechanism to bind China to the status quo has been the ASEAN proposal for a Code of Conduct (CoC), which was a product of the track-two workshops on the South China Sea organized by the Indonesian foreign ministry beginning in 1990. The CoC proposal was first mentioned in the ASEAN Declaration on the South China Sea adopted at the twenty-fifth ASEAN Ministerial Meeting in Manila on July 22, 1992. Point four of the declaration called upon the concerned parties to apply the principles contained in the Treaty of Amity and Cooperation as the "basis for establishing a code of international conduct over the South China Sea."[2]

The difficulty was that China, which had little interest in a proposal that would tie its hands in the South China Sea, resisted the CoC; it simply procrastinated and obliged ASEAN delegates to schedule meeting after meeting to discuss the issue to little purpose. The CoC could not be implemented while Beijing maintained this attitude, but it was the only measure that ASEAN, with its divergent interests, could accept. While ASEAN struggled with the CoC proposal, affected claimants have sought support from external powers to compensate for the deficiencies of the grouping. For Vietnam and the Philippines, security links with external powers were a necessary response to the inability of ASEAN to provide support and to strengthen their positions and claims against Chinese pressure.

China sidestepped the ASEAN proposal for a CoC but eventually accepted the Declaration on Conduct of the Parties (DoC), which was concluded between ASEAN and China on November 4, 2002. The DoC included the points that ASEAN had been seeking in a formal code, but it was not legally binding, which was a salient ASEAN demand. Nevertheless, the DoC was important in that it was the first multilateral document on the South China Sea that China had signed, as it had previously declared that it would deal with the claimants bilaterally. ASEAN members had various views as to why China signed the DoC. Optimists claimed that China was now willing to accept multilateral negotiations with ASEAN, which would bring resolution of the issue closer. Realists thought that China had intended to head off pressure within ASEAN to involve the United States in this dispute, as the Philippines had done earlier. Later, ASEAN was buoyed by China's accession to the association's Treaty of Amity and Cooperation on October 8, 2003, which seemed to verify the first interpretation. Within ASEAN, it was believed that China had been successfully engaged and induced to accept norms of behavior that would defuse tensions and stabilize the issue.

For ASEAN, however, the DoC was regarded as a stepping stone to a full-fledged CoC. The DoC was only a declaration that did not detail actions to be avoided or procedures to be adopted to avoid conflict. Moreover, it fell short of the legally binding commitment that ASEAN had expected. To be legally binding, a declaration of this kind would have to be incorporated in a formal treaty and subject to ratification according to the procedures of the countries concerned. ASEAN has regularly concluded legally binding agreements among its members, with the instruments of ratification deposited with the secretary general of the organization in Jakarta. Two major treaties concluded by ASEAN included the Treaty of Amity and Cooperation (signed on February 24, 1976) and the Southeast Asian Nuclear Free Zone (signed on December 15, 1995), both of which went through this ratification procedure. Making the CoC a legally binding treaty in a similar way would present particular difficulties.

For a start, ASEAN members were not in agreement on some of the key issues. One issue was the geographic scope of the code. Vietnam wanted the Paracel Islands covered, but others resisted so that the area to which the code would apply was left undefined and understood by activity and not geography. A second issue was China's insistence that it would only meet with the ASEAN claimants individually and not with ASEAN collectively over the proposed code. It demanded that ASEAN members not consult among themselves before meeting with China since the issue only concerned the individual claimants. A third issue was the dispute resolution mechanism. In the negotiations leading to the DoC, Vietnam and the Philippines had proposed a dispute resolution mechanism that would draw upon Article 2 of the 1976 Treaty of Amity and Cooperation, which mentioned a High Council. It was envisaged that this council could function as a dispute resolution mechanism for the South China Sea, but this proposal failed to receive ASEAN endorsement.[3] As ASEAN habitually proceeded by avoiding contentious issues and formal institutionalization, problems went unresolved, which gave the CoC proposal a declaratory significance but not the legality that Vietnam and the Philippines in particular were seeking. While the ASEAN intention in the CoC was to bind China to the existing status quo, Beijing had little incentive to agree since it would leave the ASEAN claimants—Vietnam, the Philippines, and Malaysia—in occupation of most of the features in the Spratly Islands. Indeed, China would be excluded from the area.[4]

ASEAN: A HOUSE DIVIDED

ASEAN has been divided as Vietnam and the Philippines have persistently demanded support for their claims in the South China Sea, while Cambodia and Laos have openly sided with China. The other members, such as Thailand, have been either indifferent to the issue or, like Malaysia, unwilling to risk exacerbating relations with Beijing. Cambodia prevented the Philippines from raising the issue of China's occupation of Scarborough Shoal in April 2012. China had ejected the Philippines from the shoal and objected when Manila lobbied hard for ASEAN support. Cambodia was ASEAN chair in 2012 and kept the issue out of the communiqué of the twentieth ASEAN summit held in April. The chairman's statement mentioned the need to "intensify efforts to ensure the effective and full implementation of the DoC based on the Guidelines for the implementation of the DoC."[5] Those guidelines were agreed with China in July 2011 and included eight points that were vague but acceptable to the parties anyway.[6] Just before the ASEAN summit in April 2012, Hu Jintao visited Phnom Penh and, according to Hun Sen's adviser Sri Thamrong, pressed Cambodia to go slowly over the CoC and not to "internationalize" the issue. China had become an important economic partner for Cambodia and its main investor. Chinese foreign direct investment in the country reached $1.19 billion in 2011.[7] The Chinese leader pledged to double bilateral trade to $5 billion by 2017 and declared that Chinese aid for Cambodia would increase.[8] Cambodia also prevented any mention of the dispute in the forty-fifth Annual Ministerial Meeting of ASEAN Foreign Ministers (AMM) in July 2012, which failed to issue a communiqué for the first time in the organization's history. The meeting was described as "acrimonious," and Philippine foreign minister Albert del Rosario stressed that he took "strong exception" to Cambodia's statement that the inability to issue a communiqué was due to "bilateral conflict between some ASEAN member states and a neighboring country."[9] Cambodian deputy prime minister and foreign minister Hor Namhong defended his performance at the annual meeting by claiming that there was "a plan behind the scenes against Cambodia."[10]

The ASEAN claimants, Vietnam and the Philippines, saw Cambodia as a proxy for China, which had successfully prevented ASEAN from forging a consensus against Chinese actions in the South China Sea. Cambodia scrambled to repair the damage to ASEAN unity by declaring that progress had been made on the CoC. Cambodian secretary of state Kao Kim Hourn stated that the code would spell out the rules governing maritime rights and navigation in the South China Sea and that it would cover China as well as ASEAN. He cautioned, however, that agreement had been reached only within ASEAN and that the task from then on would be to persuade China.[11]

Indonesia's foreign minister Marty Natalegawa acted to overcome the divisions within ASEAN after the AMM failed to issue a communiqué. Marty engaged in thirty-six hours of shuttle diplomacy and visited Manila, Hanoi, and Phnom Penh with a six-point proposal as a basis for a common position. The proposal was broad and general and did not touch on any of the current disputes; the first point restated the ASEAN commitment to the DoC and the United Nations Convention on the Law of the Sea (UNCLOS), and the third called for an early conclusion to the CoC.[12] Though broad, these points were sufficiently noncontroversial to obtain a collective ASEAN endorsement.

Predictably, China revealed little interest in a proposal that would tie it to an ASEAN-defined status quo and consistently resisted ASEAN entreaties. It called for implementation of the DoC before discussion on the CoC could proceed. In July 2011, ASEAN and China agreed to guidelines on the implementation of the DoC that mentioned joint cooperative activities concerned with navigational safety, communication at sea, and search and rescue operations. China demanded to participate with ASEAN in the drafting of the CoC, which some within ASEAN supported as a way of ensuring its acceptance. The Philippines rejected this approach and insisted that ASEAN draft the document first and then present it to China.[13] In the Philippine view, Chinese involvement in the drafting of the code would be a sure way to weaken it. ASEAN hopes for a binding CoC would be dashed, as it would be transformed into an anodyne document that would simply restate the same broad ideas found in the DoC. ASEAN's consensus-builder Marty Natalegawa reconciled these approaches and argued that ASEAN had to hear China's views on the CoC before it was presented with a draft of a code.[14] In this connection he circulated a draft of the code to ASEAN foreign ministers who met in the United Nations General Assembly in New York in September 2012. This was the first time that ASEAN foreign ministers had seen a full draft, which included procedures to govern the conduct of parties and measures to promote confidence and respect for the exclusive economic zone (EEZ) and continental shelves of coastal states.[15] After meeting Chinese foreign minister Wang Yi, Marty was optimistic that the CoC could be concluded within three years and declared that China had shown an inclination to pursue a "peaceful solution" to the dispute.

After this meeting, the CoC proposal was sent to the ASEAN-China Working Group mechanism for negotiation.[16] During the group's meetings, China circulated its own working draft of the code that said that "the CoC is not aimed at resolving disputes." The Chinese draft stated that "relevant disputes should be resolved by the sovereign states directly concerned through friendly consultations and negotiations in a commonly accepted manner." The Chinese draft noted that the purpose of the CoC was to "enhance mutual trust and promote cooperation, so as to create conditions for the countries to resolve their disputes." China also called for implementation of the DoC to supplement the negotiations over the CoC in a "simultaneous and mutually reinforcing manner."[17] This draft was an indication of Chinese thinking on the issue and revealed the extent to which China continued to insist on bilateral negotiations with the ASEAN claimants. In effect, China used the CoC proposal as a lever to move the discussions with ASEAN to bilateral negotiations.

The two sides were talking past each other and continued with the discussions with different expectations. ASEAN had no way other than the CoC of dealing with China that was acceptable to all its members. China, however, had no intention of allowing itself to be tied down by ASEAN in this way and resorted to the time-honored technique of prolonging the negotiations to avoid commitment. ASEAN swayed between the demand for a legally binding document, as pressed for by both Vietnam and the Philippines, and the opposition of Thailand and Cambodia, which sought to avoid controversy with China. The Indonesian draft reflected the differences between members in managing existing tensions without including provisions that China would oppose.[18] China avoided ASEAN demands for a document that would bind it in any way or that would shift the focus away from its preferred approach for bilateral negotiations. ASEAN leaders were heartened by what they regarded as China's acceptance of multilateralism since the conclusion of the DoC in 2002. They thought that ASEAN's role in the issue had been strengthened, and that China would come around to accept the CoC.

While the code was intended to tie China to the status quo, the problem was that the status quo was constantly changing as China brought more features in the South China Sea under its control. China encouraged ASEAN hopes that it would agree to an association-drafted CoC, but it used multilateralism to shift the focus to bilateral negotiations with the claimants without going so far as to downgrade ASEAN and everything it had attempted to do over this issue. Simply by stalling, prolonging negotiations, and engaging in repetitive meetings over the issue, China could exploit the ASEAN desire for a tangible document to demonstrate success. It could dilute the idea of a CoC to the point where it would become a restatement of general principles like the DoC, and through its very ineffectiveness it would swing attention to China's preferred approach for bilateral negotiations with the claimants. This effort to weaken ASEAN's original conception of a CoC and transform it into a diplomatic formality struck at ASEAN's role and relevance as a regional organization. Without a meaningful CoC ASEAN's diplomatic weakness in the face of China would be revealed, and though it may continue with the formality of regular and elaborate meetings over the issue, it would become aimless.

CHINA'S RECLAMATION PROJECTS: THE DILEMMA FOR ASEAN

China's reclamation projects in the Spratly Islands were first observed in 2014. Photographs were taken of dredging activities around seven reefs that were transformed into militarized artificial islands.[19] These developments have posed an acute dilemma for ASEAN as it attempts to position itself to avoid entanglement in Sino-U.S. rivalry. ASEAN unity and solidarity have in large measure depended upon the ability of its leaders to demonstrate autonomy and distance from the great powers—particularly the United States as the recognized regional hegemon. As long as ASEAN could preserve its autonomy in this way, it would promote the multilateral engagement of the great powers, China included. It could enhance its relevance as a regional grouping, elevate its diplomatic role, and remain in the "driver's seat" of Asian regionalism. Organizational unity depended upon the absence of conflict and an agreement between these great powers that would tie them to the multilateral structures that ASEAN had been sponsoring. However, the prospect of conflict between the major powers jeopardizes that unity and exposes immobilizing fissures within the grouping.

To preserve organizational unity, ASEAN had to avoid siding with external powers that may come into conflict with China. Nonclaimants such as Cambodia, Laos, and Thailand valued their relationship with China more highly than the South China Sea issue and prevented the organization from developing a consensus over it. ASEAN could not simply ignore the issue and dismiss it as a subject that should not be on the agenda, as the nonclaimant members have argued, since that would push the claimants into a deeper relationship with the United States and Japan. ASEAN struggled to maintain some semblance of unity over the South China Sea issue as the fissiparous forces within the grouping have deepened. Philippine foreign affairs secretary Albert del Rosario attempted to rouse ASEAN into action when to the assembled foreign ministers he asserted that China should be told that its actions are wrong and that the "massive reclamations should be immediately stopped." He declared that China was "poised to consolidate de facto control of the South China Sea" with wide-ranging implications for and beyond the region.[20] Cambodian leader Hun Sen openly endorsed the Chinese position when he declared that "ultimately, it is not an issue for ASEAN as a whole. It is a bilateral issue between the concerned countries, which need to talk between themselves."[21] Thailand's normal indifference toward the issue was intensified by its tilt toward China after the military under Prayuth Chan-ocha took control of the government in May 2014. Under criticism from the United States, Thailand's military rulers turned toward China for support following a well-established pattern of behavior in Thai foreign policy dating to pre-modern times. China's defense minister Chang Wanquan visited Bangkok in February 2015 and agreed to discounted arms sales and an expansion in joint military training and technology sharing. Chang made a point of saying that Beijing had no intention of interfering in Thailand's internal affairs, a clear reference to the United States and its demand for the restoration of democracy.[22]

How ASEAN could manage these widening differences and still maintain coherence has been a test of diplomatic skill. Malaysia chaired the twenty-sixth ASEAN summit on April 28, 2015, and saw to it that mention was made of the South China Sea, but without censuring China in the way the Philippines and Vietnam had sought. The chairman's report noted that "we share the serious concerns expressed by some leaders on the land reclamation being undertaken in the South China Sea." It also reaffirmed "freedom of navigation in and over-flight over the South China Sea" while also "noting the progress made in the consultations on the Code of Conduct," though little progress was made.[23] Malaysian foreign minister Datuk Seri Anifah Aman opined that the CoC could "provide the necessary rules of engagement for all parties in managing their activities in the South China Sea." He said it was "imperative that ASEAN and China make meaningful and tangible progress in the development of the CoC."[24] Singapore's defense minister Ng Eng Hen called for a CoC that would forbid the use of force and reduce miscalculations since conflict in the area would disrupt maritime trade routes affecting Singapore and the global economy.[25]

At the Shangri-La Dialogue in Singapore in late May 2015, defense ministers from Malaysia, Indonesia, and Cambodia were more explicit in the need for a CoC. Cambodian deputy prime minister and defense minister Tea Banh differed from Hun Sen when he declared that the CoC could ensure the peaceful settlement of disputes in the South China Sea. Malaysian defense minister Hishammuddin Tun Hussein similarly stressed that the CoC is the "best way to deal with the issue" and asked if the small countries of the region had any choice. Indonesian defense minister Ryamizard Ryacudu called for more dialogue and proposed joint or "peace patrols" involving the ASEAN claimants, which could at a later stage involve China as well.[26]

ASEAN's one bargaining card with China has been its diplomatic autonomy and its collective distance from U.S. military strategy. Through the CoC, ASEAN hoped to persuade China that it should accept constraints on its activities in the South China Sea to ensure a stable relationship with the grouping and that a CoC was preferable to the intrusion of external powers such as the United States and Japan in the South China Sea. The unstated assumption was that an autonomous ASEAN that was clearly not under U.S. influence was of greater value to China than the gains that it might achieve through unilateral action in the South China Sea. It was further assumed that it was in China's interest to preserve ASEAN as an autonomous regional grouping in this sense to avoid the alternative scenario of a greater U.S. and Japanese presence in the region. However, China's activities in the South China Sea and its reclamation projects show that Beijing has reassessed its relationship with ASEAN in line with its growing power. ASEAN's diplomatic autonomy could be taken for granted and would not be challenged or undermined by China's behavior in the South China Sea. China's leaders have apparently decided that they can manage the consequences of a strengthened presence in the South China Sea and deal with the involvement of external powers without ASEAN.

CENTRIFUGAL PRESSURES WITHIN ASEAN INTENSIFY

Vietnam joined ASEAN in July 1995 for various reasons, one of which was the hope that the group would provide support against China in the South China Sea. For a while it seemed that ASEAN membership would act as a deterrent against Chinese activities. In March 1997, Vietnam formally protested to China about the Kan Tan III drilling rig that was positioned in Vietnam's EEZ, sixty-five nautical miles off the coast of central Vietnam. On March 25, Vietnam summoned ASEAN ambassadors to protest and publicize the incident, and on April 1, the oil rig was withdrawn.[27] The coincidence of events revealed to the Vietnamese that ASEAN membership had some deterrent value with China. Vietnam had high hopes of making progress on the CoC when it was the ASEAN chair in 2010, but it was let down by the divisions within the group and thwarted by Chinese resistance. Consequently, some Vietnamese diplomats regarded the CoC as a futile effort that would make no headway with China.[28] The Vietnamese party leadership is strongly committed to party-to-party ties with China and has hoped that this relationship would act as a constraint upon it in the South China Sea. The belief was that China would not want to jeopardize its relationship with its brother party by challenging Vietnam in this dispute and moving against its claims. At the same time, however, Vietnam has been developing security ties with the United States, which reveals that the Vietnamese have reservations about their relationship with China and seek to use external powers as a hedge against it. Reflecting its historical experience of protecting its independence against what its leaders have regarded as the overwhelming pressure and peremptory demands of its northern neighbor, Vietnam moves on three levels in dealing with China: the party-to-party relationship, the ASEAN relationship, and the security relationship with the United States. The Vietnamese juggle these to reduce the conflicts between them.

Disappointed by ASEAN, the Vietnamese moved to develop security ties with the United States, which was keen to respond, particularly after President Barack Obama announced the pivot to Asia or rebalancing strategy in November 2011. However, the American connection was not a deterrent the Vietnamese could rely on, since their concern for Chinese reactions and the impact upon party ties with Beijing placed constraints on the relationship. The oil rig incident of 2014 presented Vietnam with a crisis that tested its response to a Chinese intrusion and prompted some reassessment in the Vietnamese system. On May 2, China Oilfield Services, a subsidiary of China National Offshore Oil Corporation, moved the HD-981 oil rig into position seventeen nautical miles from Triton

Island and within Vietnam's claimed EEZ, provoking a storm of protest from the Vietnamese. The rig was withdrawn ahead of schedule by July 15, but the incident had raised doubts not only about the constraining effect of the relationship with China but about ASEAN as well. ASEAN foreign ministers met on May 10 to deal with this incident and managed to express "serious concerns over the on-going developments in the South China Sea, which have increased tensions in the area." They urged both sides "to resolve disputes by peaceful means without resorting to threat or use of force."[29] Within Vietnam, voices were raised that the country should reach out more to the international community, loosen the shackles of the party relationship with China, and not expect support from a divided ASEAN.[30] While tensions subsided following the withdrawal of the rig, Vietnamese leaders resorted to their usual way of mollifying China by dispatching Politburo member Le Hong Anh to meet Xi Jinping in Beijing.[31] The lesson was not lost on the Vietnamese, who were prompted to further develop security ties with the United States and Japan in response to the Chinese reclamation projects. The United States partially lifted its arms embargo on Vietnam in October 2014, and when Defense Secretary Ashton Carter visited Hanoi in June 2015, he concluded a joint vision statement on defense relations with Vietnamese defense minister Phung Quang Thanh. This agreement would expand defense trade with Vietnam and allow for the coproduction of defense equipment.[32] When President Obama visited Vietnam in May 2016, he announced the lifting of the arms embargo on that country.

The Philippines has had similar disappointments with ASEAN. After the Chinese occupied Mischief Reef in 1995, Manila turned to ASEAN, expecting that the grouping would offer support under the 1992 ASEAN Declaration on the South China Sea, which called for all parties to exercise restraint. ASEAN foreign ministers at the twenty-eighth AMM in July 1995 "expressed their concern over recent events in the South China Sea" and called upon the parties to "reaffirm their commitment to the 1992 ASEAN Declaration on the South China Sea" but otherwise gave the Philippines no real support.[33] The Philippines attempted to raise the issue in the ASEAN Regional Forum, only to discover that senior officials would not allow it to be placed on the agenda for fear of offending China. From the Philippine perspective, ASEAN was prepared to sacrifice its own maritime territorial rights for the sake of the relationship with China, which greatly lessened the value of the association as a diplomatic support group. This experience prompted Manila to strengthen the security relationship with the United States, despite the troubled relations with its former colonial master. After the

Philippine senate voted to remove the U.S. presence from Subic Bay in 1991, concern about China induced the senate to approve the visiting forces agreement with the United States in 1999. The agreement allowed for port visits by U.S. naval vessels and training exercises that were intended to signal a U.S. commitment to Philippine defense.

The Philippines again found little consolation from ASEAN after the Chinese occupation of Scarborough Shoal in April 2012, when the Cambodian chair blocked ASEAN discussion of the issue. President Benigno Aquino reacted strongly against Chinese activities in the South China Sea and signed an Enhanced Defense Cooperation Agreement (EDCA) with President Obama when he visited Manila in April 2014. Under this agreement, the United States would strengthen Philippine maritime security and U.S. forces would be given access to facilities in the Philippines on a rotational basis.[34] In another move taken outside the ASEAN context, the Philippines appealed to an arbitral tribunal under Annex VII of UNCLOS in January 2013. The Philippines was criticized within ASEAN circles for taking unilateral action that might exacerbate the situation with China without consulting the grouping. In the Philippine view, ASEAN could not have it both ways. It could not ignore the legitimate concerns of the Philippines for the sake of good relations with China and then criticize Manila for resorting to legal action to protect its legal maritime claims. In this appeal, the Philippines sought legal adjudication of its rights within its EEZ and the legal status of the features occupied by China, though China refused to be a party to the proceedings.[35] On May 14, 2014, the Philippine department of foreign affairs issued a statement saying that China's reclamation projects would bolster Beijing's naval and air force mobility in the South China Sea region. The department submitted a memorial to the tribunal to rule on China's reclamation project on Mabini (also known as Johnson South) Reef.[36] Former Philippine national security council advisor Roilo Golez thought that China's completion of military installations on Mabini Reef could be a "game-changer" since it would threaten vital Philippine installations.[37] The Philippines was gradually losing its maritime territory in a process that began with the Chinese occupation of Mischief Reef; if the process continued, the Philippines would indeed be excluded from its own EEZ.[38]

As China steadily increases its activities in the area and engages in reclamation projects, it presents Malaysia and Indonesia with a dilemma. Both countries have pursued nonaligned policies and have avoided open identification with the United States, but Chinese pressure induces tolerance of an upgraded American presence in the region and stimulates the development of limited security ties with the United States. In previous decades, Malaysia was the major proponent of the integration of China into multilateral regional institutions such as the ASEAN Regional Forum. As a founding member of ASEAN, a nonaligned Malaysia had promoted regional autonomy to keep the major powers at a distance, and it had criticized Vietnamese and Philippine efforts to strengthen security ties with the United States. Malaysia insisted that ASEAN had to maintain good relations with China as a way of obligating Beijing to maintain and pursue its good neighbor policy toward the region. Malaysian prime minister Najib Razak declared that Malaysia had to "look at the big picture and not define relations with China on a single-issue basis," and he said that the territorial issue "should not be an impediment to the growing ties between Malaysia and China." Najib told the twenty-sixth ASEAN summit in April 2015 that China would continue engaging the association since it was not in Chinese interests to be seen as confronting it.[39]

However, Malaysia has also faced Chinese pressure in the South China Sea but has struggled to maintain its relationship with China. In March 2013, four Chinese naval vessels reached as far south as James Shoal, eighty kilometers from the Sarawak coastline and within the Malaysian claim. The Chinese subsequently left markers on this shoal to indicate their claim to the feature. In January 2014, three Chinese vessels again visited James Shoal, which stimulated uneasiness within Malaysian security circles.[40] In fact, the number of Chinese intrusions into the Malaysian claim area has been publicly understated, stimulating concerns in Kuala Lumpur, which had previously regarded the Chinese presence in the area as benign.[41] Navy chief Admiral Abdul Aziz Jaafar said that intrusions by Chinese vessels had been occurring daily since 2014 and had even reached Luconia Shoal, well inside Malaysia's EEZ.[42] After the first Chinese incursion, defense minister Hishammuddin Tun Hussein in October 2013 announced that a naval base would be established at Bintulu on the Sarawak coast facing James Shoal. He also declared that a marine corps would be created for amphibious operations involving all three services.[43] The Malaysian military has developed closer defense cooperation with the United States and intends to conduct amphibious training exercises with U.S. Marines, an area in which the Malaysians have been deficient.[44] U.S. naval vessels have also been visiting Malaysian ports with greater frequency; the *Nimitz*-class carrier *John C. Stennis* visited Kota Kinabalu in 2012, and in February 2015, the amphibious assault ship USS *Bonhomme Richard* docked at Sepanggar naval base with 1,600 Marines on board.[45]

U.S. Chief of Naval Operations Adm. Jonathan Greenert stated publicly that Malaysia had offered use of its bases for surveillance flights of P-8A aircraft, which

Malaysia denies. However, U.S. surveillance flights have operated from Malaysia on an ad hoc basis according to a memorandum of understanding of June 1990.[46] Kuala Lumpur has been careful to avoid the appearance of moving too close to the United States, which could damage relations with Beijing. Malaysia participated in a five-day exercise on "Managing Non-Traditional Threats and Humanitarian and Disaster Relief" in the Strait of Malacca in September 2015, which was the first bilateral exercise involving the military forces of both countries.[47] On November 10, 2015, Malaysia offered Chinese naval vessels the use of docking facilities at Kota Kinabalu, where U.S. naval vessels had previously docked.[48] In light of Malaysia's nonaligned foreign policy, any move toward the United States should be balanced by a gesture toward Beijing. In the meantime, Chinese intrusions into Malaysia's EEZ continue. The Malaysian Maritime Enforcement Agency declared on March 29, 2016, that it had driven away more than one hundred foreign fishing boats, mostly Chinese, from around Luconia Reef since March 24, which illustrated how persistent the problem was.[49]

Indonesia has regarded itself as a nonclaimant in this dispute, which has allowed it to act as a mediator both within ASEAN and between ASEAN and China. As the largest member of ASEAN, Jakarta has assumed that China would value its nonaligned status and its distance from the United States and thus give it special consideration. However, Indonesian apprehensions have been stimulated by Chinese maps of the South China Sea, which show the Chinese claim line cutting across the EEZ of the Natuna Islands. The issue first arose when these maps were published in 1993, prompting a protest from Foreign Minister Ali Alatas. In November 1994, the Indonesian state oil company Pertamina concluded a contract with Exxon to exploit the gas fields around the Natuna Islands, which were located in the area the Chinese had claimed.[50] The Indonesian military was prompted to organize naval exercises in the area in 1995 and 1996 to signal a determination to defend the islands. The problem erupted again in 2012 when the Chinese included the "nine-dash line" on their passports, which worried the Indonesians. Armed forces chief General Moeldoko announced that military forces would be strengthened around the Natuna Islands; he mentioned an army battalion, fighter aircraft, and the upgrading of the naval base there.[51] A *Jakarta Post* editorial noted that Indonesia had no territorial or border problems with China but that its "national strategic interests are also at stake with China's new military posture."[52] Before his visit to Japan in May 2015, Indonesia's new president Joko "Jokowi" Widodo said in an interview that China's nine-dash line had no basis in international law, the first time an ASEAN leader had publicly questioned the Chinese claim.[53] In Japan, Jokowi signed a defense agreement to increase cooperation in military technology, training and peacekeeping operations, and probably the exchange of intelligence.[54] The Indonesian navy announced that it wanted to conduct regular military exercises with the United States around the Natuna Islands, but because of the lack of facilities there, they had to be held elsewhere.[55]

Incidents involving Chinese fishing vessels around the Natuna Islands continue unabated. On March 19, 2016, Chinese fishing vessels again intruded into these waters. The Indonesian navy detained one such vessel with seven crew members, but two Chinese coast guard ships arrived and attempted to release the vessel, creating a diplomatic incident.[56] On June 17, the Indonesian navy noted some ten to twelve foreign fishing vessels in the area but did not identify how many were Chinese. Fishing vessels from Vietnam, Thailand, and the Philippines are also found in these waters, but only the Chinese vessels have the protection of their own coast guard, which forces the release of any intercepted vessels.[57] Jakarta is indeed troubled by these developments. The military decided to send five naval vessels to the area, to deploy five F-16 fighter aircraft in the Natuna Islands, and to extend port facilities there to accommodate three frigates.[58] President Jokowi called upon his ministers to formulate a policy on the South China Sea, but the fact that this was not done earlier demonstrated that Indonesia was basically ill prepared to deal with the situation.[59] Jakarta officials declared that Indonesia should push for implementation of the CoC, but this was not a meaningful response to the specific issue that they faced. However, Foreign Minister Retno Marsudi stressed that Indonesia's claim to the EEZ around the Natuna Islands was based on UNCLOS and that in legal terms, there was no overlap with China's claim.[60]

China cannot press its claims in the area or expand its presence by reclaiming features without subjecting ASEAN unity to severe strain. ASEAN leaders such as Malaysia's Najib had long assumed that an autonomous ASEAN was in China's interest and that Beijing would be constrained by its need to preserve that autonomy. This assumption was important in guiding ASEAN engagement of China in previous decades, but its relevance has been called into question by the Chinese reclamation activities and harassment tactics in the South China Sea. China's sense of confidence has outgrown the good neighbor policy, and its leaders may feel that ASEAN has no choice but to be on good terms with them anyway. If the good neighbor policy meant that ASEAN had the bargaining advantage by reason of its autonomy and unity, the new reality of a more powerful

China means that ASEAN is regarded as a supplicant and increasingly dependent on good ties with Beijing. Beijing understood that ASEAN's autonomy and distance from the United States were dictated by its founding charter and that as a group, it would avoid falling under American influence anyway. Moreover, China unveiled new economic inducements to attract the ASEAN countries and to mitigate the impact of its presence in the South China Sea. Beijing declared that these countries could be integrated into the twenty-first-century Maritime Silk Road, which Xi Jinping announced to the Indonesian parliament in October 2013. Premier Li Keqiang proposed a treaty of friendship and cooperation with the ASEAN countries in 2014 and offered $20 billion in loans for infrastructure development.[61] Whether China can follow through with these extravagant promises is another matter.

Nonetheless, Chinese pressure in the South China Sea has consequences for ASEAN that cannot easily be contained by diplomatic confidence or removed by economic inducements. Members such as Cambodia, Laos, and Thailand may continue to gravitate to Beijing and would be ready to take advantage of the economic benefits offered. ASEAN claimants Vietnam and the Philippines will continue to seek support outside the grouping, and although they may not break from ASEAN, they will use external support in their attempt to press the organization into offering more tangible support for their positions. Should ASEAN falter or remain unable to provide that support, they can be expected to strengthen their relationships with the United States as well as Japan. Both Malaysia and Indonesia came to ASEAN from a nonaligned foreign policy background and were committed to upholding the autonomy of the organization in great power rivalry. However, Chinese pressure in the South China Sea has released forces within the militaries of both countries that seek to develop security relationships with external powers as well. China's activities challenge Indonesia's and Malaysia's commitment to nonalignment as they grope for compensating support that can no longer be provided by ASEAN.

ASEAN AND THE ARBITRAL TRIBUNAL

The Arbitral Tribunal made its ruling public on July 12, 2016, and accepted fourteen of the fifteen points raised by the Philippines. Two main points are of relevance here. First, it decided that China may have had historic rights to the resources of the South China Sea, but "such rights were extinguished to the extent they were incompatible with the exclusive economic zones provided for in the Convention." The tribunal sidestepped the sovereignty issue that was not within its remit by deciding that China's historical claim had been superseded by

UNCLOS, which China had signed in December 1982 and ratified on June 7, 1996. The tribunal also noted that there was no evidence that China had actually exercised exclusive control over the South China Sea or the resources there in a way that could sustain a claim for sovereignty. Second, the tribunal found that none of the features in the Spratly Islands are capable of generating extended maritime zones, including those occupied and artificially reclaimed by China. The tribunal clarified the meaning of Article 121 of the Convention and the definition of an island by saying that "this provision depends upon the objective capacity of a feature, in its natural condition, to sustain either a stable community of people or economic activity that is not dependent on outside resources." The tribunal also found that Chinese activities had "violated the Philippines' sovereign rights in its exclusive economic zone" and that China had "inflicted irreparable harm to the marine environment" during its reclamation projects.[62]

The ruling triggered an outburst of ugly and hostile rhetoric from Beijing, which had vowed to reject it, but the response from ASEAN members was much more muted. Claims made under UNCLOS to EEZs were confirmed by the ruling, which gave the ASEAN claimants greater confidence in their positions. However, Beijing's rejection of the ruling and the expectation that it would become increasingly assertive to demonstrate its defiance has dampened the claimants' reactions and made them hesitant to use the ruling to strengthen their positions before China. The first meeting of ASEAN foreign ministers after the ruling was made public was held in Vientiane on July 24, 2016. The Philippines attempted to have the tribunal's decision mentioned in the communiqué, but Cambodia vetoed every effort in this direction and ensured that references to the militarization of the South China Sea were kept out. Chinese premier Li Keqiang had promised $600 million in grant aid to Cambodia over 2016–18, which explained the Cambodian leader's loyalties.[63] China-allied Laos chaired the meeting and avoided public controversy. Always indifferent to the issue, both Thailand and Myanmar held to the position that ASEAN relations with China went beyond the South China Sea, which should not act as an obstacle. The foreign ministers could at least reiterate that they were "seriously concerned over recent and ongoing developments" in the South China Sea, but this was as far as they could go. The media regarded the result as a "diplomatic victory" for China and one that put "ASEAN unity at risk."[64]

China expects the ASEAN claimants to ignore the tribunal's ruling and to negotiate individually with it. However, bilateral negotiations with Beijing over an unspecified agenda would not be in their interests while their rights to maritime zones have been recognized by a duly constituted legal tribunal. Beijing may hope to intimidate the claimants into submission by unleashing a vitriolic public relations campaign against the tribunal and by resorting to threats of confrontation. There are, however, fundamental issues at stake that would make the claimants resistant to such intimidation. China may increase its military presence in the South China Sea and may conduct military exercises there to demonstrate defiance of the tribunal's ruling, but aggressive behavior will not alter the fact that its activities and position in the Spratly area of the South China Sea have lost any legal justification.

ASEAN claimants have had to weigh their options in dealing with a more bellicose China that has enhanced its military position in the Spratly Islands through its reclamation projects. Philippine foreign minister Perfecto Yasay Jr. revealed that Chinese foreign minister Wang Yi called for bilateral negotiations without reference to the tribunal's ruling to resolve the issue. Wang Yi warned that the Philippines risked possible "confrontation" with China if it insisted on the ruling.[65] Philippine president Rodrigo Duterte rapidly accepted Wang Yi's offer of negotiations, seemingly moving toward China and away from the United States and ASEAN, largely because of American criticisms of his promotion of extrajudicial killings of drug offenders and personal pique. In October 2016, Duterte declared during a visit to Beijing that he had "realigned" himself with China and Russia and announced a "separation" from the United States.[66] He also declared that he would review the EDCA concluded with the United States in 2014 and that military exercises with the United States would be terminated. Duterte seemed to disavow his remarks upon his return to the Philippines, which added to the confusion He said that he had no intention of cutting ties with the United States and that by "separation" he meant charting "another way" in foreign policy. Not surprisingly, his declarations were described as "incoherent" by the *Philippine Star*, which opined that if this incoherence continued, the Philippines would become the "laughing stock of the world."[67] Indeed, presidential spokesperson Ernesto Abella issued a public statement that the Philippines would not break any established alliances, particularly with the United States. Presidential aides and foreign policy officials have explained and reinterpreted Duterte's impulsive statements to allay American concerns.[68]

Duterte claimed that his visit to Beijing was a success because he reached a verbal agreement with Beijing to allow Philippine fishing vessels to return to the Scarborough Shoal area from which they had been excluded over the past four years. On October 28, 2016, Ernesto Abella declared that Chinese coast guard vessels had left the area and Philippine fishermen could move in. In November, two Philippine coast guard vessels began patrolling the Scarborough Shoal area while Chinese coast guard vessels were also present.[69] This development boosted Duterte's standing as a populist president and gave rise to speculation in the Philippines that China was complying with the Arbitral Tribunal's ruling. However, allowing fishing vessels into the area was not the same as accepting the ruling since Beijing could always say that Philippine fishing vessels were there not by rights affirmed by the Arbitral Tribunal but with China's permission. Their presence under this arrangement would be tantamount to Philippine acknowledgment of China's sovereign claims. China had everything to gain and little to risk in this arrangement, as Duterte's populist credentials would be reaffirmed, encouraging him along an anti-American path. Beijing could threaten to rescind the agreement and hold the president hostage to his own populism unless he disowned the tribunal's ruling and accepted China's sovereign claim. Before the oral agreement took effect, China moved dredging and construction vessels into the area with the aim of reconstructing Scarborough Shoal in much the same way as the other reefs.[70] Sometime in the future, the work currently on hold would be completed and the populist president would realize that he had become a captive of his own rhetoric. In any case, Duterte's foreign policy populism conflicts with the views of the Philippine security establishment for whom the alliance with the United States is essential for the country's security.

THE FUTURE

China's local strategy toward the South China Sea has undermined its grand strategy of removing the U.S. military presence from the Western Pacific, and its own actions have deepened American involvement in the issue. The United States had little interest in the South China Sea until China resorted to coercive tactics to expand its presence there incrementally. Not until April 2010 did Secretary of State Hillary Clinton respond to ASEAN entreaties about Chinese pressure and express a new U.S. position of closer involvement in the issue and support for the claimants. In past decades, China pursued a good neighbor policy toward the region, and ASEAN leaders responded by attempting to integrate China into multilateral regional institutions in which the South China Sea dispute might be resolved. China has moved on from that era and has attempted to shape the relationship with ASEAN on its own terms and place it in the position of a supplicant, dependent upon reassurance from China as well as its economic favors and largesse. In doing so, China has exacerbated the divisions within ASEAN over this issue in the effort to prevent it from forming an undesirable consensus over the South China Sea that would not support Beijing's position. However, in undermining ASEAN unity over the issue, China has encouraged the claimants to seek support from external powers. In particular, Vietnam and the Philippines have strengthened their security ties with the United States and Japan as well. Despite the populism expressed by leaders such as Duterte, those ties are unlikely to be broken. As China increases its physical presence in the South China Sea through its reclamation projects, the dispute outgrows the regional context within which ASEAN had attempted to confine it and becomes an issue for Sino-U.S./Japan rivalry. China could have adopted a different policy of seeking a multilateral resolution of the issue with ASEAN based on UNCLOS in which the Deng Xiaoping formula of setting aside disputes and engaging in joint development could have been applied. ASEAN would have responded with gratitude, and there would have been no need for U.S. involvement or "freedom of navigation" patrols, and current tensions over the issue would have been avoided. Chinese ambitions, however, extended beyond what such a multilateral resolution would allow in the South China Sea, with results that the Chinese had hoped to avoid: a fragmented ASEAN and the deepening involvement of the United States and Japan in the dispute.

Notes

1. On China's good neighbor policy toward ASEAN, see David Shambaugh, "China Engages Asia: Reshaping the Regional Order," *International Security* 29, no. 3 (Winter 2004/2005); Brantly Womack, "China and Southeast Asia: Asymmetry, Leadership, and Normalcy," *Pacific Affairs* 76, no. 4 (Winter 2003/2004).
2. "ASEAN Declaration on the South China Sea adopted by the Foreign Ministers at the 25th ASEAN Ministerial Meeting in Manila, Philippines, on 22 July 1992," http://cil.nus.edu.sg/rp/pdf/1992%20ASEAN%20Declaration%20on%20 the%20South%20China%20Sea-pdf.pdf.
3. Nguyen Hong Thao, "Vietnam and the Code of Conduct for the South China Sea," *Ocean Development and International Law* 32, no. 2 (2001).
4. On the DoC, see Nguyen Hong Thao, "The 2002 Declaration on the Conduct of Parties in the South China Sea: A Note," *Ocean Development and International Law* 34, no. 3–4 (2003).
5. "Declaration on the Conduct of Parties in the South China Sea," ASEAN.org, http://www.asean.org/asean/external-relations/china/item/declaration-on-the-conduct-of-parties-in-the-south-china-sea; "Chairman's Statement of the 20th ASEAN Summit, Phnom Penh, 3–4 April 2012," ASEAN.org, http://www.asean.org/archive/documents/20th%20summit/FINAL%20Chairman%20 Statement1330.pdf.

6. Point six of the guidelines stated that "the decision to implement concrete measures or activities of the DoC should be based on consensus among parties concerned, and lead to the eventual realization of a Code of Conduct." See "Guidelines for the Implementation of the DOC," ASEAN.org, http://www.asean.org/archive/documents/20185-DOC.pdf.
7. "Cambodia Reassures China over Regional Maritime Row," Yahoo news, April 1, 2012, https://sg.news.yahoo.com/cambodia-reassures-china-over-regional-maritime-row-165640705.html.
8. Prak Chan Thul, "Hu Wants Cambodia Help on China Sea Dispute, Pledges Aid," Reuters, March 31, 2012, http://www.reuters.com/article/2012/03/31/us-cambodia-china-iduSBRE82u04Y20120331.
9. Prak Chan Thul and Stuart Grudgings, "SE Asia Meeting in Disarray over Sea Dispute with China," Reuters, July 13, 2012, http://www.reuters.com/article/2012/07/13/us-asean-summit-iduSBRE86C0BD20120713.
10. Bagus BT. Saragih, "RI Finds Common ASEAN Ground in Sea Dispute," *Jakarta Post*, July 23, 2012, http://www.thejakartapost.com/news/2012/07/23/ri-finds-common-asean-ground-sea-dispute.html#sthash.w3KykGPl.dpuf.
11. "ASEAN Agrees on Rules for South China Sea Conduct," AP News, July 10, 2012, http://asiancorrespondent.com/85615/asean-agrees-on-rules-for-south-china-sea-conduct.
12. Donald K. Emmerson, "Indonesia Saves ASEAN's Face," *Asia Times,* July 24, 2012, http://www.atimes.com/atimes/Southeast_Asia/NG24Ae01.html.
13. Christine O. Avendaño, "Aquino Wants 'First Crack' at Code," *Philippine Daily Inquirer,* April 4, 2012, http://globalnation.inquirer.net/31719/aquino-wants-%E2%80%98first-crack%E2%80%99-at-code; "Philippines Urges United ASEAN Stand on South China Sea," *Straits Times*, April 3, 2012, https://sg.news.yahoo.com/philippines-urges-united-asean-stand-south-china-sea-174416389.html.
14. Delon Porcalla, "Phl Wants ASEAN Stand on Spratlys," *Philstar*, April 3, 2012, http://www.philstar.com/Article.aspx?articleId=793837&publicationSubCategoryId=63.
15. Yohanna Ririhena, "RI Circulates Draft Code of Conduct on South China Sea," *Jakarta Post*, September 29, 2012, http://www.thejakartapost.com/news/2012/09/29/ri-circulates-draft-code-conduct-south-china-sea.html#sthash.5F11omXv.dpuf; Mark Valencia, "Navigating the Differences," *Global Asia* 8, no. 1 (Spring 2013), http://www.globalasia.org/wp-content/uploads/2013/03/43.pdf.
16. Bagus BT. Saragih, "China Closer to South China Sea Code of Conduct, Marty Says," *Jakarta Post*, May 3, 2013, http://www.thejakartapost.com/news/2013/05/03/china-closer-south-china-sea-code-conduct-marty-says.html#sthash.OP98mRy0.dpuf.
17. China's working draft (unpublished), dated February 2014.
18. See Valencia, "Navigating the Differences."
19. Photographs were obtained by Fairfax media; see Lindsay Murdoch, "Photos Reveal China Building on Reefs in Disputed Waters," *Sydney Morning Herald*, September 15, 2014, http://www.smh.com.au/world/photos-reveal-china-building-on-reefs-in-disputed-waters-20140915-10h4r0.html.

20. Simone Orendain, "Philippines Urges Strong ASEAN Statement Against China," *Voice of America*, April 26, 2015, http://www.voanews.com/content/philippines-urges-strong-asean-statement-against-china/2735093.html.
21. Kong Sothanarith, "Cambodia Publicly Endorses China Position on South China Sea," *Voice of America*, March 25, 2015, http://www.voanews.com/content/cambodia-publicly-endorses-china-position-on-south-china-sea/2694301.html.
22. Wassana Nanuam and Patsara Jikkham, "Thailand, China Bolster Military Ties as U.S. Relations Splinter," *Bangkok Post*, February 8, 2015, http://www.bangkokpost.com/news/security/468332/thailand-china-bolster-military-ties-as-us-relations-splinter.
23. "Chairman's Statement of the 26th ASEAN Summit," ASEAN.org, http://www.asean.org/news/asean-statement-communiques/item/chairman-s-statement-of-the-26th-asean-summit?category_id=26.
24. "ASEAN Chair Malaysia Wants Efforts on South China Sea Code of Conduct to Be Hastened," *Straits Times*, April 23, 2015, http://www.straitstimes.com/asia/se-asia/asean-chair-malaysia-wants-efforts-on-south-china-sea-code-of-conduct-to-be-hastened.
25. "ASEAN, China Should Conclude Pact to Ease Tensions in South China Sea: Ng Eng Hen," *Straits Times*, May 19, 2015, http://www.straitstimes.com/singapore/asean-china-should-conclude-pact-to-ease-tensions-in-south-china-sea-ng-eng-hen.
26. Nur Asyiqin Mohamad Salleh, "Three ASEAN Ministers Urge Unified Action, Code of Conduct," *Straits Times*, May 31, 2015, http://www.straitstimes.com/singapore/three-asean-ministers-urge-unified-action-code-of-conduct?page.
27. AFP, "Beijing agrees to meet Hanoi over offshore claims," *Straits Times*, April 1, 1997, p.31; Le Hong Hiep, "Chinese Assertiveness in the South China Sea: What Should Vietnam Do?" *National Interest*, May 15, 2014, http://nationalinterest.org/blog/the-buzz/chinese-assertiveness-the-south-china-sea-what-should-10468.
28. Interview sources, Ministry of Foreign Affairs, Hanoi, May 3, 2014.
29. "ASEAN Foreign Ministers' Statement on the Current Developments in the South China Sea," ASEAN.org, May 10, 2014, http://www.asean.org/news/asean-statement-communiques/item/asean-foreign-ministers-statement-on-the-current-developments-in-the-south-china-sea?category_id=26.
30. Interview sources, Danang, Vietnam, June 2014.
31. An Dien, "Vietnam, China Seek to Repair Ties Ruptured by East Sea Dispute," *Thanh Nien News*, October 27, 2014, http://www.thanhniennews.com/politics/vietnam-china-seek-to-repair-ties-ruptured-by-east-sea-dispute-33197.html.
32. Embassy of the Socialist Republic of Vietnam in the United States of America, "Secretary of Defense Ashton Carter Visited Vietnam," June 1, 2015, vietnamembassy-usa.org/news/2015/06/secretary-defense-ashton-carter-visited-vietnam.
33. "Joint Communique of the Twenty-Eighth ASEAN Ministerial Meeting Bandar Seri Begawan," ASEAN.org, July 29–30, 1995, http://www.asean.org/communities/asean-political-security-community/item/joint-communique-of-the-twenty-eighth-asean-ministerial-meeting-bandar-seri-begawan-29-30-july-1995.
34. Government of the Philippines, Department of Foreign Affairs, "DFA Fact Sheet: Philippine-U.S. Bilateral Relations," April 28, 2014, http://www.gov.ph

/2014/04/28/dfa-fact-sheet-philippine-united-states-bilateral-relations/; Thomas Maresca, "Obama Visits Philippines; U.S. Announces Defense Pact," *USA Today*, April 27, 2014, http://www.usatoday.com/story/news/world/2014/04/27/us-philippines-defense-pact/8299491/; Ernest Z. Bower, "Enhanced Defense Cooperation Agreement: Manila's Most Credible Deterrent to China," cogitASIA.com, May 29, 2015, http://cogitasia.com/enhanced-defense-cooperation-agreement-manilas-most-credible-deterrent-to-china/.

35. The main issues in the appeal were Philippine rights within its EEZ, China's right to maritime zones from the features it claims as islands under Article 121, whether China has illegally occupied and claimed sovereignty over submerged features that are not islands but part of the seabed, whether the features occupied by China are rocks and not entitled to a maritime zone, whether China has occupied features that are not above water at high tide but part of the Philippine continental shelf, and whether China can make a maritime claim based on the nine-dash line. Robert C. Beckman, "The Philippines v. China Case and the South China Sea Disputes," in *Territorial Disputes in the South China Sea: Navigating Rough Waters*, ed. Jing Huang and Andrew Billo (New York: Palgrave Macmillan, 2015), 54–68.

36. Marlon Ramos and Tarra Quismundo, "China Building Airstrip on Reef in PH Waters," *Philippine Daily Inquirer*, May 15, 2014, http://globalnation.inquirer.net/104333/manila-says-china-reclaiming-land-in-disputed-sea.

37. David Dizon, "Why China Military Base in West PH Sea is a 'Game-Changer,'" ABS-CBN News, June 6, 2014, http://www.abs-cbnnews.com/focus/06/10/14/why-china-military-base-west-ph-sea-game-changer.

38. Nikko Dizon, "Historian: Reef's Reclamation China's Way to Assert 9 Dash Line," *Philippine Daily Inquirer*, June 8, 2014, http://globalnation.inquirer.net/106049/historian-reefs-reclamation-chinas-way-to-assert-9-dash-line-claim.

39. "Najib Stresses China Ties Despite Growing Asia Territorial Disputes," *The Star*, May 22, 2014, http://www.thestar.com.my/News/Nation/2014/05/22/najib-razak-malaysia-china-japan-territorial-disputes/; "Sea Spat No Benefit to China," *The Star*, April 28, 2015, http://www.thestar.com.my/News/Nation/2015/04/28/Sea-spat-no-benefit-to-China-PM-Constructive-approach-is-best-so-as-not-to-destabilise-Asean/.

40. "Chinese Ships Patrol Area Contested by Malaysia," Reuters, January 26, 2014, http://uk.reuters.com/article/2014/01/26/uk-china-malaysia-iduKBREA0P06X20140126.

41. Interview sources, Kuala Lumpur, Malaysia, October 31, 2015; see also Dzirhan Mahadzir, "Malaysian Maritime Claims in the South China Sea," in *Entering Uncharted Waters? ASEAN and the South China Sea*, ed. Pavin Chachavalpongpun (Singapore: Institute of Southeast Asian Studies, 2014), 220.

42. Raul Dancel, "China's Intrusion into Malaysia More Extensive than Reported: Analyst," *Straits Times*, June 20, 2015, http://www.straitstimes.com/asia/se-asia/chinas-intrusion-into-malaysia-more-extensive-than-reported-analyst; Jenifer Laeng, "China Coast Guard Vessel Found at Luconia Shoals," *Borneo Post*, June 3, 2015, http://www.theborneopost.com/2015/06/03/china-coast-guard-vessel-found-at-luconia-shoals/.

43. "Malaysia to Establish Marine Corps, Naval Base Close to James Shoal," *Malaysia Today*, October 18, 2013, http://www.malaysia-today.net/malaysia-to-establish-marine-corps-naval-base-close-to-shoal/.
44. Stuart Grudgings, "Insight—China's Assertiveness Hardens Malaysian Stance in Sea Dispute," Reuters, February 26, 2014, http://uk.reuters.com/article/2014/02/26/uk-malaysia-china-maritime-insight-iduKBREA1P1Z020140226.
45. "U.S. Navy Ship's Visit Marks Growing Ties," *Borneo Post*, February 26, 2015, http://www.theborneopost.com/2015/02/26/us-navy-ships-visit-marks-growing-ties/.
46. "U.S. Says Malaysia Offers to Host Spy Planes that Irk China," Reuters, September 12, 2014, http://www.reuters.com/article/2014/09/12/us-malaysia-usa-spyplanes-iduSKBN0H72CN20140912; "Malaysia Denies Naval Base Offer to U.S.," *Borneo Post*, October 10, 2014, http://www.theborneopost.com/2014/10/10/malaysia-denies-naval-base-offer-to-us/.
47. Sumathy Permal, "China and Malaysia's First-ever Joint Military Exercise Is an Important Strategic Move," *The Star*, September 28, 2015, http://www.thestar.com.my/news/nation/2015/09/28/friendship-and-peace-on-the-waterway/.
48. Shannon Teo, "Malaysia to Allow PLA Navy Use of Strategic Port," *Straits Times*, November 22, 2015.
49. "MMEA Drives Away 100 Foreign Fishing Vessels from Malaysian Waters," *The Star*, March 29, 2016, http://www.thestar.com.my/news/nation/2016/03/29/mmea-drives-away-100-foreign-fishing-vessels-from-malaysian-waters/.
50. See *Sunday Times* (Singapore), April 9, 1995; Johan McBeth, "Oil Rich Diet," *Far Eastern Economic Review*, April 27, 1995.
51. "Indonesia's Military Flexes Muscle as S. China Sea Dispute Looms," *Jakarta Globe*, March 13, 2014, http://jakartaglobe.beritasatu.com/news/indonesia-military-flexes-muscle-s-china-sea-dispute-looms/.
52. "Editorial: Facing China's Claim," *Jakarta Post*, January 24, 2014, http://www.thejakartapost.com/news/2014/01/24/editorial-facing-china-s-claim.html.
53. "Indonesia's President Jokowi Says China Has No Legal Claim to South China Sea: Yomiuri," *Straits Times*, March 23, 2015, http://www.straitstimes.com/asia/se-asia/indonesias-president-jokowi-says-china-has-no-legal-claim-to-south-china-sea-yomiuri.
54. Steve Herman, "Indonesia, Japan to Sign a Defense Agreement," Voice of America, March 20, 2015, http://www.voanews.com/content/indonesia-to-sign-a-defense-agreement-with-japan/2688101.html.
55. Kanupriya Kapoor and Randy Fabi, "Indonesia Eyes Regular Navy Exercises with U.S. in South China Sea," Reuters, April 13, 2015, http://www.reuters.com/article/2015/04/13/us-indonesia-us-southchinasea-iduSKBN0N40O320150413.
56. Haeril Halim, Anggi M. Lubis, and Stefani Ribka, "RI Confronts China on Fishing," *Jakarta Post*, March 21, 2016, http://www.thejakartapost.com/news/2016/03/21/ri-confronts-china-fishing.html.
57. Devina Heriyanto, "Q&A: Is Indonesia Finally Confronting China over Natuna?" *Jakarta Post*, July 2, 2016, http://www.thejakartapost.com/academia/2016/07/02/qa-is-indonesia-finally-confronting-china-over-natuna.

58. Margareth S. Aritonang and Ina Parlina, "Govt. Boosts Natuna Defenses," *Jakarta Post,* July 19, 2016, http://www.thejakartapost.com/news/2016/07/19/govt-boosts-natuna-defenses.html.
59. Ayomi Amindoni, "Gov't to Formulate Official Stance on South China Sea Dispute," *Jakarta Post,* June 13, 2016, http://www.thejakartapost.com/seasia/2016/06/13/govt-to-formulate-official-stance-on-south-china-sea-dispute.html.
60. Liza Yosephine, "Minister Echoes Indonesia's Stance on South China Sea," *Jakarta Post,* June 21, 2016, http://www.thejakartapost.com/news/2016/06/21/minister-echoes-indonesias-stance-on-south-china-sea.html.
61. "China Offers ASEAN Friendship Treaty, Loans as South China Sea Tension Bubbles," *Straits Times,* November 13, 2014, http://www.straitstimes.com/asia/south-asia/china-offers-asean-friendship-loans-as-south-china-sea-tension-bubbles; Jiang Zhida, "ASEAN Will Gain from Maritime Silk Road Updated," *China Daily,* March 31, 2015, http://www.chinadaily.com.cn/kindle/2015-03/31/content_19961494.htm.
62. Permanent Court of Arbitration, "The South China Sea Arbitration," press release, The Hague, July 12, 2016, https://pca-cpa.org/wp-content/uploads/sites/175/2016/07/PH-CN-20160712-Press-Release-No-11-English.pdf.
63. Cheang Sokha, "China Gives $600 Million After South China Sea Support," *Khmer Times,* July 15, 2016, http://www.khmertimeskh.com/news/27292/china-gives--600-million-after-south-china-sea-support/.
64. Tama Salim, "ASEAN Unity at Risk," *Jakarta Post,* July 25, 2016, http://www.thejakartapost.com/news/2016/07/25/asean-unity-risk.html; Vijay Joshi and Daniel Malloy, "China Scores Diplomatic Victory, Avoids Criticism from ASEAN," *Associated Press,* July 25, 2016, http://globalnation.inquirer.net/141842/china-scores-diplomatic-victory-avoids-criticism-from-asean.
65. Patricia Lourdes, "Philippines Rejects Talks Not Based on Arbitral Ruling; China Warns of Confrontation," *Philippine Star,* July 19, 2016, http://www.philstar.com/headlines/2016/07/19/1604466/philippines-talks-hague-verdict-confrontation-china.
66. Gabriel Dominguez, "Philippine Leader Announces 'Separation' from U.S.," *Jane's Defence Weekly,* October 21, 2016.
67. Ana Marie Pamintuan, "Incoherent," *Philippine Star,* October 24, 2016, http://www.philstar.com/opinion/2016/10/24/1636759/incoherent.
68. Elena L. Aben, "PH Allays U.S. Fears, Says Treaties Will Remain in Place," *Manila Bulletin,* October 25, 2016, http://www.mb.com.ph/ph-allays-us-fears-says-treaties-will-remain-in-place/.
69. Camille Abadicio, "Filipino Fishermen Still Facing Challenges in Scarborough Shoal," CNN Philippines, November 12, 2016, http://cnnphilippines.com/news/2016/11/12/Scarborough-Shoal-Filipino-fishermen.html.
70. "Confirmation of Imminent Chinese Construction on Scarborough Shoal Would Increase Risk of Armed Conflict," *Jane's Country Risk Daily Report,* September 8, 2016; Gabriel Dominguez, "Philippines Gravely Concerned about Chinese Activity around Scarborough Shoal," *Jane's Defence Weekly,* September 6, 2016.

5

The Evolution of U.S. Strategy in the South China Sea

Tacking with Regional Strategic Winds

Sean R. Liedman

Since the end of World War II, U.S. grand strategy toward the People's Republic of China (hereafter China or PRC) has tacked between three central policy themes: containment, cooperative engagement, and competition. Additionally, a fourth unstated strategic theme undergirds the above: prevailing in conflict, which since 1949 has principally revolved around the threat of forceful reunification of Taiwan but is expanding to include the potential for conflict over disputed sovereignty and maritime claims in the South China Sea.

Before examining the current situation in the South China Sea and U.S. policy and strategy options, it is necessary to briefly review the history of the military aspects of the U.S.-China relationship, as some historical themes continue to shape both U.S. and Chinese strategy today. Additionally, any study of the substrategies in the South China Sea must include the context of the broader political, economic, and military relationship at that time. In the interest of brevity, this review will start with the end of World War II, although earlier themes such as the "Century of Humiliation" in the latter half of the nineteenth and first half of the twentieth century continue to influence Chinese strategic thinking.[1]

One other note: there are many different contextual definitions of the words "policy" and "strategy." For the purposes of this chapter, I will use the following framework: *strategy* is defined as "the *ways* in which the available *means* will be employed to achieve the *ends* of *policy*."[2]

1945–50: CIRCUMSPECT ENGAGEMENT

In the aftermath of the destruction of the war against Japan, Allied powers led the effort to restore the sovereignty of states and territories that were occupied by the Imperial Japanese Army during the war, including the Republic of China (ROC). U.S. strategy during this period is best described as "circumspect" cooperative engagement, due to the fact that many U.S. policymakers and military leaders loathed Chiang Kai Shek's mismanagement, corruption, and human rights abuses.[3] In light of the billions of dollars in cash and military equipment that the United States granted in aid to the ROC during this period, the defeat of Chiang's Nationalist Forces during the summer of 1949 by Mao's People's Liberation Army (PLA) triggered a vigorous public debate in the United States over "who lost China."[4]

Hard-liner "China hawks" (mostly Republicans) argued that more ardent support for Nationalist China could have stopped the spread of communism and blamed the Harry S. Truman administration's "China Hands," who insisted that the rot of Chiang's regime was too deep to be salvaged.[5] While the terms of reference have changed slightly, echoes of this divide persist in U.S. policy and strategy making today. In 2013, Justin Logan wrote that the "optimists (liberal doves)" favor a policy of engagement, while the "pessimists (conservative hawks)" favor a policy of containment. The compromise between the two has resulted in a muddled policy of "congagement" during the history of the relationship.[6]

Within the broader context of this period, following the surrender of Japan the authority of the South China Sea islands was put under ROC jurisdiction in December 1945, and ROC troops occupied Woody Island in the Paracels.[7] The Republic of China published a "Map of South China Sea Islands" in 1947 that depicted eleven dashes around the perimeter of the South China Sea, within which China claimed the island features.[8]

1950–72: CONTAINMENT

The defeat of Chiang's Nationalist forces by the PLA in 1949 and the Chinese intervention in the Korean War in the fall of 1950 triggered a hard shift by the Dwight Eisenhower administration to an explicit strategy of containment.[9] The United States refused to formally recognize Mao's Communist People's Republic of China as the legitimate government of China, and Washington intervened with naval forces of the U.S. Seventh Fleet in the Taiwan Straits three times in the 1950s to protect Chiang's Republic of China (now encamped solely on the island of Taiwan and a few islands in the Taiwan Straits) from PRC aggression.[10] Chinese resentment of this era of containment continues to resonate in today's U.S.-China strategic relationship, as discussed below.

Against the backdrop of the Communists' battlefield victories on the mainland, ROC troops retreated from the Paracel Islands to Taiwan on May 8, 1950, out of tactical considerations.[11] However, the Republic of China did not renounce its authority over the Paracel Islands at that time or later.[12] China usurped the Republic of China's claims to the island features in the South China Sea and published the same map, although two dashes in the Tonkin Gulf were subsequently removed, creating China's "nine-dash line" claim that is maintained to the present.[13] Additionally, China occupied Woody Island in the Amphitrite Group of the Paracel Islands in 1950—its first territorial expansion in the South China Sea.[14]

1972–86: HOLLOW ENGAGEMENT

President Richard Nixon's historic visit to China in 1972 and resultant policy shift from containment to détente led to the execution of a strategy of cooperative engagement. However, there was practically no Chinese military activity with which to engage, as the PLA had been focusing inward on lingering internal security issues stemming from the Cultural Revolution and a violent border clash with the Soviet Union on the Xinjiang and Manchurian borders in 1969.[15]

U.S. diplomatic recognition of China in 1979 and the Ronald Reagan administration's staunch anti-Soviet stance triggered a series of policy debates about the merits of selling military arms to China to deepen Sino-American cooperation and provide China with the means to serve as a bulwark against the mutual fear of further Soviet expansion in Asia.[16] June Teufel Dreyer, testifying before the Senate Committee on Foreign Relations in 1981, labeled the People's Liberation Army Navy (PLAN) "mainly a coastal defense force" that "rarely venture[s] beyond the PRC's territorial waters." Additionally, she stated that "the PLA Air Force (PLAAF) has been judged relatively weaker during the 1970s than it was in the 1950s."[17] By 1985, the debates over arms sales had matured into the sale and delivery of twenty-four S-70 Sikorsky helicopters and substantive negotiations of Chinese purchases of advanced antitank weapons, surface-to-air missiles, naval sonar systems, and naval ship self-defense systems.[18]

In the South China Sea during this period, there was an armed clash between China and the Republic of Vietnam (South Vietnam) in 1974 over sovereignty of the Crescent Group in the Paracel Islands. The United States, reeling from its strategic defeat in the Vietnam conflict and eager to deepen détente with China, stood by passively while China militarily ejected the Vietnamese and consolidated its control over the Paracels.[19]

1986–2001: ACCELERATING BUT INTERRUPTED ENGAGEMENT

U.S. Secretary of the Navy John Lehman's visit to China in August 1984 paved a path to accelerate naval engagement with China. After two years of internal wrangling within Chinese Communist Party leadership, including recollections of foreign naval domination during the "Century of Humiliation," three U.S. Navy ships pulled into the port of Qingdao on November 5, 1986, the first visit to China by U.S. Navy ships in more than forty years.[20] Secretary Lehman found a willing partner in General Liu Huaqing, who as commander of the PLAN was determined to transform it from a coastal defense force into a blue-water navy.[21]

During this period of increasing cooperative engagement, China had another naval clash with Vietnam over contested land features in the South China Sea in 1988, this time in the Spratly Archipelago. China devised a plan to occupy nine vacant features in the Spratlys in 1987, and after a deadly clash on March 14, 1988, at Johnson South Reef in which seventy-four Vietnamese sailors and marines were killed, China had gained control of six of those features.[22] In the same fashion as the 1974 Sino-Vietnamese clash in the Paracels, the United States did not intervene to prevent the use of force to resolve a sovereignty dispute in the South China Sea.[23]

Arms sales negotiations and senior defense leadership engagements continued at a quickening pace until halting abruptly following the Tiananmen Square massacre in June 1989, when the United States and Europe enacted an arms embargo against China and the United States severed all military contacts. The embargo generated four strategic consequences that linger in the U.S.-China relationship today. The first is a Chinese sense of betrayal by the United States in that a series of good faith negotiations were terminated due to disagreement over an issue that was purely an internal affair of China—in stark violation of China's stated "noninterference" principle of foreign policy. This sense of betrayal was further aggravated by the U.S. sale of 150 F-16 fighter aircraft to Taiwan in 1992.[24] Second, the Chinese perceived that the United States was officially retrenching to a strategy of containment, a perception inflamed by articles in the Western media such as "Why We Must Contain China."[25] Third, the Chinese turned back to Russia to procure advanced weaponry. Flush with cash from double-digit gross domestic product growth rates beginning in 1992 but struggling to build a mature technology base, the Chinese proceeded to purchase Russian-built Su-27 and Su-30 fighter–ground attack aircraft, T-72 tanks, S-300 (SA-10 in North Atlantic Treaty Organization terminology) surface-to-air missiles, Il-76 transport aircraft, *Kilo*-class diesel submarines, and *Sovremennyi*-class destroyers over the next five years.[26] Additionally, the cash-strapped Russians granted licenses to build Su-27 and Su-30 aircraft in China, which provided manufacturing expertise and multiple technology spinoffs for the Chinese defense industrial base. Finally, the arms embargo accelerated the pace of Chinese "illicit technology acquisition" efforts, principally aimed at the United States. The Chinese effectively used ethnic Chinese targeting, Chinese moles in the U.S. government, false front companies, and transactions with unscrupulous arms dealers to acquire U.S. technologies before discovering the "holy grail" of illicit acquisition: cyber theft.[27] It is no coincidence that the Chinese J-20 and J-31 fifth-generation stealth fighter aircraft strongly resemble Lockheed Martin's F-22 and F-35 fighters respectively; China reportedly digitally pilfered terabytes of data from Lockheed Martin and six subcontractors.[28]

U.S.-Chinese military cooperation in the 1990s resembled a roller coaster ride. Military dialogue resumed in October 1993 but then halted again during the Taiwan Straits crisis of 1996. Military contacts were revived on the heels of two presidential summits between Bill Clinton and Jiang Zemin in October 1997 but were suspended yet again after the accidental U.S. bombing of the Chinese embassy in Belgrade during Operation Allied Force in May 1999.[29] Military contacts were restarted in May 2000 when Adm. Dennis Blair (commander, U.S. Pacific Command) visited China but were suspended again less than a year later due to the EP-3 incident, a tactical incident that had strategic consequences (discussed below).[30]

On the diplomatic and economic fronts, trade negotiators in the Clinton administration paved the way for China's entry into the global economy during the 1990s, which was formalized with China's accession into the World Trade Organization in 2001. U.S. policymakers believed that it was in their nation's interest to continue the rapid expansion of free trade with the formerly closed economies of the communist bloc; however, this decision would ultimately accelerate the U.S. trade deficit with China and accelerate China's economic growth.[31]

China's entry into the Spratlys sparked increased tensions and competition in the South China Sea as various claimant states took measures to stake out and defend their claims.[32] China occupied Mischief Reef in 1994—its seventh occupied feature in the Spratly Archipelago—while the Republic of the Philippines ran a navy ship (BRP *Sierre Madre*) aground on Second Thomas Shoal in 1999 to defend its claim.[33]

2001–PRESENT: "COOPETITION"[34]

The first foreign policy crisis of President George W. Bush's administration was the EP-3 incident off Hainan Island on April 1, 2001, when a U.S. Navy EP-3 surveillance aircraft conducting a reconnaissance mission in international air space suffered a mid-air collision with a PLAN J-8 fighter jet. The Chinese pilot was killed, and the crew of the EP-3 executed an emergency landing at Lingshui Air Field on Hainan Island. Twenty-four U.S. Navy aircrew members were detained and interrogated by the Chinese for eleven days before being released into U.S. custody.

China's increasing military capabilities and assertive military operations, many of which were clearly designed to counter U.S. and allied interests in the Asia-Pacific region, were spawning a new era of strategic competition. In recognition of China's growing economic and military might, the Bush administration inferred in its 2001 Quadrennial Defense Review that China was emerging as a competitor: "Although the United States will not face a peer competitor in the near future, the potential exists for regional powers to develop sufficient capabilities to threaten stability in regions critical to U.S. interests. In particular, Asia is gradually emerging as a region susceptible to large-scale military competition. . . . Maintaining a stable balance in Asia will be a complex task. The possibility exists that a military competitor with a formidable resource base will emerge in the region."[35]

The September 11, 2001, attacks and resultant war in Afghanistan, followed by the initiation of the war in Iraq, diverted massive amounts of U.S. military resources from the Asia-Pacific region and reduced the U.S. attention span for managing the military relationship with China. Secretary of Defense Donald Rumsfeld's first visit to China occurred in October 2005, and military ties between senior defense officials subsequently resumed.[36]

The 2006 Quadrennial Defense Review acknowledged this emerging environment of "coopetition" by using the words "compete" and "partner" in the same paragraph: "Of the major and emerging powers, China has the greatest potential to compete militarily with the United States and field disruptive military technologies that could over time offset traditional U.S. military advantages absent U.S. counter strategies. U.S. policy remains focused on encouraging China to play a constructive, peaceful role in the Asia-Pacific region and to serve as a partner in addressing common security challenges, including terrorism, proliferation, narcotics, and piracy."[37]

U.S. leadership expressed similar concerns of growing Chinese competition on the diplomatic and economic fronts; Deputy Secretary of State Robert Zoellick famously urged China to become a "responsible stakeholder" in the international system during a speech in 2005 amidst concerns over China's role in the proliferation of nuclear weapons and missile technology to North Korea, Iran, and Pakistan; intellectual property theft and counterfeiting; and currency manipulation.[38]

Soon after the Barack Obama administration assumed office, Secretary of State Hillary Clinton declared that "the United States is back" in Asia in a number of fora in summer 2009 to signal that the administration believed that the geostrategic center of gravity for the United States lies in the Asia-Pacific region.[39] The Obama administration's 2010 Quadrennial Defense Review continued to echo the cooperative side of the strategy but painted a harsher picture of the increasingly competitive side of the relationship, along with the potential for conflict:

> As part of its long-term, comprehensive military modernization, China is developing and fielding large numbers of advanced medium-range ballistic and cruise missiles, new attack submarines equipped with advanced weapons, increasingly capable long-range air defense systems, electronic warfare and computer network attack capabilities, advanced fighter aircraft, and counter-space systems. China has shared only limited information about the pace, scope, and ultimate aims of its military modernization programs, raising a number of legitimate questions regarding its long-term intentions.
>
> China's growing presence and influence in regional and global economic and security affairs is one of the most consequential aspects of the evolving strategic landscape in the Asia-Pacific region and globally. In particular, China's military has begun to develop new roles, missions, and capabilities in support of its growing regional and global interests, which could enable it to play a more substantial and constructive role in international affairs. The United States welcomes a strong, prosperous, and successful China that plays a greater global role. The United States welcomes the positive benefits that can accrue from greater cooperation.[40]

In the fall of 2012, the Obama administration announced in a series of articles and speeches that the United States was strengthening its commitment to Asia, and the 2012 Defense Strategic Guidance formally labeled this policy initiative the "rebalance toward the Asia-Pacific region."[41] The Congressional Research Service summarized the major elements of the rebalance as increasing military presence in the Asia-Pacific region, strengthening security relationships with regional allies, building new security partnerships in the region, and strengthening economic ties by joining the East Asia Summit and negotiating the Trans-Pacific Strategic Economic Partnership.[42]

Predictably, some Chinese media commentators reacted to this U.S. rebalance to Asia as an effort to "restrain" or "contain" China's rise and influence. For example, noted Chinese military expert Liu Jiangping suggested in China's *Global Times* newspaper that the United States was "tightening up" a "containment circle" along mainland China's periphery.[43] U.S. senior officials attempted to dispel this notion of containment; Secretary of Defense Leon Panetta, speaking at the Engineering Academy of the PLA in September 2012, stated, "Our rebalance to the Asia-Pacific region is not an attempt to contain China. It is an attempt to engage China and expand its role in the Pacific. It's about creating a new model in the relationship of our two Pacific powers. It's about renewing and revitalizing our role in a part of the world that is rapidly becoming more critical to our economic, diplomatic, and security interests. And as I've made clear, essential to all of these goals—essential to these goals is a constructive military-to-military relationship with China."[44]

Despite lingering mistrust based on the tumultuous history of the relationship, military cooperation was deepening on many fronts. With the PLAN eager to demonstrate that it had matured from a regional to a global navy, China has sustained a counterpiracy naval task force in the Horn of Africa region since 2009, and the U.S. and Chinese navies demonstrated tactical cooperation during those counterpiracy operations. Additionally, the PLAN sent four ships to participate in the U.S. Pacific Fleet's crown jewel Rim of the Pacific (RIMPAC) exercise in waters off Hawaii in 2014. As a reflection of the "coopetitive" nature of the relationship, the PLAN also sent an uninvited *Dongdiao*-class auxiliary general intelligence ship that monitored U.S. and allied navy radar, sonar, and radio emissions and tactics during the exercise.[45] Military contacts also accelerated at the tactical level in 2015 as PLAN ships conducted port visits in Honolulu, Hawaii, San Diego, California, and Mayport, Florida, while twenty-seven officers from the U.S. Navy were afforded the opportunity to tour the PLAN aircraft carrier *Liaoning*, which had been purchased from Russia in 2002 as the ex-*Varyag*.[46]

RISING TENSIONS IN THE SOUTH CHINA SEA

Ironically, the deepening levels of U.S.-China military cooperation have also been accompanied by deepening levels of competition, particularly in the South China Sea. The 1990s witnessed a race by coastal states to stake out claims in the South China Sea and fortify them where possible.

That situation was temporarily stabilized by the Declaration on the Conduct of Parties in the South China Sea in 2002, whereby the Association of Southeast Asian Nations (ASEAN) and China agreed on a ten-point code that included affirming their commitment to the United Nations Convention on the Law of the Sea (UNCLOS), the peaceful resolution of disputes without resorting to the threat or use of force, and "self-restraint in the conduct of activities that would complicate or escalate disputes and affect peace and stability including, among others, refraining from action of inhabiting on the presently uninhabited islands, reefs, shoals, cays, and other features and to handle their differences in a constructive manner."[47]

The situation in the South China Sea remained relatively stable until 2009 when the deadline for submitting claims to the United Nations Commission on the Limits of the Continental Shelf (CLCS) arrived. The CLCS prompted the six claimant states (China, Taiwan, Vietnam, the Philippines, Malaysia, and Brunei) to file claims and counterclaims that significantly elevated tensions.[48] In a *note verbale* in response to Vietnam's CLCS filing, China reiterated its claim that "China has indisputable sovereignty over the islands in the South China Sea and the adjacent waters, and enjoys sovereign rights and jurisdiction over the relevant waters as well as the seabed and subsoil thereof (see attached map [of the nine-dash line])."[49]

China began acting aggressively to defend its claims in the South China Sea, including the dangerous harassment of the USNS *Impeccable* in international waters in 2009; the interdiction and expulsion of 147 foreign fishing boats from disputed waters in 2009; and the severing of towed cables of commercial seismic survey ships that were conducting hydrocarbon surveys within Vietnam's exclusive economic zone (EEZ) in 2011.[50] The *Global Times* captured the spirit of this more assertive Chinese behavior in a September 29, 2011, op-ed titled "Time to Teach Those Around the South China Sea a Lesson."[51] Tensions reached a new high between China and the Philippines in April 2012 over fishing rights at Scarborough Shoal, which is located 470 nautical miles from the coast of China but only 125 nautical miles from the mainland archipelago of the Philippines—well within the Philippines' two-hundred-nautical-mile EEZ.[52]

After the Philippines dispatched navy and coast guard ships to evict Chinese vessels that were unlawfully fishing within its EEZ, China responded by dispatching two Chinese marine surveillance ships (equivalent to coast guard ships) that interposed themselves between the Philippine ships and Chinese fishing vessels. A negotiated settlement to defuse the crisis was violated by the Chinese in July 2012, and China has maintained a continuous presence of marine surveillance vessels to scare off any non-Chinese fishing vessels ever since—in effect exercising de facto sovereignty through the use of force.[53]

On the heels of the Scarborough Shoal incident, the Philippines initiated arbitral proceedings in the Permanent Court of Arbitration (PCA) of the International Tribunal for the Law of the Sea (ITLOS) at The Hague in January 2013. The Philippines sought three distinct rulings in the case:

1. declaration that the parties' respective rights in the South China Sea are governed by UNCLOS and that China's claims based on "historic rights" with the nine-dash line are inconsistent with UNCLOS and therefore invalid
2. determination whether certain maritime features are characterized as islands, rocks, low tide elevations (LTEs), or submerged banks, which will subsequently clarify the maritime entitlements of those features and their impact on proximate features
3. declaration that China has violated UNCLOS by interfering with the exercise of the Philippines' rights and freedoms and through construction and fishing activities that have harmed the marine environment.[54]

In March 2014, tensions were further elevated when Chinese coast guard ships attempted to blockade the resupply of the Philippine marines stationed aboard the BRP *Sierra Madre* outpost on Second Thomas Shoal.[55] A Philippine supply vessel was ultimately able to sneak past the blockade, and the Filipinos also resorted to resupplying the marines on the outpost via air drops. Additionally, the Chinese response to the filing of the arbitration suit further inflamed tensions when a position paper issued in December 2014 reiterated the Chinese policy position of "three *no*s" regarding the Philippines' filing: nonacceptance of the filing, no participation in the proceedings, and no implementation of any findings.[56]

However, the most provocative and threatening Chinese actions in the South China Sea have been the execution of artificial island construction projects on the seven occupied maritime features (Cuarteron, Fiery Cross, Gaven, Hughes, Johnson, Mischief, and Subi Reefs) in the Spratlys beginning in 2014.[57] While other claimant states such as Malaysia, Vietnam, and the Philippines have undertaken island-expansion projects in the South China Sea, they were of a small scale (approximately 115 acres over 45 years) and did not include airfield and port infrastructure for basing military ships and aircraft.[58] In contrast, the Chinese have created more than 3,000 acres of land, which includes airfields capable of basing tactical military aircraft on Fiery Cross, Mischief, and Subi Reefs. Additionally, the Chinese have dredged the harbor and built a pier on Subi Reef that is suitable for the largest PLAN vessels to moor, which enables future naval basing options.[59]

During a news conference in Washington, D.C., in September 2015, Chinese president Xi Jinping stated, "Relevant construction activities that China is undertaking in the Nansha [Spratly] islands do not target or impact any country and China does not intend to pursue militarization."[60] However, the *Washington Post* revealed that China built radar and communications infrastructure on all seven features in the Spratlys, including a possible high-frequency radar on Cuarteron Reef that would extend its maritime surveillance capability deep into the South China Sea.[61] Additionally, the fact that China deployed J-11 fighter jets and two HQ-9 (derivative of Russian S-300) surface-to-air missile batteries on Woody Island in the Paracels as of January 2016 raises doubt that China will refrain from deploying missiles, aircraft, and ships to the newly reclaimed features in the Spratlys.[62]

On March 19, 2016, Reuters reported that the U.S. Navy had seen signs of Chinese maritime survey activity at Scarborough Shoal that could be a precursor to starting construction of another artificial island.[63] The case of Scarborough Shoal is unique in that no state has built any facilities on the exposed rocks, although the Chinese have exercised de facto maritime jurisdiction in the surrounding waters since 2012. This would be a game-changer in that the Chinese posture would transform from de facto maritime jurisdiction to physical occupation of a feature that lies only 125 nautical miles from the coast of the Philippines.

The election of President Rodrigo Duterte in the Philippines in May 2016 portended a strong shift away from the United States and toward China in Philippine foreign policy. While running as a candidate, Duterte said in March 2016, "I have a similar position as China's. I don't believe in solving the conflict through an international tribunal. China has said it will not abide by whatever that tribunal's decision will be. That's the same case with me, especially if the ruling will be against the Philippines."[64] The PCA issued a unanimous ruling on the Philippines' suit on July 12, 2016, finding that

1. there was no legal basis for China to claim historic rights to resources within the sea areas falling within the nine-dash line
2. none of the maritime features in the South China Sea meet the UNCLOS definition of an "island" and therefore do not generate EEZs that could infringe upon the two-hundred-nautical-mile EEZs of coastal states
3. China had violated the Philippines' sovereign rights in its exclusive economic zone by (a) interfering with Philippine fishing and petroleum exploration, (b) constructing artificial islands, and (c) failing to prevent Chinese fishermen from fishing in the zone
4. China had caused severe harm to the coral reef environment and violated its obligation to preserve and protect fragile ecosystems and the habitat of depleted, threatened, or endangered species
5. China's recent large-scale land reclamation and construction of artificial islands were incompatible with the obligations on a state during dispute resolution proceedings, insofar as China has inflicted irreparable harm to the marine environment, built a large artificial island in the Philippines' exclusive economic zone, and destroyed evidence of the natural condition of features in the South China Sea that formed part of the parties' dispute.[65]

The PCA ruling could not have been more favorable for both the Philippines and the broader principle of the rule of law; however, the Philippine, Chinese, and American responses completely undermined the ruling's effects. Philippine foreign minister Perfecto Yasay Jr. "welcomed the issuance" but then went on to remind Filipinos "to exercise restraint and sobriety."[66] Duterte further undermined the ruling in December 2016 when he stated at a news conference, "In the play of politics, now, I will set aside the arbitral ruling. I will not impose anything on China."[67] The Chinese foreign ministry released a statement saying that "China's territorial sovereignty and maritime rights and interests in the South China Sea shall under no circumstances be affected by those awards. China opposes and will never accept any claim or action based on those awards."[68] Additionally, China violated President Xi's pledge to not militarize the islands by building anti-aircraft radar and gun facilities on each of the seven maritime features.[69] Finally, the U.S. State Department released a statement saying that the United States "strongly supports the rule of law," "supports the peaceful resolution of disputes," "expresses its hope and expectation that both parties will comply with their obligations," and "urge[s] all claimants to avoid provocative statements or actions." This timid diplomatic statement by the Obama administration and subsequent lack of any tangible economic or military actions to support the ruling imposed no costs on China and ultimately legitimized its rejection of the tribunal process and its findings.

ASSESSING U.S. STRATEGY IN THE SOUTH CHINA SEA

The U.S. response to Chinese expansion in the Spratly Islands and its rejection of the findings of the PCA can be characterized by the word "restraint," and the results of that restraint have been mixed. On the heels of the Mischief Reef seizure in 1994, the U.S. State Department pronounced in 1995 that the United States

> strongly opposes the use or threat of force to resolve competing claims and urges all claimants to exercise restraint and to avoid destabilizing actions. . . . has an abiding interest in the maintenance of peace and stability in the South China Sea. . . . has a fundamental interest in maintaining freedom of navigation in the South China Sea. . . . takes no position on the legal merits of the competing claims to sovereignty over the various islands, reefs, atolls, and cays in the South China Sea; and . . . would view with serious concern any maritime claim or restriction on maritime activity in the South China Sea that was not consistent with international law, including the 1982 United Nations Convention on the Law of the Sea.[70]

The United States has maintained this policy for the past twenty years.[71]

Any assessment of U.S. policy and strategy in the South China Sea must begin with an understanding of the *ends*. In a speech in July 2015, a senior U.S. State Department official summarized U.S. objectives in the South China Sea as

- protecting unimpeded freedom of navigation and overflight and other lawful uses of the sea by all, not just the U.S. Navy
- honoring our alliance and security commitments and retaining the full confidence of our partners and the region in the United States
- aiding the development of effective regional institutions, including a unified ASEAN
- promoting responsible marine environmental practices

- fostering China's peaceful rise in a manner that promotes economic growth and regional stability, including through consistency with international law and standards
- more generally, an international order based on compliance with international law and the peaceful resolution of disputes without the threat or use of force.[72]

The U.S. record of achievement of those objectives has been mixed.

Freedom of Navigation and Overflight

Achievement of this objective has been mixed. While the Chinese have not restricted the freedom of navigation and overflight of commercial vessels and aircraft transiting the South China Sea, they have warned light civil aircraft transiting to and from the Philippine territory of Pagasa Island in the Spratlys.[73] Additional examples of how the Chinese have denied other claimant states their rights to the lawful use of international waters in the South China Sea have already been highlighted in this chapter.

The U.S. Navy has executed four maritime Freedom of Navigation Operations (FONOPs) and countless aerial missions in the South China Sea. In May 2015, a U.S. Navy P-8A Poseidon maritime patrol aircraft with a CNN television crew embarked was aggressively challenged eight times by "the Chinese Navy" to "go away" and "leave immediately to avoid misunderstanding" while conducting a surveillance mission in the vicinity of reclaimed features in the Spratlys but clearly from the sanctuary of international airspace outside of twelve nautical miles of any territorial claims.[74]

The first maritime FONOP in the vicinity of Subi Reef in the Spratlys on October 27, 2015, was heavily criticized for not being clear in its intent and prompted Senator John McCain to write a letter to Secretary of Defense Ashton Carter asking to clarify the purpose of the FONOP.[75] In his response issued fifty-six days after the operation, Carter clarified that this FONOP "challenged attempts by claimants to restrict navigation rights and freedoms around features they claim, including policies by some claimants requiring prior permission or notification of transits within territorial seas."[76] The second maritime FONOP was executed on January 30, 2016, in the vicinity of Triton Island within the Paracels and accompanied by a Department of Defense press release that clearly stated its intent: "This operation challenged attempts by the three claimants,

China, Taiwan, and Vietnam, to restrict navigation rights and freedoms around the features they claim by policies that require prior permission or notification of transit within territorial seas. The excessive claims regarding Triton Island are inconsistent with international law as reflected in the Law of the Sea Convention."[77] A third maritime FONOP was executed near Fiery Cross Reef on May 10, 2016.

In essence, all three of these FONOPS challenged the Chinese, Vietnamese, and Taiwanese demands for prior notification of entry of military ships into their EEZ and territorial waters, which is in contravention of UNCLOS. Julian Ku pointed out that the second FONOP in the vicinity of Triton Island received tacit support from Taiwan and Vietnam when each country released statements that did not condemn the United States for failing to provide prior notification, thereby isolating China as the only state to issue a condemnation.[78] A fourth maritime FONOP was executed on October 21, 2016, in the vicinity of Triton and Woody Islands within the Paracel Island group. In this FONOP, the USS *Decatur* executed a high seas freedom passage to challenge the straight baselines drawn by the Chinese in the Paracels. However, it is important to note that the *Decatur* did not pass within twelve nautical miles of those islands.[79]

Executing FONOPs to challenge prior notification requirements and excessive straight baselines does not address the root tensions in the South China Sea, which are the excessive Chinese maritime claims and the UNCLOS legal status of the seven reclaimed features and their associated maritime entitlements in the sea. Gregory Poling suggested that an innocent passage to challenge the prior notification requirement was "low-hanging fruit" and that executing a high seas transit regime within twelve nautical miles of a reclaimed feature that was formerly a low tide elevation—for example, Mischief Reef—would get at the heart of the matter, which is excessive Chinese maritime claims.[80]

The United States could increase the impact of FONOPs by modifying two current practices. The first is the "pre-announcement" of intent to conduct FONOPs; this has been done ostensibly to forewarn the Chinese and reduce the risk of escalation but has insidiously reduced the assertive effect of the freedom to "fly, sail and operate wherever international law allows," Secretary Carter had proclaimed in numerous public fora. The second is preserving some strategic ambiguity in its post-execution press releases. If the United States were to be ambiguous as to the purpose of the FONOP, the Chinese would have to guess which claims were being challenged and would be forced to clarify the nature of their claims.

Honoring Alliances and Security Commitments

The United States has succeeded in strengthening its alliances and partnerships in the South China Sea region. It has recently negotiated an Expanded Defense Cooperation Agreement with the Philippines that will enable further security cooperation assistance and basing rights, although the Duterte administration's position on this agreement is unclear.[81] The United States has also announced a Comprehensive Partnership with Vietnam (2013) and Malaysia (2014), a Joint Statement on Comprehensive Defense Cooperation Agreement with Indonesia, and an enhanced basing agreement with Singapore, and it has continued to sell arms to Taiwan in accordance with the provisions of the Taiwan Relations Act of 1979.

The United States has also succeeded in strengthening its relationships with regional institutions such as ASEAN, including hosting the annual U.S.-ASEAN summit in the United States for the first time in February 2016.

Promotion of Responsible Marine Environmental Practices

The United States has clearly failed to achieve this objective. The construction of the seven features in the Spratlys has been labeled "the quickest rate of permanent loss of coral reef area in human history," with a claim that "a substantial amount of this damage is irrecoverable and irreplaceable."[82] It will take some time for marine biologists to assess the damage to the regional marine ecosystem due to the loss of coral and shallow water habitat.

Compliance with International Law and the Peaceful Resolution of Disputes

The United States has also failed to bring Chinese behavior into accord with UNCLOS. The majority of legal scholars seem to have concluded that China's maritime claims do not conform to UNCLOS.[83] Additionally, the Chinese denial of claimant rights to the lawful use of the sea and their refusal to submit to arbitration of their territorial disputes are also in contravention of UNCLOS. Finally, while the Chinese have not used lethal military force in the enforcement of their claims, vessels from the China marine surveillance and China coast guard have used a variety of coercive, nonlethal techniques such as water cannons, shouldering, and ramming.[84] The ruling of the PCA presented the United States and regional allies and partners with an opportunity to strengthen the principle of adherence to the rule of international law, but the feckless response to enforce the outcomes of the ruling had the opposite effect in that it undermined the principle of adherence to the rule of international law.

U.S. POLICY AND STRATEGY OPTIONS FOR THE FUTURE

The United States has essentially three broad policy options for the South China Sea: continued concession to Chinese sovereignty claims and further expansion in the South China Sea in an effort to preserve Chinese cooperation on broader regional and global issues; freezing the status quo; or rolling back Chinese expansion and excessive sovereignty claims.

Option 1: Continued Concession

This policy option can be described as a continuance of the policy of the Obama administration, which argued that the South China Sea is not the central issue in the U.S.-Chinese relationship and that the benefits of curtailing Chinese expansion in the sea were not worth the costs of losing Chinese cooperation on other U.S. interests, including the Iran nuclear deal, the denuclearization of North Korea, global nuclear nonproliferation, climate change, cyber security and theft, intellectual property rights, fair trade, equitable monetary policy, and peaceful relations with Taiwan.[85] Advocates of this policy option also point out that the domestic credibility of Chinese president Xi Jinping and his Communist Party leaders has been strained as economic growth slows and the stock market plummets; therefore, provoking a confrontation in the South China Sea that sparks an ultra-nationalist outburst from China would not be prudent. From a military perspective, the militarization of the seven features in the South China Sea does not fundamentally alter China's anti-access/area denial strategy, because in the event of armed conflict between the United States and China, the islands are indefensible and could be neutralized quickly.[86]

The U.S. strategy for achieving this policy could consist of the following diplomatic and military *ways* and *means*. In the diplomatic arena, the United States could

- continue to warn against further militarization of the reclaimed features in the Spratlys
- make relatively weak diplomatic statements against the Chinese rejection of any results of the PCA
- encourage bilateral negotiations to resolve the disputes over maritime and sovereignty claims
- continue to invest in multilateral institutions and relationships—and include China in their design
- emphasize the benefits of continued Chinese cooperation on broader issues in the U.S.-China relationship.

In the military sphere, the United States could

- continue maritime and aerial FONOPs that challenge the requirement for prior notification of entry into territorial seas and EEZs, but not challenge excessive Chinese maritime claims. Take no risk of actual confrontation; back off if it appears that the Chinese are willing to risk escalation
- continue to execute multilateral security cooperation exercises and encourage Chinese participation (for example, invite the Chinese to RIMPAC 2018)
- continue to provide security cooperation assistance to treaty allies to maintain the status quo.

The downside of this policy option is that it will continue to deliver mixed results on the U.S. stated policy objectives for the South China Sea. It will also continue to weaken the time-honored U.S. principle of adherence to the rule of law. Any bilateral negotiations will start with the Chinese in a position of strength and will only reinforce the realist notion that "might makes right" in international relations. They will not compel China to curtail its claims and activities that are in contravention of UNCLOS. Additionally, bilateral negotiations would not reassure jittery allies and partners in the region that their interests are protected against further Chinese expansion. Claimant states will be left to ponder, "Where next?" Dredging sand and coral to stake out a claim and militarize Scarborough Shoal? Seizing Second Thomas Shoal from the squad of Philippine marines guarding the claim? Evicting the Taiwanese from Itu Aba? Annexing and beginning artificial island construction activities on Malaysia's Swallow Reef or James Shoal to extend China's operational reach farther south? While the notion of each of those Chinese actions may seem far-fetched, nobody anticipated in 2012 that the Chinese would execute a massive artificial island construction operation that would generate more than three thousand square kilometers in the Spratlys by the end of 2015.

Option 2: Freezing the Status Quo

This policy option is best described as an "all stop" order that could colloquially be described as "possession is nine-tenths of the law," or "if you occupy it today, you own it." This option acknowledges that the Chinese have presented the region with a fait accompli for the seven reclaimed features in the Spratlys and that the best-case outcome is to freeze it through balancing.

Under this policy, for example, China would retain possession of the seven features it has reclaimed in the Spratlys and all of the Paracels; the Philippines would be granted sovereignty over Pagasa, Lawak, Parola, Likas, and Patag Reefs; Taiwan would be granted sovereignty over Itu Aba; and Vietnam would be granted Great Discovery, London, Pearson, and Pigeon Reefs.[87] This policy would accept the transgressions of the past but would attempt, with a show of credible military power, to strengthen and preserve the rules-based order going forward. The diplomatic elements of achieving this policy could include

- continuing to warn against further militarization of any features in the South China Sea
- emphasizing the "win-win" nature of this policy in that all claimant states retain their current possessions
- threatening to curtail cooperation on regional issues and impose economic sanctions in the event of any Chinese attempts to change the status quo
- declaring unequivocally that any Philippine military personnel are covered under Article V of the Philippines Mutual Defense Treaty, including personnel stationed on any feature in the South China Sea.[88]

Military elements of the strategy would include

- continuing maritime and aerial FONOPs that challenge the requirement for prior notification and assert freedom of navigation outside of twelve nautical miles of any maritime feature that is deemed to be an island or a rock under UNCLOS
- encouraging multilateral nonclaimant state participation in FONOPs, including the Japanese, South Koreans, and Australians, to emphasize regional commitment to stability and the peaceful resolution of disputes
- threatening to curtail Chinese participation in multilateral security cooperation exercises in the event of any further Chinese expansion
- increasing security cooperation assistance to treaty allies and partner claimant states, particularly to their naval and coast guard forces through foreign military sales and training
- discouraging all claimant states from deploying military forces on any maritime feature
- defending against any attacks or aggression by the Chinese with gradual escalation of the use of force.

The downside of this policy option is that it would be difficult to execute without triggering another frenzy of artificial island construction and occupation prior to its implementation date. It would require negotiation between China and other claimant states, and China has demonstrated a propensity to use prolonged negotiations as a cover for achieving its desired policy objectives while the negotiations are taking place. This option also leaves open the question of those features that are disputed but not occupied, such as Scarborough Shoal. Even if successfully implemented, as Greg Poling opined, "The status quo is now inherently unstable. A new round of escalation is always just over the horizon."[89]

Option 3: Rolling Back

U.S. secretary of state Rex Tillerson publicly hinted at this policy option during his confirmation hearing in January 2017 when he stated, "We're going to have to send China a clear signal that, first, the island-building stops. And second, your access to those islands also is not going to be allowed."[90] Chinese state-run media predictably howled with indignation; for example, the *Global Times* editorialized, "Unless Washington plans to wage a large-scale war in the South China Sea, any other approaches to prevent Chinese access to the islands will be foolish." However, numerous observers have subsequently outlined policy options to roll back excessive Chinese claims without resorting to the use of military force. James Kraska invoked President Ronald Reagan's 1983 "Oceans Policy," which stated, "In this respect, the United States will recognize the rights of other states in the waters off their coasts, as reflected in UNCLOS, so long as the rights and freedoms of the United States and others are recognized by such coastal states."[91] In other words, the United States would withdraw recognition of China's lawful rights under UNCLOS as a lawful countermeasure until China came into compliance with its obligations under UNCLOS. Alexander Vuving suggested targeted economic sanctions against state-owned Chinese companies that support the reclaimed features in the Spratlys, such as China Southern and Hainan airlines, which provide commercial air transport; China Mobile, China Telecom, and China United Telecom, which provide communications services; or the China Communications Construction Company, which performed the dredging of the islands.[92]

In reality, there is a broad range of statecraft options that could roll back excessive Chinese maritime claims and prevent further territorial expansion with acceptable levels of risk. Since the PCA ruled that the nine-dash-line claim is void, the United States and other regional partners could exercise the full range of high seas freedoms in waters that lie beyond twelve nautical miles from any feature and outside of the two-hundred-nautical-mile EEZ of any of the coastal states, including military operations, fishing, and seabed exploration. Additionally, the United States and other regional partners could conduct high seas freedoms within twelve nautical miles of those features that the PCA ruled as LTEs.

The diplomatic elements of a strategy for achieving this policy could include:

- affirming the PCA's jurisdiction and the obligations of all parties to implement its rulings
- building international diplomatic consensus to compel China into accepting the implementation of the PCA rulings
- curtailing cooperation with China on regional issues
- continuing to denounce the militarization of any maritime features in the South China Sea
- making the case that Scarborough Shoal is "different" and making it clear that the United States will not accept Chinese construction of an artificial island on the shoal
- acknowledging the fact that this option will induce "moderate friction" in the broader U.S.-China relationship.[93]

Military elements to support the strategy would include:

- executing maritime and aerial FONOPs that affirm the PCA rulings, including high seas transit within twelve nautical miles of any maritime feature that was ruled to be an LTE, regardless of sovereignty claims
- encouraging multilateral participation in FONOPs, including by the Japanese, South Koreans, and Australians
- terminating Chinese participation in multilateral security cooperation exercises, including RIMPAC 2018
- utilizing U.S. and regional coast guard vessels to guarantee the free exercise of Philippine "historic fishing rights" at Scarborough Shoal in accordance with the PCA ruling
- increasing security cooperation assistance to treaty allies and claimant state partners, particularly by bolstering their naval and coast guard forces with foreign military sales and training.

In the economic realm, targeted economic sanctions could be imposed on companies and personnel that support Chinese operations in contravention of the PCA ruling.

The downside of this policy option is that it would elevate the strategic risk in the U.S.-Chinese relationship; the Chinese have invested significant resources and national pride in reclaiming those seven features. The United States and its allies and partners would have to closely monitor Chinese reactions to each of the ways and means listed above to avoid sparking a broader conflict. However, failing to fully implement the rulings of the PCA will undermine the credibility of ITLOS and UNCLOS and of the broader principle of applying international law to peacefully resolve disputes.

SUMMARY

The Chinese campaign to construct seven artificial islands in the Spratly Island chain in the South China Sea has inexorably changed "the facts on the ground" in the region in the span of just three years. The PCA ruling negated the excessive Chinese maritime claims in the South China Sea, including those claims derived from the newly reclaimed islands. The United States and its regional allies and partners will face a series of difficult policy and strategy choices in the face of the Chinese refusal to implement the arbitral rulings. While the Donald Trump administration has not issued any clear statements of South China Sea policy to date, which of the three broad policy options the administration chooses (continued concession, status quo, or roll back) will become apparent by key observables in its behavior.

The key observables in the U.S. diplomatic realm will be the degree of inclusion or isolation of China in regional institutions and consultations and the threat of using military and nonmilitary tools of statecraft (such as economic sanctions) to attempt to compel the Chinese to adhere to international law and the principle of the peaceful resolution of disputes. The key observables in the military realm will be the continued inclusion of China in multilateral security exercises such as RIMPAC, and whether or not U.S. and allied military operations challenge excessive Chinese maritime claims such as the twelve-nautical-mile territorial sea claims around maritime features that were formerly LTEs.

These three policy options have been presented in order of ascending strategic risk of conflict with China, and also of ascending degree of compliance with the principle of adherence to international law. The Trump administration will have to decide how much risk it is willing to accept in the South China Sea to achieve broader regional and global U.S. strategic interests, which include not only its relationship with China but also the foundational principle of adherence to the rule of law upon which the post–World War II international system is built.

Notes

1. For example, see William A. Callahan, "National Insecurities: Humiliation, Salvation, and Chinese Nationalism," *Alternatives* 29, no. 2 (2004): pp. 199–218.
2. Mackubin Thomas Owens, "Strategy and the Strategic Way of Thinking," *Naval War College Review* 60, no. 4 (Autumn 2007), https://www.usnwc.edu/getattachment/d73f1c33-649a-41e4-93e5-28ce624fd041/Strategy-and-the-Strategic-Way-of-Thinking--Commen.aspx.
3. Jonathan D. Spence, *The Search for Modern China* (New York: W. W. Norton and Company, 1999), 446, 453.
4. "Who Lost China?" *Washington Post,* May 4, 1950, p. 10.
5. Robert L. Beisner, *Dean Acheson: A Life in the Cold War* (New York: Oxford University Press, 2006), 173–205.
6. Justin Logan, "Optimists (Liberal Doves) vs. Pessimists (Conservative Hawks) on China," *USA Today Magazine* 141, issue 2816 (May 2013): pp. 32–34.
7. H. Y. Chen, "Territorial Disputes in the South China Sea Under the San Francisco Peace Treaty," *Issues and Studies* 50, no. 3 (2014): pp. 174–75.
8. Kevin Baumert and Brian Melchior, "China: Maritime Claims in the South China Sea," *Limits in the Seas* no. 143 (Washington, D.C.: Department of State, December 5, 2014), 3, http://www.state.gov/documents/organization/234936.pdf.
9. Wooseon Choi, "Structural Realism and Dulles's China Policy," *Review of International Studies* 38, no. 1 (2012): pp. 119–40.
10. Michael M. Sheng, "Mao and China's Relations with the Superpowers in the 1950s: A New Look at the Taiwan Strait Crises and the Sino-Soviet Split," *Modern China* 34, no. 4 (2008): pp. 477–507.
11. Chen, "Territorial Disputes in the South China Sea," 175.
12. Ibid.
13. Baumert and Melchior, "China: Maritime Claims in the South China Sea," 3.
14. M. Taylor Fravel, "China's Strategy in the South China Sea," *Contemporary Southeast Asia* 33, no. 3 (2011): p. 297.
15. Spence, *The Search for Modern China,* 580, 584.
16. U.S. Senate Foreign Relations Committee and Congressional Research Service, *The Implications of U.S. China Military Cooperation: A Workshop* (Washington, D.C.: U.S. Government Printing Office, 1982), VII.
17. Kerry B. Dumbaugh and Richard F. Grimmet, *U.S. Arms Sales to China* (Washington, D.C.: Congressional Research Service, July 8, 1985), 41–43.
18. Ibid.
19. Ngo Minh Tri and Koh Swee Lean Collin, "Lessons from the Battle of the Paracel Islands," *The Diplomat,* January 23, 2014, http://thediplomat.com/2014/01/lessons-from-the-battle-of-the-paracel-islands.
20. Andrew C. A. Jampoler, "The Politics of Port Visits," U.S. Naval Institute *Proceedings* (August 2004): pp. 66–69.
21. John W. Garver, "China's Push Through the South China Sea: The Interaction of Bureaucratic and National Interests," *China Quarterly,* no. 132 (December 1992): pp. 1020–24.
22. Fravel, "China's Strategy in the South China Sea," 298.

23. Andrew S. Erickson, "America's Security Role in the South China Sea," *Naval War College Review* 69, no. 1 (Winter 2016): p. 8.
24. Guangqiu Xu, "Anti-Western Nationalism in China," *World Affairs* 163, no. 4 (Spring 2001): p. 160.
25. Charles Krauthammer, "Why We Must Contain China," *Time*, July 31, 1995, http://content.time.com/time/magazine/article/0,9171,983245,00.html.
26. Rajan Menon, "The Strategic Convergence Between Russia and China," *Survival* 39, no. 2 (1997): pp. 101–25.
27. Dallas Boyd et al., *Advanced Technology Acquisition Strategies of the People's Republic of China* (Fort Belvoir, Va.: Defense Threat Reduction Agency, September 2010), 33–40, https://fas.org/irp/agency/dod/dtra/strategies.pdf.
28. "China's Cyber-Theft Jet Fighter," *Wall Street Journal*, November 12, 2014.
29. Kurt Campbell and Richard Weitz, "The Limits of U.S.-China Military Cooperation: Lessons from 1995–1999," *Washington Quarterly* 29, no. 1 (2005): p. 181.
30. George Galdorisi and George Capen, "Military Contact Is Lynchpin in Sino-U.S. Relations," U.S. Naval Institute *Proceedings* 127/9/1 (September 2001): pp. 70–72.
31. Nicholas Lardy, "Issues in China's WTO Accession," May 9, 2001, https://www.brookings.edu/testimonies/issues-in-chinas-wto-accession/.
32. Fravel, "China's Strategy in the South China Sea," 298.
33. Gregory B. Poling, "Rationalizing U.S. Goals in the South China Sea," *Journal of Political Risk* 3, no. 9 (September 2015), https://www.jpolrisk.com/rationalizing-u-s-goals-in-the-south-china-sea.
34. The word "coopetition" is used in the literal portmanteau sense as the state of simultaneously cooperating while also competing, not in the classic game theory sense where participants cooperatively compete to improve the outcome for all participants.
35. U.S. Department of Defense, *Quadrennial Defense Review 2001* (Washington, D.C.: Department of Defense, 2001), 4, http://archive.defense.gov/pubs/qdr2001.pdf.
36. Campbell and Weitz, "The Limits of U.S.-China Military Cooperation," 170.
37. U.S. Department of Defense, *Quadrennial Defense Review 2006* (Washington, D.C.: Department of Defense, February 2006), 29, http://archive.defense.gov/pubs/pdfs/QDR20060203.pdf.
38. Robert Zoellick, "Whither China? From Membership to Responsibility," remarks to National Committee on U.S.-China Relations, September 21, 2005, https://www.ncuscr.org/sites/default/files/migration/Zoellick_remarks_notes06_winter_spring.pdf.
39. Dong Wang and Chengzhi Yin, "Mainland China Debates U.S. Pivot/Rebalancing to Asia," *Issues and Studies* 50, no. 3 (September 2014): pp. 58–60.
40. U.S. Department of Defense, "Quadrennial Defense Review Report," February 2010, 29, 31, http://www.defense.gov/Portals/1/features/defenseReviews/QDR/QDR_as_of_29JAN10_1600.pdf.
41. Department of Defense, "Sustaining U.S. Global Leadership: Priorities for 21st Century Defense," January 2012, 2, http://archive.defense.gov/news/Defense_Strategic_Guidance.pdf.
42. Mark E. Manyin et al., *Pivot to the Pacific? The Obama Administration's "Rebalancing" Toward Asia* (Washington, D.C.: Congressional Research Service, March 28, 2012), 1.

43. Wang and Yin, "Mainland China Debates U.S. Pivot," 75.
44. Leon Panetta, speech, September 19, 2012, http://archive.defense.gov/transcripts/transcript.aspx?transcriptid=5117.
45. Sam LaGrone, "China Sends Uninvited Spy Ship to RIMPAC," USNI News, July 18, 2014, http://news.usni.org/2014/07/18/china-sends-uninvited-spy-ship-rimpac.
46. Christopher Bodeen, "Senior U.S. Navy Officers Visit Chinese Aircraft Carrier," *Navy Times*, October 21, 2015, http://www.navytimes.com/story/military/2015/10/21/senior-us-navy-officers-visit-chinese-aircraft-carrier/74318652.
47. "2002 Declaration on the Conduct of Parties in the South China Sea," November 4, 2002, http://cil.nus.edu.sg/rp/pdf/2002%20Declaration%20on%20the%20Conduct%20of%20Parties%20in%20the%20South%20China%20Sea-pdf.pdf.
48. Fravel, "China's Strategy in the South China Sea," 300.
49. "Note Verbale of the People's Republic of China," May 7, 2009, http://www.un.org/depts/los/clcs_new/submissions_files/vnm37_09/chn_2009re_vnm.pdf. (Author note: The attached map was the nine-dash line map.)
50. Fravel, "China's Strategy in the South China Sea," 305, 306, 313.
51. S. S. Kao, "Scarborough Shoal Dispute, China's Assertiveness, and Taiwan's South China Sea Policy," *International Journal of China Studies* 5, no. 1 (2014): pp. 153–54.
52. Ibid., 158.
53. Jane Perlez and Keith Bradsher, "In High Seas, China Moves Unilaterally," *New York Times*, May 9, 2014, http://www.nytimes.com/2014/05/10/world/asia/in-high-seas-china-moves-unilaterally.html?_r=0/.
54. Permanent Court of Arbitration, "Arbitration Between the Republic of The Philippines and the People's Republic of China," press release, October 29, 2015, http://www.pcacases.com/web/sendAttach/1503.
55. Erik De Castro and Roli Ng, "Philippine Ship Dodges China Blockade to Reach South China Sea Outpost," Reuters, March 31, 2014, http://www.reuters.com/article/us-philippines-china-reef-idUSBREA2U02720140331.
56. "Position Paper of the Government of the People's Republic of China on the Matter of Jurisdiction in the South China Sea Arbitration Initiated by the Republic of the Philippines," December 7, 2014, http://www.fmprc.gov.cn/mfa_eng/zxxx_662805/t1217147.shtml.
57. The Asia Maritime Transparency Initiative (AMTI) at the Center for Strategic and International Studies maintains an up-to-date "island tracker" at this site: http://amti.csis.org/island-tracker.
58. Harry B. Harris Jr., "Statement Before the Senate Armed Services Committee on U.S. Pacific Command Posture," February 23, 2016, http://www.armed-services.senate.gov/imo/media/doc/Harris_02-23-16.pdf.
59. AMTI island tracker.
60. Jeremy Page et al., "China's President Pledges No Militarization in Disputed Islands," *Wall Street Journal*, September 25, 2015, http://www.wsj.com/articles/china-completes-runway-on-artificial-island-in-south-china-sea-1443184818.
61. Simon Denyer, "Satellite Images Show China May Be Building Powerful Radar on Disputed Islands," *Washington Post*, February 22, 2016, https://www.washingtonpost.com/news/worldviews/wp/2016/02/22/satellite-images-show-china-may-be-building-powerful-radar-on-disputed-islands.

62. "China's Missile Offense," *Wall Street Journal*, February 19, 2016, http://www.wsj.com/articles/chinas-missile-offense-1455824757.
63. David Brunnstrom and Andrea Shalal, "Exclusive: U.S. Sees New Chinese Activity around South China Sea Shoal," Reuters, March 19, 2016, http://www.reuters.com/article/us-southchinasea-china-scarborough-exclu-idUSKCN0WK01B.
64. Raissa Robles, "Dear Mayor Duterte, Pls Disclose What You Told Chinese Officials," May 8, 2016, ABS-CBN News, http://news.abs-cbn.com/blogs/opinions/05/08/16/opinion-dear-mayor-duterte-pls-disclose-what-you-told-chinese-officials.
65. Permanent Court of Arbitration, "The South China Sea Arbitration: The Republic of the Philippines v. the People's Republic of China," press release, July 12, 2016, https://pca-cpa.org/wp-content/uploads/sites/175/2016/07/PH-CN-20160712-Press-Release-No-11-English.pdf.
66. Kristine Angeli Sabillo, "PH Welcomes 'Milestone Decision' on West Philippine Sea," Inquirer.net, July 12, 2016, http://globalnation.inquirer.net/140963/ph-welcomes-milestone-decision-on-west-philippine-sea-calls-for-restraint-sobriety.
67. Associated Press, "Philippines to 'Set Aside' South China Sea Ruling to Avoid Imposing on Beijing," *The Guardian*, December 17, 2016, https://www.theguardian.com/world/2016/dec/17/philippines-to-set-aside-south-china-sea-tribunal-ruling-to-avoid-imposing-on-beijing.
68. "Statement of the Ministry of Foreign Affairs of the People's Republic of China on the Award of 12 July 2016 of the Arbitral Tribunal in the South China Sea Arbitration Established at the Request of the Republic of the Philippines," July 12, 2016, http://news.xinhuanet.com/english/2016–07/12/c_135507744.htm.
69. Asia Maritime Transparency Initiative, "China's New Spratly Island Defenses," December 13, 2016, http://www.npr.org/sections/thetwo-way/2016/12/15/505721549/in-south-china-sea-islands-anti-aircraft-and-radar-systems-emerge-in-full-color.
70. Daily Press Briefing, U.S. Department of State, May 10, 1995, http://dosfan.lib.uic.edu/ERC/briefing/daily_briefings/1995/9505/950510db.html.
71. M. Taylor Fravel, "U.S. Policy Toward the Disputes in the South China Sea Since 1995," March 2014, http://taylorfravel.com/documents/research/fravel.2014.RSIS.us.policy.scs.pdf.
72. Daniel R. Russel, "Remarks at the Fifth Annual South China Sea Conference," Washington, D.C., July 21, 2015, http://www.state.gov/p/eap/rls/rm/2015/07/245142.htm.
73. Jim Gomez, "Philippine Plane Warned by 'Chinese Navy' in Disputed Sea," Associated Press, January 18, 2016, http://bigstory.ap.org/article/f3d87ed0feaa42ad97d188ad39c2716c/philippine-plane-warned-chinese-navy-disputed-sea.
74. Jim Sciutto, "Behind the Scenes: A Secret Navy Flight Over China's Military Buildup," CNN, May 26, 2015, http://www.cnn.com/2015/05/26/politics/south-china-sea-navy-surveillance-plane-jim-sciutto/.
75. Ankit Panda, "Everything You Wanted to Know About the USS *Lassen*'s FONOP in the South China Sea," *The Diplomat*, January 6, 2016, http://thediplomat.com/2016/01/everything-you-wanted-to-know-about-the-uss-lassens-fonop-in-the-south-china-sea/.
76. Ibid.

77. Julian Ku, "Isolating China: Why the Latest U.S. Freedom of Navigation Operation May Have Already Succeeded," Lawfareblog.com, February 1, 2016, https://www.lawfareblog.com/isolating-china-why-latest-us-freedom-navigation-operation-may-have-already-succeeded.
78. Ibid.
79. Julian Ku, "U.S. Defense Department Confirms USS *Decatur* Did Not Follow Innocent Passage and Challenged China's Excessive Straight Baselines," Lawfareblog.com, November 4, 2016, https://www.lawfareblog.com/us-defense-department-confirms-uss-decatur-did-not-follow-innocent-passage-and-challenged-chinas.
80. Gregory Poling, "South China Sea FONOP 2.0: A Step in the Right Direction," Asia Maritime Transparency Initiative, February 2, 2016, http://amti.csis.org/south-china-sea-fonop-2-0-a-step-in-the-right-direction/.
81. U.S. Department of State, "2016 Joint Statement of the United States-Philippines Ministerial Dialogue," January 12, 2016, http://www.state.gov/r/pa/prs/ps/2016/01/251503.htm.
82. Oliver Holmes, "South China Sea Images Reveal Impact on Coral of Beijing's Military Bases," *The Guardian*, September 17, 2015, http://www.theguardian.com/world/ng-interactive/2015/sep/17/south-china-sea-images-reveal-impact-on-coral-of-beijings-military-bases.
83. For example, see Robert Beckman, "The UN Convention on the Law of the Sea and the Maritime Disputes in the South China Sea," *American Journal of International Law* 107, no. 1 (January 2013): p. 161.
84. Vijay Sakhuja, "China's Big South China Sea Gamble," *National Interest*, July 8, 2015, http://nationalinterest.org/blog/the-buzz/chinas-big-south-china-sea-gamble-13283.
85. For example, see Michael McDevitt, *The South China Sea: Assessing U.S. Policy and Options for the Future* (Arlington, Va.: Center for Naval Analyses, November 2014), vi.
86. Poling, "Rationalizing U.S. Goals in the South China Sea."
87. Source of current status of occupation: Mark E. Rosen, *Philippine Claims in the South China Sea: A Legal Analysis* (Arlington, Va.: Center for Naval Analyses, August 2014), https://www.cna.org/CNA_files/PDF/IOP-2014-U-008435.pdf.
88. Poling, "Rationalizing U.S. Goals in the South China Sea."
89. Ibid.
90. Michael Forsythe, "Rex Tillerson's South China Sea Remarks Foreshadow Foreign Policy Crisis," *New York Times*, January 12, 2017, https://www.nytimes.com/2017/01/12/world/asia/rex-tillerson-south-china-sea-us.html.
91. James Kraska, "Tillerson Channels Reagan on the South China Sea," Lawfareblog.com, January 12, 2017, https://lawfareblog.com/tillerson-channels-reagan-south-china-sea.
92. Alexander Vuving, "How America Can Take Control in the South China Sea," *Foreign Policy*, February 13, 2017, http://foreignpolicy.com/2017/02/13/how-the-u-s-can-take-control-in-the-south-china-sea/.
93. Erickson, "America's Security Role in the South China Sea," 13.

6

U.S. Rebalancing Strategy and Disputes in the South China Sea

A Legacy for America's Pacific Century

Tongfi Kim

During his visit to Japan in November 2009, U.S. president Barack Obama declared that he, as "America's first Pacific President," would ensure that the United States strengthened its leadership in the Asia-Pacific region.[1] The region has been important to the United States since at least the late nineteenth century, but the Obama administration's new emphasis was arguably a shift in U.S. grand strategy.[2] As Secretary of State Hillary Clinton put it in her influential article in 2011, the Obama administration's pivot or rebalancing strategy aimed to "lock in a substantially increased investment—diplomatic, economic, strategic, and otherwise—in the Asia-Pacific region."[3]

Although there is significant uncertainty over the direction of U.S. foreign policy under President Donald Trump, the rebalancing strategy remains important as a reference point to future U.S. strategy in the Asia-Pacific.[4] This chapter first analyzes the background to the U.S. strategy. It then explains how diplomatic, economic, and military dimensions of the strategy are related to the disputes in the South China Sea, with a special focus on the People's Republic of China (hereafter referred to as China). The subsequent sections describe the responses of the territorial disputants and other regional states. I argue that China's economic allure is shaping U.S. and other states' policies toward the South China Sea disputes, that the United States has had moderate success without provoking China too much, and that geography and U.S. naval dominance influence the regional states' responses to the American strategy. The conclusion briefly discusses the implications of this chapter's findings.

BACKGROUND TO THE REBALANCING/PIVOT

From a long-term perspective, the rising economic power of Asia-Pacific states has necessitated U.S. engagement in the region for economic and geopolitical reasons. For commercial interests alone, the United States cannot neglect the region's large population (Asia accounts for about 60 percent of the global total) and fast economic growth.[5] Moreover, because the new wealth translates into military capabilities and geopolitical influence (as in the case of China), the United States has politico-strategic reasons to prioritize the region. Granted, Asia was an important battleground during the Cold War, and the United States in the early post–Cold War era also strived to prevent the emergence of a superpower in the region.[6] However, by the time President Obama took office in 2009, Asia's strategic importance had further grown relative to other regions—not least due to the rise of China.

China's economic importance to the United States and the global economy—in addition to its role in diverse issues such as climate change and nuclear nonproliferation—means that Washington needs to maintain and improve its ties with Beijing while also competing with it as a rival. At the first meeting of the U.S.-China Strategic and Economic Dialogue in 2009, Obama stated that the "relationship between the United States and China will shape the twenty-first century, which makes it as important as any bilateral relationship in the world."[7]

China overtook Japan as the second-largest economy in the world in 2010, but China presents a different challenge than did Japan in the past. Beijing's views on democracy and the current international order are significantly different from those of Washington, and China does not acquiesce to U.S. primacy. Through its economic power, China is competing with the United States for influence across the globe, and the competition is most intense in the Asia-Pacific. China replaced the United States as the largest trading partner (in goods) of the Association of Southeast Asian Nations (ASEAN) countries in 2007, and China's goods trade with ASEAN countries in 2014 was more than double that of the United States.[8]

The region provides the United States with various options to counter the strategic weight of China, but these options need reinforcement and cultivation. The United States has treaty alliances with Australia, Japan, the Philippines, South Korea, and Thailand, and it also has friendly relationships with other emerging powers such as India and Indonesia. These regional states might have their own reasons to balance against the rise of China, but to many Americans, it does not seem prudent to count on such balancing. Aaron Friedberg, for example, advocates stronger U.S. military commitment in Asia for the following reason:

"Without active cooperation from its regional partners, Washington cannot hope in the long run to balance against a rising China. On the other hand, without strong tokens of its continuing commitment and resolve, America's friends may grow fearful of abandonment, perhaps eventually losing heart and succumbing to the temptations of appeasement."[9] Thus, at least in part, the U.S. rebalancing strategy can be seen as a long-term adjustment of the U.S. grand strategy in response to the growing importance of cooperation and competition in the Asia-Pacific.

From a shorter-term perspective, there were two specific reasons for the Obama administration's Asia-Pacific foreign policy: the wars in Afghanistan and Iraq and the global financial crisis of 2007–9.[10] Despite the increasing importance of the Asia-Pacific, the foreign policy resources of the George W. Bush administration (2001–9) were focused on the wars in Afghanistan and Iraq. For example, Asian leaders saw a wavering of U.S. commitment to the region in Secretary of State Condoleezza Rice's (2005–9) absence at the annual ministerial gatherings of the ASEAN Regional Forum in 2005 and 2007. As the wars became less popular in the United States, a renewed emphasis on the Asia-Pacific made political sense for the Obama administration.[11] Michael Green and Dan Twining, for example, suspect that the pivot strategy was "a convenient political frame for the White House to try to explain that the Obama administration remains muscular and strategic, despite its accelerated retreat from Iraq and Afghanistan."[12]

In terms of military resources, the winding down of the two wars was a precondition for the rebalancing toward Asia; Noboru Yamaguchi argues that the strategy was "fundamentally a demobilization from a wartime posture rather than a mere geographic change in U.S. policy priorities."[13] As supporters of the strategy in the region complained, measures to strengthen the military dimension of the rebalancing strategy were rather modest. Although the limited nature of the military measures was partially attributable to U.S. policymakers' desire to avoid provoking China, it is essential to take into account the domestic aftereffect of the two wars. Thus, pivoting "away" from Afghanistan and Iraq may have been more important than pivoting "toward" the Asia-Pacific.

The Obama administration's strategy was also significantly affected by the global financial crisis of 2007–9. The crisis increased the importance of economic engagement in the Asia-Pacific and imposed constraints on the U.S. military budget, which was already strained by the costly wars in Afghanistan and Iraq.[14] In response to the global economic downturn, the Obama administration introduced the National Export Initiative in 2010, for which Asian nations were major targets.[15] The Trans-Pacific Partnership (TPP) was a central piece of the rebalancing strategy. There was a competitive element in the TPP, especially over the long term; as President Obama declared, the United States "can't let countries like China write the rules of the global economy."[16] But the urgency of economic recovery from the financial crisis was no less important to the Obama administration's economic foreign policy.

In the face of budget constraints after the financial crisis, the U.S. government was forced to cut its military spending; the rebalancing strategy therefore aimed to preserve military resources in the Asia-Pacific by shifting priorities. Perhaps the most prominent among the military components of the strategy is the planned reinforcement of naval capabilities in the Asia-Pacific region. At the annual Shangri-La Dialogue in June 2012, U.S. defense secretary Leon Panetta declared that the U.S. Navy would redeploy its forces from its current 50/50 percent split between the Pacific and the Atlantic to a 60/40 percent split.[17] As the financial crisis and subsequent budget cuts cast doubt on U.S. staying power in the Asia-Pacific (and China appeared to be triumphant in the wake of the global crisis), such rebalancing of priorities was important to the military credibility of the United States.

U.S. policymakers have repeatedly emphasized that the rebalancing strategy was not targeted against China and that rebalancing was not just about military objectives. Asia-Pacific states, however, were most interested in the strategy's implications for Sino-American relations and U.S. military presence in the region. Many states in the region seek to benefit economically from China's rise, but they are also anxious to keep the United States in regional affairs as a counterweight to the increasing power of China. As will be explained in the following sections, maritime and territorial disputes in the South China Sea have intensified the competitive aspects of U.S. strategy.

COMPONENTS OF THE U.S. REBALANCING STRATEGY
The South China Sea Disputes
Disputes in the South China Sea involve multiple states over multiple issues. China, the Philippines, Vietnam, Malaysia, Brunei, and the Republic of China (hereafter referred to as Taiwan) have conflicting claims over various islands and maritime features in the South China Sea. Because China's vague maritime claim based on the "U-shaped line" includes much of the South China Sea, it also worries countries such as Indonesia, which is not part of the current territorial disputes.

In addition to having interests in these disputes as a third party, the United States has an important disagreement with China in the South China Sea over China's rights to regulate foreign military activities within its exclusive economic zone (EEZ).[18] In March 2009, for instance, five Chinese ships obstructed the U.S. survey ship USNS *Impeccable* in China's EEZ in the South China Sea.[19]

Maritime and territorial disputes in the South China Sea have a decades-old history, but tensions in these waters have intensified in the last several years due to China's increased presence. Even Alastair Iain Johnston, who criticizes the discourse of China's "new assertiveness," acknowledges that China has become more assertive in these waters since around 2010.[20] Although Southeast Asian states have conflicting claims among themselves as well, international attention has been mostly drawn to China's disputes with those nations and the United States because of China's growing power and increasing maritime presence.[21]

In addition to increasing the activities of its maritime agencies in the waters, China has executed highly visible actions that challenged the status quo.[22] For example, after months of standoff with the Philippines, China extended its control over Scarborough Shoal in 2012 by reneging on a U.S.-negotiated agreement.[23] In 2014, China moved an oil platform to waters near the Paracel Islands, which are claimed by China, Taiwan, and Vietnam, triggering large anti-China protests and riots in Vietnam. Since September 2013, China has also been engaging in massive island-building and construction of military facilities in the disputed Spratly islands.[24] Although other disputants have also engaged in similar activities in the past, the much larger scale and faster pace of the Chinese endeavor have alarmed many states.[25] China's broad and vague claims based on historical rights have also been worrying the disputants. For instance, in his visit to Singapore in November 2015, Chinese president Xi Jinping asserted that the South China Sea has been Chinese territory since ancient times and that protecting it is a matter of China's territorial sovereignty.[26] In July 2016, an international tribunal in The Hague decided against Beijing's broad claims to the South China Sea, but, as it had previously declared, the Chinese government rejected the ruling.[27]

Diplomatic Rebalancing

Although the U.S. rebalancing strategy had been launched before these moves by China, the South China Sea disputes have been an important focus of the strategy from its inception. One of the important features of the strategy was increased attention to Southeast Asia, in addition to the traditionally strong U.S. engagement in Northeast Asia.[28] In his memoir, Jeffrey Bader, who was the director of

Asian affairs on Obama's National Security Council, describes how Obama's team formed its foreign policy partially in response to the dissatisfaction of Southeast Asian governments with U.S. engagement in the region during the George W. Bush administration.[29]

Thus, the signs of the rebalancing strategy could already be identified in the early days of the Obama administration, especially in diplomacy. In February 2009, after she was confirmed as secretary of state, Hillary Clinton chose Asia as her first overseas destination and became the first U.S. secretary of state to visit ASEAN headquarters. ASEAN secretary general Surin Pitsuwan commended Clinton by saying that her "visit shows the seriousness of the United States to end its diplomatic absenteeism in the region."[30] Clinton continued her active Asia diplomacy and visited Asia-Pacific states significantly more than her predecessors.[31] Unlike previous U.S. administrations, which had been reluctant to sign the ASEAN Treaty of Amity and Cooperation, the Obama administration pleased Southeast Asian states by signing the treaty in July 2009.[32] This, in turn, paved the way for the United States to join the East Asia Summit in 2011.

As the United States engaged Southeast Asia more closely, it became more vocal on the disputes in the South China Sea. At the ASEAN Regional Forum in July 2010, Clinton made a declaration that caused chagrin and consternation in China. She said that the United States "has a national interest in freedom of navigation, open access to Asia's maritime commons, and respect for international law in the South China Sea." Clinton repeated the U.S. position, which is framed as neutrality and adherence to international law but collides with China's positions on the disputes. While claiming not to take sides on the competing territorial claims, Clinton clearly took a position against China's U-shaped line as it is not based on land features:

> The United States supports a collaborative diplomatic process by all claimants for resolving the various territorial disputes without coercion. We oppose the use or threat of force by any claimant. While the United States does not take sides on the competing territorial disputes over land features in the South China Sea, we believe claimants should pursue their territorial claims . . . and rights to maritime space in accordance with the [United Nations] convention on the law of the sea. Consistent with customary international law, legitimate claims to maritime space in the South China Sea should be derived solely from legitimate claims to land features.[33]

Clinton later declared that "the United States helped shape a regionwide effort to protect unfettered access to and passage through the South China Sea, and to uphold the key international rules for defining territorial claims in the South China Sea's waters."[34]

President Obama himself, of course, was an important part of the diplomatic component of the rebalancing strategy. He aimed to reassure Asian states about U.S. leadership in the region by increasing the visibility of U.S. diplomacy. In November 2009, Obama attended the first U.S.-ASEAN summit meeting, which previous administrations had resisted.[35] Because the disputes in the South China Sea have been worrying many states in the region, he also addressed the issue despite his administration's simultaneous need for improved China-U.S. relations. In November 2011, before Obama became the first U.S. president to attend the East Asia Summit, China's assistant foreign minister Liu Zhenmin explicitly argued against discussing the disputes at the meeting. Obama, however, declared that "cooperation in the South China Sea" was one of the "shared challenges" to be discussed at the summit meeting.[36] In February 2016, Obama hosted the first U.S.-ASEAN summit meeting held in the United States, and many believed that the U.S. goal in the meeting was to counter China's influence in Southeast Asia.[37]

Economic Rebalancing

The rebalancing strategy also had a strong emphasis on economic engagement because "economics and trade are both causes of and instruments for the pivot toward the Asia-Pacific."[38] China, India, Indonesia, and Vietnam were some of the most important targets of the Obama administration's National Export Initiative. The Trade Promotion Coordinating Committee identified the entire Asia-Pacific region as "next tier markets," which were expected to grow quickly in the coming years.[39] The economic component of the U.S. rebalancing strategy involved competitive elements, but it should be noted that economic cooperation with China was a major goal of the strategy as well.

Arguably, the crown jewel of U.S. economic rebalancing was the Trans-Pacific Partnership, which was agreed in October 2015 among twelve states in the Pacific Rim.[40] It did not include China. The broad scope of the issues covered by the TPP was controversial within and outside the United States, but many appreciated the long-term significance of the agreement. Even before Japan joined the TPP negotiations in July 2013, a U.S. analyst pointed out that "the relatively small immediate economic benefits from liberalizing trade with the current TPP members should not obscure the importance of designing the rules of the game, so to speak, for trade and investment in what will likely be the most dynamic and fastest growing region of the world over the coming decades."[41]

The economic element of the rebalancing strategy had links to incentives and disincentives that have affected U.S. policy in the South China Sea. On one hand, the importance of economic cooperation with China has prevented the United States from taking a confrontational stance on the South China Sea disputes. Hillary Clinton took a relatively firm stance on the disputes in the South China Sea, but she still acknowledged that the United States should not make an enemy out of China: "Today's China is not the Soviet Union. We are not on the brink of a new Cold War in Asia. Just look at the ever expanding trade between our economies, the connections between our peoples, the ongoing consultations between our governments. . . . Geopolitics today cannot afford to be a zero-sum game. A thriving China is good for America and a thriving America is good for China, so long as we both thrive in a way that contributes to the regional and global good."[42]

On the other hand, the economic importance of the Asia-Pacific region to the United States means that Washington has strong incentives to sustain its leadership in the region against China's challenges. For its long-term economic growth, the United States needs to be part of Asia-Pacific politics. This requires the United States to avoid disillusioning Asia-Pacific states about its strategic engagement, including the South China Sea disputes. The growing economic importance of the Asia-Pacific region has also been linked to the strategic value of the South China Sea. A U.S. Congressional Research Service report explained that "with an increasing volume of U.S. exports and imports flowing in and out of the region, it has become critical that the United States maintains free navigation from the Arabian Sea across to the eastern edge of the Pacific Ocean. This has been one of the arguments made for U.S. interest in a peaceful resolution of the territorial disputes over the South China Sea."[43]

Military Rebalancing

The strategic value of the South China Sea, in combination with the importance of maintaining U.S. military prestige in Asia, prompted the United States to engage in military rebalancing as well. The military component of the rebalancing strategy had direct relevance to the disputes in the South China Sea. In his speech to the Australian parliament in November 2011, Obama emphasized that the Asia-Pacific was prioritized in U.S. military policy: "As we end today's wars, I have directed my national security team to make our presence and mission in the

Asia Pacific a top priority. As a result, reductions in U.S. defense spending will not—I repeat, will not—come at the expense of the Asia Pacific."[44]

In addition to shifting capabilities to the Asia-Pacific, the 2012 Strategic Guidance of the U.S. Department of Defense focused reductions on Army and Marine ground forces while preserving U.S. naval capabilities.[45] This was consistent with the rebalancing strategy because naval power is considered to be particularly important for the Asia-Pacific.[46] The guidance also emphasized the need to maintain power projection capabilities in the face of anti-access/area denial challenges from states such as China and Iran. Building on his predecessor Leon Panetta's pledge to assign 60 percent of U.S. naval forces to the Asia-Pacific by 2020, Secretary of Defense Chuck Hagel stated in 2013 that the United States had committed and would continue to commit 60 percent of overseas air forces to the region.[47] The Pentagon confirmed the shift in naval and air forces in the Asia-Pacific Maritime Security Strategy released in August 2015, and Secretary of the Navy Ray Mabus requested an 8 percent increase in the 2016 budget for the Navy.[48]

The military component of the U.S. rebalancing strategy also involved closer cooperation with allies and partners in the Asia-Pacific. Starting in April 2012, the U.S. Marines have been deployed on a rotation basis in Darwin, Australia; the deployment began with 200 Marines and is scheduled to increase to 2,500.[49] In April 2014, the United States and the Philippines signed the Enhanced Defense Cooperation Agreement, which facilitates the deployment of American military personnel in the Philippines on a rotational basis. The agreement builds on the Visiting Forces Agreement signed in 1998.[50] By 2018, 4 U.S. littoral combat ships are scheduled to be deployed rotationally in Singapore.[51] The new Guidelines for U.S.-Japan Defense Cooperation released in April 2015 are more relevant to the Sino-Japanese disputes in the East China Sea but may also have some significance in the South China Sea. At his meeting with Obama on November 19, 2015 in Manila, Japanese prime minister Shinzo Abe expressed strong support for the U.S. position in the South China Sea and stated that his government would consider dispatching the Japan Self-Defense Forces to the South China Sea.[52] In September 2016, Japanese defense minister Tomomi Inada stated that Japan would "increase its engagement in the South China Sea through . . . Maritime Self-Defense Force joint training cruises with the U.S. Navy."[53]

Another important military component of the U.S. rebalancing was its efforts to expand "cooperation with emerging partners throughout the Asia-Pacific to ensure collective capability and capacity for securing common interests."[54] Put differently, capacity building of Southeast Asian states is one way of balancing the rising Chinese presence in the South China Sea without the United States risking direct conflict.[55] The United States has provided assistance to the maritime capacity building of countries such as the Philippines, Vietnam, Malaysia, and Indonesia. At the Shangri-La Dialogue in 2015, in the same speech where he criticized China's land reclamation in the Spratly Islands, U.S. secretary of defense Ashton Carter announced the Southeast Asia Maritime Security Initiative, which would provide equipment and training to Southeast Asian states.

In the context of China's increased presence in the South China Sea, the U.S. efforts to enforce freedom of navigation work as implicit support for other claimants in the area. According to Carter, "On October 27, 2015, the U.S. Navy destroyer USS *Lassen* (DDG-82) conducted a FONOP [Freedom of Navigation Operation] in the South China Sea by transiting inside 12 nautical miles of five maritime features in the Spratly Islands—Subi Reef, Northeast Cay, Southwest Cay, South Reef, and Sandy Cay—which are claimed by China, Taiwan, Vietnam, and the Philippines."[56] What was at stake was the credibility of the United States as the protector of the status quo in the South China Sea. It remains to be seen how U.S. policy will develop with respect to China's artificial islands.

In sum, the U.S. rebalancing strategy was linked to the South China Sea disputes in diplomatic, economic, and military affairs. Strategy involves consideration of others' actions, and so the next section examines the reactions of other states to the U.S. strategy, especially with respect to the disputes in the South China Sea.

REACTIONS TO THE U.S. REBALANCING

With the notable exception of China, Asia-Pacific states generally see the U.S. rebalancing strategy in a positive light. According to a survey of strategic elites in the Asia-Pacific in 2014, the following percentages of experts in each country supported the Obama administration's goal of a strategic rebalance: the United States, 96; Singapore, 96; Japan, 92; South Korea, 92; Taiwan, 90; Indonesia, 87; India, 82; Australia, 81; Thailand, 54; and China, 23.[57] Although not part of this survey, many Philippine and Vietnamese experts are likely to support the strategy as well due to high tension between their countries and China. Overall, 51 percent of respondents answered that rebalance was "the right policy but is not being resourced or implemented sufficiently, followed by 24 percent who felt it is reinforcing regional stability and prosperity."[58] China was the only country where a majority of respondents (74 percent) perceived the rebalancing strategy to be too confrontational toward China.

China's Response

China in the post–Cold War era has been generally critical of what it characterizes as a domineering U.S. presence in Asia. Because China is by far the strongest state that has maritime and territorial claims in the South China Sea, it prefers to deal with the other disputants on a bilateral basis to obtain advantage in negotiations. Thus, China opposes U.S. rebalancing to the Asia-Pacific in general and U.S. interventions in the South China Sea in particular. For instance, an article in the *China Daily* criticized Clinton's remarks on the South China Sea disputes at the ASEAN Regional Forum in July 2010, arguing that her "seemingly impartial remarks were in effect an attack on China and were designed to give the international community a wrong impression that the situation in the South China Sea is a cause for grave concern."[59] The article then lauds Chinese foreign minister Yang Jiechi's response to Clinton, namely, that the situation is peaceful and stable, the United States should not coerce nonclaimant states into taking sides, and turning the issue into a multilateral one will only make matters worse.

From the Chinese perspective, along with Sino-Japanese disputes in the East China Sea, the South China Sea disputes are probably the most important factor that drives the competitive aspect of U.S. rebalancing. An article in the *People's Daily*, an official newspaper of the Chinese Communist Party, criticized the U.S. strategy as follows:

> Are the actions of the United States sailing its warships to the South China Sea, frequently holding military drills clearly against China with the countries around the sea and trying to form a military alliance with them responsible actions? Are the actions of the United States forcing Asian countries to take side[s] between the United States and China and even deliberately smearing normal cooperation between China and its surrounding countries responsible actions? . . . the so-called "freedom of navigation of the South China Sea" issue . . . is just a step taken by the United States to implement its "returning to Asia" strategy.[60]

Naturally, there are debates in China over the U.S. strategy. Dong Wang and Chengzhi Yin provide an extensive survey of the debates, explaining positions of both moderates and hardliners. In 2014, they argued that "the moderates' more optimistic assessments are largely shared by mainland Chinese policy makers" despite "the hardliners' dire and pessimistic analyses of the U.S. pivot or rebalancing to Asia."[61] With heightened tensions over China's land reclamation activities, the competitive aspect will likely become more pronounced in coming years.

In terms of the effects of the U.S. strategy on Chinese policy in the South China Sea, two contrasting views are conceivable. On one hand, as the Chinese government itself likes to warn, the U.S. strategy may provoke China and escalate maritime tensions. Robert Ross argues that the rebalancing strategy is "unnecessary and counterproductive"; among other things, "Beijing will push back against countries that rely on the United States to support them in sovereignty disputes."[62] On the other hand, as the U.S. government would like to believe, the U.S. rebalancing strategy may deter China from taking aggressive actions and lead to a more conciliatory policy from Beijing. For example, a Congressional Research Service report in 2012 made the following observation: "After the United States, Vietnam, and other East Asian countries diplomatically pushed back in 2010 against what they saw as Chinese encroachment in the South China Sea, China chose to join multilateral negotiations with Southeast Asian countries over a Code of Conduct in the South China Sea. More recently, Vietnam's move to strengthen U.S.-Vietnamese ties (as well as deepen its ties to India and Japan) appears to have led Beijing to try to patch up its relationship with Hanoi, contributing to an easing of tensions."[63]

Both of these contrasting views may be partially correct, because competing dynamics could coexist in Chinese foreign policy. The U.S. rebalancing strategy may indeed provoke China and increase tension in the South China Sea, but it is hard to imagine that the absence of the U.S. strategy would have induced China to claim less in the disputes. In a counterfactual world where the United States did not rebalance to the region, Southeast Asian states may have more readily conceded to China, thereby reducing tensions over the disputes, but the status quo might have been more dramatically revised in favor of China.

Responses of the Philippines and Vietnam

The Philippines and Vietnam were in the most desperate need for U.S. support through the rebalancing strategy. Despite the commonality, however, their approaches varied significantly. While the Philippines under former president Benigno Aquino III openly defied China and sought U.S. support, Vietnam was cautious to avoid provoking China. Geography probably played an important role in this difference.[64] The Philippines can count on the ocean as a protective barrier against China, and the Philippines is a treaty ally of the United States, the dominant naval power for the foreseeable future. In contrast, Vietnam shares a land border with China, and it has fought numerous costly wars against China throughout its history, most recently in 1979. Although Vietnam normalized its diplomatic relations with the United States in 1995 and continues to improve ties, it does not have a U.S. security commitment.

In expressing desire for deeper U.S. engagement in the South China Sea, the Philippine government's position was the most clear-cut among Southeast Asian states, especially after Aquino took office in 2010. Aside from China's increasing activities in the South China Sea, Philippine domestic politics also pushed the Aquino administration (2010–16) to take a harder stance in the disputes. Sino-Philippine relations were relatively good under former president Gloria Macapagal Arroyo (2001–10), who took an "equi-balancing" strategy between China and the United States.[65] In his "anything-but-Arroyo" campaign, Aquino shifted the Philippine policy decidedly in favor of the United States, partially to dissociate himself from his predecessor.[66]

The rebalancing strategy presented an excellent opportunity for the Philippines to seek stronger U.S. support for its position on the disputes in the South China Sea. Whereas the U.S. government publicly declared that the U.S.-Japan alliance covers the Senkaku/Diaoyu Islands, it has left the applicability of the U.S.-Philippines Mutual Defense Treaty to the Philippine-claimed territories in the South China Sea at best unclear.[67] By fully embracing the U.S. rebalancing strategy, the Philippine government sought to influence the U.S. position. Moreover, even if the U.S. government did not change its stance on the Philippine claims, increased U.S. military presence in the Philippines and the South China Sea was a welcome development to the Philippines, which had sought to balance the rising Chinese presence.[68]

According to Jeffrey Bader, "Of all the countries in the region, Vietnam was arguably the most determined to see the United States play a greater role there because of its anxiety over China."[69] Although they have been relatively low key, Vietnam and the United States have conducted joint naval exercises since 2010. Secretary Clinton suggested a strategic partnership between the United States and Vietnam in her visit to Hanoi in October 2010. Instead, in July 2013, the two countries formed a "comprehensive partnership," which seemed to fall short of a full strategic partnership.[70] In July 2015, Nguyen Phu Trong became the first secretary general of the Vietnamese Communist Party to visit the White House, where he shared his concern about the South China Sea disputes with President Obama.[71] The United States lifted a decades-old arms embargo on Vietnam in May 2016.[72]

While Vietnam has strong strategic reasons to align with the United States, its attitude toward the U.S. strategy (and China) was not as clear as that of the Philippines. Vietnamese political leaders have historical and ideological reasons to be suspicious of U.S. intentions. Moreover, they have much to lose if the U.S. strategy does not work out in the long run. As Carl Thayer points out, "Vietnam cannot choose its neighbors and one enduring axiom of Vietnamese national security policy is to avoid having permanent tensions in relations with China."[73] Thus, Vietnam actively engages China and other states such as Russia, India, and Japan while also seeking a stronger U.S. presence in the region. Finally, Vietnam and the Philippines have been increasing cooperation on the South China Sea disputes: in November 2015, the two countries issued a Joint Statement on the Establishment of a Strategic Partnership, which repeatedly refers to cooperation in the South China Sea.[74]

Responses of the Other Disputants

So far, the other claimants in the South China Sea disputes have had a much lower level of tension with China. They took softer stances toward China while still supporting the U.S. rebalancing strategy. Malaysia, for example, has taken a "conscious and deliberate policy of not viewing China as a threat."[75] While Malaysia has strengthened security relations with the United States in the last several years, it has balanced these efforts by increasing security cooperation with China. Malaysia and China held their first defense and security consultation in September 2012 and their first joint military exercise in September 2015. Perhaps as a diplomatic tactic vis-à-vis China, "the rebalancing has not featured high-profile bilateral initiatives with Malaysia," even though "most observers say U.S.-Malaysia relations have warmed considerably in recent years."[76] Brunei, another Southeast Asian claimant and TPP member, welcomed the U.S. rebalancing, especially its economic aspect. Brunei is also increasing maritime cooperation with the United States, but it is less enthusiastic about military rebalancing.[77]

Because Taiwan receives informal U.S. military protection against China and seeks to expand economic ties with the United States, the U.S. rebalancing strategy was clearly a welcome development for Taipei. It was, however, concerned that Sino-American competition might damage cross-Strait relations, which improved significantly after Ma Ying-jeou took the Taiwanese presidential office in 2008.[78] Taiwan's position in the South China Sea is complicated by its historical relations with China, which inherited the Republic of China's claims.[79] While China is the main threat against the security of Taiwan, it is sometimes seen as being on the same side in the South China Sea disputes. With respect to U.S. rebalancing and China, Taiwan simply had bigger fish to fry than the disputes in the South China Sea.

Responses of Other Southeast Asian States

Singapore warmly welcomed the U.S. rebalancing strategy. The U.S. policy was consistent with Singapore's grand strategy, which relies on the United States as "an external balancer capable of preserving a stable distribution of power in Southeast Asia and the wider Asian region." Singapore, however, "wants to preserve its independence of manoeuvre with China and to avoid a situation where it would eventually have to 'choose' between Washington and Beijing."[80] Thus, while serving an important role in U.S. military rebalancing, Singapore closely engaged China. In May 2015, for instance, Singapore and China conducted their first bilateral naval exercise.

Consistent with its emphasis on independence from superpowers, Indonesian foreign policy has avoided taking sides with either the United States or China. Both Washington and Beijing have been courting Jakarta, and Indonesia probably benefits from this competitive dynamic. Indonesia's maritime and territorial disputes with China are only latent, but Jakarta is suspicious of China's broad claims in the South China Sea.[81] As the largest member of ASEAN, Indonesia is also wary of China's challenge against the centrality of ASEAN in regional politics. On balance, disputes in the South China Sea have pushed it toward the United States and increased security cooperation between the two countries. For example, Indonesia and the United States have conducted surveillance exercises since 2012. In April 2015, the Indonesian navy also revealed its desire to hold regular naval exercises with the United States near the Natuna Islands.[82] Not coincidentally, China claims waters in the islands' EEZ.

Despite the U.S.-Thai alliance, Thailand was ambivalent toward U.S. rebalancing, especially in military affairs.[83] Thailand has maintained highly cordial relationships with both the United States and China, but U.S.-Thai relations have experienced setbacks since the coups d'état in Thailand in 2006 and 2014. Thailand has been an informal ally of China since they began balancing against the unified Vietnam in the late 1970s. Thailand's military relations with China, therefore, are significantly warmer than those of other Southeast Asian states. Thailand's economic and military dependence on China has been increasing even more in recent years.[84] Reportedly, in a closed-door meeting of Thai strategic elites in 2012, three dozen participants unanimously agreed that Thailand must look beyond the U.S. alliance and strengthen Sino-Thai relations.[85]

Other mainland Southeast Asian states are not supportive of the U.S. rebalancing strategy, as they have deep economic and military dependence on China and do not have much at stake in the South China Sea disputes. The opening of

Myanmar has been a big success for the U.S. strategy, but Myanmar is still highly dependent on China and is reluctant to embrace the United States wholeheartedly. Cambodia's pro-China stance led to ASEAN's first-ever failure to issue a joint statement after its annual meeting in 2012. Although the United States has made progress in improving its relations with Laos, it still has not matched Chinese influence there.[86]

Japanese and Indian Responses

Although not part of the South China Sea disputes, Japan and India have watched U.S. policy toward the South China Sea with keen interest. These two states are major powers with significant interests in the South China Sea and share concerns about the rising power of China. Even before the U.S. rebalancing strategy, the United States, India, Japan, and Australia initiated the Quadrilateral Security Dialogue in 2007, which prompted a diplomatic protest from China. Yet Japanese and Indian attitudes toward the U.S. rebalancing strategy have important differences.

Along with the Philippines under former president Benigno Aquino III, Japan was the most passionate supporter of the U.S. rebalancing strategy. The U.S.-Japan alliance and American military presence in Asia are the most important bases of Japanese defense policy. Moreover, Japan has maritime and territorial disputes of its own with China. Consequently, Japan fully and publicly embraced the U.S. strategy, and it is eager to assist U.S. engagement in the South China Sea.[87] The Japanese government is contributing to the maritime capacity building of the Philippines, Vietnam, Indonesia, and Malaysia by, for example, providing patrol ships and training to these countries' maritime agencies. In addition to discussing a possible status of forces agreement, Japan and the Philippines held joint naval exercises in the South China Sea in May and June 2015. Furthermore, Japan signed a defense agreement with Indonesia in March 2015 and established a strategic partnership with Malaysia in May 2015. In April 2016, two destroyers of the Japan Maritime Self-Defense Force made a port call at Vietnam's Cam Ranh Bay, which faces the South China Sea.[88] With the United States, Japan held their first bilateral naval exercise in the South China Sea in October 2015. China has sternly opposed and warned against Japan's involvement in the sea.[89]

The U.S. rebalancing strategy seemed to bring geopolitical benefits to India as well, but India has been more cautious in its approach toward the United States than Japan. Although India does play a role in the South China Sea disputes, for example, through its security cooperation with Vietnam, its support for the U.S.

strategy was less public than that of Japan.[90] On one hand, India clearly benefits from a greater U.S. presence in the South China Sea and the broader Asia-Pacific because "the greater the U.S. pressure in the Pacific, the more likely that China would want to keep its southwestern frontiers tranquil."[91] On the other hand, India recognizes the danger of provoking China, and its domestic politics and tradition of nonalignment also hinder its approach to the United States. Geographically, the land border with China, which remains disputed, gives India incentives to align with the United States against China. The geographical contiguity, however, also makes India more cautious in handling its strong neighbor, against which it lost a war in 1962.

CONCLUSION

The U.S. rebalancing toward the Asia-Pacific was motivated by multiple factors, but its development was significantly influenced by the maritime and territorial disputes in the South China Sea. Due to the high visibility of China's activity in these waters, the disputes have become a litmus test for the U.S. commitment to its Asian allies and partners. Although both supporters and opponents of the strategy can criticize its implementation, it seems to have had at least moderate success in a difficult task—namely, reassuring regional states without provoking China too much.

Although each state's response to the U.S. rebalance needs to be understood in the context of its foreign policy tradition as well as its relationship with the United States and China, geography seems to have a systematic influence: namely, countries that are closer to China and on mainland Asia are more cautious of embracing the U.S. strategy.[92] Maritime states have more incentives to support the United States because their maritime and territorial interests are threatened by China's advances in the South China Sea. Moreover, maritime states are able to take a more defiant policy against China because they are not too threatened by China's land forces and are not yet vulnerable to China's naval forces as a result of U.S. naval dominance. If China establishes naval dominance in the South China Sea, their attitude may well change.

Although Donald Trump's foreign policy will differ significantly from that of Barack Obama, the legacy of the U.S. rebalancing strategy will remain in the dynamics of the South China Sea disputes. The long-term factors that encouraged the Obama administration's rebalance to Asia will continue in the coming decades, and the strategy had fairly broad bipartisan support in U.S. foreign policy circles. Moreover, "By routinely participating in leaders' and Cabinet-level officials' meetings such as the [East Asia Summit], the Obama Administration has raised costs to it and successor administrations of not participating in the future, thereby helping to lock in U.S. engagement in the future."[93] This was a welcome development to the Southeast Asian disputants in the South China Sea, as the disputes in these waters are unlikely to disappear any time soon.

Notes

1. Barack Obama, "Remarks by President Barack Obama at Suntory Hall," November 14, 2009, https://www.whitehouse.gov/the-press-office/remarks-president-barack-obama-suntory-hall.
2. See, for example, Douglas Stuart, "Obama's 'Rebalance' in Historical Context," in *The New U.S. Strategy towards Asia: Adapting to the American Pivot,* ed. William T. Tow and Douglas Stuart (London and New York: Routledge, 2015).
3. Hillary Clinton, "America's Pacific Century," *Foreign Policy,* October 11, 2011, http://foreignpolicy.com/2011/10/11/americas-pacific-century/. The strategy was initially termed "pivot to the Asia-Pacific," but the term faced criticism from both American and foreign observers. Pivot implied U.S. disengagement from other regions of the world, and supporters of the strategy in Asia disliked the impression that the United States can pivot away from Asia in the future. For criticism against the term "pivot," and to a lesser extent "rebalancing," see Michael Green and Dan Twining, "Dizzy Yet? The Pros and Cons of the Asia 'Pivot,'" *Foreign Policy,* November 21, 2011; Mark E. Manyin, Stephen Daggett, Ben Dolven, Susan V. Lawrence, Michael F. Martin, Ronald O'Rourke, and Bruce Vaughn, *Pivot to the Pacific? The Obama Administration's "Rebalancing" Toward Asia* (Washington, D.C.: Congressional Research Service, March 28, 2012), 9–10; Michael D. Swaine, "Chinese Leadership and Elite Responses to the U.S. Pacific Pivot," *China Leadership Monitor,* no. 38 (2012): p. 16; and Ralf Emmers, "Security and Power Balancing: Singapore's Response to the U.S. Rebalance to Asia," in Tow and Stuart, *The New U.S. Strategy towards Asia,* 148. For an analysis that documents a shift of U.S. strategy during the George W. Bush administration, see Nina Silove, "The Pivot before the Pivot: U.S. Strategy to Preserve the Power Balance in Asia," *International Security* 40, no. 4 (2016): pp. 45–88.
4. So far, it is hard to discern a grand strategy in President Trump's policy. In fact, some argue that Trump's approach is "explicitly anti-strategic." See Micah Zenko and Rebecca Friedman Lissner, "Trump Is Going to Regret Not Having a Grand Strategy," *Foreign Policy,* January 13, 2017, http://foreignpolicy.com/2017/01/13/trump-is-going-to-regret-not-having-a-grand-strategy/.
5. See Population Division of the Department of Economic and Social Affairs of the United Nations Secretariat, "2015 Revision of World Population Prospects," http://esa.un.org/unpd/wpp/.
6. On the U.S. post–Cold War strategy to prevent the emergence of a rival superpower, see an excerpt of the February 18, 1992, draft Defense Planning Guidance, http://nsarchive.gwu.edu/nukevault/ebb245/doc03_extract_nytedit.pdf.

7. Barack Obama, "Remarks by the President at the U.S.-China Strategic and Economic Dialogue," July 27, 2009, https://www.whitehouse.gov/the-press-office/remarks-president-uschina-strategic-and-economic-dialogue.
8. See U.S. Government Accountability Office, "Southeast Asia: Trends in U.S. and Chinese Economic Engagement," August 2015.
9. Aaron Friedberg, *A Contest for Supremacy: China, America, and the Struggle for Mastery in Asia* (New York: W. W. Norton, 2011), 275.
10. China's perceived assertiveness impacted the development of the rebalancing strategy as well, but Obama's foreign policy team had formulated the strategy before China's "new assertiveness," which began around 2010. For critical assessments of the discourse on China's new assertiveness, see Alastair Iain Johnston, "How New and Assertive Is China's New Assertiveness?" *International Security* 37, no. 4 (2013): pp. 7–48; Andrew Scobell and Scott W. Harold, "An 'Assertive' China? Insights from Interviews," *Asian Security* 9, no. 2 (2013): pp. 111–31; and Björn Jerdén, "The Assertive China Narrative: Why It Is Wrong and How So Many Still Bought into It," *Chinese Journal of International Politics* 7, no. 1 (2014): pp. 47–88.
11. See, for example, Pew Research Center, "More See Failure than Success in Iraq, Afghanistan," January 2014, http://www.people-press.org/2014/01/30/more-now-see-failure-than-success-in-iraq-afghanistan/.
12. Green and Twining, "Dizzy Yet? The Pros and Cons of the Asia 'Pivot,'" http://foreignpolicy.com/2011/11/21/dizzy-yet-the-pros-and-cons-of-the-asia-pivot/.
13. Noboru Yamaguchi, "A Japanese Perspective on U.S. Rebalancing toward the Asia-Pacific Region," *Asia Policy* 15 (2013): p. 7.
14. "Based on funding enacted from the 9/11 attacks through fiscal year 2014, CRS estimates a total of $1.6 trillion has been provided to the Department of Defense, the State Department, and the Department of Veterans [Affairs] for war operations, diplomatic operations and foreign aid, and medical care for Iraq and Afghan war veterans over the past 13 years of war." Amy Belasco, *The Cost of Iraq, Afghanistan, and Other Global War on Terror Operations since 9/11* (Washington, D.C.: Congressional Research Service, December 8, 2014), 5.
15. Shayerah Ilias, Ian F. Fergusson, Wayne M. Morrison, and M. Angeles Villarreal, *Boosting U.S. Exports: Selected Issues for Congress* (Washington, D.C.: Congressional Research Service, November 29, 2011), 1–29.
16. Barack Obama, "Statement by the President on the Trans-Pacific Partnership," October 5, 2015, https://www.whitehouse.gov/the-press-office/2015/10/05/statement-president-trans-pacific-partnership.
17. Leon Panetta, "The U.S. Rebalance Towards the Asia-Pacific," June 2, 2012, https://www.iiss.org/en/events/shangri%20la%20dialogue/archive/sld12-43d9/first-plenary-session-2749/leon-panetta-d67b.
18. Ronald O'Rourke, *Maritime Territorial and Exclusive Economic Zone (EEZ) Disputes Involving China: Issues for Congress* (Washington, D.C.: Congressional Research Service, September 18, 2015), 11–15.
19. Kevin Baron, "Pentagon: Five Chinese Vessels Harass U.S. Ship," *Stars and Stripes*, March 10, 2009, http://www.stripes.com/news/pentagon-five-chinese-vessels-harass-u-s-ship-1.89046.

20. Johnston, "How New and Assertive Is China's New Assertiveness?" 19, 45–46.
21. On intra-ASEAN disputes as a South China Sea "blindspot," see Liow Joseph Chinyong, "The South China Sea Disputes: Some Blindspots and Misperceptions," ASAN Forum, July 31, 2015, http://www.theasanforum.org/the-south-china-sea-disputes-some-blindspots-and-misperceptions/.
22. On the activities of China's maritime agencies in the South China Sea, see, for example, International Crisis Group, "Stirring up the South China Sea (I)," *Asia Report* no. 223, April 23, 2012, http://www.crisisgroup.org/~/media/Files/asia/north-east-asia/223-stirring-up-the-south-china-sea-i.pdf; and Linda Jakobson, *China's Unpredictable Maritime Security Actors* (Sydney: Lowy Institute for International Policy, December 2014).
23. M. Taylor Fravel, "China's Island Strategy: 'Redefine the Status Quo,'" *The Diplomat*, November 1, 2012, http://thediplomat.com/2012/11/chinas-island-strategy-redefine-the-status-quo/.
24. Ben Dolven, Jennifer K. Elsea, Susan V. Lawrence, Ronald O'Rourke, and Ian E. Rinehart, *Chinese Land Reclamation in the South China Sea: Implications and Policy Options* (Washington, D.C.: Congressional Research Service, June 18, 2015).
25. Reuters, "China's Land Reclamation in South China Sea Grows: Pentagon Report," August 21, 2015, http://www.reuters.com/article/2015/08/21/us-southchinasea-china-pentagon-idUSKCN0QQ0S920150821#euO6oIWP1fPs2bv4.97; and Derek Watkins, "What China Has Been Building in the South China Sea," *New York Times*, October 27, 2015, http://www.nytimes.com/interactive/2015/07/30/world/asia/what-china-has-been-building-in-the-south-china-sea.html?r=0.
26. Ben Brumfield, "China's President Xi: South China Sea Is Chinese Territory," CNN, November 7, 2015, http://edition.cnn.com/2015/11/07/china/south-china-sea-xi-jinping-comments/.
27. Jane Perlez, "Tribunal Rejects Beijing's Claims in South China Sea," *New York Times*, July 12, 2016, http://www.nytimes.com/2016/07/13/world/asia/south-china-sea-hague-ruling-philippines.html?_r=0.
28. Robert G. Sutter, Michael E. Brown, and Timothy J. A. Adamson, with Mike M. Mochizuki and Deepa Ollapally, *Balancing Acts: The U.S. Rebalance and Asia-Pacific Stability* (Washington, D.C.: Sigur Center for Asian Studies, George Washington University, August 2013).
29. Jeffrey Bader, *Obama and China's Rise: An Insider's Account of America's Asia Strategy* (Washington, D.C.: Brookings Institution Press, 2012).
30. Hillary Clinton, "Beginning a New Era of Diplomacy in Asia," remarks with ASEAN Secretary General Surin Pitsuwan, Jakarta, Indonesia, February 18, 2009, http://www.state.gov/secretary/20092013clinton/rm/2009a/02/119422.htm.
31. Manyin et al., *Pivot to the Pacific?* 16–17.
32. "The ASEAN countries had long tried to cajole previous administrations into joining other non-ASEAN signatories, Russia, China, Australia, India, Japan, and France, as a member, but the U.S. had showed little interest for reasons as negligible as the treaty itself. Some believed accession would tie America's hands in Burma because U.S. sanctions might be labeled treaty violations. Some in the Defense

Department felt the treaty's emphasis on noninterference in countries' internal affairs could negatively affect U.S. alliance commitments. With North Korea's accession to the [Treaty of Amity and Cooperation] in 2008, some also argued that it could also affect America's North Korea policy." Bader, *Obama and China's Rise*, 13.

33. U.S. Department of State, "Comments by Secretary Clinton in Hanoi, Vietnam," July 23, 2010, http://iipdigital.usembassy.gov/st/english/texttrans/2010/07/201 00723164658su0.4912989.html#axzz3rfM8Qosc. It should be noted that the United States has not ratified the United Nations Convention on the Law of the Sea.
34. Clinton, "America's Pacific Century."
35. John J. Brandon, "ASEAN Summit Promises First-Ever Full U.S. Engagement," Asia Foundation, November 11, 2009, http://asiafoundation.org/in-asia/2009/11/11 /asean-summit-promises-first-ever-full-u-s-engagement/.
36. Jeremy Page, "Beijing Resists Sea Debate During East Asia Summit," *Wall Street Journal*, November 16, 2011, http://www.wsj.com/articles/SB100014240529702 03503204577039892130094070; Barack Obama, "Remarks by President Obama to the Australian Parliament," November 17, 2011, https://www.whitehouse.gov /the-press-office/2011/11/17/remarks-president-obama-australian-parliament.
37. Jeff Mason and Bruce Wallace, "Obama, ASEAN Discuss South China Sea Tensions, but No Joint Mention of China," Reuters, February 17, 2016, http://www .reuters.com/article/us-usa-asean-idUSKCN0VP1F7.
38. Manyin et al., *Pivot to the Pacific?* 20.
39. Ilias et al., *Boosting U.S. Exports*, 17.
40. Despite the significance of the agreement, newly elected U.S. president Donald Trump withdrew the United States from the TPP in January 2017.
41. Joshua Meltzer, "The Significance of the Trans-Pacific Partnership for the United States," testimony, U.S. House Small Business Committee, May 16, 2012, http:// www.brookings.edu/research/testimony/2012/05/16-us-trade-strategy-meltzer.
42. Hillary Clinton, "Forrestal Lecture at the Naval Academy," Annapolis, Md., April 10, 2012, http://www.state.gov/secretary/rm/2012/04/187693.htm.
43. Manyin et al., *Pivot to the Pacific?* 21.
44. Obama, "Remarks by President Obama to the Australian Parliament."
45. See Department of Defense, "Sustaining U.S. Global Leadership: Priorities for 21st Century Defense," January 2012, http://www.defense.gov/news/Defense _Strategic_Guidance.pdf.
46. Sutter et al., *Balancing Acts*.
47. David Alexander, "U.S. Rebalance to Asia-Pacific Gaining Steam, Pentagon Chief Says," Reuters, June 1, 2013, http://www.reuters.com/article/2013/06/01/us -security-asia-usa-idUSBRE95002820130601#xT7uZgbwEb0OXPYe.97; also see Sutter et al., *Balancing Acts*.
48. See "Sea Power: Who Rules the Waves?" *The Economist*, October 17, 2015, http:// www.economist.com/news/international/21674648-china-no-longer-accepts -america-should-be-asia-pacifics-dominant-naval-power-who-rules?fsrc=scn /tw_ec/who_rules_the_waves_.
49. Australian Defence Facilities, "U.S. Marine Rotational Force—Darwin," September 30, 2013, http://nautilus.org/briefing-books/australian-defence-facilities

/us-marine-rotational-force-darwin/. Starting in April 2017, the sixth rotation brought 1,250 Marines to Darwin. See Nancy Notzon and Stephanie Zillman, "U.S. Marines Arriving in NT Ready 'For Anything' in Wake of North Korean Threat," ABC News, April 18, 2017, http://www.abc.net.au/news/2017-04-18/us-marines-ready-for-anything-as-latest-rotation-arrives-in-nt/8450218.

50. The Philippines had closed U.S. bases in the early 1990s and still does not allow the establishment of permanent bases by foreign states: "After the expiration in 1991 of the Agreement between the Republic of the Philippines and the United States of America concerning Military Bases, foreign military bases, troops, or facilities shall not be allowed in the Philippines except under a treaty duly concurred in by the Senate and, when the Congress so requires, ratified by a majority of the votes cast by the people in a national referendum held for that purpose, and recognized as a treaty by the other contracting State." See the Philippine constitution, http://www.gov.ph/constitutions/1987-constitution/. In practice, however, the Philippine government has hosted U.S. forces as guests in the Philippine bases. Also see Thomas Lum and Ben Dolven, *The Republic of the Philippines and U.S. Interests—2014* (Washington, D.C.: Congressional Research Service, May 15, 2014).

51. Franz-Stefan Gady, "4 U.S. Littoral Combat Ships to Operate out of Singapore by 2018," *The Diplomat*, February 19, 2015, http://thediplomat.com/2015/02/4-us-littoral-combat-ships-to-operate-out-of-singapore-by-2018/.

52. Kyodo and Bloomberg, "Abe to Mull SDF Dispatch to South China Sea," *Japan Times*, November 20, 2015, http://www.japantimes.co.jp/news/2015/11/20/national/politics-diplomacy/abe-obama-discuss-anti-terrorism-steps-light-paris-attack-weigh-beijings-south-china-sea-moves/#.WUJg9euGPIU. See Jesse Johnson, "Chinese State Media Blasts Japan over South China Sea 'Patrols,' but Experts See No Change in Policy," *Japan Times*, September 18, 2016, http://www.japantimes.co.jp/news/2016/09/18/national/chinese-state-media-blasts-japan-south-china-sea-patrols-experts-see-no-change-policy/#.V-VSSvl96Uk.

53. Johnson, "Chinese State Media Blasts Japan over South China Sea 'Patrols'."

54. Department of Defense, "Sustaining U.S. Global Leadership: Priorities for 21st Century Defense."

55. Nontraditional security problems such as piracy and terrorism have been popular targets of maritime security initiatives in Southeast Asia, partially in order to reduce the impression of containing China. On nontraditional security threats and maritime security in Southeast Asia, see, for example, Carolin Liss, *Oceans of Crime: Maritime Piracy and Transnational Security in Southeast Asia and Bangladesh* (Singapore: International Institute for Asian Studies and Institute of Southeast Asian Studies, 2011), and Carolin Liss, "New Actors and the State: Addressing Maritime Security Threats in Southeast Asia," *Contemporary Southeast Asia* 35, no. 2 (2013): pp. 141–62.

56. Ankit Panda, "Everything You Wanted to Know About the USS *Lassen*'s FONOP in the South China Sea," *The Diplomat*, January 6, 2016, http://thediplomat.com/2016/01/everything-you-wanted-to-know-about-the-uss-lassens-fonop-in-the-south-china-sea/.

57. Michael Green and Nicholas Szechenyi, *Power and Order in Asia: A Survey of Regional Expectations* (Washington, D.C.: Center for Strategic and International

Studies, 2014), 12. At the public opinion level, U.S. military rebalancing to Asia is less popular but still welcomed by many. See Pew Research Center, "Global Publics Back U.S. on Fighting ISIS, but Are Critical of Post-9/11 Torture," June 2015. Philippine and Vietnamese publics are the most welcoming toward the defense pivot (71 percent welcome increased U.S. military resources in Asia).

58. Green and Szechenyi, *Power and Order in Asia*, 12.
59. "Chinese FM Refutes Fallacies on the South China Sea Issue," *China Daily*, July 25, 2010, http://www.chinadaily.com.cn/china/2010-07/25/content_11046054.htm.
60. Zhong Sheng, "U.S. Should Not Muddy the Waters Over South China Sea," *People's Daily*, March 20, 2012, http://en.people.cn/90780/7762712.html/.
61. Dong Wang and Chengzhi Yin, "Mainland China Debates U.S. Pivot/Rebalancing to Asia," *Issues and Studies* 50, no. 3 (2014): p. 85. In addition to the debates over the benign or hostile nature of the U.S. strategy, the Chinese have also debated whether the United States actually can implement the strategy in the face of resource constraints.
62. Robert Ross, "The Problem with the Pivot: Obama's New Asia Policy Is Unnecessary and Counterproductive," *Foreign Affairs* 91, no. 6 (2012): p. 80.
63. Manyin et al., *Pivot to the Pacific?* 8.
64. Tongfi Kim, "Balancing the Risks of U.S. Rebalancing," in Tow and Stuart, *The New U.S. Strategy towards Asia*, 201–6.
65. In relation to her corruption scandal, Arroyo was criticized for giving China undue influence in the Philippines. See, for example, Jojo Malig, "Arroyo Corruption Scandal Weakened China Influence—WikiLeaks Cables," ABS-CBN News, August 29, 2011, http://news.abs-cbn.com/-depth/08/29/11/arroyo-corruption-scandal-weakened-china-influence-leaked-us-cables-say.
66. Renato Cruz De Castro, "The Aquino Administration's Balancing Policy against an Emergent China: Its Domestic and External Dimensions," *Pacific Affairs* 87, no. 1 (2014): pp. 5–27. Sino-Philippine relations have improved under the presidency of Rodrigo Duterte, but it is too soon to tell if the rapprochement will have a long-term impact.
67. See Tongfi Kim, "U.S. Alliance Obligations in the Disputes in the East and South China Seas: Issues of Applicability and Interpretations," *PRIF Report*, no. 141 (2016): pp. 1–34.
68. The Philippines is eager to increase security cooperation with Japan as well. The two countries are seeking to increase maritime security cooperation through equipment transfer and joint exercises and are even discussing a status of forces agreement for the Japan Self-Defense Forces' deployment in the Philippines. See, for example, Renato Cruz de Castro, "Philippine Navy and Japan's Maritime Self Defense Forces in the South China Sea," Asia Maritime Transparency Initiative, July 1, 2015, http://amti.csis.org/philippine-navy-and-japans-maritime-self-defense-forces-in-the-south-china-sea/.
69. Bader, *Obama and China's Rise*, 102.
70. For "possible explanations for why the United States and Vietnam opted for a comprehensive partnership rather than a strategic partnership," see Carl Thayer, "The

U.S.-Vietnam Comprehensive Partnership: What's in a Name?" cogitASIA.com, July 30, 2013, http://cogitasia.com/the-u-s-vietnam-comprehensive-partnership-whats-in-a-name/.
71. Carl Thayer, "8 Developments in U.S.-Vietnam Relations Show Emerging Partnership," *The Diplomat*, July 13, 2015, http://thediplomat.com/2015/07/8-developments-in-us-vietnam-relations-show-emerging-partnership/.
72. Oliver Holmes, "U.S. Lifts Decades-long Embargo on Arms Sales to Vietnam," *The Guardian*, May 23, 2016, https://www.theguardian.com/world/2016/may/23/us-lifts-decades-long-embargo-on-arms-sales-to-vietnam.
73. Carl Thayer, "Is Vietnam Pivoting Toward the United States?" *The Diplomat*, July 6, 2015, http://thediplomat.com/2015/07/is-vietnam-pivoting-toward-the-united-states/.
74. "Viet Nam, Philippines Issue Joint Statement on Strategic Partnership," Viet-NamNews, November 19, 2015, http://vietnamnews.vn/politics-laws/278770/viet-nam-philippines-issue-joint-statement-on-strategic-partnership.html.
75. A Malaysian diplomat's remark in February 2010, quoted in Cheng-Chwee Kuik, "Making Sense of Malaysia's China Policy: Asymmetry, Proximity, and Elite's Domestic Authority," *Chinese Journal of International Politics* 6, no. 4 (2013): p. 463.
76. Ian E. Rinehart, *Malaysia: Background and U.S. Relations* (Washington, D.C.: Congressional Research Service, May 23, 2014), 1.
77. David Berteau, Michael Green, and Zack Cooper, *Assessing the Asia-Pacific Rebalance* (Washington, D.C.: Center for Strategic and International Studies, 2014), 31, http://csis.org/files/publication/150105_Berteau_AssessingAsiaPacificRebal_Web.pdf; and Rahul Mishra, "The U.S. Rebalancing Strategy: Responses from Southeast Asia," in *Asian Strategic Review 2014: U.S. Pivot and Asian Security,* ed. Vivek Chadha and S. D. Muni (New Delhi: Pentagon Press, 2014), 158–59.
78. Fu-Kuo Liu, "The U.S. Pivot to Asia: Taiwan's Security Challenges and Responses," in Tow and Stuart, *The New U.S. Strategy towards Asia*, 102–11. Tsai Ing-wen, who took the Taiwanese presidency in May 2016, is less pro-China than her predecessor, but the direction of the cross-Strait relations under her administration is yet to be seen.
79. Lynn Kuok, *Tides of Change: Taiwan's Evolving Position in the South China Sea*, East Asia Policy Paper 5 (Washington, D.C.: Brookings Institution, May 2015), http://www.brookings.edu/~/media/research/files/papers/2015/05/taiwan-south-china-sea-kuok/taiwan-south-china-sea-kuok-paper.pdf.
80. Emmers, "Security and Power Balancing," 143–44.
81. See, for example, Ann Marie Murphy, "Indonesia Responds to China's Rise," in *Middle Powers and the Rise of China,* ed. Bruce Gilley and Andrew O'Neil (Washington, D.C.: Georgetown University Press, 2014), 126–48.
82. Sheldon Simon, "U.S.-Southeast Asia Relations: South China Sea Wariness," *Comparative Connections* 17, no. 1 (2015).
83. Kitti Prasirtsuk and William Tow, "A Reluctant Ally? Thailand in the U.S. Rebalancing Strategy," in Tow and Stuart, *The New U.S. Strategy towards Asia,* 129–42.
84. Amy Freedman, "Malaysia, Thailand, and the ASEAN Middle Power Way," in Gilley and O'Neil, *Middle Powers and the Rise of China*, 104–25.

85. Kavi Chongkittavorn, "Thailand Looks Beyond the U.S. Alliance," *The Nation*, April 2, 2012, http://www.nationmultimedia.com/opinion/Thailand-looks-beyond-the-USalliance-30179152.html.
86. Phuong Nguyen, "In Laos, a Strategic Opening the United States Cannot Miss," *Southeast Asia from Scott Circle* 6, no. 7 (April 2, 2015), http://csis.org/files/publication/150402_SoutheastAsia_Vol_6_Issue_7.pdf.
87. Japan has been seeking new security partnerships with Southeast Asian states as well as others (most notably, Australia). Although these new partnerships will be diplomatically useful to Japan, I suspect that the main goal of the Japanese policy is to please the United States by assisting U.S. engagement in the Asia-Pacific.
88. Simon, "U.S.-Southeast Asia Relations: South China Sea Wariness"; and Sheldon Simon, "U.S.-Southeast Asia Relations: Courting Partners," *Comparative Connections* 17, no. 2 (2015): pp. 53–64. For more on Japan's activities related to the South China Sea, see Inoguchi and Panda's chapter in this volume.
89. See, for example, Ankit Panda, "China's 'Red Line' Warning to Japan on South China Sea FONOPs Is Here to Stay," *The Diplomat*, August 29, 2016, http://thediplomat.com/2016/08/chinas-red-line-warning-to-japan-on-south-china-sea-fonops-is-here-to-stay/.
90. David Scott, "India's Incremental Balancing in the South China Sea," *E-International Relations*, July 26, 2015, http://www.e-ir.info/2015/07/26/indias-incremental-balancing-in-the-south-china-sea/.
91. C. Raja Mohan, "India: Between 'Strategic Autonomy' and 'Geopolitical Opportunity,'" *Asia Policy* 15 (2013): p. 23. Also see Mahesh Shankar, "India and the U.S. 'Pivot' to Asia," in Tow and Stuart, *The New U.S. Strategy towards Asia*, 184–200.
92. For similar views on the division between maritime and continental Southeast Asia, see Euan Graham, "Southeast Asia in the U.S. Rebalance: Perceptions from a Divided Region," *Contemporary Southeast Asia* 35, no. 3 (2013): p. 325; and Thitinan Pongsudhirak, "Obama's Southeast Asia Visit: Reengaging with the Region," *East Asia Forum*, November 2, 2012, http://www.eastasiaforum.org/2012/11/20/obamassoutheast-asia-visit-re-engaging-with-the-region/.
93. Manyin et al., *Pivot to the Pacific?* 19–20.

7

Japan's Grand Strategy in the South China Sea

Principled Pragmatism

Takashi Inoguchi and Ankit Panda

THE SOUTH CHINA SEA AND JAPAN

The South China Sea, though not geographically proximate to Japan, has grown increasingly important for Tokyo's geopolitical and grand strategic outlook in recent years. Three primary impulses have historically driven Tokyo's strategic thinking toward the South China Sea, which has emerged in the early twenty-first century as one of Asia's foremost flashpoints as a rising China looks to assert its claims over disputed waters and maritime features.[1] First, Japan's position as a status quo middle power or a stakeholder great power means that it wishes to see the post–World War II order persist unaltered in Asia.[2] This translates to support for the norms of customary and formal international law and multilateral treaties, including the 1982 United Nations Convention on the Law of the Sea (UNCLOS) in the South China Sea.[3] Second, Japan's decades-long alliance with the United States means that Tokyo's attention will naturally follow Washington's—as tension has risen in the South China Sea, the United States, eager to "rebalance" to Asia, has looked to preserve the status quo in the region.[4] Finally, as Japan's foreign policy evolves under a new generation of leadership, Tokyo's own security interests and geopolitical considerations for its position within the Asian security order—in particular, its competition with a rising China—drive its approach toward the South China Sea.[5]

Furthermore, Japan's perspective toward the South China Sea, through which $5 trillion in maritime trade traverses annually, is informed by the overall importance of the region for global commerce.[6] In particular, as a net importer of energy,

Japan's energy security is highly dependent on commercial sea lanes crossing the South China Sea.[7] Keeping sea lanes open to free navigation and overflight is thus central to Japan's grand strategic thinking about the South China Sea. Following China, Japan is the world's largest net importer of fossil fuels.[8] Notably, 83 percent of Japan's energy imports originate in the Middle East and pass through the strategically pivotal Malacca Strait before making their way through the South China Sea to access the waters of the western Pacific, between the First and Second Island Chains, on their way to Japanese ports.[9] Furthermore, following the catastrophic 2011 Tohoku earthquake and tsunami and the ensuing nuclear meltdown at the Fukushima Daiichi nuclear power plant, public opinion and policy in Japan led to reduced dependence on nuclear power in the country, increasing Japan's reliance on fossil fuels.[10] As a result, liquid natural gas imports rose by 24 percent between 2010 and 2012.[11] Liquid natural gas, like oil, makes its way to Japan via the South China Sea. Thus, energy security weighs heavily on Tokyo's strategic calculus for this region.[12] Any threat to the freedom of navigation for commercial vessels could raise energy import costs considerably for Japan, with potentially major ramifications for the economy.[13]

Japan's strategic thinking toward the South China Sea also needs to be considered in light of a substantial increase in regional tensions in recent years. In particular, China's newest generation of leaders, while alluding to Deng Xiaoping's advice to "set aside disputes and pursue joint development" in the region, has focused disproportionately on the latter over the former.[14] Starting in 2012 but as early as the late 1990s, China started to assert its claims in the region, disrupting relations with other South China Sea claimant states, including Brunei, Malaysia, the Philippines, Taiwan, and Vietnam.[15] In particular, in the Japanese strategic view, the South China Sea will be an important test case for the universalism of various multilateral frameworks, most importantly UNCLOS.[16] Japan's interests lie in preserving freedom of navigation and overflight in the South China Sea and avoiding the emergence of an Asian Mediterranean Sea, where a few countries claim exclusive sovereignty over maritime areas, impeding international civilian and military access. In March 2014, following the Philippines' decision to move ahead with filing arbitral proceedings against China at the Permanent Court of Arbitration in The Hague, the Japanese government issued the following statement on the South China Sea:

> The Government of Japan believes that the South China Sea issue is directly related to peace and stability of the region. More importantly, however, Japan recognizes the possibility of conflict in the region as a

threat to the integrity of the international maritime order as a whole. It therefore sees resolution of tensions in the South China Sea as a common concern for the wider international community, regarding it as important for the parties concerned to act on the basis of the principle of "the rule of law" for the maintenance and enhancement of the international order in the region.[17]

In addition to UNCLOS, Japan regards efforts by the Association of Southeast Asian Nations (ASEAN)—an organization to which all South China Sea claimants except China and Taiwan belong—to manage tensions in the South China Sea positively.[18] Notably, Tokyo views the existing but unimplemented 2002 Declaration on the Conduct of Parties in the South China Sea and ongoing progress between ASEAN and China toward a binding Code of Conduct as positive developments.[19]

FIRST EAST CHINA SEA, THEN SOUTH CHINA SEA

While in recent years Tokyo's gaze has shifted toward the South China Sea as tensions have increased over Chinese irredentism, it would be wrong to ignore the salience of ongoing tensions between China and Japan in the East China Sea as a contributing factor to Japan's approach toward the South China Sea issue.[20] Scholars have argued that China brought the East China Sea disputes to bear on the bilateral relationship as it gained power primarily due to reasons of nationalism-derived legitimacy.[21] A watershed event sparking a nearly two-year-long high-level diplomatic freeze between Tokyo and Beijing was the 2012 decision of the Japanese government, then led by the Democratic Party of Japan with Yoshihiko Noda as prime minister, to purchase the disputed Senkaku Islands (known and claimed as the Diaoyu Islands in China).[22] The Japanese government's decision to purchase the islands, thereby nationalizing them, was spurred not by any overt intention to increase tensions with China, but to prevent the islands, which were owned privately, from falling into the hands of the highly nationalist governor of Tokyo, Shintaro Ishihara. One scholar, Toru Horiuchi, notes that Ishihara's plans, which could ultimately have been much worse for China-Japan relations, had public support in Japan, thereby prompting the Japanese government's decision to act preemptively.[23] The islands, which are administered by Japan, had previously been at the center of a 2010 dispute in which Japan's coast guard arrested a Chinese fisherman near the islands.[24] That incident drew Chinese criticism and resulted in a temporary freeze on the export of Chinese rare earth minerals to Japan. However, it did not spark a broader and long-term diplomatic freeze like the 2012 nationalization, which came at a time of extreme fragility between China and Japan.[25]

The Noda government's 2012 decision to nationalize the islands was followed by a period of political change in Japan where the conservative, nationalist-leaning Liberal Democratic Party (LDP), led by Shinzo Abe, who had served as prime minister from 2006 to 2007, returned to power.[26] Abe's return to the fore in Tokyo began a period during which Beijing and Tokyo seldom spoke at a high level.[27] At one point, no high-level contact between Japanese and Chinese diplomats had occurred for at least fourteen months.[28] Tensions rose through 2013 and the early months of 2014, eventually stabilizing as China began shifting its own attention toward the South China Sea. However, in late 2013, China unilaterally declared the imposition of an air defense identification zone (ADIZ) over the East China Sea, including over the disputed islands.[29] Chinese sources, as Michael D. Swaine has documented, justified the move as a "legitimate national security–related measure similar in function to ADIZs established by other nations and intended to strengthen Chinese security and increase regional safety."[30] The Japanese government, along with the United States, condemned the move and instructed its civilian aviators to avoid complying with Chinese ADIZ requirements. The United States, to emphasize the perceived illegitimacy of the ADIZ, flew two B-52 bombers over the East China Sea in November 2013.[31] The bombers did not originate from U.S. bases in Tokyo, however—they flew from the U.S. Andersen Air Force Base in Guam.[32] In anticipation of heightened tensions in the region as a result of international arbitration filed by the Philippines, China shifted its attention to the South China Sea, where it embarked on extensive island-building and construction projects—euphemistically dubbed "land reclamation." Beginning roughly in early 2014, Japanese attention shifted accordingly.[33] Still, the East China Sea continues to feature as an area of primary interest for national security planners in Tokyo. For example, Japan's Defense White Paper released in July 2015 emphasizes Chinese resource exploration activity along disputed gas fields in the East China Sea.[34]

At the same time, it should be noted that the white paper devotes extensive attention to the East and South China Sea issues, emphasizing the extent to which it appears to have captured the attention of Japanese leaders, including, most importantly, Shinzo Abe's cabinet.[35] Reports in the Japanese press ahead of the release of the white paper noted that the *kantei*, the prime minister's office manned by approximately three hundred officials and parliamentarians close to and working for Abe, were unwilling to approve a preliminary draft of the white paper due to what they perceived as an inadequate amount of attention devoted to the East China Sea issue. The paper was revised accordingly and was released with roughly one-third of its more than four hundred pages devoted to Chinese activities in the East and South China Seas, including Beijing's provocative island-building activities in the latter. Japan's 2016 White Paper echoed these themes, emphasizing maritime difficulties in both seas.[36]

It is plausible that strategic planners in Tokyo, including those within the Self-Defense Forces (SDF), have noted that China generally has avoided the pursuit of destabilizing activities in more than one area at once. Thus, when Chinese island-building, patrols, and other activities, including the controversial May 2014 deployment of an oil rig into waters disputed with Vietnam, occurred, the East China Sea remained relatively calm.[37] In fact, late 2014 witnessed the resumption of high-level diplomatic ties between Tokyo and Beijing, paving the way for the first official meeting between Japanese prime minister Shinzo Abe and Chinese president Xi Jinping on the sidelines of the Asia-Pacific Economic Cooperation Summit in 2014. Leading up to that encounter, Japanese national security chief Shotaro Yachi met Chinese state councilor Yang Jiechi in November 2014.[38] The two senior officials agreed to a "four-point consensus," which created a path back to diplomatic normalcy after a nearly two-year freeze in high-level contact following the Senkaku nationalization.[39] For China, this was ostensibly driven by a desire to restore good ties across the East China Sea as the South China Sea began to heat up in late 2014 and early 2015.

Thus, in thinking about Japan's shifting perspective toward the South China Sea, it is important to remember the centrality of the East China Sea, including the dispute over the sovereignty of the Senkaku Islands and the final delimitation of Chinese and Japanese EEZs, in Japanese strategic thought. The East China Sea is an area with direct relevance to Japan's national security and defense interests. Meanwhile, the South China Sea is relevant to Japan insofar as it is an area where the sinews underlying the contemporary Asian order risk being frayed by Chinese irredentism. In what follows, we offer a broader discussion of the recent trends in Japanese domestic politics, regional diplomacy, and U.S. alliance dynamics that have informed Tokyo's strategic approach to the South China Sea issue.

A TRANSFORMATION IN DOMESTIC AND ALLIANCE POLITICS

Recent trends in Japanese domestic politics have seen the country head toward a complete recalibration of its security policy under the LDP government of Shinzo Abe.[40] To understand Japan's broader perspective toward the South China Sea issue, it is first worth considering these trends. Notably, Abe, as prime minister, has spent considerable political capital in posturing Japan as a "normal" country. Since its adoption following Japan's defeat in World War II, the constitution has forbidden the country from ever engaging in war; specifically, Article 9 of the constitution states that "the Japanese people forever renounce war as a sovereign right of the nation and the threat or use of force as means of settling international disputes." Abe has sought to stretch the meaning of Article 9 so as to allow Japan to act as a "proactive pacifist" country—an objective that Beijing views negatively.[41] He has made little secret of his intentions to recalibrate Japan's national defense policies. In fact, Abe attempted to do so during his first term (2006–7) but was resolutely unsuccessful at the time. Nevertheless, he was able to establish a ministry of defense for Japan. The country up to that point did not have a cabinet-level ministry to handle the country's defense portfolio.

Shortly after returning to the prime minister's office in late 2012, Abe moved to implement a national security council for Japan, modeled after the institution of the same name within the U.S. national security apparatus. Japan's 2014 white paper described the council, which was established formally in December 2013, as "the control tower of [Japan's] foreign and defense policies."[42] The economic agenda and the implementation of "Abenomics" mostly topped the *kantei's* agenda in 2013, but in 2014, the Abe cabinet moved to lift Japan's self-imposed ban on exporting weapons.[43] The ban, put into place in 1967, was based on "three principles": Japan would not export weapons to communist states, countries under United Nations sanctions, and countries in armed conflict. In practice, Japan exported no weapons initially, pursuing limited defense research and development for its own SDF. In April 2014, the export ban was overturned, although conditions remain. First, no weapons can be exported to countries under United Nations Security Council sanctions, such as North Korea and Iran. Second, defense exports, especially those with a joint research and development component, with such countries as the United States, the United Kingdom, France, Australia, India, and some Southeast Asian countries, can be allowed by the Japanese government's decision as long as they are deemed to contribute to Japan's security. Third, weapons exports are allowed only when the governments of importing countries are obligated to abide by an agreement governing the use of the technology. In 2015, Japan started discussions about the export of defense technology with Australia, the United Kingdom, the United States, and India.

Another watershed moment in recent Japanese defense reforms included the *kantei's* decision to reinterpret Article 9 of the constitution as allowing Japan to practice the right of collective self-defense.[44] The reinterpretation move drew controversy in Japan but was consistent with how Japanese cabinets and legislators had previously handled unprecedented military deployments, including the participation of noncombatant SDF units in the 2003 Iraq war under the Junichiro Koizumi administration. Alongside these domestic reforms, Abe embarked on a diplomatic "charm offensive" across Asia, approaching states that were like-minded on China's potential threat to the status quo Asian order. These states included India, Australia, and the Southeast Asian claimant states in the South China Sea. The outreach also included, naturally, Japan's decades-long ally, the United States. Abe's efforts in Washington culminated with a historic speech before a joint session of Congress in April 2015, the first ever by a Japanese prime minister, where he delivered assurances that his defense reforms would move forward.[45]

Specifically, during his address before U.S. legislators, Abe outlined a large substantive scope for his reform agenda. He noted that his government was "working hard to enhance the legislative foundations for our security," and that once the reforms were in place, "Japan will be much more able to provide a seamless response for all levels of crisis." Abe, pointing to the U.S.-Japan alliance itself, noted that the "enhanced legislative foundations should make the cooperation between the U.S. military and Japan's Self Defense Forces even stronger, and the alliance still more solid, providing credible deterrence for the peace in the region."[46]

Abe's defense reforms culminated in an uproar regarding a national defense legislation package that would effectively legalize the *kantei*'s controversial 2014 reinterpretation of Article 9 to allow for collective self-defense. The lower house's decision to approve the package in July 2015 was so controversial that it resulted in the largest public protests in Japan since the Fukushima Daiichi fiasco in 2011. The legislative package passed in the upper house on September 19 by a simple majority of the LDP-Komeito party coalition. Despite widespread protests and a commensurate dip in Abe's approval ratings, scholars familiar with Japanese defense policy over the decades note that the Abe administration's approach represents continuity rather than change in how Japan goes about evolving its SDF to meet new challenges. Others, such as Yuki Tatsumi, noted that the Abe government could have seized the opportunity of the legislative debate to clarify Japan's shifting security environment since the end of the Cold War, justifying the defense reform package in terms "beyond the vague notion of 'proactive contribution to international peace.'"[47]

Reactions to the lower house debate in July 2015 overstated Japan's pacifist history and the extent to which the proposed legislative package is revolutionary. Despite Article 9, Japan has never practiced strict pacifism—indeed, the very existence of the SDF is a testament to this fact. Jennifer Lind, a scholar of Japanese foreign policy, offered a sober reaction to the legislative package. Writing for the *Wall Street Journal* shortly after protests erupted in Tokyo, she noted that "Tokyo decisively rejected pacifism by adopting a grand strategy of limited remilitarization and alliance with the U.S."[48] Recalling this and acknowledging Japan's perception of Asia's shifting geopolitical architecture and growing threats, the Abe national security legislative package is a reaction to changing times wholly consistent with Japan's postwar approach to its military. As Lind noted at the time, "The new security legislation is merely Tokyo's most recent calibration of a grand strategy in which Japan does less when it can, and more when it must."[49] As Tokyo sees a potential need to fight alongside the United States to preserve maritime security and freedom of navigation in the region—including in the South China Sea—the administration sees this legislative package as central.[50]

Following the lower house debates focused on constitutional issues from the coalition government's point of view, upper house debates focused on the assessment of the security environments Japan faces. One pronounced feature of upper house debates should be singled out: the expeditionary nature of proposed SDF security operations was neither diluted nor deleted. Proposed regular Maritime Self Defense Forces (MSDF) patrols of the South China Sea were not specified.

Japan's alliance with the United States has been a key linchpin of the country's thinking about its national defense since the two countries signed their Treaty of Mutual Cooperation and Security in 1960. Given Japan's constitutional limitations on maintaining an active and offensive-capable military, its alliance with the United States—the world's foremost military power—has been considered central to securing its defense interests. Unsurprisingly, therefore, doubts about the U.S. willingness and ability to guarantee extended deterrence for Japan, increasing at the same time as China's acceleration of assertive military activity in the East and South China Seas, have resulted in some voices within Japan—certainly within the more conservative LDP—calling for the country to prepare for the day where it has to account for its own defense.[51]

The *kantei*'s reinterpretation of Article 9 as permitting collective self-defense is of direct relevance to the U.S.-Japan alliance. In the wake of the announcement, the United States and Japan worked toward a revision of their Bilateral Defense Guidelines, a set of stipulations outlining their defense cooperation in peacetime and wartime. The guidelines, untouched since 1997, were modified to reflect Japan's new defense posture, highlighting a more "global" role for the U.S.-Japan alliance. This has been interpreted to mean that, as far as Japan's role in the South China Sea is concerned, any potential U.S. involvement in a future conflict there could mean a role for Japan, so long as the Japanese government is able to substantiate a direct threat to the welfare and safety of the Japanese people. Masahiko Komura, vice president of the LDP, noted in March 2015 that the collective self-defense reinterpretation was predicated on the constitutional imperative of the Japanese government to protect the lives and happiness of the Japanese people.[52] Though the South China Sea is not geographically proximal to the Japanese people (unlike the Senkakus, which are a stone's throw from the populated islands of the Ryukyu chain, including Okinawa), Japan's reliance on South China Sea–borne commerce could form the basis of the government's legal argument for kinetic involvement in a conflict there.

Moreover, heading into mid-2015, senior U.S. military officials began to openly allude to the prospect (which was eventually realized) of Japanese patrols in the South China Sea. In January 2015, Adm. Robert Thomas, the commander of the U.S. Seventh Fleet and the top U.S. naval officer for Asia, told reporters that the United States would welcome an expanded Japanese role in the South China Sea. "I think allies, partners, and friends in the region will look to the Japanese more and more as a stabilizing function," he told the press at the time.[53] In April 2015, U.S. secretary of defense Ashton Carter and his Japanese counterpart Gen Nakatani agreed that both their countries opposed any attempts to change the status quo through the use of force—a message implicitly directed at China.[54] Reports as early as May 2015 highlighted that the idea of joint U.S.-Japan patrols in the South China Sea were raised during the defense guideline revision process.[55] Echoing earlier reports, Japan's highest-ranking military officer, Admiral Katsutoshi Kawano, the chief of the joint staff of Japan's SDF, confirmed his country's interest in expanding operations in the South China Sea: "Of course, the area is of the utmost importance for Japanese security. We don't have any plans to conduct surveillance in the South China Sea currently but depending on the situation, I think there is a chance we could consider doing so. . . . In the case of China, as we can see with the South China Sea problem, they are rapidly expanding their naval presence and their defense spending is still growing. Also because there is a lack of transparency, we are very concerned about China's actions."[56]

From the U.S. perspective, an expanded role for Japan in the South China Sea is consistent with the Obama administration's "Rebalance to Asia" strategy. Particularly given trends in domestic U.S. politics, including defense spending sequestration, Washington is eager to see its Asian allies bear a greater proportion of the burden for their own defense. In the South China Sea in particular, Washington is eager to see a broader role for Tokyo to add legitimacy to its calls to preserve the regional status quo amid China's island-building and construction work.

In August 2015, the U.S. Department of Defense released a strategic document, *The Asia-Pacific Maritime Security Strategy*, that, inter alia, outlined how Washington continues to see Japan as the linchpin of its forward military presence in Asia.[57] "The cornerstone of our forward presence will continue to be our presence in Japan, where the United States maintains approximately 50,000 military personnel, including the U.S. Navy's Seventh Fleet and the only forward-stationed Carrier Strike Group in the world," the report notes.[58] It also asserts that in order to ensure that the U.S. presence in Asia is "sustainable," the United States and Japan are working to "develop a new laydown for the U.S. Marine Corps in the Pacific," which includes a shift toward a more geographically distributed model across Australia, Hawaii, Guam, and mainland Japan.[59] Implicit in this outline of the United States' shifting military geography is a bid to improve the "readiness of our forward forces to respond to regional crises," including in the South China Sea.[60]

Finally, in October 2015, three days after the United States staged its first freedom of navigation operation in the South China Sea by sailing an *Arleigh Burke*–class guided missile destroyer within twelve nautical miles of a Chinese artificial island in the South China Sea, the Japanese Maritime Self-Defense Force joined the U.S. Navy for the first-ever bilateral naval exercise in the region between the allies.[61] The exercise represented a culmination of a range of the processes in the U.S.-Japan alliance that we describe above.

EXTENT OF JAPAN'S SOUTH CHINA SEA–RELATED ACTIVITIES

In what follows, we detail Japan's posture and activities in the South China Sea and its diplomatic relations with continental and maritime Southeast Asian states. As already noted, the stakes in the South China Sea have risen dramatically in the second decade of the twenty-first century. The current period of increased tensions originated with the 2012 standoff between the Philippines and China over Scarborough Shoal.[62] That year coincided with the tipping point in Japanese security and defense policy that the LDP's return to power ushered in.

Japan and the Philippines

In 2015, Japan drastically increased its security cooperation with the Philippines, another U.S.-allied Asian state and a South China Sea territorial claimant. In 2014, Tokyo came out in support of the Philippines' decision to file arbitral proceedings against China at the Permanent Court of Arbitration: "The Government of Japan supports the Philippines' use of procedures under the United Nations Convention on the Law of the Sea aiming at peaceful settlement of disputes on the basis of international law, as such an action contributes to the maintenance and enhancement of the international order in the region based on the rule of law."[63]

From June 22 to June 26, 2015, a Japanese MSDF P3-C Orion landed on the Philippines' Palawan Island to engage in a training exercise with the Philippine navy.[64] Nominally, the exercise was intended to increase maritime security cooperation and interoperability between the two navies. Instead, much attention focused on the P3-C Orion's flight over the frontier of Reed Bank in the Spratly Islands with a Philippine naval crew on board. According to the Philippines, Reed Bank is incontrovertibly within its exclusive economic zone per UNCLOS, but this remains disputed by China. The Reed Bank component of the MSDF-Philippine navy exercises was intended to simulate a search for a shipwrecked vessel.

The MSDF surveillance flight did not go unnoticed in China. Chinese commentator Wang Haiqing, writing for China's state-run Xinhua news agency, called the exercise the "latest sequel to Tokyo's meddling in the South China Sea."[65] Wang goes on to accuse Japan of diverting its military attention to the South China Sea to force China to in turn move its resources away from the East China Sea, where Japan and China dispute the sovereignty of the Senkaku/Diaoyu Islands. He also notes that Abe's rapprochement with the Philippines is a ploy to win broader public support for Abe's contentious defense reforms in Japan, where public opinion on the issue has been divided.[66]

Tokyo and Manila will continue to increase their military contacts with the United States' blessing. The Balikatan joint exercise in 2015, which included more than 15,000 U.S., Philippine, and Australian troops, featured personnel from Japan's SDF as observers.[67] Also, in a first, in August 2015, as part of the U.S.-led Pacific Partnership series of exercises involving seven regional states, Japan joined humanitarian vessels from the Philippines and the United States for a refueling and humanitarian assistance exercise off Subic Bay, the site of a former U.S. naval base in the Philippines and a strategically located South China Sea littoral port.[68] The U.S. commander leading the exercise, Rear Adm. Charles Williams of the

U.S. Seventh Fleet's Task Force 73, noted that the fact that Tokyo had sent Admiral Katsutoshi Kawano, its most senior military official, spoke "volumes about their commitment to the region and their commitment to being part of a multilateral engagement."[69] The optics of Tokyo's participation were an unmistakable sign of its increasing engagement with the Philippines and the United States in and around the South China Sea.

For the Philippines, the rapprochement with Tokyo is both necessary and strategically sound given its broader regional position. Manila's hard power resources are limited—an inconvenient reality given the rise in tensions in the region and, in particular, China's willingness to use kinetic assertion to emphasize its maritime and territorial claims in the South China Sea. As a result, Manila has to hedge its position by banding together with its traditional ally, the United States, and now also with Japan. Japan's recalibrated defense posture and gradual shift toward a more expeditionary role for the SDF makes it a natural partner for the Philippines in the South China Sea. Underpinning this convergence is the fact that Japan continues to be the Philippines' most important trading partner and official development assistance donor among Southeast Asian states.[70]

Security commentators have noted that Japan and the Philippines have established a de facto alliance given mutual concerns over China's rise. In 2015, the year marking the seventieth anniversary of the end of World War II in Asia, many countries in the region exhibited a major focus on history. In particular, observers across Asia were looking to see if Abe would continue the trend of apologizing for Japan's wartime atrocities in line with the statements by Prime Ministers Tomiichi Murayama in 1995 and Junichiro Koizumi in 2005. One of the few remaining areas of tension between the Philippines and Japan is over this history issue. Philippine "comfort women," like their South Korean counterparts, have demanded recognition and compensation from the government of Japan. Overall, however, following Abe's 2015 statement on the war, the Philippines issued no comment—abstaining from either praising or criticizing the agreement.[71] Tellingly, neither Tokyo nor Manila sent any high-level representation to a September 3 parade held in Beijing to commemorate the seventieth anniversary of the war's end; Japan saw the parade as a Chinese attempt to emphasize Japanese wartime atrocities. For Manila, in order to realistically cooperate with Tokyo over the South China Sea, historical issues have to be set aside in favor of pragmatic cooperation.

Critically, when in July 2016 a five-judge tribunal based at the Permanent Court of Arbitration ruled overwhelmingly in favor of Manila's submissions in its 2013 case against China over maritime entitlements in the South China Sea,

Japan voiced strong and enthusiastic support for the ruling. Foreign Minister Fumio Kishida immediately released a statement on the award, noting that Japan considered it "final and legally binding on the parties to the dispute under the provisions of UNCLOS." He added that "the parties to this case are required to comply with the award. . . . Japan strongly expects that the parties' compliance with this award will eventually lead to the peaceful settlement of disputes in the South China Sea."[72] Tokyo's strong position in the aftermath of the ruling left it as the only nonclaimant Asian state to describe the ruling as final and legally binding on China—a position shared by claimant states the Philippines and Vietnam. The July 2016 ruling is the most significant international legal development concerning the disputed maritime claims in the South China Sea. That Tokyo immediately staked out a principled position based on the legitimacy of international law suggests that Japan's grand strategic thinking about the South China Sea will continue to be framed in the language of the rules-based global order.

Viewed over a longer term, Manila's pursuit of a policy compatible with U.S. and Japanese approaches in the South China Sea is not guaranteed—something that Tokyo, like other regional states, has had to reckon with, especially with Philippine president Rodrigo Duterte. Duterte, early in his first term, showed signs of breaking with the internationalist approach to resolving disputes championed by the Benigno Aquino administration. Moreover, Duterte has questioned the utility of the Philippines' closeness to the United States.[73] In particular, should the Philippines pursue a longer-term approach of pursuing bilateralism with China over the South China Sea without conditions stemming from the July 2016 ruling, Tokyo may have to reconsider its longer-term engagement with Manila.

Japan and Indonesia

The election of Indonesian president Joko "Jokowi" Widodo in late 2014 led to a shift in Indonesia's maritime policy.[74] Though the state is not an active claimant in the South China Sea, it has grown concerned about the ambiguity surrounding China's "U-shaped line" claim to waters near the Natuna archipelago.[75] Some commentators and analysts have described Jokowi's approach to maritime issues as heavy-handed, primarily with reference to his administration's early move to sink illegal fishing vessels operating in Indonesian waters.[76] In mid-2016, Jokowi, demonstrating an intention to buttress Jakarta's position in the Natunas following repeated encounters involving Indonesian maritime law enforcement vessels and China's coast guard, announced the start of a massive government-backed initiative to tap the Natuna archipelago's rich natural gas reserves.[77]

In March 2015, Jokowi and Abe signed a new defense partnership and set out to establish a high-level bilateral maritime forum to discuss a range of issues related to maritime security, commerce, and the preservation of "free, open, and stable seas."[78] This initiative was in part spurred by the Jokowi administration's push to turn Indonesia into a "global maritime fulcrum," an objective he announced at the 2014 East Asia Summit.[79] In the same speech, he called on all parties in the South China Sea maritime territorial disputes to exercise restraint, respect the 2002 Declaration on the Conduct of Parties in the South China Sea, and seek a solution within the framework of existing international law.[80] For Japan, it was immediately apparent that Jokowi's perspective had much in common with Tokyo's own goals in the South China Sea. Additionally, given Indonesia's status as primus inter pares in ASEAN, coordination with the Jokowi government would be necessary for any long-term Japanese influence within the organization.

However, Indonesia—building on its history as a leader within the nonaligned movement—remains interested in maintaining a degree of neutrality in the region, particularly with regard to relations between China and the rest of the ASEAN member states. Indonesia applies neutrality to its relations with Japan as well. Jokowi visited both Beijing and Tokyo on the same trip, lest it appear that Indonesia was pivoting too far either way.[81] In Beijing, Jokowi showed that Indonesia would continue to work with China as a maritime partner. The Xi-Jokowi joint statement set out an agenda on defense and maritime cooperation.[82] Jokowi's approach to Indonesia's position in Asia seems to be driven by a combination of pragmatism and a populist impulse to appear strong on issues concerning Indonesia's sovereignty. Abe's Japan has demonstrated its willingness to appeal to both impulses in its approach toward Jakarta in late 2014 and early 2015.

Japan and Vietnam

In the summer of 2014, Vietnam seemed to be the most likely state to have a kinetic faceoff with China over disputed claims in the South China Sea. Starting in early May, after China moved its state-owned *Hai Yang Shi You* 981 (HD-981) oil rig, flanked by scores of civilian, coast guard, and naval vessels, into an area off the disputed Paracel Islands, relations between Vietnam and China hit their lowest point since the two countries fought a war in 1979.[83] Conflict became increasingly likely due to the elevated nationalist rhetoric in both countries over the sovereignty of the Paracel Islands.[84]

In August 2014, toward the end of the Vietnam-China flareup, Japanese foreign minister Fumio Kishida visited Hanoi and announced a ¥500 million (roughly $5 million) deal for Vietnam to purchase Japanese maritime surveillance vessels. In his statement publicizing the deal, Kishida further noted that Tokyo and Hanoi had agreed to "maintaining peace and stability" measures in regional waters.[85] In addition to the sale, Japan agreed to provide training and equipment to help the Vietnamese enhance their maritime surveillance capabilities using the vessels as soon as possible.[86]

The summer 2014 incident between Vietnam and China was an important exogenous factor for helping to drive Japan and Vietnam closer together. Vietnam had maintained generally cordial relations with Beijing until the incident, owing to a general degree of solidarity between the ruling communist parties in both countries. The oil rig saga transformed Vietnam's thinking about the threat China posed in the South China Sea, which, combined with the resulting rise in Vietnamese nationalism, prompted a foreign policy shift. Coverage of the HD-981 incident included reports of Chinese vessels ramming and capsizing Vietnamese ships, sparking outrage across Vietnam that included protests against Chinese citizens and Chinese-owned businesses in the country.[87] The incident irreparably drove Hanoi and Beijing apart, leaving the door open for Tokyo to initiate a well-timed strategic overture toward Vietnam.

For Vietnam, the post–HD-981 period has also included a rapprochement with the United States, which has had implications for Japan's perspective toward Vietnam. Emblematic of this shift was the October 2014 announcement, following Vietnamese deputy prime minister Pham Binh Mih's visit to the United States, that the decades-long U.S. embargo on arms sales to Vietnam would be partially lifted, specifically to allow sales that would help Vietnam bolster its maritime security.[88] In June 2015, U.S. defense secretary Ashton Carter traveled to Vietnam—having just delivered a stirring defense of the status quo in the South China Sea at the 2015 Shangri-La Dialogue in Singapore—to announce $18 million in U.S. financing to help Vietnam acquire coast guard patrol vessels.[89] As a capstone to this era of swift strategic rapprochement between the United States and Vietnam, roughly forty years after the fall of Saigon marked an end to the Vietnam War, the general-secretary of Vietnam's ruling Communist Party visited the United States.[90]

For Japan, the United States' ongoing strategic rapprochement with Vietnam is a strong vote of confidence that Hanoi can be enlisted in the broader project to preserve the status quo in the South China Sea. As a result, going forward, Tokyo is likely to expand its cooperation with Hanoi on maritime security matters and actively assist Vietnam in its bid to administer its claimed exclusive economic zone in the South China Sea. Interestingly, as some observers have noted, there is a burgeoning track-two trilateral process incorporating the United States, Japan, and Vietnam, which could signal a formal track-one trilateral on the horizon.[91]

Japan and Malaysia

In May 2015, during Malaysian prime minister Najib Razak's visit to Tokyo, Japan and Malaysia signed a new strategic partnership designed to raise the status of their bilateral relationship.[92] Notably, the joint statement devoted considerable attention to two topics relevant to the current situation in the South China Sea: "Cooperation for Peace and Stability" and "Achieving Free, Open, and Stable Seas."[93] Specifically, the statement noted that "Prime Minister Abe supported Malaysia's continued efforts in ensuring the safety and security of Malaysia's maritime zones, in particular the SLOC [Sea Line of Communication] in [the] Straits of Malacca and the South China Sea."[94] The two sides also agreed to begin discussions on the transfer of defense equipment and other sensitive technology, signaling a shift in Malaysia's approach toward Tokyo.

Malaysia, more so than the other major claimants in the South China Sea, has taken a nuanced approach to its dispute with China, often avoiding direct confrontation with Beijing over the issue. Malaysia has also directly cooperated with China—in August 2015, the Chinese defense ministry announced that Chinese and Malaysian armed forces would host their first joint live-troop exercise.[95] That announcement, however, came just after Malaysia began the CARAT (Cooperation Afloat Readiness and Training) Malaysia 2015 bilateral naval exercise with the United States.[96] Malaysia has pursued a strategy of "playing it safe" when it comes to the South China Sea, favoring cordial diplomacy with China while also pursuing its claims and interests in the region.[97] In this sense, Malaysia has found it valuable to increase its cooperation with Japan.

Japan and "Continental" ASEAN: Cambodia, Laos, Myanmar, Thailand

Early in July 2015, Abe joined his counterparts from Cambodia, Laos, Myanmar, Thailand, and Vietnam—the five continental members of ASEAN as well as five of the six states through which the Mekong River runs—to announce a comprehensive strategy outlining Japan's cooperation with this group of states, known as the "Mekong Five."[98] The 2015 strategy built on Japan's legacy of robust overseas development assistance to Southeast Asian states but focused specifically on the idea of "quality infrastructure," a concept Abe had emphasized earlier and Japan had developed based on consultation with the Mekong Five.

Along with the announcement of the Mekong strategy, Japan appropriated an additional ¥750 billion (approximately $6.1 billion) in assistance and aid to the Mekong Five through 2020. Mainstream reporting on the development sought to color it as a Japanese attempt for sustained relevance through a source of development assistance for infrastructure projects, given the launch of the China-led Asian Infrastructure Investment Bank in October 2014. In fact, this would be a misleading assessment. Tokyo's new Mekong strategy was an important update to, and entirely consistent with, Japan's approach to the region.

The joint statement on the "New Tokyo Strategy 2015 for Mekong-Japan Cooperation" details Japan's plans for "quality infrastructure" provision in the region via four pillars. These include "industrial infrastructure development; soft infrastructure; sustainable development; and the coordination of frameworks."[99] Uniquely, Japan will focus its resources on helping the region develop soft infrastructure—industrial structures and human resource development—in addition to more fundamental hard infrastructure such as roads, railways, and ports.

With regard to the South China Sea, it is notable that the Mekong Five—all members of ASEAN—do not hold a consistent position on how the Southeast Asian organization should approach the issue of disputed maritime territory. For example, Vietnam's experience with China in May 2014, when the two states reached a nadir in their bilateral ties resulting from the HD-981 incident, stands diametrically opposed to Thailand's and Cambodia's perfectly amicable ties with China. In 2016, during Laos' chairmanship of ASEAN, Cambodia in particular acted as a spoiler, preventing ASEAN unity on the question of the South China Sea disputes.

As far as Japan is concerned, among the Mekong Five, only Vietnam will be receptive to Japan's interests in the South China Sea over the long term. Laos is landlocked, and even if it had an interest in maritime issues, its proximity to China dampens any interest in ruffling Beijing's feathers over the South China Sea. Myanmar, also without maritime access to the South China Sea, has undergone a period of political reform following the historic triumph of the National League for Democracy and seeks to rebalance its ties with China amid its broader opening to Western states and Chinese competitors like India.

CONCLUSION

Two primary trends ensure that Japan will continue to remain a strategically interested and important actor in the South China Sea issue. First, Japan's evolving security posture and ongoing shifts in how Tokyo perceives the United States' long-term approach to the Asia-Pacific region lead it to take a greater interest in the South China Sea. It will continue to build ties with ASEAN states, including claimant states that have experienced difficult episodes with China in recent years, notably the Philippines and Vietnam. Secondly, as Japan's 2015 Defense White Paper proves, Japan perceives China as its primary security threat and strategic challenge. This threat perception does not manifest in narrow concerns about sovereignty and maritime delimitation in the South China Sea. Indeed, Japan, as a status quo middle power in Asia, has an important stake in preserving the contemporary order in the region and seeing the universality of international law upheld. To this end, Tokyo will continue to advocate at global and regional forums for the resolution of ongoing disputes in the South China Sea through peaceful means, and for all claimants in the region to uphold universal principles in customary and formal international law, including freedom of navigation and overflight.

Having acknowledged Tokyo's sustained interest in the South China Sea issue, the authors believe that three critical dynamics and events will largely determine Tokyo's strategic thinking regarding the South China Sea. First, given the continued salience of the U.S.-Japan alliance, Tokyo will avoid making any public statements or taking any policy positions that contravene the United States' considered position on the South China Sea issue. The Japanese government reads Washington's October 2015 initiation of regular freedom of navigation patrols in the South China Sea as a positive development that tested and revealed China's reaction to having its excessive maritime claims challenged. Second, as a long-term grand strategy, Tokyo will avoid putting undue pressure on China in the South China Sea to avoid a deterioration of the status quo in the East China Sea or in the general bilateral relationship. As China's 2010 decision to suspend commerce over the arrest of a Chinese fisherman demonstrates, Beijing is willing to impose costs on Tokyo for moves it perceives as threatening or worrisome. Third, like all stakeholders in the South China Sea (including the United States), Tokyo will continue to take a particular interest in bilateral developments between the Philippines and China in the South China Sea. The tribunal's strong award in the Philippines' favor and nullification of China's U-shaped line claim will factor into Tokyo's calculus for its moves in the South China Sea leading into the 2020s.

Overall, Tokyo recognizes that in order to remain a strategically relevant power in Asia and to protect its broader interests, Japan must understand, react to, and shape the regional conversation around the South China Sea. In particular, for Shinzo Abe's vision of a "proactively pacifist" Japan to persist beyond his time as prime minister, Tokyo will have to afford the South China Sea sustained strategic attention.

Notes

1. Robert D. Kaplan, *Asia's Cauldron: The South China Sea and the End of a Stable Pacific* (New York: Random House, 2014); Bill Hayton, *The South China Sea: The Struggle for Power in Asia* (New Haven: Yale University Press, 2014).
2. Hiroki Takeuchi, "Sino-Japanese Relations: Power, Interdependence, and Domestic Politics," *International Relations of the Asia-Pacific* 14, no. 1 (2014): pp. 7–32; Takashi Inoguchi, "A Call for a New Japanese Foreign Policy," *International Affairs* 90, no. 4 (2014): pp. 943–58, and "War Occurrence: Hyper-insecurity and Multilateral Institutions," *Japanese Journal of Political Science* 16, no. 3 (2015): pp. 388–98.
3. Reinhard Drifte, "The Senkaku/Diaoyu Islands Territorial Dispute between Japan and China: Between the Materialization of the China Threat and Japan Reversing the Outcome of World War II?" *UNISCI Discussion Papers* 32 (2014): pp. 9–62; Inoguchi, "A Call for a New Japanese Foreign Policy"; Takashi Inoguchi, "The Rise of 'Abegeopolitics': Japan's New Engagement with the World," *Global Asia* 9, no. 3 (2014): pp. 30–36.
4. For a broader discussion of the U.S. rebalance to Asia, see Patrick Cullen, *The Long, Short, and Breadth of It: Mapping the Pentagon's Rebalance to Asia* (Oslo: Norwegian Institute of Policy Affairs, 2014); Gary J. Schmitt, *Challenges to the U.S. Rebalance to Asia* (Washington, D.C.: American Enterprise Institute, 2014); Takashi Inoguchi, G. John Ikenberry, and Yoichiro Sato, eds., *The Troubled Triangle: Economic and Security Concerns for the United States, Japan and China* (New York: Palgrave Macmillan, 2013); Takashi Inoguchi, "Speculating on Asian Security, 2013–2033," *European Review of International Studies* 1, no. 1 (2014): pp. 46–56.
5. For background, see Siguar Center and Affiliated Experts, "Shinzo Abe's Foreign Policy and Reactions from Asian Powers," *POLICY* (2015), http://www.risingpowersinitiative.org/shinzo-abes-foreign-policy-and-reactions-from-asian-powers/; Tung-Chieh Tsai, "Abe's New Foreign Strategy and Its Challenges," *Prospect Journal* 11 (2014): pp. 99–125; Tomohiko Taniguchi, "China's Rise: Changing Contours of Japan's Foreign Policy," in *Emerging China: Prospects of Partnership in Asia*, ed. Sudhir T. Devare, Swaran Singh, and Reena Marwah (London: Taylor and Francis, 2014), 182; Purnendra Jain and Peng Er Lam, *Japan's Strategic Challenges in a Changing Regional Environment* (Singapore: World Scientific, 2012).
6. Paul Midford, "Japan's Approach to Maritime Security in the South China Sea," *Asian Survey* 55, no. 3 (2015): pp. 525–47.
7. Ibid.
8. Candace Dunn and Mark J. Eshbaugh, "Japan Is the Second Largest Net Importer of Fossil Fuels in the World," U.S. Energy Information Administration, November 7, 2013, http://www.eia.gov/todayinenergy/detail.cfm?id=13711.
9. Paul B. Stares, ed., *Rethinking Energy Security in East Asia* (Tokyo: Nihon Kokusai Koryu Center, 2000); Dunn and Eshbaugh, "Japan Is the Second Largest Net Importer of Fossil Fuels in the World"; Norani Zulkifli, Sharifah Munirah Alatas, and Zarina Othman, "The Importance of the Malacca Straits to Japan: Cooperation and Contributions Toward Littoral States," *Jebat: Malaysian Journal of History, Politics, and Strategy* 41, no. 2 (2014): pp. 80–98.

10. Yoshihiko Shinoda, Tsutida Shouji, and Kimura Hiroshi, "Periodical Public Opinion Survey on Nuclear Energy (Inhabitants Living in the Tokyo Metropolitan Area)," *Transactions of the Atomic Energy Society of Japan* 13, no. 3 (2014): pp. 94–112, doi:10.3327/taesj.j13.018.
11. Dunn and Eshbaugh, "Japan Is the Second Largest Net Importer of Fossil Fuels in the World."
12. Joshua P. Rowan, "The U.S.-Japan Security Alliance, ASEAN, and the South China Sea Dispute," *Asian Survey* 45, no. 3 (2005): pp. 414–36.
13. Ibid.
14. Ministry of Foreign Affairs of the People's Republic of China, "Set Aside Dispute and Pursue Joint Development," http://www.fmprc.gov.cn/mfa_eng/ziliao_665539/3602_665543/3604_665547/t18023.shtml.
15. Leszek Buszynski, "The South China Sea: Oil, Maritime Claims, and U.S.-China Strategic Rivalry," *Washington Quarterly* 35, no. 2 (2012): pp. 139–56; Ian James Storey, "Creeping Assertiveness: China, the Philippines, and the South China Sea Dispute," *Contemporary Southeast Asia* 21, no. 1 (April 1999): pp. 95–118.
16. Ministry of Foreign Affairs of Japan, "Statement by the Press Secretary, Ministry of Foreign Affairs of Japan, on an Issue concerning the South China Sea (Arbitral Proceedings by the Philippines under the United Nations Convention on the Law of the Sea)," March 31, 2014.
17. Ibid.
18. Tomotaka Shoji, 'The South China Sea: A View from Japan," *NIDS Journal of Defense and Security,* no. 15 (December 2014), http://www.nids.go.jp/english/publication/kiyo/pdf/2014/bulletin_e2014_7.pdf.
19. Leszek Buszynski, "ASEAN, the Declaration on Conduct, and the South China Sea," *Contemporary Southeast Asia* (2003): pp. 343–62. For the full document, see Association of Southeast Asian Nations, "Declaration on the Conduct of Parties in the South China Sea," http://www.asean.org/asean/external-relations/china/item/declaration-on-the-conduct-of-parties-in-the-south-china-sea.
20. Mark J. Valencia, "The East China Sea Dispute: Context, Claims, Issues, and Possible Solutions," *Asian Perspective* 31, no. 1 (2007): pp. 127–67; Inoguchi, "War Occurrence."
21. Erica Strecker Downs and Phillip C. Saunders, "Legitimacy and the Limits of Nationalism: China and the Diaoyu Islands," *International Security* 23, no. 3 (1999): pp. 114–46, doi:10.1162/isec.23.3.114.
22. Linus Hagström, "China–Japan Tensions over Senkaku Purchase an Orchestrated Affair," *East Asia Forum* 17 (September 2012), http://www.eastasiaforum.org/2012/09/17/china-japan-tensions-over-senkaku-purchase-an-orchestrated-affair/; Takashi Inoguchi, "Japan in 2012: Voters Swing, and Swing Away Soon," *Asian Survey* 53, no. 1 (2013): pp. 184–97.
23. Toru Horiuchi, "Public Opinion in Japan and the Nationalization of the Senkaku Islands," *East Asia* 31, no. 1 (2014): pp. 23–47.
24. Linus Hagström, "'Power Shift' in East Asia? A Critical Reappraisal of Narratives on the Diaoyu/Senkaku Islands Incident in 2010," *Chinese Journal of International Politics* 5, no. 3 (2012): pp. 267–97.

25. Takashi Inoguchi, "Introduction to Special Issue: Japan-China Fragile Partnership: at Fortieth Anniversary of Diplomatic Normalization," *Japanese Journal of Political Science* 14, no. 1 (2013): pp. 1–7, doi:10.1017/s146810991200031x.
26. Martin Fackler, "Ex-Premier Is Chosen to Govern Japan Again," *New York Times*, December 26, 2012.
27. Chico Harlan, "As Japan and China Clash, Their Diplomats See Little Chance to Talk It Out," *Washington Post*, December 7, 2013.
28. Ibid.
29. Qiang Hou, "Announcement of the Aircraft Identification Rules for the East China Sea Air Defense Identification Zone of the P.R.C.," Xinhua, November 23, 2013; Inoguchi, "War Occurrence."
30. Michael D. Swaine, "'Chinese Views and Commentary on the East China Sea Air Defense Identification Zone (ECS ADIZ)," *China Leadership Monitor* 43, no. 1 (2014): pp. 24–25.
31. Julian Beijing, "U.S. Sends B-52s on Mission to Challenge Chinese Claims," *Wall Street Journal*, November 27, 2015, http://www.wsj.com/articles/SB10001424052702303281504579221993719005178.
32. Ibid.
33. Derek Watkins, "What China Has Been Building in the South China Sea," *New York Times*, July 30, 2015, http://www.nytimes.com/interactive/2015/07/30/world/asia/what-china-has-been-building-in-the-south-china-sea.html.
34. Ministry of Defense of Japan, "Defense of Japan 2015," http://www.mod.go.jp/e/publ/w_paper/2015.html.
35. Ibid.
36. Franz-Stefan Gady, "Japan's Defense White Paper Highlights Growing Threat from China," *The Diplomat*, August 2, 2016, http://thediplomat.com/2016/08/japans-defense-white-paper-highlights-growing-threat-from-china/.
37. Carl Thayer, "China's Oil Rig Gambit: South China Sea Game-Changer," *The Diplomat*, May 12, 2014, http://thediplomat.com/2014/05/chinas-oil-rig-gambit-south-china-sea-game-changer/.
38. Foreign Ministry of the People's Republic of China, "Yang Jiechi Meets National Security Advisor of Japan Shotaro Yachi: China and Japan Reach Four-Point Principled Agreement on Handling and Improving Bilateral Relations," November 11, 2014, http://www.fmprc.gov.cn/mfa_eng/zxxx_662805/t1208360.shtml.
39. Shannon Tiezzi, "A China-Japan Breakthrough: A Primer on Their 4-Point Consensus," *The Diplomat*, November 7, 2014, http://thediplomat.com/2014/11/a-china-japan-breakthrough-a-primer-on-their-4-point-consensus/.
40. Tung-Chieh Tsai, "Abe's New Foreign Strategy and Its Challenges," *Prospect Journal* 11 (2014): pp. 99–125; Inoguchi, "The Rise of 'Abegeopolitics'."
41. Xiaoming Zhang, "China's Perceptions of and Responses to Abe's Foreign Policy," *Asian Perspective* 39, no. 3 (2015): pp. 423–40.
42. Ministry of Defense of Japan, "Defense of Japan 2014," http://www.mod.go.jp/e/publ/w_paper/2014.html.
43. Eric Pfanner, "Japan Inc. Now Exporting Weapons," *Wall Street Journal*, July 20, 2014, http://www.wsj.com/articles/japans-military-contractors-make-push-in-weapons-exports-1405879822.

44. Adam P. Liff, "Japan's Defense Policy: Abe the Evolutionary," *Washington Quarterly* 38, no. 2 (2015): pp. 79–99; William Choong, "Defence and Japan's Constitutional Debate," *Survival* 57, no. 2 (2015): pp. 173–92; Axel Berkofsky, "Hijacking Japan's Security and Defence Policy Agenda?" *Security and Conflict in East Asia* (2015): p. 142.
45. Shannon Tiezzi, "Hope and History: Shinzo Abe's Speech to Congress," *The Diplomat*, April 30, 2015, http://thediplomat.com/2015/04/hope-and-history-shinzo-abes-speech-to-congress/.
46. Shinzo Abe, "Full Text of Abe's Speech before U.S. Congress," *Japan Times*, April 30, 2015, http://www.japantimes.co.jp/news/2015/04/30/national/politics-diplomacy/full-text-abes-speech-u-s-congress/.
47. Yuki Tatsumi, "Japan's New Security Legislation: A Missed Opportunity," *The Diplomat*, July 16, 2015, http://thediplomat.com/2015/07/japans-new-security-legislation-a-missed-opportunity/.
48. Jennifer Lind, "Japan's Security Evolution, Not Revolution," *Wall Street Journal*, July 20, 2015, http://www.wsj.com/articles/japans-security-evolution-not-revolution-1437410475.
49. Ibid.
50. Richard L. Armitage and Joseph S. Nye, *The U.S.-Japan Alliance: Anchoring Stability in Asia* (Washington, DC: Center for Strategic and International Studies, 2012), 2; Go Ito, "The U.S.-Japan Partnership for Maritime Security in the East and the South China Seas," *Journal of Contemporary East Asia Studies* 3, no. 2 (2012).
51. David J. Trachtenberg and Herman Kahn, "U.S. Extended Deterrence: How Much Strategic Force Is Too Little?" *Strategic Studies Quarterly* 6 (2012): pp. 62–92; Mira Rapp Hooper, "Uncharted Waters: Extended Deterrence and Maritime Disputes," *Washington Quarterly* 38, no. 1 (2015): pp. 127–46; Andrew O'Neil, "Extended Nuclear Deterrence in East Asia: Redundant or Resurgent?" *International Affairs* 87, no. 6 (2011): pp. 1439–57; James L. Schoff, *Realigning Priorities: The U.S.-Japan Alliance and the Future of Extended Deterrence* (Washington, D.C.: Institute for Foreign Policy Analysis, March 2009), http://www.ifpa.org/pdf/RealignPriorities.pdf.
52. Mina Pollman, "Japan's Argument for Collective Self-Defense," *The Diplomat*, March 30, 2015, http://thediplomat.com/2015/03/japans-argument-for-collective-self-defense/.
53. Tim Kelly and Nobuhiro Kubo, "U.S. Would Welcome Japan Air Patrols in South China Sea," Reuters, January 29, 2015.
54. "Japan, U.S. Consider Joint Surveillance in South China Sea," *Japan Times*, April 19, 2015, http://www.japantimes.co.jp/news/2015/04/19/national/japan-u-s-consider-joint-surveillance-in-south-china-sea/#.VUF2DZOGPT8.
55. Ibid.
56. Katsutoshi Kawano, quoted in Franz-Stefan Gady, "Japan's Top Military Officer: Joint U.S.-Japanese Patrols in South China Sea a Possibility," *The Diplomat*, June 26, 2015, http://thediplomat.com/2015/06/japans-top-military-officer-joint-u-s-japanese-patrols-in-south-china-sea-a-possibility/.

57. U.S. Department of Defense, *Asia-Pacific Maritime Security Strategy: Achieving U.S. National Security Objectives in a Changing Environment* (Washington, D.C.: Department of Defense, 2015), http://www.defense.gov/Portals/1/Documents/pubs/NDAA%20A-P_Maritime_SecuritY_Strategy-08142015-1300-FINAL FORMAT.PDF.
58. Ibid., 22.
59. Ibid.
60. Ibid., 23.
61. Ankit Panda, "A First: Japanese and U.S. Navies Hold Exercise in South China Sea," *The Diplomat*, October 31, 2015, http://thediplomat.com/2015/10/a-first-japanese-and-us-navies-hold-exercise-in-south-china-sea/.
62. Tina G. Santos, "PH, Chinese Naval Vessels in Scarborough Shoal Standoff," *Philippine Daily Inquirer* 11 (2012); Shawn Shaw-fawn Kao, "Scarborough Shoal Dispute, China's Assertiveness, and Taiwan's South China Sea Policy," *International Journal of China Studies* 5, no. 1 (2014): p. 153.
63. Ministry of Foreign Affairs of Japan, "Statement by the Press Secretary, Ministry of Foreign Affairs of Japan, on an Issue Concerning the South China Sea (Arbitral Proceedings by the Philippines under the United Nations Convention on the Law of the Sea)," March 31, 2014.
64. Manuel Mogato, "Japanese Plane Circles over China-claimed Region in South China Sea," Reuters, June 23, 2015.
65. Haiqing Wang, "Commentary: Japan's Meddling in South China Sea Nothing but Miscalculation," Xinhua, June 22, 2015, http://news.xinhuanet.com/english/2015-06/22/c_134346280.htm.
66. Ibid.
67. U.S. Department of Defense, *Asia-Pacific Maritime Security Strategy*.
68. Ankit Panda, "A First: Japan Joins U.S.-Philippines Humanitarian Drills in Subic Bay," *The Diplomat*, August 16, 2015.
69. Manuel Mogato, "Japan Joins U.S.-Philippine Humanitarian Drills amid China Sea Dispute," Reuters, August 15, 2015.
70. Renato Cruz de Castro, "Philippine Navy and Japan's Maritime Self Defense Forces in the South China Sea," Asia Maritime Transparency Initiative, July 1, 2015, http://amti.csis.org/hilippine-navy-and-japans-maritime-self-defense-forces-in-the-south-china-sea/.
71. Xinhua, "Philippines Declines to Criticize Abe over WWII Statement," August 16, 2015, http://www.wantchinatimes.com/news-subclass-cnt.aspx?id=20150816000085&cid=1101.
72. Ministry of Foreign Affairs of Japan, "Arbitration between the Republic of the Philippines and the People's Republic of China regarding the South China Sea (Final Award by the Arbitral Tribunal) (Statement by Foreign Minister Fumio Kishida)," July 12, 2016, http://www.mofa.go.jp/press/release/press4e_001204.html.
73. Ankit Panda, "Anything But 'Rock Solid': U.S.-Philippines Alliance in for Difficult Times," *The Diplomat*, September 14, 2016, http://thediplomat.com/2016/09/anything-but-rock-solid-us-philippines-alliance-in-for-difficult-times/.

74. Adelle Neary, "Jokowi Spells out Vision for Indonesia's 'Global Maritime Nexus,'" *Southeast Asia from Scott Circle* 24 (2014).
75. Prashanth Parameswaran, "Natuna Is Indonesian, Not Chinese: Jokowi Adviser," *The Diplomat*, December 11, 2014, http://thediplomat.com/2014/12/natuna-is-indonesian-not-chinese-jokowi-adviser/.
76. Prashanth Parameswaran, "Explaining Indonesia's 'Sink the Vessels' Policy under Jokowi," *The Diplomat*, January 13, 2015, http://thediplomat.com/2015/01/explaining-indonesias-sink-the-vessels-policy-under-jokowi/.
77. Nithin Coca, "What Indonesia's Natuna Gas Means," *The Diplomat*, September 5, 2016, http://thediplomat.com/2016/09/what-indonesias-natuna-gas-means/.
78. Natalie Sambhi, "Jokowi's Trip to Tokyo and China," *The Strategist*, March 30, 2015, http://www.aspistrategist.org.au/jokowis-trip-to-tokyo-and-china/.
79. Rendi A. Witular, "Jokowi Launches Maritime Doctrine to the World," *Jakarta Post*, November 13, 2014, http://www.thejakartapost.com/news/2014/11/13/jokowi-launches-maritime-doctrine-world.html.
80. Ibid.
81. A. Ibrahim Almuttaqi, "Jokowi's Trip to Japan and China: A Game-Changer?" *Jakarta Post*, April 13, 2015.
82. Ministry of Foreign Affairs of the People's Republic of China, "Joint Statement on Strengthening Comprehensive Strategic Partnership between the People's Republic of China and the Republic of Indonesia," March 27, 2015, http://www.fmprc.gov.cn/mfa_eng/zxxx_662805/t1249201.shtml. The statement noted a granular level of maritime cooperation between Indonesian authorities and Chinese vessels: "The Indonesian side is ready to continue providing facilitation for Chinese vessels to carry out telemetry, tracking and control missions in Indonesian waters in accordance with the Indonesian national laws and bilateral agreements."
83. Katherine Hui-Yi Tseng, "The China-Vietnam Clashes in the South China Sea: An Assessment," *East Asian Policy* 6, no. 3 (2014): pp. 81–89.
84. Randall L. Schweller, "China's Aspirations and the Clash of Nationalisms in East Asia: A Neoclassical Realist Examination," *International Journal of Korean Unification Studies* 23, no. 2 (2014).
85. Ankit Panda, "Vietnam to Acquire Japanese Maritime Surveillance Ships," *The Diplomat*, August 2, 2014, http://thediplomat.com/2014/08/vietnam-to-acquire-japanese-maritime-surveillance-ships/.
86. Ibid.
87. Shannon Tiezzi, "Rioters in Vietnam Attack Chinese, Taiwanese Factories," *The Diplomat*, May 14, 2014, http://thediplomat.com/2014/05/rioters-in-vietnam-attack-chinese-taiwanese-factories/.
88. Ankit Panda, "United States Lifts Vietnam Arms Embargo (With a Catch)," *The Diplomat*, October 3, 2014, http://thediplomat.com/2014/10/united-states-lifts-vietnam-arms-embargo-with-a-catch/.
89. Ankit Panda, "U.S. to Help Vietnam Bolster Maritime Security," *The Diplomat*, June 2, 2015, http://thediplomat.com/2015/06/us-to-help-vietnam-bolster-maritime-security/.

90. Carl Thayer, "Is Vietnam Pivoting Toward the United States?" *The Diplomat*, July 6, 2015, http://thediplomat.com/2015/07/is-vietnam-pivoting-toward-the-united-states/.
91. Prashanth Parameswaran, "The Future of U.S.-Japan-Vietnam Trilateral Cooperation," *The Diplomat*, June 23, 2015, http://thediplomat.com/2015/06/the-future-of-us-japan-vietnam-trilateral-cooperation/.
92. Prashanth Parameswaran, "Japan and Malaysia's New Strategic Partnership," *The Diplomat*, May 27, 2015, http://thediplomat.com/2015/05/japan-and-malaysias-new-strategic-partnership/.
93. Ministry of Foreign Affairs of Japan, "Japan-Malaysia Joint Statement on Strategic Partnership," May 25, 2015, http://www.mofa.go.jp/s_sa/sea2/my/page3e_000342.html.
94. Ibid.
95. Prashanth Parameswaran, "China, Malaysia to Hold First Ever Joint Live-Troop Exercise," *The Diplomat*, August 31, 2015, http://thediplomat.com/2015/08/china-malaysia-to-hold-first-ever-joint-live-troop-exercise/.
96. Prashanth Parameswaran, "U.S., Malaysia Launch Naval Exercise," *The Diplomat*, August 18, 2015, http://thediplomat.com/2015/08/us-malaysia-launch-naval-exercise/.
97. Prashanth Parameswaran, *Playing It Safe: Malaysia's Approach to the South China Sea and Implications for the United States* (Washington, D.C.: Center for a New American Security Maritime Strategy Series, February 2015), http://www.cnas.org/sites/default/files/publications-pdf/CNAS%20Maritime%206_Parameswaran_Final.pdf.
98. Ministry of Foreign Affairs of Japan, "New Tokyo Strategy 2015 for Mekong-Japan Cooperation (MJC2015)," July 4, 2015, http://www.mofa.go.jp/s_sa/sea1/page1e_000044.html.
99. Ibid.

8

India's "Grand Strategy" and the South China Sea

New Delhi's Evolving Response to Chinese Expansionism

Gordon G. Chang

In August 2016, India's state-owned Oil and Natural Gas Corporation (ONGC) announced that its subsidiary had received from PetroVietnam, Hanoi's national oil giant, a third extension of a license to explore Block 128 in the South China Sea. ONGC Videsh Limited (OVL), the subsidiary, had been looking for energy in the block since 2006 and has yet to find hydrocarbons.[1]

It makes little sense for India to drill in faraway water with so little potential of a major find, especially at a time of historically low prices. What explains the extraordinary patience? Block 128 is in an area Beijing claims as its own, and OVL is acting as a proxy for New Delhi. As the *Times of India* reported, the extension allows "India to maintain its presence there purely for strategic reasons."[2]

India has gone to great lengths to maintain its presence off Vietnam's coast, and Hanoi has made it easy for New Delhi to stay close. Over the years, the two countries have signed several arrangements cementing their relationship, largely because each identifies the same state—the People's Republic of China—as its most dangerous adversary.[3]

China challenges Vietnam by maintaining competing territorial claims in the South China Sea. Official Chinese maps show an area defined by nine or ten dashes, and Beijing believes every island, shoal, rock, reef, and other feature inside the "nine-dash line" is part of China. It has attempted periodically to exclude other nations from sailing vessels and flying planes inside its perimeter, which includes about 85 percent of that body of water.

India has no territorial claims inside the nine-dash line but now considers it has vital interests there. For one thing, as a trading nation, it believes it has a stake in freedom of navigation. Also, Beijing has been exerting influence westward into the Indian Ocean, so New Delhi is looking east into the South China Sea. The two powers are acting on each other's periphery and appear locked in long-term struggle.

The clashing maritime initiatives suggest that ties between the two giants will remain troubled. China's diplomats like to use the phrase "win-win outcomes," but the South China Sea is turning into a classic zero-sum contest for China and India. The International Crisis Group has called the body of water "the cockpit of geopolitics in East Asia," and scholar Robert Kaplan called it "Asia's Cauldron," a location "on the way to becoming the most contested body of water in the world."[4]

Indian analysts debate whether New Delhi has a "grand strategy," but it certainly has immediate interests.[5] And at this time, provoked by China, it also has grand tactics, to defend itself in a more assertive fashion across a broader geographic area, land and sea. India has long played defense against the Chinese state, but it is now doing so in locations distant from its borders.

CHINA LOOKS WESTWARD INTO THE INDIAN OCEAN

For decades, China and India had almost no interaction in international water. New Delhi had announced a "Look East" policy in 1991, but the initiative was more aspirational than substantial.[6] New Delhi envisioned Look East as an outreach to the member states of the Association of Southeast Asian Nations (ASEAN), not a tactic to oppose China.[7]

At the time, neither China nor India tried to control sea lanes. The phrase "South China Sea" rarely passed the lips of Indian diplomats or security analysts, and the Indian navy did not venture far from its ports. China's fleet also stayed in coastal waters. The Indian Ocean then was well beyond its capabilities.

This quiet period did not last long, however, as ambitions expanded. Before the turn of the century, Beijing scouted the Indian Ocean. In 1999, for instance, China leased Marao Island in Maldives for "maritime traffic management" purposes.[8]

New Delhi feared Beijing would turn maritime traffic management facilities into surveillance posts and berths for container vessels into havens for vessels of war. The concern was not misplaced. China now uses Marao to monitor Indian and U.S. warship movements, and many believe Beijing will convert it into a submarine base "in the near future."[9] Moreover, in September and October 2014, a Chinese submarine and its tender docked in Sri Lanka, at the Chinese-funded Colombo International Container Terminal.

Beijing looks like it will employ the same stratagem elsewhere. China is constructing facilities in Payra in Bangladesh, Gwadar in Pakistan, and Kyaukpyu in Burma. There is a Chinese-funded port with obvious military applications in the Seychelles, and Beijing in the middle of 2017 formally opened a military base in Obock in Djibouti. Walvis Bay, Namibia, in the South Atlantic near the Cape of Good Hope, anchors the western end of Beijing's facilities.

In November 2014, a Namibian newspaper noted that China was setting up eighteen "naval bases" in the Indian Ocean.[10] The Chinese military termed the report "utterly groundless."[11] Beijing has repeatedly said it will never establish such presences overseas, but China's Indian Ocean facilities look military-related.[12] Some call them "overseas strategic support bases"; Chinese analysts use the term "depots," and foreigners liken them to a "string of pearls." Whatever they are called, the facilities concern New Delhi. If India does not have a grand strategy, it is because its moves are defensive, a reaction to Chinese expansion in both surrounding waters and along its land borders.

Henry Kissinger explained Beijing's strategy by comparing it to *wei qi*, the Chinese game of encirclement.[13] In fact, India's analysts say that China's port-building in the Indian Ocean is proof of Beijing's "strategic encirclement theory."[14] According to Harsh Pant of King's College, "China's strategy toward South Asia is premised on encircling India and confining her within the geographical coordinates of the region. This strategy of using proxies started off with Pakistan and has gradually evolved to include other states in the region, including Bangladesh, Sri Lanka, and Nepal."[15]

Beijing officials, understandably, deny a hostile motive toward the Indian giant. "There is no strategic competition between China and India in our relationship and there is certainly no such word as 'surround'," said Liu Jianchao, assistant foreign minister, in September 2014. China, he said, "has never, and will not, use so-called military or other means to try and hem in India."[16]

Yet hemming in India looks to be a consequence of China's grand strategy. President Xi Jinping's "21st Century Maritime Silk Road," unveiled in October 2013, is designed to connect the great cities of China's coast to Africa, the Middle East, and ultimately Europe. This initiative, now known as the "Road," is only half of a broad plan. There is also a "Belt." Xi, in the preceding month, announced his "Silk Road Economic Belt," which seeks to build a trade route through Central Asia.

China's "One Belt, One Road" flows around, and possibly constricts, India.[17] "The idea of one belt and one road is based mainly on the economy, but has political and strategic components and implications," admitted Zhuang Jianzhong of Shanghai's Jiao Tung University.[18]

The effort, said to involve 3 continents, 65 countries, and 4.4 billion people, is not only considered the centerpiece of Xi's foreign policy but is also touted as defining China's role as a world leader.[19] As Wendell Minnick notes, One Belt, One Road "could usher in a new era that sees China as the undisputed geopolitical powerhouse in the region."[20] Many have already accepted Chinese dominance. "There is no alternative for India but to become a part of this order or remain unintegrated, since it is too late for India to set up its own Asian order," writes Akhilesh Pillalamarri.[21]

That assessment, however, sounds premature, because there are many reasons why One Belt, One Road could fail. For one, the Chinese economy, already delinking from the rest of the world, is trending down and may not be able to support the $1 trillion cost of the planned Belt and Road transportation infrastructure.[22] Moreover, China's generally aggressive geopolitical policies are triggering a reaction that could lead to concerted action against the Chinese economy, as an increasing number of voices have urged.[23] Even in the absence of such concerted action, the unusually slow start to Belt and Road projects is fueling doubt.[24]

And then there is Indian opposition to China's grand plan. Prime Minister Narendra Modi has his "Mausam Maneuver" and "Spice Route and Cotton Route" projects connecting ports in the Indian Ocean region and beyond, alternatives to Xi's Maritime Silk Road. Beijing wants to coordinate its Silk Road with Modi's initiatives, but two rounds of maritime dialogue between Beijing and New Delhi have shown almost no progress.[25] When called on to do so, the Indian prime minister did not endorse Xi's plan.[26] India did not participate in Xi's Belt and Road Forum in May 2017.

From Modi's perspective, there is no advantage in being absorbed into a project directed from the Chinese capital, especially because Beijing's scheme has military implications. China, to dominate the seas surrounding India, has expanded its presence there, moving from diplomatic port calls to training cruises to regular operations and missions in that expansive body of water.[27]

Chinese naval vessels began continuous operations in the Indian Ocean in 2006 after starting participation in the anti–Somali piracy patrols. Since then, the activity off India's shores has increased "exponentially," according to Indian navy chief Admiral Robin Dhowan in December 2014, and now Chinese vessels regularly patrol the Indian Ocean.[28] Many in India, therefore, view the Silk Road initiative as a trojan horse, a precursor to a permanent Chinese presence just off their shores.[29]

NEW DELHI LOOKS EAST TO THE SOUTH CHINA SEA

India's leaders have, over the years, increasingly appreciated the importance of the South China Sea to their security. In 2000, India sent naval vessels into that body of water for the first time.[30] In 2007, the Indian navy, after designating the Indian Ocean its "primary responsibility," recognized the South China Sea as an area of "secondary importance."[31]

As a practical matter, the Indian Ocean and South China Sea have become an integrated area of operation, best symbolized by a long deployment of four vessels in mid-2015. The Indian warships visited ports in both bodies of water—Jakarta in Indonesia, Kuantan in Malaysia, Sattahip in Thailand, and Sihanoukville in Cambodia—as well as participated in Singapore's Simbex exercise.[32]

India now appreciates the interconnections of Asia's waters. According to New Delhi–based author and analyst Brahma Chellaney, "China's consolidation of power in the South China Sea will have a direct bearing on India's interests in its own maritime backyard, the Indian Ocean. . . . In fact, China's quiet maneuvering in the Indian Ocean, where it is chipping away at India's natural geographic advantage, draws strength from its more assertive push for dominance in the South China Sea." Moreover, some Indian analysts are becoming alarmed. As Chellaney has noted, "If China gets its way in the South China Sea, it will become far more assertive against its other neighbors, including India."[33]

Yet this is not just about the Indian Ocean. "The South China Sea," Chellaney explains, "is critical to the contest for influence in the Indian Ocean and the larger Indo-Pacific region, which extends from the Indian Ocean through the South China Sea to the Pacific Ocean. That contest is central to China's intent to fashion a Sino-centric Asia."[34]

The phrase "Indo-Pacific" became popular in New Delhi as Indian leaders began to realize they could not compartmentalize waters. India's eastern islands are only about ninety miles from the western approach to the Strait of Malacca, and the South China Sea connects the two great oceans on which India increasingly depends for its prosperity and security.

India's diplomacy, therefore, has become increasingly focused on the South China Sea. In 2011, the "usually meek" Indian prime minister Manmohan Singh in Bali told the Chinese in no uncertain terms that, despite how they might feel, his country would continue to explore for oil and gas in that body of water.[35] The following year, New Delhi abandoned traditional reluctance on the matter at the ASEAN Regional Forum in Phnom Penh by expressing support for freedom of navigation.[36]

In 2014, Singh went further, assuming a broader role in South China Sea matters: "We welcome the collective commitment by the concerned countries to abide by and implement the 2002 Declaration on the Conduct of Parties in the South China Sea and to work towards the adoption of a Code of Conduct in the South China Sea on the basis of consensus."[37]

At the same time, Shankar Menon, Singh's national security adviser, signaled that India also had an interest in the East China Sea. "What happens in the South China Sea or the East China Sea concerns and affects the entire region," Menon said. "Conflict would roll back the gains to each of our countries of 40 years of stability and peace."[38]

Modi, Singh's successor, has continued these initiatives. He has, for example, publicly issued four joint statements on freedom of navigation in the South China Sea, one in connection with his October 2014 meeting with his Vietnamese counterpart, Nguyen Tan Dung, and two others with U.S. president Barack Obama, in September 2014 and January 2015.[39] The fourth statement was issued in September 2016 when the Indian prime minister traveled to Hanoi and met with Prime Minister Nguyen Xuan Phuc.[40]

New Delhi has recently released comments directed against China's controversial reclamation activities and has condemned Beijing's refusal to arbitrate its South China Sea sovereignty claims.[41] The Modi government then called on China to honor the July 2016 arbitral award in Philippines vs. China.[42] In a leak to a Mumbai newspaper, New Delhi signaled it would "resist" any moves by Beijing to establish an air defense identification zone over that body of water.[43]

India, in short, now sees itself as a stakeholder in China's coastal waters. Modi has indicated that his country will progress beyond symbolism and rhetoric to a policy of substance. "My government," he said in November 2014 at the East Asian Summit in Naypyidaw, "has moved with a great sense of priority and speed to turn our 'Look East Policy' into 'Act East Policy.'"[44]

Moreover, New Delhi's concept of "east" has broadened in recent years. India has signed security cooperation agreements with Singapore, Indonesia, Malaysia, Vietnam, Thailand, Cambodia, and the Philippines, and there are now extensive military links with ASEAN.[45]

Indian leaders are looking even farther afield. Modi, notably, is building relations with island nations in the Pacific. He went to Fiji in 2014 and in the following year announced a plan to establish a space research and satellite monitoring station there. Then he hosted the second summit of the Forum for India-Pacific Islands Co-operation on Indian soil, in Jaipur.[46] India has been slow to recognize the importance of the fourteen Pacific Islands states, but Modi realizes they are "real countries, not postcards" and is making inroads in the region, which covers almost a sixth of the surface of the earth.[47] New Delhi's Pacific initiatives are in direct competition with China's.

Then there is the country that sits east of the Pacific Ocean. Modi, looking past decades of Cold War–era hostility and abandoning more than a half century of nonalignment, is building security links with the United States. Not only did the Indian leader turn Look East into Act East, he also extended Act East to "Look East, Link West."[48] Linking West means, in the first instance, working with Washington. As Modi said at the White House during his 2014 visit, "America is an integral part of our Look East and Link West policies."[49]

India is fully embracing the United States. New Delhi's new outlook permits Washington, in the words of Cleo Paskal of Chatham House, to view that country "as the stable partner it has been looking for in the Indian Ocean—and possibly even in the Indo-Pacific."[50] So India and the United States are increasingly acting together. In August 2016, for example, the two states signed the Logistics Exchange Memorandum of Agreement when Indian defense minister Manohar Parrikar visited the Pentagon to meet Defense Secretary Ashton Carter. The agreement provides for unprecedented defense cooperation, including the sharing of base facilities.[51]

The linking of the world's most populous democracy with its most powerful one is, by far, the grandest of Modi's bold strategies. And if New Delhi has a grand strategy, building a partnership with Washington is it. In any event, the relationship is one of the core elements of his foreign policy and will, in all likelihood, endure. As Modi said of America, "We are natural allies."[52]

NEW DELHI'S MOTIVATIONS

At some point, India was bound to take an interest in waters far beyond its shores. There is, of course, a natural broadening of ambition when a nation goes from weak and poor to rich and strong. India has by no means completed that transition, but Modi apparently believes his country will eventually do so. He repeatedly talks about this era as "India's century."

Chinese thinkers, to no one's surprise, fault India for the rivalry in the South China Sea. Shen Dingli of Shanghai's Fudan University believes, as the Chinese Communist Party's *Global Times* puts it, that "India is not happy about the rise of China."[53] That comment makes New Delhi look like it is acting out of jealousy. In a similar vein, Wang Dehua of the Shanghai Municipal Center for

International Studies has taken the international relations concept of balancing one step further. "By playing the card of the South China Sea issue, [New Delhi] wants Beijing to make compromises on the border disputes or Pakistan-related issues," writes Wang.[54]

India's interest in the South China Sea, however, looks like it came at an early stage in its economic development, suggesting its policy is more a reaction to Chinese moves than the result of a perception of its own strength. Srikanth Kondapalli of Jawaharlal Nehru University confirms this: he believes New Delhi's interest in the South China Sea—and the East China Sea—are merely "counter-strategies."[55]

Indian diplomacy has in fact been reactive—something evident, for example, from the exchange of visits of Xi Jinping and Narendra Modi in 2014 and 2015. Before coming to India in September 2014, Xi visited Maldives and Sri Lanka, two countries where China's maritime presence has irritated New Delhi. Modi, as Chellaney told the *Financial Times*, repaid Xi "in the same coin" after touring China in May 2015.[56] From the Middle Kingdom he went to Mongolia, the first official visit by an Indian prime minister to that nation, and South Korea.

"India's trying to augment its limited power by joining hands with countries around China's periphery," Chellaney noted.[57] Modi was surely talking to Beijing when he agreed with Prime Minister Chimed Saikhanbileg that India is Mongolia's "third neighbor."[58] Mongolia in fact is landlocked and completely surrounded by China and Russia.[59]

So India is also playing *wei qi* across the Asian landmass. Yet "counter-containment" is not the only story. In reality, New Delhi's interests are broader than merely countering, in a tit-for-tat way, China's expansive moves. Modi's foreign policy seeks to accomplish big objectives.

For one thing, New Delhi is shifting its focus from reinvigorating traditional relationships—"revisiting its civilizational links," in the words of former Indian diplomat Amit Dasgupta—to a much bigger project, "crafting an Asian architecture."[60] And India's concepts do not look like those promoted by China's Xi. For one thing, India's world is an open one.

India's architecture is directed to protecting trade flows, especially to and from Japan, South Korea, China, Taiwan, and the ASEAN states, and to ensuring the transportation of oil and gas to Indian ports from Russia's Sakhalin and the exclusive economic zone of Vietnam.[61] In fact, 55 percent of India's trade passes through the Strait of Malacca, either entering or exiting the South China Sea in the narrow band of water separating Malaysia and Singapore to the north from Indonesia to the south.

"India's prosperity is dependent, almost exclusively, on sea trade," writes Rajeev Ranjan Chaturvedy. "Land routes from the Indian subcontinent are few and provide little facility for commerce. Safeguarding the sea lanes is therefore indispensable for India's development as its future is dependent on the freedom of the vast water surface."[62] As Madhav Nalapat of Manipal University in India points out, "Modi's ambition is to replicate the success of Deng Xiaoping in India, and for this, freedom of transit through land, air, and sea is crucial."[63]

As Nalapat notes, there is great concern that Beijing will seek to deny to India and others "unfettered access" to the South China Sea.[64] Freedom of navigation in that body of water is not just an abstract notion to New Delhi. In July 2011, INS *Airavat*, an Indian amphibious assault ship, was heading to Haiphong in northern Vietnam from the Nha Trang port in the southern portion of the country. A caller identifying himself as the "Chinese navy" on an open channel demanded the Indian vessel leave the area: "You are entering Chinese waters. Move out of here."[65] The ship was forty-five nautical miles from the coast at the time and therefore in international seas.

The *Airavat* ignored the unwarranted demand, but the call, almost certainly made on the instructions of Beijing, forced the Indian policy establishment to realize it had interests in the South China Sea.[66] India's Ministry of External Affairs soon issued a statement on "freedom of navigation in international waters, including in the South China Sea."[67]

More recently, China has renewed its efforts to push India out of those waters. In August and September 2015, for instance, Beijing launched a barrage of articles in state and Communist Party media complaining of India's exploration for energy off Vietnam's coast. The most significant of these complaints, an editorial in the official *China Daily*, told New Delhi that Indian activities were "illegal" and "unwise." The move, the paper warned, would jeopardize ties, so India should "rethink" its actions.[68] In sum, the Chinese leadership, both civilian and military, is leaving New Delhi little choice but to work with other nations to protect India's right to ply international waters.

At the same time, nations worried about Beijing's sea provocations have wanted to work with India, pulling it into the fray. In March 2015, Singapore's defense minister Ng Eng Hen publicly called on New Delhi to take a more active role in his region. "We hope that their presence and participation will increase—that really adds up to engagement and confidence building and mutual understanding," he said. "We've said so to our Indian counterparts, we feel that we benefit from their presence, from their voice, and we'll continue to take that line."[69] Laura

Del Rosario, a Philippine deputy minister, said, "India should go East, and not just Look East."[70] Moreover, in July 2015, Philippine foreign secretary Evan Garcia encouraged India to ignore Chinese attempts to "rewrite the narrative of the region" and "keep on doing what it has always been doing."[71]

India is an ideal partner for the many countries threatened by China in the South China Sea. It has the heft to oppose Chinese expansionism but has no territorial claims of its own. Therefore, there is no "strategic trust deficit," as one diplomatic source put it, and "the bilateral cooperation seems to have got a new boost from India's current Look East and Act East policy."[72] With Narendra Modi, a leader willing to act, India has become the security provider of choice of nearby nations.

New Delhi, through its intensified diplomacy, is "creating strategic opportunities" for countries surrounding the South China Sea, writes Rajeev Ranjan Chaturvedy. As a result, India is now "an indispensable element in the strategic discourse of this region."[73]

Not only South China Sea parties want India to take a larger role. Australian foreign minister Julie Bishop in April 2015 talked about maritime cooperation with India and said the two countries should together work for the adoption of a South China Sea Code of Conduct.[74]

Moreover, Washington is looking to India. "The South China seas are international waters and India should be able to operate freely wherever India wants to operate," said Adm. Harry Harris Jr., former commander of the U.S. Pacific Fleet and now commander of U.S. Pacific Command. "If that means the South China Sea, then get in there and do that."[75]

Furthermore, there is support from the normally Beijing-friendly U.S. State Department. In December 2014, Assistant Secretary of State for East Asian and Pacific Affairs Daniel Russel called Modi's activist policies "appealing to me and my colleagues. . . . He has shown in word and deed his interest in involving India in the thinking and the affairs of the broader region. . . . That's very much to be welcomed."[76] Washington, says Richard Rossow of the Center for Strategic and International Studies, is beginning to look at India "as a global provider of security."[77]

As India becomes more closely integrated in the South China Sea, an informal coalition is forming in the region. Modi, by virtue of working with Washington, is cooperating with a network of states defending the global commons in the seas off China's coast. The product of this coordination has been termed "the Quad," a progressively close working relationship among India, Australia, Japan, and the United States.

Shinzo Abe, during his first term as Japanese prime minister in 2007, argued for a "quadrilateral" of democracies. Beijing was able to derail the effort with pressure on India and Australia, but the pair is now beginning to support the concept. Since 2011, India and Japan have maintained a trilateral dialogue with the United States. A similar dialogue exists among the United States, Japan, and Australia, and now India, Japan, and Australia have formed a similar grouping. As Harsh Pant suggested, these various dialogues can morph into the long-awaited Quad spanning the Indo-Pacific.[78] Significantly, India invited Japan to the October 2015 Malabar naval exercises it holds each year with the United States, and the three participated in Malabar 2016.[79]

The Quad, as it forms, could become the nucleus of the coalition described by Taro Aso, who proposed an "arc of freedom and prosperity" for Asia when he was Japan's foreign minister in 2006. The concept, however, was soon forgotten as regional diplomats were optimistic they could maintain cooperative relations with China.

Yet as questions about China have turned into doubts that are fast becoming fears, Aso's arc of freedom is forming. As it does, nations in East Asia are looking to India, which anchors the arc's western end. India, not surprisingly, featured in Aso's speech announcing the concept, and New Delhi is also an integral part of the "values diplomacy" introduced by Shinzo Abe early in his second term as prime minister.[80] Moreover, India is one of the four corners—along with Japan, Hawaii, and Australia—of Abe's "democratic security diamond."[81]

It has become clear, as Shashank Joshi of the Royal United Services Institute said in May 2015, that India has picked sides.[82] Beijing, in one of its more self-defeating geopolitical moves, forced New Delhi to abandon its long-held notions of nonalignment and throw in its lot with Beijing's adversaries.

The South China Sea is one of the most important reasons why democracies are coming together, as envisioned by Aso a decade ago and supported by Abe now. As a result of Beijing's provocative behavior there, vessels of Japan's Maritime Self-Defense Force may end up patrolling those waters, and India could be drawn more deeply into that area as well. After all, Modi sees India's future linked with that of the region's democratic states. As Victor Mallet wrote about the prime minister's outreach to Mongolia, "He not only emphasized defense co-operation, upgraded Mongolia to a 'strategic partner' and said India would help the country's armed forces with cybersecurity, but also praised Mongolia as the 'new bright light of democracy' in the world, implicitly linking his hosts to India and the U.S. and distancing them from authoritarian Communist China."[83]

Democratic states—and others—are looking to New Delhi for support, giving India a prominence that otherwise would not have come so soon. Beijing has noticed India's participation and now publicly tells New Delhi it has no legitimate interest in South China Sea issues.[84]

Statements of that sort almost require Modi to respond when he would prefer to address other matters. The South China Sea, as important as it is to India, does not define the prime minister's external policies, and his external policies have not defined his tenure in office. He is focused on what he was elected in 2014 to do: deliver prosperity to more than a billion restless, ambitious people.

His economic focus was evident from his May 2015 three-day, three-city China visit, which the *New York Times* aptly described as "essentially a business trip filled out with displays of good will and ancient cultural kinship."[85] The highlight of that trip, at least from the Indian side, was the signing of twenty-six memos of understanding, valued by New Delhi at $22 billion, between Indian and Chinese businesses. Modi's trip to the United States—New York and Silicon Valley—in September of that year also looked like a series of investment promotion events.[86]

Modi "needs a window of relative strategic calm in his backyard to build the Indian economy."[87] Because the potential disturber of the regional peace is Beijing, India's prime minister will do his best to not allow the South China Sea to derail his high-priority goal. As Sadanand Dhume noted about Modi on the eve of the 2015 trip, "He is certainly not looking to pick a fight with China."[88] That would be bad politics. Nobody in India, Dhume says, wants to do that. Nor did Modi pick that fight at the China-hosted Group of 20 (G20) meeting in September 2016, something Beijing feared he might do.

Nonetheless, the rivalry between the two countries is unmistakable, with competition now the defining theme of each country's policy toward the other. Significantly, despite all the goodwill gestures Modi extended to Xi in September 2014 and Xi extended to him the following May, neither has given an inch on the central issues, such as the South China Sea, that divide their countries.

The Indian leader's assertive stance signals a slow-forming but nonetheless fundamental shift in thinking in the Indian capital about China. There is a sense that although India needs Chinese investment to develop its economy, it should no longer try to placate Beijing because, among other reasons, China cannot be moved by gestures of friendship.

In 2005, Manmohan Singh said, "India and China can together reshape the world order."[89] He was correct, but these two titans are not cooperating on the

South China Sea. They are, if anything, challenging each other in those strategic sea lines of communication. That body of water may not be where Modi would want to focus his energies, but the controversies there are becoming impossible for his India, with its broad economic ambitions, to avoid.

Robert Kaplan believes Asians do not fight over ideas.[90] Even if he is correct—and many do not think he is—they do fight over interests, and that struggle is often grounded in principles. The coalition forming against China is a grouping of states supporting the principles of an unrestricted global commons and open international system, and most of these states are democracies. The South China Sea dispute for India and its friends concerns far more than just "space on the map."

Two visions of the international system—one of an open architecture and the other a closed one—are in competition in and over the South China Sea. India, asserting its principles, will increasingly shape the outcome in the waters where Asia decides its future.

INDIAN SUPPORT OF VIETNAM

In the weeks before the G20 meeting in September 2016, a commentary appearing in the *Global Times* praised India for being "neutral" on the South China Sea.[91] Beijing, in anticipation of the event, worked hard to scrub the formal agenda of this controversial geopolitical issue.

Despite what the Chinese newspaper said, Modi has not been neutral about that body of water. On his way to Hangzhou, the G20 site, he stopped in Hanoi to meet his Vietnamese counterpart, Nguyen Xuan Phuc. South China Sea issues dominated the conversations even though Modi and Phuc rarely uttered the word "China" in public.

The Vietnamese welcomed Modi with open arms. Just as India looks at Vietnam as a way to assert its interests in the South China Sea, Vietnam since the 1980s has seen India as a shield from Chinese encroachments. Beijing grabbed the Paracel Islands from Hanoi and killed more than seventy Vietnamese servicemen in 1974, and then the country lost about sixty more when China occupied Johnson Reef, which Vietnam claimed, in 1988.

Hanoi's general strategy has worked. Vietnam has not lost a possession in the South China Sea to China since 1988, the first year of Indian exploration in Vietnamese waters. As Ton Sinh Thanh, Hanoi's ambassador to India, noted in April 2015, because India is drilling off his country's shores, "Nobody can prevent it."[92]

Hanoi's stratagem is continuing. Vietnam has apparently offered India berthing facilities in Haiphong and Nahthrong, and the Modi-Phuc joint statement issued after their September 2016 meeting noted that the two prime ministers "agreed to further enhance cooperation in the oil and gas sector."[93]

The prime ministers also talked about defense cooperation. Modi and Phuc witnessed the signing of twelve agreements, including one for the sale of Indian-built fast patrol boats to Vietnam, which paid for the craft with a $100 million line of credit New Delhi had previously extended. Moreover, for the purpose of "facilitating deeper defense cooperation," Modi in September 2016 provided another $500 million credit line.

Modi was making good on promises to Hanoi made during his first months in office. "India remains committed to the modernization of Vietnam's defense and security forces," he declared in October 2014.[94] The Indian leader, it appears, is willing to more than just irk the Chinese to keep his word. His government, for instance, looks to be on the verge of selling to Vietnam the BrahMos antiship missile, which could change the power equation off Vietnam's coast and would make tangible the cementing of ties between New Delhi and Hanoi.[95]

At the moment, those ties look especially strong. Modi and Phuc declared the strategic partnership of India and Vietnam, announced in 2007, was upgraded to a "comprehensive" one. Previously, Vietnam had only two "comprehensive strategic partnerships," one with China and the other with Russia. Those two special relationships, however, are now in doubt. China, with its expansive claims in the South China Sea, poses a serious threat to Vietnam's security by demanding territory and waters over which Hanoi believes it has sovereignty, and Russia's long-standing friendship is open to question due to its growing alignment with Beijing. New Delhi, therefore, looks like Hanoi's most reliable partner at this moment.

That brings us back to India's search for hydrocarbons in Vietnam's waters. Modi and Phuc covered a wide range of issues in their September meeting, and one of them was Block 128, the dry hole.[96] Phuc wanted OVL, the Indian driller, to stay and had no trouble in getting Modi to agree. Perhaps that more than anything else showed that New Delhi and Hanoi were strategic partners in deed as well as in words.

Vietnam expects India to use force to protect its drilling rights if need be, and it is unlikely New Delhi will disappoint its Vietnamese friends. On the eve of Navy Day in 2012, Indian naval chief Admiral D. K. Joshi talked about the South China Sea this way: "Not that we expect to be in those waters very frequently, but when the requirement is there for situations where the country's interests are involved, for example ONGC Videsh, we will be required to go there and we are prepared for that."[97]

India, at this moment, looks prepared for most anything in the South China Sea. More so than many other nations, it is willing to oppose, if not confront, Chinese expansionism, even if it must do so in China's peripheral waters.

CONCLUSION

China and India are locked in a competitive dynamic. As the competition intensifies, New Delhi's foreign policies will inevitably change quickly.

One of the consequences of rapid change is a historic move from nonalignment to close cooperation with the United States and its allies and partners. The other result is the expansion of New Delhi's horizons. Because of that expansion, India is exerting its influence far beyond its borders into seas that do not touch its shores.

Some may call that "grand strategy," but, looking back over the course of decades, Indian policy has been a series of responses to an assertive China. The defense of the Indian homeland, whether one calls that "strategy," is now taking place in seas far to its east.

Notes

1. "ONGC Gets One-Year Extension to Explore Vietnam Block in South China Sea," *Economic Times*, August 27, 2016, http://articles.economictimes.indiatimes.com/2015-08-27/news/65929043_1_block-128-block-127-south-china-sea.
2. Sachin Parashar, "ONGC Videsh Ltd to Stay Put in South China Sea for Strategic Reasons," *Times of India*, August 24, 2016, http://timesofindia.indiatimes.com/india/ONGC-Videsh-Ltd-to-stay-put-in-South-China-Sea-for-strategic-reasons/articleshow/53836408.cms.
3. Michelle FlorCruz, "Vietnam and India Sign Oil, Naval Agreement Amid South China Sea Disputes, Angering Beijing," *International Business Times*, October 29, 2014, http://www.ibtimes.com/vietnam-india-sign-oil-naval-agreement-amid-south-china-sea-disputes-angering-beijing-1715677. China's reaction to the drilling has been both mild and harsh. In September 2011, an editorial in the *Global Times*, controlled by the Communist Party, urged Beijing to stop Indian exploration by diplomacy or "means outside diplomacy." Indian analysts were upset by the apparent call for the use of force. See, for example, Ananth Krishnan, "South China Sea Project a 'Serious Political Provocation,' Chinese Paper Warns India," *Hindu*, September 16, 2011, http://www.thehindu.com/news/international/article2459736.ece.
4. Robert Kaplan, *Asia's Cauldron: The South China Sea and the End of a Stable Pacific* (New York: Random House, 2014), 14. For more, see International Crisis Group, "Stirring Up the South China Sea (III): A Fleeting Opportunity for Calm," Asia Report No. 267, May 7, 2015, http://www.crisisgroup.org/~/media/Files/asia/north-east-asia/267-stirring-up-the-south-china-sea-iii-a-fleeting-opportunity-for-calm.pdf.

5. Among the doubters of an Indian "grand strategy" is Srikanth Kondapalli of Jawaharlal Nehru University. See "India's Role in Solving East Sea Disputes," VietnamNet Bridge, May 11, 2014, http://english.vietnamnet.vn/fms/special-reports/115704/india-s-role-in-solving-east-sea-disputes.html.
6. India "had failed to put much meat on the bones of the policy." Simon Denyer, "China, India Perform Dangerous New Dance," *Washington Post*, November 26, 2011, http://www.washingtonpost.com/world/asia_pacific/china-india-perform-dangerous-new-dance/2011/11/22/gIQAMdFrzN_story.html?wpisrc=nl_cuzheads.
7. Rajeev Ranjan Chaturvedy, "South China Sea: India's Maritime Gateway to the Pacific," *Strategic Analysis*, June 26, 2015, http://www.tandfonline.com/doi/full/10.1080/09700161.2015.1047218.
8. "Close to China but India Ties Precious: Maldives President," *Indian Express*, January 6, 2014, archive.indianexpress.com/news/close-to-china-but-india-ties-precious-maldives-president/1215800.
9. Deepak Sinha, "India and the Maldives: Not Just Another Day in Paradise," *Indian Defence Review*, March 10, 2015, http://www.indiandefencereview.com/news/india-and-the-maldives-not-just-another-day-in-paradise/.
10. Adam Hartman, "Chinese Naval Base for Walvis Bay," *Namibian*, November 19, 2014, http://www.namibian.com.na/indexx.php?archive_id=130693&page_type=archive_story_detail&page=1.
11. "China Denies Reports to Set Up 18 Naval Bases in Indian Ocean," *Economic Times*, November 27, 2014, http://articles.economictimes.indiatimes.com/2014-11-27/news/56515685_1_gwadar-port-hambantota-port-docking.
12. For a discussion of China's pledge in connection with the Indian Ocean, see Mandip Singh, "The Proposed PLA Naval Base in Seychelles and India's Options," Institute for Defense Studies and Analyses, December 15, 2011, http://www.idsa.in/idsacomments/TheProposedPLANavalBaseinSeychellesandIndiasOptions_msingh_151211.
13. Henry Kissinger, *On China* (New York: Penguin Press, 2011), 23–25. Pentagon analyst Michael Pillsbury has also commented on the significance of the game: "Today, China's leaders operate on the belief that rival states are fundamentally out to encircle one another, the same objective as in *wei qi*." Michael Pillsbury, *The Hundred-Year Marathon: China's Secret Strategy to Replace America as the Global Superpower* (New York: Henry Holt, 2015), 36.
14. Singh, "The Proposed PLA Naval Base in Seychelles and India's Options."
15. Harsh V. Pant, "India and China Slugging It Out in South Asia," *Japan Times*, December 21, 2014, http://www.japantimes.co.jp/opinion/2014/12/21/commentary/world-commentary/india-china-slugging-south-asia/#.VKFu5cDYU.
16. Atul Aneja, "China Woos Maldives to Join Maritime Silk Road," *Hindu*, September 15, 2014, http://www.thehindu.com/news/international/south-asia/chinese-president-xi-jinping-woos-maldives-to-join-maritime-silk-road/article6412585.ece. Beijing's position on this point has been consistent. See comments of Zhang Yan, Chinese ambassador to India, in He Huifeng, "Port Projects in Indian Ocean 'Not Strategic,'" *South China Morning Post*, June 19, 2008.

17. India, in addition to China's Road initiative, is concerned about its Belt projects, especially the China-Pakistan Economic Corridor. The corridor, a series of north-south transportation links bisecting Pakistan, connects China's Xinjiang Uygur Autonomous Region with the Indian Ocean at the strategic port of Gwadar. These links cut through territory—Kashmir—India claims as its own. Prime Minister Modi indirectly signaled his interest in the corridor in his Independence Day address in August 2016. Manu Balachandran, "Balochistan Is Now Officially an Arrow in India's Quiver Against Pakistan," *Quartz India*, September 16, 2016, http://qz.com/782147/narendra-modis-message-to-the-un-balochistan-is-now-officially-an-arrow-in-indias-quiver-against-pakistan/.

18. Wendell Minnick, "China's 'One Belt, One Road' Strategy," *Defense News*, April 12, 2015, http://www.defensenews.com/story/defense/2015/04/11/taiwan-china-one-belt-one-road-strategy/25353561/. Indian analysts have similar views. For instance, Abhijit Singh of the Institute for Defense Studies and Analyses in New Delhi writes, "Still, with an impending $40 billion investment plan, it seems highly unlikely China would have assumed responsibility for the onerous projects without the promise of future strategic gains." Abhijit Singh, "A 'PLA-N' for Chinese Maritime Bases in the Indian Ocean," PacNet no. 7, January 26, 2015, http://csis.org/publication/pacnet-7-pla-n-chinese-maritime-bases-indian-ocean.

19. Editorial, "'One Belt, One Road' Initiative Will Define China's Role as a World Leader," *South China Morning Post*, April 2, 2015, http://www.scmp.com/comment/insight-opinion/article/1753773/one-belt-one-road-initiative-will-define-chinas-role-world?utm_source=edm&utm_medium=edm&utm_content=20150402&utm_campaign=scmp_today. The *Post* writes: "It is the most significant and far-reaching project the nation has ever put forward, having domestic and foreign policy implications that impact the economy and strategic and diplomatic relations. Importantly, it provides an opportunity for the nation to take a regional and global leadership role."

20. Minnick, "China's 'One Belt, One Road' Strategy."

21. Akhilesh Pillalamarri, "India Needs to Join Asia's Emerging 'Chinese Order,'" *The Diplomat*, November 20, 2014, http://thediplomat.com/2014/11/india-needs-to-join-asias-emerging-chinese-order/.

22. China's two-way trade fell 8.0 percent in 2016. For more on the limits of China's ability, see Vikram Mansharamani, "China Is Spending Nearly $1 Trillion to Rebuild the Silk Road," PBS NewsHour, March 2, 2016, http://www.pbs.org/newshour/making-sense/china-is-spending-nearly-1-trillion-to-rebuild-the-silk-road/.

23. Jennifer M. Harris, "The Best Weapon Against Chinese Expansionism Is Not a Weapon," *Washington Post*, September 2, 2016, https://www.washingtonpost.com/news/in-theory/wp/2016/09/02/the-best-weapon-against-chinese-expansionism-is-not-a-weapon/?utm_term=.cc763bc6159b.

24. Christopher K. Johnson, "President Xi Jinping's 'Belt and Road' Initiative: A Practical Assessment of the Chinese Communist Party's Roadmap for China's Global Resurgence," Center for Strategic and International Studies, March 2016, https://csis-prod.s3.amazonaws.com/s3fs-public/publication/160328_Johnson_PresidentXiJinping_Web.pdf.

25. Dipanjan Roy Chaudhury, "India, China May Sign a Pact on Joint Deep Sea Research in Indian Ocean Region," *Economic Times*, April 24, 2015, http://articles.economictimes.indiatimes.com/2015-04-24/news/61493750_1_south-china-sea-indian-ocean-region-oil-blocks; "Ready to Link Silk Road Plans with India's 'Mausam': China," *Economic Times*, April 5, 2015, http://articles.economictimes.indiatimes.com/2015-04-05/news/60833337_1_maritime-silk-road-indian-ocean-defence-dialogue. Beijing has also talked about coordinating its Maritime Silk Road with Jakarta's Global Maritime Fulcrum. See Atul Aneja, "China's Silk Road Diplomacy Willing to Enmesh India's Projects," *Hindu*, April 6, 2015, http://www.thehindu.com/news/international/china-silk-road-india-mausam-spice-route/article7073804.ece.
26. India "remained reticent" on the "One Belt, One Road" initiative, which Indian foreign secretary Subrahmanyam Jaishankar called "a Chinese initiative." Jaishankar said China had not raised the issue with India: "We are open to discussing this with the Chinese whenever they want to." Chris Buckley and Ellen Barry, "Modi Calls on China to Rethink Stances that Strain Ties to India," *New York Times*, May 15, 2015, http://www.nytimes.com/2015/05/16/world/asia/narendra-modi-urges-china-to-rethink-policies-that-strain-ties-to-india.html?_r=0.
27. Vijay Sakhuja, "Chinese Submarines Taste Indian Ocean," Center for International Maritime Security, October 1, 2014, http://cimsec.org/chinese-submarines-taste-indian-ocean/13257. The development of the Chinese navy to protect the country's overseas commercial interests is one of the most important themes in China's first white paper on military strategy. See Information Office of the State Council of the People's Republic of China, "China's Military Strategy," May 2015, http://news.xinhuanet.com/english/china/2015-05/26/c_134271001.htm. The paper is notable because it evidences a shift from land to the maritime domain. On the seas, the paper signals a turn away from an emphasis on defense of coastal waters to "open seas protection." As Ni Lexiong, a naval analyst based in Shanghai, explained, "The white paper aims to tell the world China has formally become a great sea power and transitioned from a traditional agricultural country to a modern commercial state, which will focus on maritime development to defend its overseas interests." Andrea Chen, "China Charts Course for Blue-Water Navy, Extending Reach into Open Seas," *South China Morning Post*, May 26, 2015, http://www.scmp.com/news/china/diplomacy-defence/article/1808948/beijing-pledges-increase-range-role-navy-amid-tensions
28. Sudhi Ranjan Sen, "Chinese Activity Is Up Exponentially in Indian Ocean: Navy Chief to NDTV," New Delhi Television, December 3, 2014, http://www.ndtv.com/article/india/chinese-activity-is-up-exponentially-in-indian-ocean-navy-chief-to-ndtv-629425.
29. See comments of Kanwal Sibal, former Indian foreign secretary, in Tim Sullivan, "India, China Quietly Struggle in Indian Ocean," Associated Press, September 20, 2014. There is a reason China has been so active in the waters off India's coast. Brahma Chellaney notes this of Chinese president Xi Jinping: "Under Xi, China has moved to a proactive posture to shape its external security environment, using

trade and investment to expand its sphere of strategic influence while simultaneously asserting territorial and maritime claims against its neighbors. The Maritime Silk Road project—part of Xi's increasing focus on the seas—is driven by his belief that the maritime domain holds the key to China achieving preeminence in Asia." Brahma Chellaney, "What Are Chinese Submarines Doing in the Indian Ocean?" Huffington Post, May 19, 2015, http://www.huffingtonpost.com/brahma-chellaney/chinese-subs-in-indian-ocean_b_7320500.html.
30. Zachary Keck, "India Wades into South China Sea Dispute," *The Diplomat*, March 12, 2014, http://thediplomat.com/2014/03/india-wades-into-south-china-sea-dispute/.
31. "India's Role in Solving East Sea Disputes."
32. Rajat Pandit, "India Sends Four Warships to the East, Kicks Off Exercise with Singapore," *Times of India*, May 23, 2015, http://timesofindia.indiatimes.com/india/India-sends-four-warships-to-the-east-kicks-off-exercise-with-Singapore/articleshow/47398279.cms?from=mdr.
33. Brahma Chellaney, e-mail message to author, April 26, 2015.
34. Ibid.
35. Denyer, "China, India Perform Dangerous New Dance."
36. Jemimah Joanne C. Villaruel, "India's Interests in the South China Sea—Analysis," *Eurasia Review*, April 8, 2015, http://www.eurasiareview.com/08042015-indias-interests-in-the-south-china-sea-analysis/.
37. Keck, "India Wades into South China Sea Dispute." New Delhi noticeably emphasized the South China Sea in public comments in 2013. For instance, Singh's statement quoted in the text echoed the one he made in 2013 at the East Asia Summit in Brunei. Zachary Keck, "India Rebukes Beijing on South China Sea," *The Diplomat*, October 12, 2013, http://thediplomat.com/2013/10/india-rebukes-beijing-on-south-china-sea/.
38. Keck, "India Wades into South China Sea Dispute."
39. "PM Modi Pledges to Modernize Vietnam's Defenses, Which Could Irk China," New Delhi Television, October 28, 2014, http://www.ndtv.com/india-news/pm-modi-pledges-to-modernise-vietnams-defences-which-could-irk-china-685732; White House, Office of the Press Secretary, "U.S.-India Joint Statement," September 30, 2014, https://www.whitehouse.gov/the-press-office/2015/01/25/us-india-joint-strategic-vision-asia-pacific-and-indian-ocean-region; White House, Office of the Press Secretary, "U.S.-India Joint Strategic Vision for the Asia-Pacific and Indian Ocean Region," January 25, 2015, https://www.whitehouse.gov/the-press-office/2015/01/25/us-india-joint-strategic-vision-asia-pacific-and-indian-ocean-region.
40. Devirupa Mitra, "India and Vietnam Upgrade to Comprehensive Strategic Partnership," The Wire, September 4, 2016, http://thewire.in/63957/india-and-vietnam-upgrade-to-comprehensive-strategic-partnership/. Moreover, Modi's officials now take every opportunity to let the region know what New Delhi thinks about freedom of navigation in the South China Sea. "India supports freedom of navigation in international waters, including the South China Sea, the right of passage and

overflight, unimpeded commerce and access to resources in accordance with principles of international law, including the 1982 U.N. Convention on the Law of the Sea," said V. K. Singh, minister of state for external affairs, in an August 2015 speech at the fifth East Asia Summit in Kuala Lumpur. Dipanjan Roy Chaudhury, "India to Resist Curbs on Navigation and Flight in South China Sea," *Economic Times*, September 12, 2015, http://economictimes.indiatimes.com/news/defence/india-to-resist-curbs-on-navigation-flight-in-south-china-sea/articleshow/48930379.cms.

41. Dipanjan Roy Chaudhury, "Chinese Military Bases in South China Sea Worries India," *Economic Times*, March 26, 2015, http://articles.economictimes.indiatimes.com/2015-03-26/news/60516212_1_south-china-sea-bilateral-cooperation-artificial-islands; comments of Indian ambassador to the Philippines Lalduhthlana Ralte in Catherine S. Valente, "India Backs PH in China Sea Row," *Manila Times*, March 11, 2015, http://www.manilatimes.net/india-backs-ph-in-china-sea-row/168539/.
42. Mitra, "India and Vietnam Upgrade to Comprehensive Strategic Partnership."
43. Chaudhury, "India to Resist Curbs on Navigation and Flight in South China Sea." As Ankit Panda notes, "The rhetoric coming out of New Delhi seems to be growing more specific and pointed as time goes on." Ankit Panda, "India's Got a Plan for South China Sea Disputes (And China Won't Like It)," *The Diplomat*, March 11, 2015, http://thediplomat.com/2015/03/indias-got-a-plan-for-south-china-sea-disputes-and-china-wont-like-it/.
44. "'Look East' Policy Now Turned into 'Act East' Policy: Modi," *Hindu*, November 14, 2014, http://www.thehindu.com/news/national/look-east-policy-now-turned-into-act-east-policy-modi/article6595186.ece.
45. For a discussion of the evolution of the Look East policy, see Chaturvedy, "South China Sea: India's Maritime Gateway to the Pacific."
46. Dipanjan Roy Chaudhury, "FIPIC Summit: PM Narendra Modi Announces Plan to Open Space Research Station in Fiji," *Economic Times*, August 21, 2015, http://articles.economictimes.indiatimes.com/2015-08-21/news/65706359_1_indian-ocean-region-south-pacific-xi-jinping.
47. Cleo Paskal, "Act East, Engage Pacific Island Countries," *Sunday Guardian*, August 15, 2015, http://www.sunday-guardian.com/analysis/act-east-engage-pacific-island-countries.
48. For a discussion of Modi's new formulation of this decades-old policy, see N. K. Singh, "Let's Look East and Link West," *Hindustan Times*, September 27, 2014, http://www.hindustantimes.com/analysis/let-s-look-east-and-link-west/article1-1268845.
49. C. Raja Mohan, "Modi and the Middle East: Towards a Link West Policy," *Indian Express*, October 5, 2014, http://indianexpress.com/article/opinion/columns/modi-and-the-middle-east-towards-a-link-west-policy/99/#sthash.53ITsNHv.dpuf.
50. Cleo Paskal, e-mail message to author, September 13, 2016.
51. Lisa Ferdinando, "Carter Hosts Indian Counterpart, Praises Strong Bilateral Ties," U.S. Department of Defense, August 29, 2016, http://www.defense.gov/News/Article/Article/929603/carter-hosts-indian-counterpart-praises-strong-bilateral-ties.

52. "Exclusive Interview with Narendra Modi: 'We Are Natural Allies,'" *Time*, May 7, 2015, http://time.com/3849492/narendra-modi-interview/?xid=newsletter-brief.
53. Liu Sheng, "India Makes Waves with South China Sea Oil and Gas Exploration," *Global Times*, September 17, 2011, http://www.globaltimes.cn/content/675647.shtml. For additional comments of Chinese commentators, see "India's Entry into South China Sea Aimed at Countering China: Chinese Analysts," *Economic Times*, September 18, 2011, http://articles.economictimes.indiatimes.com/2011-09-18/news/30172047_1_south-china-sea-india-and-china-china-claims.
54. Wang Dehua, "New Delhi Makes Geopolitical Calculation in Playing South China Sea Card," *Global Times*, September 8, 2015, http://www.globaltimes.cn/content/941298.shtml.
55. "India's Role in Solving East Sea Disputes."
56. Victor Mallet, "India Plays Soft Power Game in China's Backyard," *Financial Times*, May 18, 2015, http://www.ft.com/intl/cms/s/0/c72967f8-fd52-11e4-b072-00144feabdc0.html#axzz3aWQNpRIj.
57. Ibid.
58. "'India Privileged to Be Considered Mongolia's Spiritual Neighbor' Says PM Narendra Modi," New Delhi Television, May 17, 2015, http://www.ndtv.com/india-news/india-is-privileged-to-be-considered-as-mongolias-spiritual-neighbour-says-pm-narendra-modi-763714.
59. Mongolia is, according to the *Financial Times*, "an integral part of India's 'Act East' policy." Mallet, "India Plays Soft Power Game in China's Backyard." Mallet, the *Financial Times*' South Asia Bureau chief, identifies three phases to Modi's outreach diplomacy. The first was the outreach to South Asia; the second to "global and Pacific powers," including China; and the third to China's backyard with Mongolia as the opening event.
60. Amit Dasgupta, "Despite China, India Should Look East," *Hindustan Times*, December 9, 2014, http://www.hindustantimes.com/analysis/despite-china-india-should-look-east/article1-1294571.aspx.
61. Munmun Majumdar, "India's Stakes in the South China Sea," *International Journal of Humanities and Social Science* 3, no. 13 (2013): pp. 243–44, http://www.ijhssnet.com/journals/Vol_3_No_13_July_2013/28.pdf.
62. Rajeev Ranjan Chaturvedy, "India's Maritime Gateway to the Pacific," *Hindu*, February 22, 2014, http://www.thehindu.com/opinion/op-ed/indias-maritime-gateway-to-the-pacific/article5714122.ece.
63. Madhav Nalapat, e-mail message to author, April 27, 2015.
64. Ibid.
65. Indrani Bagchi, "China Harasses Indian Naval Ship on South China Sea," *Times of India*, September 2, 2011, http://timesofindia.indiatimes.com/india/China-harasses-Indian-naval-ship-on-South-China-Sea/articleshow/9829900.cms.
66. "Chinese Warship Warns Indian Navy Vessel in South China Sea?" *Economic Times*, September 1, 2011, http://articles.economictimes.indiatimes.com/2011-09-01/news/29953708_1_ins-airavat-south-china-sea-chinese-navy.
67. Bagchi, "China Harasses Indian Naval Ship on South China Sea."

68. "India Should Rethink Its Oil Exploration Plans," *China Daily*, September 1, 2015, http://www.chinadaily.com.cn/opinion/2015-09/01/content_21764279.htm.
69. Sharon Chen, "India Should Play Bigger Role in South China Sea, Says Singapore," Bloomberg Business, March 16, 2015, http://www.bloomberg.com/news/articles/2015-03-16/india-should-play-bigger-role-in-south-china-sea-says-singapore.
70. Keck, "India Wades into South China Sea Dispute."
71. Elizabeth Roche, "Philippines Urges India to Play Bigger Role in Asia-Pacific and South China Sea," Livemint, July 18, 2015, http://www.livemint.com/Politics/97hbAHNvDvhljcBZfxjAJI/Philippines-urges-India-to-play-bigger-role-in-AsiaPacific.html.
72. Chaudhury, "Chinese Military Bases in South China Sea Worries India."
73. Rajeev Ranjan Chaturvedy, "South China Sea: India's Maritime Gateway to the Pacific," *Strategic Analysis*, June 26, 2015.
74. "Australia Wants to Be India's Energy Partner of Choice," *Hindu*, April 15, 2015, http://www.thehindubusinessline.com/news/international/australia-wants-to-be-indias-energy-partner-of-choice/article7105981.ece; "India, Australia Could Push for South China Sea Conduct Code: Bishop," *Business Standard*, April 13, 2015, http://www.business-standard.com/article/news-ians/india-australia-could-push-for-south-china-sea-conduct-code-bishop-115041300778_1.html.
75. Vishnu Som, "In South China Sea Row, Top U.S. Commander Roots for India," New Delhi Television, March 4, 2015, http://www.ndtv.com/india-news/in-south-china-sea-row-top-us-commander-roots-for-india-743991.
76. Frank Jack Daniel, "As Obama Visits, Signs that India Is Pushing Back Against China," Reuters, January 21, 2015, http://in.reuters.com/article/2015/01/21/india-usa-china-idINKBN0KU1IB20150121.
77. Ibid.
78. Harsh V. Pant, "Asia's New Geopolitics Takes Shape Around India, Japan, and Australia," *The Diplomat*, July 28, 2015, http://thediplomat.com/2015/07/asias-new-geopolitics-takes-shape-around-india-japan-and-australia/. For more on this topic, see Walter Lohman, "Responding to China's Rise: Could a 'Quad' Approach Help?" *National Interest*, June 25, 2015, http://nationalinterest.org/feature/responding-chinas-rise-could-quad-approach-help-13182.
79. Ryan J. Batchelder, "Three Nations Set Sail for Exercise Malabar 2016," U.S. Navy, June 16, 2016, http://www.public.navy.mil/surfor/cg53/Pages/Three-nations-set-sail-for-exercise-Malabar-2016.aspx#.V9G0mzUW5qC.
80. Ministry of Foreign Affairs of Japan, "Speech by Mr. Taro Aso, Minister for Foreign Affairs on the Occasion of the Japan Institute of International Affairs Seminar 'Arc of Freedom and Prosperity: Japan's Expanding Diplomatic Horizons,'" November 30, 2006, http://www.mofa.go.jp/announce/fm/aso/speech0611.html.
81. Shinzo Abe, "Asia's Democratic Security Diamond," Project Syndicate, December 27, 2012, https://www.project-syndicate.org/commentary/a-strategic-alliance-for-japan-and-india-by-shinzo-abe.
82. Natalie Obiko, "Modi in China: India PM Hopes for No Xi Surprise," Bloomberg Business, May 13, 2015, http://www.bloomberg.com/news/articles/2015-05-13/a-more-skeptical-modi-heads-to-china-after-last-xi-visit-spoiled. India, Ankit Panda

writes, has joined "a chorus of mostly democratic, mostly U.S.-aligned states in opposing Chinese irredentism." Panda, "India's Got a Plan for South China Sea Disputes (And China Won't Like It)."
83. Mallet, "India Plays Soft Power Game in China's Backyard."
84. Ministry of Foreign Affairs of the People's Republic of China, "Foreign Ministry Spokesperson Hong Lei's Regular Press Conference on October 8, 2014," October 8, 2014, http://www.fmprc.gov.cn/mfa_eng/xwfw_665399/s2510_665401/t1198634.shtml. For a more recent warning, see Sachin Parashar, "No Oil Hunt in South China Sea Without Nod, Beijing Tells Delhi," *Economic Times*, May 31, 2015, http://economictimes.indiatimes.com/news/politics-and-nation/no-oil-hunt-in-south-china-sea-without-nod-beijing-tells-delhi/articleshow/47487210.cms. For more information, see Saibal Dasgupta, "China Warns India About Taking Up Vietnam's Offer for Oil Exploration in Disputed South China Sea," *Times of India*, October 28, 2014, http://timesofindia.indiatimes.com/india/China-warns-India-about-taking-up-Vietnams-offer-for-oil-exploration-in-disputed-South-China-Sea/articleshow/44960780.cms; Ananth Kirshnan, "China Cautions India on Vietnam Overture," *India Today*, October 28, 2014, http://indiatoday.intoday.in/story/china-cautions-india-on-vietnam-overture/1/397892.html.
85. Ellen Barry and Chris Buckley, "Narendra Modi and Xi Jinping Aim to Shelve Rifts Amid Economic Courtship," *New York Times*, May 13, 2015, http://www.nytimes.com/2015/05/14/world/asia/india-and-china-aim-to-table-territorial-rifts-amid-economic-courtship.html.
86. Devjyot Ghoshal and Itika Sharma Punit, "A Guide to Narendra Modi's Trip to New York and Silicon Valley," Quartz, September 20, 2015, http://qz.com/506390/a-guide-to-narendra-modis-trip-to-new-york-and-silicon-valley/.
87. Comments of Ashok Malik of the Observer Research Foundation, in Barry and Buckley, "Narendra Modi and Xi Jinping Aim to Shelve Rifts Amid Economic Courtship."
88. Sadanand Dhume, interview by John Batchelor and Gordon Chang, The John Batchelor Show, Cumulus Media Network, May 13, 2015, http://johnbatchelorshow.com/podcasts/thurs-51315-hr-2-jbs-co-host-gordon-chang-forbescom-henry-navarro-university-california.
89. John Lancaster, "India, China Hoping to 'Reshape the World Order' Together," *Washington Post*, April 12, 2005, http://www.washingtonpost.com/wp-dyn/articles/A43053-2005Apr11.html.
90. Kaplan, the geopolitical analyst and author, writes that "it is not ideas that Asians fight over, but space on the map." *Asia's Cauldron*, 33.
91. Zhao Gancheng, "Sino-Indian Relationship Should Focus on Big Picture, Not Individual Issues," *Global Times*, August 16, 2016, http://www.globaltimes.cn/content/1000842.shtml.
92. "Nobody Can Prevent India's Oil Exploration in Our Waters: Vietnam," *Economic Times*, April 28, 2015, http://economictimes.indiatimes.com/industry/energy/oil-gas/nobody-can-prevent-indias-oil-exploration-in-our-waters-vietnam/articleshow/47084612.cms.

93. "India's Role in Solving East Sea Disputes"; Mitra, "India and Vietnam Upgrade to Comprehensive Strategic Partnership."
94. Dipanjan Roy Chaudhury, "Bolstering Act East Policy: India to Train Vietnamese Intelligence Forces," *Economic Times*, April 6, 2015, http://articles.economictimes.indiatimes.com/2015–04–06/news/60866058_1_indian-ocean-region-south-china-sea-pm-dung.
95. Sam LaGrone, "India Set to Sell Super Sonic Anti-Ship Cruise Missile to Vietnam," USNI News, June 1, 2016, https://news.usni.org/2016/06/01/india-set-sell-super-sonic-anti-ship-cruise-missile-vietnam-china-upset.
96. Mitra, "India and Vietnam Upgrade to Comprehensive Strategic Partnership."
97. Sandeep Unnithan, "Indian Navy Prepared to Defend Its Interest in South China Sea, Says Admiral DK Joshi," *India Today*, December 3, 2012, http://indiatoday.intoday.in/story/india-prepared-to-intervene-in-south-china-sea-navy-chief/1/235881.html.

9

Paradoxes Abounding

Russia and the South China Sea Issue

Stephen Blank[1]

Southeast Asia in general and the South China Sea in particular are not areas where Russia has vital interests justifying military deployments.[2] Yet Moscow persistently seeks a permanent footing there. Russia's standing remains problematic, as Southeast Asia still does not accept it as a fully invested player despite its progress in laying the institutional and legal foundations for playing a bigger role there.[3] Moreover, Russia's performance at the 2015 and 2016 Shangri-La conferences on Asian security showed that it remains detached from Asian security agendas and focused on its own parochial obsessions, such as color revolutions. Furthermore, despite Russian rhetoric about Asia, its bureaucracies and elites still focus on the West.[4] Nevertheless, Moscow steadily professes Southeast Asia's intrinsic importance to Russia and its relevance to Russia's larger Asia policy.

Russia has previously sought to project naval power into the South China Sea—for example, by reopening a logistics base at Cam Ranh Bay.[5] Moscow also still seeks naval bases or anchorages there and in the Indian Ocean. Consequently, the South China Sea is or should be important to Russia for several reasons, not just because it is vital to Moscow's regional interlocutors but also because of its interest in stationing ships there. Furthermore, resolving the disputes over that sea could constitute a precedent for other cases such as that of the Arctic, a vital Russian interest. Conversely, failure to resolve those disputes could trigger either a major conflict or a restructuring of Asian if not general international relations. A major armed conflict in Asia, especially one involving the United States and

China, would greatly harm Russia's vital interests, while constructive Russian participation in resolving maritime issues would improve its regional standing.

Many other reasons explain Southeast Asia's importance to Moscow. Since Russia's Asia policy aims to elicit international recognition of its standing as a great, independent, Asian, and global power, Russia cannot be taken seriously if it stands aloof while the South China Sea issue roils world politics.[6]

Russian commentators also discern in Southeast Asia's multiple security institutions—including the Association of Southeast Asian Nations (ASEAN), East Asia Summit (EAS), ASEAN Defense Ministers Meeting, and Asia Pacific Economic Cooperation—a major element in the alleged powerful and ascendant tendency toward multipolarity in Asia and world politics.[7] Therefore, Russia cannot detach itself from these institutions and should credibly contribute to resolving some of the most outstanding and difficult regional issues.

Moscow understands that because Asia is the global economy's dynamic center, Russia must expand its minimal presence in Southeast Asia. Having hitherto failed to achieve its goals in the region, Russia must constantly persuade its audiences that it is an important country so that others will take it seriously and see it as it wants to be seen. Unfortunately, Southeast Asian governments do not share Russia's self-estimate.[8] Meanwhile, Moscow's continuing inability to address regional security issues coherently only intensifies this dichotomy between Russian ambitions and regional realities.[9] This situation leads to a paradox in Russian policy. Russia either seeks to evade discussion of the South China Sea issue or publicly inclines toward Beijing's stance that this question is exclusively one for local powers and thus not the United States. But either of these stances, evasion or exclusion of nonregional players, undermines Russia's claim to be taken seriously as a great Asian power in Southeast Asia. This is one of the abiding paradoxes in Russia's approach to Southeast Asia and the South China Sea.

RUSSIAN OBJECTIVES IN SOUTHEAST ASIA

Moscow's quest for status, standing, influence, and a lasting voice in Southeast Asian affairs is rife with unresolved (and possibly unresolvable) paradoxes that thwart Russia's realization of its self-imposed goals in Asia. Indeed, Russia finds it difficult to find its footing in Southeast Asia. In the 1990s, Southeast Asia and Russia were marginal to each other's concerns.[10] Despite its economic revival from 1998 to 2007, aggressive great power politics, and pivot to Asia since 2008, Russia still punches below its weight throughout Southeast Asia. Its contradictory policies hobble it in grappling with China's threat in the South China Sea.

Southeast Asian economies offer raw materials and resources that are increasingly valuable in the face of the Western sanctions and Russian retaliation that are curtailing Western imports. Indeed, since sanctions began, Russia has solicited ASEAN members' investment in Russia's energy holdings in Siberia and the Arctic.[11] In 2013, Russia and Vietnam agreed to explore for oil in each other's continental shelf.[12] By September 2015, Vietnamese firms had reportedly invested $2.4 billion in eighteen projects in Russia. Recent Russian commentary has argued that Vietnamese elites have been talking about investing in Russia since "dewesternization" became Russia's watchword.[13] And whenever senior Russian officials appear at an Asian conference, they invoke Russia's investment and/or trade potential. Nevertheless, little investment is occurring. Moreover, in January 2016, Russian oil producer Gazprom Neft withdrew from negotiations to buy a 49 percent share of the Dung Quat refinery because Hanoi would not give it preferential conditions.[14]

Southeast Asia is also a significant Russian market for arms and energy sales.[15] Moscow must concurrently engage with states possessing energy assets and states that need to buy them. Russia either helps discover energy sources and shares in their proceeds, thereby gaining influence in a country, or else it sells its energy, thus creating another avenue of revenue and influence. Russian arms sales link with energy deals and the quest for military bases as components of Russia's grand strategy to advance its interests.[16]

Arms sales also help elicit recognition of Russia as it wants to be seen. An independent competitive defense sector not only lowers unit costs and assists indigenous technological innovation but also enables an independent foreign and defense policy. Should Russia lose ground in the military exports field, and implicitly in its military competitiveness and independence, it will encounter increasing pressure to align with either China or the West and yield some if not most of that independence. Thus, an independent defense industry is not only an economic factor for Russia but also an essential element of its ability to conduct an independent foreign policy.

Russian military exports initiate and strengthen relations in regions in which it wants influence, such as Asia and the Middle East. Vice premier Dmitri Rogozin stated, "The FSVTS [Federal Service for Military-Technical Cooperation, the institution responsible for negotiating arms sales] at the moment is, it can be said, the country's second foreign policy agency, a second MID [ministry of foreign affairs], a second Smolensk Square, because it strengthens what the diplomats do today, not just in political terms, but rather authenticated in material, treaty relations, contracts, maintenance services, equipment repair, and its maintenance in a suitable state."[17] Rogozin confirmed this stance when he said, "They [the FSVTS] trade arms only with friends and partners."[18]

President Vladimir Putin himself stated, "We see active military technical cooperation as an effective instrument for advancing our national interests, both political and economic."[19] Russia exports military systems abroad to achieve the following objectives: to uphold its image as a global power, maintain an independent foreign policy, expand its influence in these regions, obtain resource extraction rights, initiate and strengthen defense relations, and secure military basing rights. Therefore, if Russia cannot compete with its rivals in arms sales to Asia, it will lose ground regionally and globally. But these arms sales, especially to Vietnam—its largest customer and partner in Southeast Asia—embody another paradox, because the purpose of those weapons is to defend against Chinese threats and encroachments to Vietnam's territory, energy platforms, and vital interests, even as Russia becomes increasingly dependent on China.

Further paradoxes appear in Russia's military policy toward Southeast Asia. Russian military leaders clearly want a naval base there. Russia previously sought access to Vietnam's Cam Ranh Bay and still seeks to continue its temporary right of access, even if not as a base.[20] In 2014, Defense Minister Sergei Shoigu announced progress in talks with eight governments to establish a global network of air bases, including Singapore and the Seychelles, to extend the reach of Russia's long-range maritime and strategic aviation assets and global military presence.[21] Shoigu cited Russia's need for refueling bases near the equator and said that "it is imperative that our navy has the opportunities for replenishment."[22] Clearly, Moscow still desires to project power into the South China Sea. From the Seychelles and/or Singapore, a combined force of Su-34s and Tu-22Ms, armed with cruise missiles, could strike throughout the Indian Ocean, West Pacific, and East Africa. A base at Cam Ranh Bay would further enhance that capability. Yet long-term sustainment of the fleet in Southeast Asia is well beyond Russia's capability, and Russia cannot take sides in any maritime conflict in Southeast Asia without jeopardizing its relationship with the other side. Neither is it clear what mission its forces could perform. Once again, Moscow craves the aura of great power status but lacks the means or the reasons to attain it. These three paradoxes are only a few of the many that bedevil Russian foreign policy throughout Southeast Asia and the South China Sea.

The identification of Russia as a great power remains an article of faith and obsession of Russian elites.[23] Ambassador extraordinaire and former deputy foreign minister Nikolai Spassky wrote that "the problem is that the Russians still do not see any other worthy role for their country in the twenty-first century other than the role of a superpower, or a state that realizes itself principally through influence on global processes. Characteristically such sentiments are widespread not only among the elites, but also among the public at large."[24]

Dmitri Trenin, director of the Moscow Center of the Carnegie Endowment, observed that Russian analysts argued in the 1990s that current difficulties were transient but Russia was entitled to this "presidium seat" in Europe, the Middle East, Asia, and on global issues.[25] Today, it is no less true that Russia's obsession with great power status continues to dominate elite perceptions. As Nikolai Gvosdev observed in 2006, "Unlike in any of the other established or rising great powers, the question as to whether or not Russia is a great power is seen as an existential matter, that Russia cannot exist apart from being a great power, lest it cease to be Russia."[26] Moreover, Russian analysts still believe that Russian policy in Asia is succeeding. Sergei Karaganov recently wrote that Russia has "turned itself from a peripheral European country into a great Asian-Pacific Eurasian one."[27] Others have stated that although the "Russian Federation's 'critical mass' remains small" in the Asia-Pacific, "the correct choice of a path and the readiness to follow it to the end is a guarantee of ultimate success."[28] But the multiplicity and stridency of such assertions reveal their inherently problematic nature. Postulating this entitlement today actually presupposes that Russia never had, and still does not have, this status, either in its own eyes or those of others. Moreover, few external observers accept this Russian assertion, least of all in Southeast Asia.

Western (especially U.S.) policy analysts omit Russia as a factor in Asian security.[29] Washington refuses to view Russia as an Asian great power.[30] If these analysts are correct, Russia neither is nor can be an independent sovereign power in Asia. Even some prominent Russian experts believe this outcome may ensue. Institute of World Economy and International Relations director Aleksandr Dinkin writes that absent radical reform, Russia by 2030 will be only a middle power, like Turkey.[31]

Many statements by Putin, leading officials, and analysts of Russia's foreign policy demonstrate that much, if not all, of Putin's overall project depends on convincing domestic and foreign audiences that Russia truly is such a great power; otherwise, it risks disintegration.[32] Consequently, much of Russian foreign policy is a determined and obsessive quest for status as Russia strives to make others see and accept it as Moscow wants to see itself and be seen.[33] The quest for bases and Russia's arms sales policy exemplify this desire to be seen as a great power without possessing the means to enforce this claim. Therefore, Russia is at least equally concerned with being able to do something to justify its claims. The real attributes of great powers are commonly considered to be not only military power but also large-scale economic power, which Russia lacks. Russia regularly solicits China, Japan, South Korea, India, and ASEAN investments to obtain desperately needed capital and technology. While hardly the sign of a great power, such solicitation is a core element in the overall agenda of Russian foreign policy; without it, Russia cannot develop the Russian Asia that is the precondition for any serious daily engagement with Asia.[34]

Consequently, the quest for economic investment and technology transfer is not just to make Russia richer but to also make it a more effective strategic competitor.[35] Russia's quest for multipolarity and recognition by Southeast Asian states and organizations as a self-standing if not self-sufficient pole is a second key objective of Russian policy. Ever since Yevgeny Primakov became foreign minister in 1996, Russian discourse has argued that multipolarity most comports with Asia's international realities.[36] Consequently, ASEAN's multilateral organizations allegedly embody this trend in action and justify vigorous Russian efforts to join those groups and engage individual Southeast Asian governments.[37]

However, in practice, Russia's concept of multipolarity amounts to what Dmitri Trenin calls a "benign oligarchy."[38] Not surprisingly, Russia's concept of multilateral or network diplomacy means "collective leadership of leading states 'who objectively bear responsibility for the state of world affairs.'"[39] This openly advocates an exclusionary great power concert where a few big states decide matters for the small states, which, from Russia's standpoint, are not truly sovereign states anyway. Only the truly sovereign states—Russia, the United States, India, China, and possibly some European states and/or members of the United Nations Security Council—make the rules for smaller states.[40] Some Russian writers even explicitly invoke the example of the Congress of Vienna or the Yalta system.[41] Putin's 2015 speech to the United Nations General Assembly, which frequently referred to the Yalta summit, shows that this analogy still haunts the official mind of Russian policymaking.[42]

Moreover, each pole should respect each other pole's sovereign democracy in their domain and not intervene in their politics.[43] Russia should not only be a pole but should also be exempt from other powers' scrutiny and criticism. While this concept may accord with China's idea for a multipolar order, it hardly is palatable to the United States, Japan, or Southeast Asian nations. But these expressions also reflect the tension between wish or emotion and reality. For example, the anti-American emotion behind these statements is clear. As Spassky writes, "There is no greater joy for a Russian intellectual than to speculate about a decline of America."[44] He is not alone in that sentiment.[45]

In practice, Russia cannot live up to its own plans for a structure for Asia's overall security. In September 2010, Russia and China jointly proposed a multipolar Asian order. In June 2011, they declared that as the world was steadily evolving toward multipolarity, they would advance their earlier joint proposal and comprehensively deepen their partnership, which was a factor for peace in the Asia-Pacific region. Both governments recognized each other's territorial claims upon Japan and denounced efforts to "undo" the post-1945 territorial status quo. Accordingly, both governments agreed to promote multilateral mechanisms across Asia.[46] Moscow's diplomats immediately began pushing these ideas on Asian audiences.[47] This Sino-Russian proposal is based on "mutual trust, mutual benefit, equality, and cooperation." All states would respect each other's sovereignty (that is, no criticism of domestic politics) and integrity (that is, support for Russian and Chinese postures on outstanding territorial issues, the Kuril Islands, the Senkakus, Taiwan, and possibly even China's claims on the Spratly Islands, nonalliance principles, equal and transparent security frameworks, and equal and indivisible security).[48] Since the vagueness of the proposal benefits only Russia and China, denounces the U.S. alliance system in Asia, and greatly resembles Moscow's European Security Treaty of 2009–2010, it epitomizes Russia's shallow, self-serving concept of Asian, if not global, multipolarity.[49]

Equally important, it shows that Moscow demands equality and inclusion based solely on Russia's assertion of its status as a great Asian and global power irrespective of actual Asian conditions. Moscow demanded an exalted status on the basis of a proposal that disregarded contending claims in Asian security issues. It associated itself with Beijing to present itself as a system-forming power regarding Asian security without doing anything specific to commit to Asia or offer genuine proposals for security there. Moreover, Moscow did so while China increased its aggressive maritime policies vis-à-vis Japan and Southeast Asia, hardly a way to convince them of Russia's power and capability for playing an independent role.

Furthermore, Moscow could not even uphold its agreement with China concerning disputed territorial claims. In 2012, when China called its sovereignty in the Senkaku Islands a core interest, Nikolai Patrushev, head of Russia's security council, told Japanese officials that Russia would not take sides in this dispute and that Japan and China had to solve this problem through mutual dialogue. Furthermore, Japan and Russia agreed to "strengthen the bilateral dialogue in a bid to expand cooperation in the fields of security and defense amid the rapidly changing security environment in the Asia-Pacific region."[50] Clearly, Moscow retreated from supporting China's territorial claims.[51] In 2013, as Chinese threats against Japan over these islands mounted, Russia conspicuously began a serious effort to normalize relations with Japan and obtain Japanese investment. Russia had good reasons for doing so, but they hardly substantiated the 2010–11 proposal or Russia's claims to an identity of interests with China or to true great power status in Asia.

At the ASEAN annual foreign ministers' meeting in Brunei in 2013, Russia, undeterred by the illogic of its first proposal, submitted a new collective security proposal for Asia that was drafted with China. This document again aimed to weaken the U.S. position, especially in Southeast Asia:

> The proposal contained not only familiar regional and international security guidelines and codes of conduct, but also offered ambitious ideas that resonated with ASEAN strategists. Since the end of 2011, ASEAN strategists have been searching for ways to deal with the U.S. rebalancing policy and, at same time, preserve the grouping's bargaining power. In other words, ASEAN too is looking for a rebalancing policy. . . . What has brought China and Russia together is their common objective to mitigate what they perceive as U.S. hegemony. Beijing and Moscow also want to ensure that Washington's revitalized security alliances and rebalancing strategy don't weaken their presence and influence in Asia.[52]

The two sides also expected to further their collaboration at the EAS, organized by ASEAN for heads of state in October 2013, and a conference to which Russia has conspicuously failed to send its president in the last four years.[53] In addition:

> Beijing and Moscow have identified the EAS as the most appropriate platform, along with the existing guidelines and codes of conduct in the region, for building a new regional structure. This is a far cry from the past when Russia was used to pushing its version of collective security without considering regional concerns. Today Russia is more willing to work with ASEAN and other regional and international groupings.

China and Russia—also pivotal dialogue partners of ASEAN—want to be on par with ASEAN in setting the agenda and shaping the future security landscape of the region. And that is a welcome and refreshing change for regional economic development and security.[54]

Unfortunately, demanding weakened U.S. alliances in Asia cannot command regional support in the face of growing Chinese aggressiveness. Neither does it benefit Russia. Weakening the U.S. presence in Asia leaves Moscow face to face with a Beijing that will soon eclipse it in practically every index of usable power and undermines chances for equilibrium in the Asia-Pacific region even if it invokes the narcotic of "equal security." Moreover, Russian officials have occasionally, perhaps without realizing it, essentially admitted that they have no concrete ideas for organizing Asian security in general. At the 2011 Shangri-La conference in Singapore, Deputy Prime Minister Sergei Ivanov said that "Russian-Chinese proposals are aimed at helping the countries of the region to realize that security is indivisible and at abandoning attempts to strengthen one's security at the expense of others. New regional security architecture should be based on the universal principles of international law, non-aligned approaches, confidence and openness, with due regard to the diversity of the [Asia-Pacific region] and an emerging polycentric balance of forces."[55]

Ivanov's suggestion that this proposal simply grow out of ASEAN and the existing EAS mechanism in whatever flexible form the members want (that is, that Russia and China retain a veto power over its ultimate manifestation) underscores this proposal's essential insubstantiality and fundamental lack of seriousness regarding a multilateral or multipolar forum that would exercise real influence on Asian security. A truly serious proposal would spell out critical details of the structure and process involved. Ivanov said:

> We do not suggest—I repeat, we do not suggest—creating a new regional organization. A flexible mechanism of multilateral interaction relying on the existing structures and forums, which could be incorporated into an extended partnership network, is likely to serve the needs of the region better. We call this approach "a network diplomacy." Besides, we consider it reasonable to establish connections not only between organizations and forums, but also between specialized agencies, notably counter-terrorism, anti-drug centers, and disaster relief centers. We would like to see ASEAN as the *primus motor* of this process and consider the Association to be a core factor of regional policy and integration.[56]

Ultimately, Russia's grandiloquent proposals for Asian security are insubstantial. Before 2014, China's aggressiveness led Russia to back away from its own promises and proposals—hardly a way to inspire confidence in Southeast Asia. And since invading Ukraine, Moscow's previous efforts to balance covertly at the regional level against China (for example, by attempting to adopt a neutral position on the Senkakus and drawing closer to Vietnam) have atrophied as Moscow's dependence upon China for economic and political support against the West and its own economic crisis has grown.

RUSSIA AND ASEAN

The visible contradictions in Moscow's overall program for Asian security manifest themselves just as strongly in regard to its approach to Southeast Asia and the South China Sea issue. About a decade ago, Russia sought to reengage with ASEAN. Each side saw the other as a partner with common interests that could balance the challenges they discerned from the United States (in Russia's case) and China (in ASEAN's case). Russia and Southeast Asian governments believed that serious bilateral engagement offered economic advantages, trade, arms sales, and, for Moscow, markets and potential investors, especially in the Russian Far East.[57] But Russia's governmental interests and capabilities relating to Southeast Asia were practically invisible, even though Southeast Asia needed as many great powers as possible to engage it and help sustain regional balances and security.[58] Today, Russian commentators admit that Russia's relationship with the region focused on political and security issues at the expense of economic issues, which were lagging behind, and that this owed much to what Vyacheslav Nikonov called "the disdainful attitude" of Russian elites to Asia in general.[59]

Nevertheless, the post-2005 engagement on political and security issues touched on political and security ideas, not least of which was the South China Sea. K. S. Nathan observed that for Malaysia, an objective of the bilateral Malaysian-Russian relationship was "reduction of the risk of war, the prevention of militarization of space, the prohibition and destruction of weapons of mass destruction, and ensuring the security of sea lanes of communication."[60] Presumably Malaysia hoped to bring Moscow to support open passage throughout the South China Sea. Of course, not all Southeast Asian observers supported such direct Russian engagement. Christopher Len of the Institute of Southeast Asian Studies in Singapore subsequently argued that Russia should shun direct involvement in the issues of the South China Sea, instead using its membership in regional security institutions such as the EAS and the ASEAN Regional Forum to foster a solution or diplomatic process.[61]

For all of its talk of an East Asian security architecture, Russia was passive on this issue through 2013.[62] Russian analysts could not formulate solutions for what Moscow should do even as it expanded its energy explorations with Vietnam in the South China Sea and its overall ties with Hanoi. All they could recommend was to increase the "overall cooperative potential of the region and to contribute to the search for its new security architecture."[63] However, events in practice were already affecting Russia's posture.

First, by 2007, Russia began its ongoing major Arctic campaign, declaring the Northern Sea Route as part of its exclusive economic zone (EEZ). Paradoxically, China opposed this posture, leading Moscow to retort by issuing military threats in 2010. In 2009, Hu Zhengyue, Chinese assistant minister of foreign affairs, said, "When determining the delimitation of outer continental shelves, the Arctic states need to not only properly handle relationships among themselves, but must also consider the relationship between the outer continental shelf and the international submarine area that is the common human heritage, to ensure a balance of coastal countries' interests and the common interests of the international community."[64]

Although not then a member of the Arctic Council, China essentially disputed any claims of sovereignty in the Arctic waters beyond littoral countries' twelve-mile limit or EEZ if they signed the United Nations Convention on the Law of the Sea (UNCLOS). Furthermore, although China lacks an Arctic coast, it stated: "The Arctic belongs to all the people around the world as no nation has sovereignty over it."[65] This statement directly challenged Russia's assertion over Arctic waters beyond its territorial limits and a cornerstone of Russian policy. Moreover, there was clearly some military interest in the Chinese navy as Rear Admiral Yin Zhuo indicated here.[66] He believed a scramble for the Arctic was under way that encroached on China's interests and that China and other nations "should find their own voices" regarding the Arctic. China should become an indispensable player in Arctic exploration, especially as exploitation of the region "will become a future mission of the navy."[67] While such sentiments have hardly become policy, they are not isolated, as there are notable exponents in China's navy and expert community of an aggressive policy to get foreign bases and to conduct missions beyond China's immediate coasts.[68] Beyond expressing such sentiments, even if China's navy remains unable to compete with the U.S. Navy in projecting power abroad, it is building quite vigorously for a power projection capability well beyond China's shores.[69] And these capabilities do not threaten only U.S. allies and interests, as Russian planners well know.

Arctic problems and issues, as China knows and admits, have hitherto been resolved by peaceful means such as the 2010 Russo-Norwegian treaty, but

> China appears to be particularly wary of Russia's intentions in the Arctic. Chinese observers have made note of Russia's decision in August 2007 to resume long-distance bomber flights over the Arctic and the planting of a Russian flag on the Arctic seabed that same month. Guo Peiqing has said that the disputes in the Arctic are in fact "Russia and some other states' challenge to the international order and international law after the end of the cold war." China and the rest of the world would be at a disadvantage if Russia's claims over the underwater terrain between the Lomonosov and Mendeleev ridges are legitimized because, in that case, Russia alone would have rights to the resources in that area. Even if that claim is unsuccessful, some Chinese Arctic specialists have expressed concern that the commercial advantage of the Arctic routes would substantially decrease if Russia were to unilaterally charge exorbitant service fees for ships passing through its EEZ waters.[70]

In response, in October 2010, Russian navy commander in chief Admiral Vladimir Vysotsky announced the continuing buildup of the Northern and Pacific fleets in the Arctic, along with efforts to build up the coastal reconnaissance surveillance system and the air forces. Likewise, submarine patrols will also continue in the Arctic.[71] And Moscow may also step up Arctic patrol flights by Il-38 and Tu-142 aircraft.[72] But surprisingly, Vysotsky, speaking with authorization from above, singled out China as a threat:

> There are a lot of people who wish to get into the Arctic and Antarctic from an economic point of view.... We have already been observing how a number of states, which are not members of the Arctic Council, are setting out their interests quite intensively and in various ways. In particular, China has already signed agreements with Norway to explore the Arctic zone. We know about the economy and infrastructure that exist in China today, which is becoming our serious partner from both positive and problematical sides.... Therefore Russia needs to form its rational position and, at the same time, not give up any of its interests. ... There are not long-standing relationships, overt opponents, or overt allies in the Arctic yet. But I believe the most problematic relations will be with those countries, which are not traditional members of the Arctic Council.[73]

These belligerent remarks and tough-minded policies suggested considerable anxiety about China's economic and military ambitions. Thus, the two states' positions here exactly reverse their stances on the South China Sea. A precedent could be set in one of these disputed areas that would then have immense legal-political significance for the other. Given the strategic priority of these two areas, the fact that both states are militarizing them and seeking to influence precedents affecting their waters should not be a surprise. If Russia intends to be a major energy provider to Southeast Asia (as it clearly hopes), uninterrupted navigation and exploration in the South China Sea become very important. Moreover, as Russian analysts know, war in Asia threatens not only local economic development but also Russia's vital interests.[74]

But the Arctic parallel was hardly the only relevant one during 2005–14. Moscow's relationship with Hanoi grew steadily as Russia and Vietnam explored for oil and gas off of Vietnam's coast in waters claimed by China. Vietnam became a major buyer of Russian weapons and recently completed negotiations for a free trade agreement with Russia's Eurasian Customs Union.[75] This is on top of Russia's previous overt efforts to attain basing at Cam Ranh Bay in Vietnam.[76] Not surprisingly, China criticized these moves that may be seen as representing (along with Moscow's parallel rapprochement with Japan) Russia's response to Xi Jinping's invitation to join China "in guaranteeing security and stability in the Asia-Pacific Region."[77] These moves demonstrated Moscow's quest for total independence and tactical flexibility and its habitual reliance on energy and arms sales to gain leverage on regional security agendas. Moreover, they also demonstrate that Russia pursued a hedging strategy against China in Asia, supporting China against the United States while working to constrain Chinese power in Asia.

The importance of Southeast Asia also steadily grew due to Russia's own pivot to Asia.[78] As early as 2008, leading regional political figures (for example, Singapore senior minister Goh Chok Tong) were urging Russia to deepen its relationship with East Asia in general and Southeast Asian countries in particular.[79] Russian acceptance of Xi Jinping's offer for joint positions on Asian security would be an admission that it has become China's "junior brother" in Asia. Thus, despite the allegedly deepening Sino-Russian friendship, in Southeast Asia Russia through 2014 had quietly but openly resisted Chinese encroachments to forge a deeper military-political relationship with Vietnam.

Beijing repeatedly demanded that Moscow terminate energy exploration in the South China Sea, clearly responding to Russia's visibly enhanced interests in

Southeast Asia. In 2012, Russia announced its interest in a naval base at Cam Ranh Bay, a step probably connected to joint Russo-Vietnamese energy projects off Vietnam's coast, and a means of checking China in the South China Sea. Gazprom also signed a deal to explore two licensed blocks in Vietnam's continental shelf in the South China Sea, taking a 49 percent stake in the offshore blocks, which hold an estimated 1.9 trillion cubic feet of natural gas and more than 25 million tons of gas condensate. Those actions precipitated Beijing's demand that Moscow leave the area. However, despite its silence, presumably to avoid antagonizing China, Moscow stayed put and increased support for Vietnam regarding energy exploration in the South China Sea, arms sales, and defense cooperation.[80]

Russia and Vietnam have been "strategic partners" since 2001 and upgraded the relationship to a comprehensive strategic partnership in 2012.[81] The most striking and consequential forms of cooperation are military. Vietnam's defense minister, General Phung Quang Thanh, called Russia "Vietnam's primary strategic military partner in the sphere of military and technical cooperation."[82] Beyond its interest in Cam Ranh Bay, Russia is helping Vietnam build a submarine base and repair dockyard to provide maintenance support for the six *Kilo*-class subs that Vietnam bought from Russia to protect its interests in the South China Sea.[83] More recently, both sides have begun discussing regular Russian port visits to Vietnam for maintenance, rest, and relaxation, although Cam Ranh Bay will not become a Russian base.[84]

Vietnam and Russia announced a third tranche of the sale of twelve new Su-30MK2 fighter aircraft that can target ships and aerial and ground targets. Vietnam has also ordered six new *Varshavyanka*-class submarines that improve on its existing *Kilo*-class submarines and can conduct antisubmarine, antiship, general reconnaissance, and patrol missions in relatively shallow waters such as the South China Sea.[85] These sales display Vietnam's defense modernization to ward off threats to its offshore energy interests, defend Vietnamese claims in the South China Sea, and deter growing Chinese aggressiveness.[86]

But perhaps the most striking aspect of these recent arms sales and ministerial talks between both states' defense ministers is Russian prime minister Dmitry Medvedev's approval of a draft Russo-Vietnamese military cooperation pact to formalize bilateral defense cooperation. Medvedev's approval orders Russia's ministry of defense to discuss the accord with Hanoi and authorizes it to sign the agreement on Russia's behalf. The accord stipulates exchanges of opinions and information, confidence-building measures, cooperation to enhance international security and ensure more effective action against terrorism, and better arms control.[87] Allegedly, nothing in the bilateral relationship aims to target a third country.[88] However, most of these announcements come from Hanoi, which has every reason to show China its ability to garner support for its military buildup and political resistance.[89]

Vietnam's efforts to forge partnerships against Chinese power are unsurprising. But Russia's activities clearly surprised and even dismayed China. They were part of Moscow's overall "pivot" to Asia (which actually preceded Washington's pivot to Asia) and aim to invigorate Moscow's economic-military-political position as an independent major Asian power in its own right. In 2012, China's media called Moscow's policies "unrighteous" and warned Russia that it appears to prefer cooperation with "ill-doers" over cooperation with China, with whom Moscow professes an identity of interests. Chinese media also stressed that Russo-Vietnamese military and energy cooperation allows Vietnam to extend energy exploration into contested area, so in some sense Russia is culpable. China also correctly accused Russia of seeking a return to Cam Ranh Bay.[90] Thus, Russia's "chess moves" suggested that ostensible Sino-Russian amity regarding Asia's regional security agenda was something of a facade.[91] Russia's comprehensive strategic partnership agreement with Vietnam amply underscored its refusal to yield to China in Southeast Asia.[92] The announcement in June 2014 that Zarubezhneft may expand its energy exploration operations on Vietnam's shelf signified Moscow's dissent to Chinese probes in the South China Sea.[93] Moscow also acknowledged Vietnam's right to buy arms from anyone it wants, including the United States.[94] The Russo-Vietnamese communiqué of Prime Minister Medvedev's visit in April 2015 opposed China's territorial claims in Asia and showed that Russia has other friends in Asia besides China.[95] According to Hanoi, "The leaders also discussed and agreed that any East Sea disputes should be addressed through peaceful means with respect to international law, including UNCLOS, as well as fully and effectively implement the Declaration on the Conduct of Parties in the East Sea and work towards the formation of a Code of Conduct in the East Sea."[96] During this visit, Russia and Vietnam expanded their trading relationship, which includes energy projects in areas claimed by China.[97]

Since then, however, Russia's policy has evolved differently. As Russian dependence on China grows, this balancing act has become progressively more difficult to sustain. Russia increasingly depends on Chinese loans, investments, and political support in return for supporting Chinese policies in Asia. This manifests first in regard to Sino-Russian relations. Dmitri Rogozin, discussing defense issues, observed that "Russia and China are now becoming *as we wanted, not only neighbors but deeply integrated countries*" (emphasis added).[98] Andrei Denisov, Russia's ambassador to China, described bilateral relations as a model for great power relations and twice supported Beijing's demand that Washington desist from involvement in the South China Sea, saying that increased U.S. military power could create a real threat for Russia.[99]

Moreover, Moscow has sought a military-political alliance with China.[100] In October 2014, Putin told Chinese prime minister Li Keqiang, "We do have great plans—we are natural partners, natural allies, we are neighbors."[101] First, we must understand what such an alliance means. As Russian foreign minister Sergei Lavrov stated in 2014, "If we talk about alliances, not in the old sense of the word, not in the sense of tough bloc discipline when [the North Atlantic Treaty Organization] was against the Warsaw Pact and everyone knew that this part of the negotiating table would raise their hands and this part would vote against it. Today such baculine discipline looks humiliating to states that preach democracy, pluralism of thought, and so on. . . . Other types of alliances—flexible network alliances—are much more in demand today."[102]

Moscow has openly solicited an alliance with Beijing, primarily against Washington, but invariably that also entails an alliance against U.S. allies in East Asia. In 2014, Sergei Shoigu said in Beijing that Russia and China confront not only U.S. threats in the Asia-Pacific but also U.S.-orchestrated "color revolutions" and Islamic terrorism. Therefore, "The issue of stepping up this cooperation [between Russia and China] has never been as relevant as it is today."[103] He specifically advocated enhanced Sino-Russian security cooperation (through unspecified means) both bilaterally and within the Shanghai Cooperation Organization.[104] Shoigu included not only Central Asia but also East Asia, as did his deputy minister Anatoly Antonov. Both men decried U.S. policies that allegedly were engendering color revolutions and support for Islamic terrorism in Southeast and Central Asia. Shoigu further stated that "in the context of an unstable international situation the strengthening of good-neighborly relations between our countries acquires particular significance. This is not only a significant factor in the states' security but also a contribution to ensuring peace throughout the Eurasian continent and beyond."[105]

This overture to China fundamentally reversed past Russian policy to exclude the People's Liberation Army from Central Asia and retain for Russia alone the option of military intervention there. It signifies Russia's growing dependence on China in Central Asia and elsewhere under mounting Western and economic pressure. This alliance would also reverse Chinese policy that has heretofore shunned military involvement in Central Asia. President Xi Jinping has already called for a new Asian security order, including Russia.[106] And while China abjures a formal alliance, a "network alliance," as Lavrov suggested, might be more palatable to it, especially as it increasingly can exploit Russia's growing economic and political dependence upon Chinese aid, trade, and investment.

Chinese reactions to Shoigu's and Antonov's calls are also interesting. On the one hand, China's ministry of defense spokesman went out of his way to deny that an alliance with Russia existed and said that "I need to emphasize here, though, [that] China and Russia adhere to the principle of no alliance, no confrontation, and not targeting a third party in military cooperation, and therefore it will not constitute threats to any country. It is inappropriate to place normal military cooperation between China and Russia in the same category as [t]he U.S.-Japan military alliance."[107]

At the 2015 Shangri-La conference, Moscow announced that it would be launching joint naval exercises in the South China Sea with its Asian partners, first Brunei and China, in 2016.[108] Although Russia may have subtly registered its concern at the mounting U.S.-China tensions and simultaneously signaled to China that Russia too has other partners and has interests in this sea that it will defend, it was also clear from this conference that Moscow will not criticize China or raise a coherent agenda that addresses the questions that interest Southeast Asian governments.

The September 2016 exercises with China in the South China Sea also suggest a retreat from Russia's previous somewhat exposed position in Southeast Asia. At the 2015 Shangri-La conference, deputy defense minister Anatoly Antonov criticized Washington for missile defenses in Asia that allegedly threaten Russia and China. He also attacked U.S. policies as representing a "systematic containment" of both Russia and China. And he even attacked Washington for its pressure on Vietnam to prevent Russia from basing the long-range Russian aircraft there that fly provocative missions against the United States and Japan.[109] And in October and November 2015, when the U.S. military openly defied Chinese claims of sovereignty of its artificial island bases in that sea, Antonov denounced these moves as inflammatory efforts to intervene and form militarized blocs and provocations in Southeast Asia.[110] In July, Vladimir Petrovsky had written that China had called for negotiations leading to "spheres of influence" in the South China Sea and welcomed the possibility that the Barack Obama administration might have to accept this concept and thus Moscow's claim for a sphere of influence in Ukraine—a telling indicator of Russia's real priorities, increasing subordination to China, and skewed perspectives on this and other Asian issues.[111]

Apart from a common anti-American alliance, these remarks simply dismissed the concerns of Southeast Asian states and displayed Russia's alarm that Washington could successfully pressure Vietnam to remove Moscow's long-range aircraft, even though Vietnam is its main partner in ASEAN. Some Western scholars believe that Vietnam may well have discounted Russia's willingness and ability to help it in anything more than a limited way because of its growing dependence on China. Therefore, talk of Vietnam and the United States being natural partners and of future defense sales and cooperation all suggests a Vietnamese reorientation toward cooperation with Washington at Moscow's expense.[112]

It is becoming impossible for Russia to deal candidly with Chinese power.[113] Russia now verbally and physically supports China's position on the South China Sea issue. By September 2016, Moscow conducted joint patrols there that included "island seizing" while studiously refraining from any challenge to China's claims despite China's recent aggressive policies.[114]

CONCLUSION

Moscow's evolving postures on Southeast Asian security and the South China Sea highlight the many paradoxes that it has failed to resolve. The first is the disparity between its grandiose objectives and *pronunciamentos* concerning Asian security and the reality of its seriously underdeveloped material and cognitive capabilities for active participation in Asia. It has also failed to make best use of ASEAN's idea to have Russia serve as a balancer in Asia. Instead, consumed by a Western orientation and obsession with a mythical U.S. enmity, Russia has excessively pursued China while trying covertly to balance against it with insufficient means in the regional security process. Ultimately, this gambit backfired, and it has reached a point where Moscow cannot and will not say anything consequential about the South China Sea lest it offend China. Analysts such as Sergei Karaganov who once openly sounded the alarm about Russia becoming a raw materials appendage to China now talk glowingly about Chinese and Eurasian vistas of cooperation.[115] Such cooperation can only generate greater Russian dependence on China and corresponding loss of influence throughout Asia despite Moscow's well-founded suspicions of Chinese goals in Asia and the Arctic. Therefore, Russia has utterly failed to garner the benefits that closer engagement with ASEAN could offer it and Southeast Asia. Even Vietnam threw in with the United States' Trans-Pacific Partnership trade group that excludes China and Russia (but was terminated by President Donald Trump in 2017).[116] Nonetheless, Vietnam continues to pursue a revived version of the Trans-Pacific Partnership by hosting a conference dedicated to that purpose.[117]

These unresolved paradoxes have consequences. For regional actors, they mean that Russia cannot balance China for the foreseeable future—hence, the turn to Washington and to cooperation with New Delhi, Tokyo, and Canberra. But Russia stands to lose much more. It has essentially deprived itself of a voice and standing on a major issue of contemporary security that could cause it harm but where it has no leverage over the participants. On a grander scale, Moscow's absenteeism on the South China Sea issue underscores the decisive failure of its own pivot to Asia since 2008. As Russian dependence upon Chinese support grows, and as that support is given only in return for lasting material concessions, it becomes clear that Moscow has failed to engage Asia or be recognized as a great Asian power. By the reckoning of Russia's own experts, this failure presages a further diminution of Russia's effective capacity in Asia, where absence and impotent equivocation are not the desired states for any self-respecting great power.

Notes

1. This work was supported by a National Research Foundation of Korea grant funded by the Korean government (NRF-2015S1A3A2046684).
2. By vital interests I mean those for which Russia is ready to commit its military forces.
3. Gennady Chufrin, Mark Hong, and Teo Kah Beng, eds., *ASEAN-Russia Relations* (Singapore and Moscow: Institute of Southeast Asian Studies and Institute of World Economy and International Relations, 2006); Victor Sumsky, Mark Hong, and Amy Lugg, eds., *ASEAN-Russia Foundations and Future Prospects* (Moscow and Singapore: State Institute of International Relations and Institute of Southeast Asian Studies, 2012).
4. Alexander Gabuev, "The Silence of the Bear: Deciphering Russia's Showing at Shangri-La Dialogue," June 1, 2015, http://carnegie.ru/eurasiaoutlook/?fa=60263.
5. *Vietnam Net Bridge*, October 19, 2010, Open Source Center, Foreign Broadcast Information Service, Central Eurasia (henceforth FBIS SOV).
6. Stephen Blank, "Is Russia a Great Power in Asia?" in *Great Powers and Geopolitics: International Affairs in a Rebalancing World*, ed. Aharon Klieman (Heidelberg and New York: Springer International, 2015), 161–82.
7. Paradorn Rangismaporn, "Russia's Search for an Enhanced Role in Southeast Asia," in Sumsky, Hong, and Lugg, 327–29.
8. "Keynote Address by Vyacheslav Nikonov," in Sumsky, Hong, and Lugg, xlii.
9. Gabuev, "The Silence of the Bear."

10. Stephen Blank, "Is There a Future for Russian Relations with Southeast Asia?" *Journal of East Asian Affairs* 12, no. 1 (Spring/Summer 1999): pp. 73–110.
11. Anton Tsvetov, "The Changing Nature of Russia-Southeast Asia Relations," Russia Beyond the Headlines, May 19, 2015, http://rbth.com/blogs/2015/05/19/the_changing_nature_of_russia-southeast_asia_relations_46133.html.
12. Interfax, FBIS SOV, November 7, 2012.
13. "Vietnam Firms Invest 2.4BN Dollars in 18 Russia Projects," Vietnamese News Agency, November 3, 2015; Tsvetov, "The Changing Nature of Russia-Southeast Asia Relations."
14. "Gazprom Neft Ceases Talks to Buy 49% Stake in Vietnam's Only Refinery," Talk Vietnam, January 11, 2016, http://www.talkvietnam.com/2016/01/gazprom-neft-ceases-talks-to-buy-49-stake-in-vietnams-only-refinery/; "Gazprom Neft Ends Talks for Refinery," *Vietnam News*, January 12, 2016, http://vietnamnews.vn/economy/281025/gazprom-neft-ends-talks-for-refinery.html.
15. Matthew Bodner, "Russia Seeks to Energize Asian Presence," *Defense News*, November 1, 2015; Franz-Stefan Gady, "Confirmed: Indonesia Will Buy 10 Russian S-35 Fighter Jets," *The Diplomat*, February 11, 2016; "Russia, Indonesia to Sign Contract of 4 Be-200 Amphibious Planes," Sputnik International, February 18, 2016, https://sputniknews.com/business/201602181034942138-indonesia-russia-amphibious-planes/.
16. Stephen Blank and Edward Levitzky, "Geostrategic Aims of the Russian Arms Trade in East Asia and the Middle East," *Defence Studies* 15, no. 1 (2015): pp. 1–18.
17. "Rogozin Discusses Glonass, Defense Order, Exports," Interfax-AVN Online, December 11, 2013.
18. Ibid.
19. Vladimir Putin, "Meeting of the Commission for Military Technology Cooperation with Foreign States," March 12, 2014, http://eng.kremlin.ru/news/4121.
20. Stephen Blank, "Russia's Ever Friendlier Ties to Vietnam—Are They a Signal to China?" *Eurasia Daily Monitor*, November 30, 2012.
21. Bruce Jones, "Russia Searches for Strategic Airbase Partner," *IHS Jane's Defence Weekly*, March 4, 2014, http://www.janes.com/article/34916/russia-searches-for-strategic-airbase-partners.
22. Ibid.
23. One cannot emphasize this point strongly enough; these elites cling to this belief as if it were the foundation of a religious faith, even if they are wholly secularized in their view of world politics.
24. Nikolai Spassky, "The Island of Russia: Can Russia Become a Superpower Again —and Does It Really Need It? *Russia in Global Affairs* 9, no. 2 (April-June 2011): p. 23.
25. For Trenin's views and other such expressions, Dmitry Trenin, "Transformation of Russian Foreign Policy: NATO Expansion Can Have Negative Consequences for the West," *Nezavisimaya Gazeta*, February 5, 1997; J. Michael Waller, "Primakov's Imperial Line," *Perspective* 7, no. 3 (January-February 1997): pp. 2–6; "Primakov, Setting a New, Tougher Foreign Policy," *Current Digest of the Post-Soviet Press* 49, no. 2 (February 12, 1997): pp. 4–7.

26. Nikolai Gvosdev, "'Because It Is': Russia, The Existential Great Power," https://www2.gwu.edu/~sigur/assets/docs/major_powers_091407/Gvosdev_on_%20Russia.pdf.
27. Sergei Karaganov and Elisabeth Hellenbroich, "Russia's Victory, New Concert of Nations," *Russia in Global Affairs*, March 31, 2017, http://eng.globalaffairs.ru/pubcol/Russias-Victory-new-Concert-of-Nations-18641.
28. Vladimir Petrovsky, "Russia and Asia-Pacific Economic Integration: Seeking a 'Point of Entry,'" *Far Eastern Affairs* 43, no. 4 (2015): p. 10.
29. Chuck Hagel, in his speech to the International Institute of Strategic Studies Shangri-La Dialogue, Singapore, June 1, 2013, http://www.defense.gov/speeches/speech.aspx?speechid=1785, completely ignores Russia in discussing Asia-Pacific security. As one State Department official told the author in 1995, "We will have a policy for Russia in Asia when Russia has a policy for Russia in Asia." Stephen Blank, "The End of Russian Power in Asia?" *Orbis* (Spring 2012): pp. 249–66; Andrew F. Cooper and Daniel Flemes, "Foreign Policy Strategies of Emerging Powers in a Multipolar World: An Introductory Review," *Third World Quarterly* 34, no. 6 (2013): p. 946; Noah Feldman, *Cool War, The Future of Global Competition* (New York: Random House, 2013), 107.
30. Blank, "The End of Russian Power in Asia?"
31. Paul Goble, "Window on Eurasia: Russia Stands to Lose World Power Status by 2020, IMEMO Director Says," Johnson's Russia List, September 21, 2010.
32. Andrei Tsygankov, "Vladimir Putin's Vision of Russia as a Normal Great Power," *Post-Soviet Affairs* 21, no. 2 (2005): pp. 132–58.
33. Yuri Ushakov, "From Russia with Like," *Los Angeles Times*, February 1, 2007.
34. "Programma Effektivnoe Ispol'zovnaiya Na Sisteme Osnove Vneshnepoliticheskikh Faktorov v Tselakh Dolgosrochnogo Razvitiia Rossisskoi Federatsii," *Russky Newsweek*, May 10–16, 2010, http://www.runewsweek.ru/country/34184/.
35. Celeste A. Wallander, "The Challenge of Russia for U.S. Policy," testimony before the Committee on Foreign Relations, U.S. Senate, June 21, 2005.
36. Mark N. Katz, "Primakov Redux? Putin's Pursuit of 'Multipolarism' in Asia," *Demokratiztsiya* 14, no. 1 (Winter 2006): pp. 141–44.
37. Vyacheslav Amirov and Evgeny Kanaev, "Russia's Policy Towards the Countries of South-East Asia and ASEAN: Positive Developments, But an Uncertain Future?" *Russian Analytical Digest* 76, no. 10 (2010): pp. 10–11.
38. Dmitri Trenin, "A Less Ideological America," *Washington Quarterly* 31, no. 4 (2008): p. 118.
39. Ibid.
40. Ibid.
41. Igor Ivanov, "Undivided Security in a Globalized World," *Security Index* 18, no. 1 (2012): p. 86.
42. Polly Mosendz, "Read: The Full Transcript of Russian President Vladimir Putin's Speech at the United Nations General Assembly," *Newsweek*, September 28, 2015, http://www.newsweek.com/transcript-putin-speech-united-nations-377586.
43. Timofei Bordachev and Fedor Lukyanov, "A Time to Cast Stones," *Russia in Global Affairs*, no. 2 (2008), http://eng.globalaffairs.ru/number/n_10937.

44. Nikolai Spassky, "The Island of Russia," http://eng.globalaffairs.ru/printnumber/The-Island-of-Russia-15237.
45. Fedor Lukyanov, "Political No-Road Map," April 3, 2008, in FBIS SOV; Mikhail Tsypkin, "Russian Politics, Policy-Making and American Missile Defence," *International Affairs* 85, no. 4 (2009): pp. 784–87. Tsypkin cites analogous examples of this; Vladimir Shlapentokh, "The Puzzle of Russian Anti-Americanism: From 'Below' or from 'Above,'" *Europe-Asia Studies* 63, no. 5 (July 2011): pp. 873–89.
46. "Joint Statement of the People's Republic of China and the Russian Federation on the Current International Situation and Major International Issues," June 16, 2011, in FBIS SOV.
47. Robert Karniol, "Russia's Place in Asia-Pac Security Set-Up," *Straits Times,* June 22, 2011, in FBIS SOV; *Interfax,* June 6, 2011, in FBIS SOV.
48. "China, Russia Call for Efforts in Asia-Pacific Security," *China Daily,* September 28, 2010.
49. *European Security Treaty,* www.kremlin.ru, November 29, 2009.
50. Stephen Blank, "Russia Plays Both Sides Against the Middle on Senkaku Islands," *Eurasia Daily Monitor,* November 14, 2012.
51. Ibid.
52. Kavi Chongkittavorn, "ASEAN Role Vital for Russia, China," *China Daily,* August 23, 2013.
53. Ibid
54. Ibid.
55. Sergei Ivanov, speech to the IISS Shangri-La Conference, Singapore, June, 2011, http://www.iiss.org/conferences/the-shangri-la-dialogue/shangri-la-dialogue-2011/speeches/sixth-plenary-session/sergei-ivanov/.
56. Ibid.
57. Chufrin, Hong, and Beng, *ASEAN-Russia Relations.*
58. Andrew Tan Tien Huat, "Security Issues in Southeast Asia: A Commentary," in ibid., 50–51.
59. "Keynote Address by Vyacheslav Nikonov," in Sumsky, Hong, and Lugg.
60. K. S. Nathan, "Malaysia and Russia: Strengthening Strategic Partnership in the 21st Century: A Malaysian Perspective," in Chufrin, Hong, and Beng, 19.
61. Christopher Len, "Russia and the ASEAN Member States: Political and Economic Cooperation in Progress," in Sumsky, Hong, and Lugg.
62. Evgeny Kanaev, "The South China Sea Issue: A View from Russia," in Sumsky, Hong, and Lugg, 97.
63. Ibid., 105.
64. "China's Perspective on Arctic Matters," *Shijie Zhishi* 55, no. 15 (2009).
65. Gordon G. Chang, "China's Arctic Play," *The Diplomat,* March 10, 2010, http://the-diplomat.com/2010/03/09/china's-arctic-play/, quoted in Caroline Muekusch, "The Arctic Sea Competition: Strategic Competition (Part 2)," Second Line of Defense, November 28, 2010, http://www.sldinfo.com/?p=11643.
66. Ibid., 7.
67. Ibid.

68. See the remarks of Shen Dingli, in Geoff Dyer and Richard MacGregor, "Beijing Builds to Hold U.S. Power at Bay," *Financial Times*, January 19, 2011, p. 6.
69. Ibid.; Ronald O'Rourke, *China Naval Modernization: Implications for U.S. Navy Capabilities—Background and Issues for Congress*, RL33153 (Washington, D.C.: Congressional Research Service, December 23, 2010), 5–7; U.S. Department of Defense, *Annual Report to Congress on Military and Security Developments Involving the People's Republic of China 2010* (Washington, D.C.: Department of Defense, 2010), 29–37; Christopher D. Yung et al., *China's Out of Area Naval Operations: Case Studies, Trajectories, Obstacles, and Potential Solutions* (Washington, D.C.: National Defense University Press, 2010); U.S. Department of Defense, *Annual Report to Congress on Military and Security Developments Involving the People's Republic of China 2011* (Washington, D.C.: Department of Defense, 2011), 27–37.
70. Linda Jakobson, "China Prepares for an Ice-free Arctic," *SIPRI Insights on Peace and Security* no. 2 (2010): p. 12.
71. *RIA Novosti,* October 1, 2010, and October 2, 2010, in FBIS SOV.
72. *RIA Novosti*, October 1, 2010, in FBIS SOV.
73. "Navy Commander Says Russia to Fight for Arctic as China Sets Its Eyes on It," ITAR-TASS News Agency, October 4, 2010, in FBIS SOV.
74. Victor Sumsky, "The Enlargement of the East Asia Summit: The Reasons and Implications of Bringing Russia In," in Sumsky, Hong, and Lugg, 73–78; Evgeny A. Kanaev and Anastasia S. Pyatachkova, *Russia and Asia-Pacific Security: The Maritime Dimension*, National Research University Higher School of Economics Working Papers Series WP BRP 17/IR/2015 (Moscow, 2015).
75. *Vietnam Investment Review Online*, March 28, 2014, in FBIS SOV.
76. Stephen Blank, "Russia's Ever Friendlier Ties to Vietnam—Are They a Signal to China?" *Eurasia Daily Monitor,* November 30, 2012.
77. Chang, "China's Arctic Play," 27.
78. Fiona Hill and Bobo Lo, "Putin's Pivot," *Foreign Affairs*, August 6, 2013.
79. Bertha Henson, "Engage East Asia SM Goh Urges Russia," *Straits Times*, June 5, 2008, in FBIS SOV.
80. Blank, "Russia's Ever Friendlier Ties to Vietnam."
81. VOV News, May 10, 2013, in FBIS SOV.
82. Vladimir Mukhin, "Preferable Tariffs for Navy Ships: Vietnam and Cuba Are Helping Russian Navy Solve Defense Missions in the World's Ocean," *Nezavisimaya Gazeta*, August 7, 2013, in FBIS SOV.
83. Jon Gravatt, "Russia to Help Vietnam Build Naval Submarines," *Jane's Defence Weekly*, March 29, 2010.
84. Mukhin, "Preferable Tariffs for Navy Ships," in FBIS SOV.
85. Thanh News Online, August 23, 2013, in FBIS SOV.
86. Jon Gravatt, "Vietnam Signs Deal with Russia to Procure Additional Su-30MK2s," *Jane's Defence Weekly*, August 23, 2013.
87. Interfax, August 29, 2013, in FBIS SOV.
88. Vietnam News Agency, August 8, 2013, in FBIS SOV.
89. Jon Gravatt, "Vietnam's Unmanned Ambitions," *Jane's Defence Weekly*, August 6, 2013.

90. Vladimir Radyuhin, "Russia Renews Interest in Vietnam Base," *The Hindu*, October 8, 2010.
91. Jeffrey Mankoff, "The Wary Chinese-Russian Partnership," *New York Times*, July 11, 2013.
92. VOV News, May 10, 2013, in FBIS SOV.
93. Interfax, June 16, 2014, in FBIS SOV.
94. Stephen Blank, "Russia's Game in Southeast Asia," *Eurasia Daily Monitor*, April 29, 2015, https://jamestown.org/program/russias-game-in-southeast-asia/.
95. Sam Skove, "Russia Expands 'Pivot' East Beyond China to Vietnam and Thailand," *Moscow Times*, April 9, 2015, http://www.themoscowtimes.com/article.php?id=518906.
96. Vietnam News Agency Online, April 7, 2015, in FBIS SOV.
97. Tuoitrenews, April 7, 2015, in FBIS SOV.
98. Bodner, "Russia Seeks to Energize Asian Presence."
99. "Raised Focus on Relations with China Predates Western Sanctions," RIA Novosti, December 8, 2015; "Ministry of Foreign Affairs of the Russian Federation," January 7, 2015, in FBIS SOV.
100. Artyom Lukin and Renssalear Lee, *Russia's Far East: New Dynamics in Asia and Beyond* (Boulder, Colo.: Lynne Rienner, 2015).
101. Michael Birnbaum, "Chinese Leader Signs Trade Deal with Russia," *Washington Post*, October 14, 2014.
102. Interfax, August 27, 2014, in FBIS SOV.
103. Interfax, November 18, 2014, in FBIS SOV.
104. Ibid.
105. "Ministry of Defense of the Russian Federation"; Nezavisimaya Gazeta Online, November 20, 2014, in FBIS SOV.
106. Xi Jinping, "New Asian Security Concept for New Progress in Security Cooperation," remarks at the Fourth Summit of the Conference on Interaction and Confidence Building Measures in Asia, May 21, 2014, http://www.fmprc.gov.cn/mfa_eng/zxxx_662805/t1159951.shtml.
107. "Ministry of National Defense of the People's Republic of China," November 27, 2014, in FBIS SOV.
108. Gabuev, "The Silence of the Bear"; Ankit Panda, "Russia Plans South China Sea Naval Exercise with China in 2016," *The Diplomat*, June 1, 2015.
109. Aaron Mehta, "Vietnamese Leader Predicts Closer U.S. Military Ties," *Defense News*, July 8, 2015; Cuong T. Nguyen, "The Dramatic Transformation in U.S.-Vietnam Relations," *The Diplomat*, July 2, 2015.
110. RIA Novosti, November 4, 2015, in FBIS SOV.
111. Vladimir Petrovsky, "Should Russia Interfere in the South China Sea Dispute?" Valdai Discussion Club, July 23, 2015, http://valdaiclub.com/opinion/highlights/should_russia_interfere_in_the_south_china_sea_islands_dispute/.
112. Conversations with Pavel Baev of the Peace Research Institute, Washington, D.C., July 8, 2015; Nguyen, "The Dramatic Transformation in U.S.-Vietnam Relations"; Shawn W. Crispin, "Limits of U.S.-Vietnam Relations Revealed in Communist

Party Leader Visit," *The Diplomat*, July 10, 2015; Ton Nu Thi Ninh, "The Right Way to Read U.S.-Vietnam Relations Today," *The Diplomat*, July 6, 2010.
113. Gabuev, "The Silence of the Bear."
114. Stephen Blank, "A Crystallizing Russo-Chinese Alliance," *Eurasia Daily Monitor*, September 9, 2016; Sam LaGrone, "China, Russia Kick Off Joint South China Sea Naval Exercise; Includes 'Island Seizing' Drill," USNI News, September 12, 2016, https://news.usni.org/2016/09/12/china-russia-start-joint-south-china-sea-naval-exercise-includes-island-seizing-drill.
115. Sergei Karaganov, "Russia's Asian Strategy," in Sumsky, Hong, and Lugg, 350–55; Sergei Karaganov, "Obeshchanie Evrazii: Povorot Kitaia na Zapad Kraine Vygoden Rossii," www.rg.ru, October 26, 2015.
116. Keith Bradsher, "Labor Reform in Vietnam, Tied to Pacific Trade Deal, Depends on Hanoi's Follow-Up," *New York Times*, November 5, 2015.
117. "Asia Pacific Trade Ministers Meet, Seek to Revive TPP," Voice of America Asia, May 20, 2017, https://www.voanews.com/a/asia-pacific-trade-ministers-meet-seek-to-revive-tpp/3863081.html.

10

The European Union

Setting a New Course for the South China Sea

Peter M. Solomon

THE EU'S STAKE IN THE SOUTH CHINA SEA

The European Union (EU) holds a vital stake in the security of the South China Sea. The magnitude of trade and investment between the EU and its strategic partners—China, Japan, and South Korea—and other regional states, along with the prospects for enhanced economic relations, requires stability in the region. Mounting territorial disputes over island chains and several localized challenges are working against the goal of security within the South China Sea. These challenges include the increasing militarization of the region, the turbulent relations between China and Taiwan, and the realization of North Korea's growing nuclear threat. Because the resolution of the South China Sea disputes would set precedents for the settlement of maritime disagreements, the EU cannot afford to stay docked at port and watch as others determine the status quo. The time for the EU to chart a new course is now.

The EU heavily relies on regional trade (see table 10-1). More than 23 percent (more than €405 billion) of EU exports are destined for China, Japan, Hong Kong, Indonesia, Malaysia, Singapore, South Korea, Taiwan, Thailand, and Vietnam. In contrast, the EU imports more than one-third of its goods from these same countries (nearly €600 billion).[1] On the one hand, the EU's mutual reliance on trade with the region creates great opportunities, but on the other hand, this dependence also comes with formidable risk. Consequently, one of the EU's foreign policy goals is to promote peace and stability in the South China Sea.

In spite of the economic hurdles Europe faces following the 2008 financial crisis, including the anticipated departure of the United Kingdom from the bloc after a July 2016 referendum, the EU remains the most successful experiment of political-economic, intergovernmental integration. The EU is in a unique position, therefore, to nurture the development of the Association of Southeast Asian Nations (ASEAN) and to establish a unique multilateral relationship that can influence regional affairs. As a whole, the ten-member political-economic association is already considered the EU's fourth-largest trade partner, behind the United States, China, and Switzerland (€207 billion in 2016).[2] ASEAN, which notably does not include China, comprises Brunei, Cambodia, Indonesia, Laos, Malaysia, Myanmar, the Philippines, Singapore, Thailand, and Vietnam. The EU's relationship with ASEAN is composed of the EU-ASEAN Dialogue, which involves exchanges among ministers and senior officials on trade, investment, and security issues.[3]

EUROPEAN UNION DIPLOMACY

The twenty-eight individual member states within the political-economic organization known as the European Union compose the world's second-largest economy ($16.40 trillion gross domestic product [GDP] compared to the U.S. $18.57 trillion).[4] The Treaty of Lisbon, the international agreement that governs the EU, dictates the rights and policies for the EU and describes its decision and voting processes.[5] At the EU level, the high representative of the union for foreign affairs and security policy is the chief diplomatic officer and heads the EU's international relations department, the European External Action Service.[6] The Foreign Affairs Council is responsible for carrying out the common foreign and security policy and the common security and defense policy.[7] Decisions related to security or defense policy generally require unanimous agreement by the European Council, which comprises the heads of member states. In some circumstances, a qualified majority vote may apply (for example, appointment of a special representative).[8] Because decision-making by the EU typically requires consensus, reaching an agreement can be a complicated and slow process.[9]

Any conflict in the South China Sea, whether major or minor, would cause grave concern for the EU and could endanger Europe's economic stake in the East Asia–Western Pacific region. A clash would also impact the EU's identity as a normative power and trigger the EU's concern for the wellbeing of three of its strategic partners: China, Japan, and South Korea. Before 2012, the defining

TABLE 10-1. THE EUROPEAN UNION'S TRADE WITH ITS TOP TEN EAST ASIAN AND SOUTHEAST ASIAN TRADE PARTNERS BY IMPORTS AND EXPORTS (2016)

Country	EU Imports in € (billions)	Percent of Total EU Imports	EU Exports in € (billions)	Percent of Total EU Exports
China	334.6	20.2	170.1	9.7
Japan	66.4	3.9	58.1	3.3
South Korea	41.4	2.4	44.5	2.6
Vietnam	33.1	1.9	9.3	0.5
Taiwan	26.1	1.5	19.6	1.1
Malaysia	22.2	1.3	13.2	0.8
Thailand	20.3	1.2	13.6	0.8
Singapore	19.4	1.1	31.4	1.8
Hong Kong	18.2	1.1	35.0	2.0
Indonesia	14.6	0.9	10.5	0.6
Total	596.3	35.5	405.3	23.2

Source: European Commission Directorate General for Trade, "Client and Supplier Countries of the EU28 in Merchandise Trade," 2016, http://trade.ec.europa.eu/doclib/docs/2006/september/tradoc_122530.02.2017pdf.

moment for the EU's diplomatic involvement in regional affairs was the July 2003 European Commission communication "A New Partnership with South East Asia." This document expresses Europe's desire to enhance economic relations and highlights common values with this region. It also seeks to identify a mutually acceptable approach to political and regulatory challenges, such as promoting regional stability and supporting human rights.[10] Looking back, the EU's economic relationship with the region has been fruitful.

As a normative or morally motivated power, the EU has stepped up its engagement over the past decade to express its staunch support for peaceful methods to maintain stability and resolve territorial disputes in the region. The attendance of Catherine Ashton, the EU's high representative for foreign affairs, at the Phnom Penh ASEAN Regional Forum in July 2012 underlined the EU's focus on the South China Sea. Following the conference, an EU-U.S. Joint Statement on the Asia Pacific Region stressed "the importance the European Union and the United States attach to this thriving region and its peaceful and dynamic development."[11] The bodies further emphasized cooperation in the resolution of South China Sea territorial disputes between ASEAN and China. Specifically, the EU and United States supported working with their regional partners to enhance maritime security "based on international law as reflected in the United Nations Convention on the Law of the Sea (UNCLOS)."[12] Both the EU and United States called for the implementation of a code of conduct that could be used to "resolve territorial and maritime disputes through peaceful, diplomatic, and cooperative solutions."[13]

Similarly, in August 2014, European Commission president José Manuel Barroso and Vietnamese prime minister Nguyen Tan Dung issued a joint press statement that recapitulated the EU's promotion of a peaceful resolution to the South China Sea dispute. The leaders agreed that a political-diplomatic mechanism, such as UNCLOS, should be implemented to settle South China Sea disagreements.[14] In response to China's recent island reclamation and runway construction, the EU joined the Group of Seven in the denouncement of "unilateral actions, such as large scale reclamation, which change the status quo and increase tensions." It is important to note, however, that China was not specified.[15] Consequently, in July 2015, the EU drew criticism from the United States for not taking a stronger stance against China's reclamation activities. The U.S. deputy assistant secretary of defense for South and Southeast Asia, Amy Searight, stated, "A little bit more forward-leaning approach that would support, for example, the idea of a halt to further reclamation, further militarization, would be very useful."[16]

In the wake of the ruling against China at The Hague, it became evident that internal dissension within the EU hamstrung the bloc from taking this "forward-leaning approach." In contrast to the more critical U.S. position, the EU published a press release on July 15, 2016, stating "The EU does not take a position on sovereignty aspects relating to claims. It expresses the need for the parties to the dispute to resolve it through peaceful means, to clarify their claims and pursue them in respect and in accordance with international law, including the work in the framework of UNCLOS."[17]

While the United Kingdom, Germany, and France favored a more targeted statement to uphold international law vis-à-vis China, such smaller countries as Greece, Hungary, Croatia, and Slovenia preferred a more measured approach. Greece and Hungary, on the one hand, rely heavily on Chinese investment. Croatia and Slovenia, on the other hand, maintain maritime territorial disputes with each other and were apprehensive about setting precedents that could affect the dispute's resolution.[18] Croatia's decision also reflects recent interest from China to improve economic relations. This was evident after China sent its largest delegation ever to Zagreb to "create a high-level platform for bilateral enterprises to increase mutual understanding, explore new business opportunities, strengthen industrial matchmaking and expand cooperation."[19] Similarly, Slovenia has experienced increased attention from China with a focus on economic and trade collaboration.[20] These examples illustrate the formidable challenge the EU faces in shaping a unanimous hardline statement, as there are twenty-eight countries with their own unique interests. As Theresa Fallon, a strategic analyst from the European Institute of Asian Studies, stated, China has "groomed them [EU member states] to advocate Beijing's position on the South China Sea.[21]

In comparison to the EU's reluctance to adopt a "forward-leaning approach," the United States clearly backed up its rhetoric with actions that promote freedom of maritime navigation. In October 2015, the U.S. Navy sent the USS *Lassen*, a guided missile destroyer, within twelve nautical miles of the Chinese-claimed Spratly Islands.[22] Similarly, in November 2015, and much to the disdain of Beijing, the United States flew two B-52 fighter-bombers over the South China Sea to demonstrate freedom of overflight and to challenge China's self-pronounced air defense identification zone.[23] Ahead of The Hague ruling, three U.S. Navy destroyers were sent to take stock of the disputed areas near the Spratly Islands.[24] The continued patrols of the U.S. Navy have helped maintain stability in the region but have done little to deter China's island building or to impede Asia's arms race.

In spite of U.S. encouragement of the EU to exert more pressure on China's reclamation activities, member states have largely remained fixed on the advancement of bilateral trade and investment relationships with Beijing.[25] Moreover, following U.S. concerns about the accountability and transparency of the recently launched Chinese-led Asian Infrastructure Investment Bank (AIIB), such key European allies as the United Kingdom, Germany, and France (among eleven other member states) were more than eager to join the infrastructure fund.[26] Along with the United States, Japan notably abstained from joining the AIIB. Regarding the swift decision of the European allies of the United States to join the AIIB, the European Council on Foreign Relations, an independent international think tank, postulated, "The transatlantic disagreement over China is not primarily about this divergence between the EU and the U.S., but about the decision of EU member states to go it alone."[27] Indeed, negotiating AIIB membership as a union likely would have resulted in both better terms for the individual member states and better relations with the United States and Japan on their foreign policies vis-à-vis China.

With respect to Germany, an October 2015 bilateral visit to China by Chancellor Angela Merkel evidenced that bilateral trade is the top priority for Germany.[28] Chancellor Merkel cemented a deal to sell China 130 Airbus jets, but her comments on the South China Sea disputes were limited. She did, however, signal her desire for maritime trade routes to remain "free and safe" and recommended that the row be settled via international courts.[29] In the wake of the USS *Lassen* patrol, Merkel's views were mirrored by senior EU spokespersons who voiced support for a commitment to the freedom of maritime navigation and support for UNCLOS.[30] An EU foreign affairs spokesperson went a step further with a showcase of support for the United States "exercising their freedom of navigation."[31]

During Merkel's June 2016 visit to China, the focus again was on investment and trade.[32] The German chancellor, however, did signal the importance for all countries to "uphold this [maritime] order and to maintain stability in the region."[33] Notwithstanding Merkel's call for order and stability, it is clear that Germany's key focus with China is trade. There are, nevertheless, great economic consequences if China's aggressive tactics are not kept in check, and it is questionable if Merkel's broad call and similar statements by other European leaders will lead to the halting of China's land reclamation in the South China Sea.

The EU's strategic partners in the region would be directly impacted in the case of greater militarized conflict in the South China Sea. Japan, in particular, would suffer because 70 percent of its oil is shipped through the region.[34] Any major unrest would drive Japan's oil tankers to chart an alternate course to avoid engagement in the South China Sea. This option, moreover, would be expensive because Japan's tankers would be forced to navigate an indirect route around Indonesia. South Korea also would be affected as two-thirds of its natural gas is transported through the South China Sea.[35] Regarding the EU's global trade interests, the freedom of maritime navigation and the welfare of international sea lanes are strategically crucial for Europe.[36] It is here that the EU can set a new course in the South China Sea. Not only can it further freedom of the seas, but it also can cultivate the cooperation of its members to realize common goals.

While the EU's economic links with Japan and with South Korea are significant, these relationships do not approach the magnitude of its trade ties with China. In fact, the EU's imports and exports with Japan and South Korea, though substantial at a combined trade total of €210.1 billion in 2016, are dwarfed in comparison to the EU's economic partnership with China, which totaled €514.8 billion in trade in 2016.[37] China also provided substantial economic support to the EU in the wake of the financial crisis and remains a firm supporter of the euro as an alternative reserve currency to the U.S. dollar.[38] China, like the EU, believes that strong EU-Sino relations can be a useful counterweight to U.S. political influence around the world.[39] Consequently, the wind behind Europe's sails is unlikely to change soon, and the EU will continue to maintain neutrality and encourage cooperative efforts to identify a peaceful solution to the South China Sea disputes.

One of the EU's goals, as outlined in the 2016 EU global strategy document, is to "deepen trade and investment with China, seeking a level playing field, appropriate intellectual property rights protection, greater cooperation on high-end technology, dialogue on economic reform, human rights and climate action."[40] Given China's economic weight, the EU goal to deepen trade and investment is understandable. It is important, nonetheless, for the EU not to allow China to use commercial incentives to "play a game of divide and conquer" with its member states.[41]

Counter to Washington's desire for the EU to develop a coordinated strategy vis-à-vis China, the trend has been the opposite: member states individually pursue favor with China for economic gains. The EU global strategy document does assert, however, that "in a more complex world of global power shifts and power diffusion, the EU must stand united" and "swiftly translate this vision into action."[42]

While shaping a unified policy—whether economic or political—challenges member states, they all have much to gain by taking on a unified role. By not charting this course, moreover, the EU's current lack of unity weakens the shared policies of the United States and Japan in Asia.

EU MILITARY CAPABILITIES

Inasmuch as the EU is the second-largest economy in the world by GDP, its defense spending as a percentage of GDP (1.5 percent) lags behind that of the United States (3.3 percent) and China (1.9 percent).[43] The EU's military spending is still significant in absolute terms because of the size of the overall economy. As a result of the diverse interests of member states and stretched national budgets, however, the EU has deepened its reliance on the United States to not only maintain world order but also secure Europe's own borders.

The EU has taken strides to develop joint military capabilities and possesses more than a dozen rapid response battlegroups.[44] Battlegroups consist of about 1,500 personnel each and can be deployed in response to emerging crises following agreement by the European Council.[45] These forces, nevertheless, have never been deployed, and in contrast to the idea of an EU army that can project power, battlegroups are primarily designed to support peacekeeping and relief efforts. Additionally, it is difficult to predict how the adverse effects of the debt crisis and slow economic recovery will affect the EU's research and development of new military capabilities.[46] Specifically, the military budgets of the United Kingdom and Germany in 2015 decreased, with France's expenditures unchanged from the prior year.[47] The United Kingdom's military expenditures fell to their lowest level as a percentage of GDP since 1980—from 2.1 percent of GDP in 2014 to 1.9 percent of GDP in 2015.[48] Given the post–financial crisis austerity measures taken by EU member states, the continued focus on internal issues, and the lack of collective power-projection capabilities, the responsibility for keeping China's expansionary behavior in check will remain largely on the United States.

Along with the United States, the EU shares a vision with Japan and South Korea to promote peace and maintain stability in East Asia. Although China encourages peace and stability as well, David Kerr, a professor of Chinese foreign policy at the University of Durham, argues that the difference between European and Chinese worldviews is a result of "the contrast between European structuralism and Asian Organicism" and the "significance of civil society."[49] On the one hand, Kerr explains, China's worldview is based on the perception of "a world of functions (law, governance, markets) and not a world of ethical properties and boundaries."[50] On the other hand, while Japan and South Korea are by nature Asian countries, the EU-Japan and EU–South Korea relationships are grounded in a similar outlook to promote peace, support the advancement of human rights, and ensure stability in the Asia-Pacific region.

The basis for EU-Japan security relations stems from a dialogue that began in the early 1970s and was highlighted by Japanese prime minister Kakuei Tanaka's 1973 visit to Europe.[51] The 1991 Hague Declaration, signed at the first EU-Japan Summit, expanded the security discourse to include nonproliferation, disarmament, and inter-regional cooperation.[52] The Joint Action Plan "Shaping Our Common Future" that was signed at the tenth EU-Japan summit in 2001 also revealed a similar security vision in "promoting peace and security."[53] In the face of their occasional differences (for example, Europe's soaring trade deficit with Japan in the late 1980s and the EU's consideration to remove its arms embargo on China in 2003), the EU-Japan relationship has grown into a formidable partnership, one that stems from a similar vision on how to approach security issues.

Another relationship devoted to ensuring peace and stability in East and Southeast Asia is the EU–South Korea partnership. The cornerstone of this security relationship lies in the Framework Agreement on Trade and Co-operation, which was signed in 1996 and ratified in 2001. The need for such a declaration arose in response to the development of nuclear weapons by North Korea in 1994. The EU and South Korea were careful not to specifically mention North Korea in the agreement, instead outlining objectives to "promote peaceful solutions to international or regional conflicts" and to intensify discussions on issues, such as "arms control and disarmament, non-proliferation and weapons of mass destruction."[54]

The EU and South Korea security partnership is also institutionalized in the form of the ASEAN Regional Forum (ARF), which highlighted maritime security in the ARF Statement on Cooperation Against Piracy and Other Threats to Security in June 2003. Additionally, this common priority among ARF members, with the inclusion of Japan, culminated in the objective to "work together to protect ships engaged in international voyages" in the Asia-Pacific region.[55] The EU–South Korea Framework Agreement, implemented in 2014, recognizes a shared commitment to cooperate on matters from nonproliferation and counterterrorism to climate change and energy security.[56] The EU–South Korea Framework Agreement also expresses a shared vision of maritime safety and regional security as a common vision.[57] These examples, moreover, set the stage for the EU to play a significant role in containing China's aggression in the South China Sea.

Whether the EU will cooperate in joint military expeditions with Japan or South Korea in the future is a question that must be answered. It appears unlikely the EU would lead a military exercise in the Western Pacific, but surely it recognizes the security of the region remains critical to Europe and the world's economy. Paul Stares, a senior fellow at the Council on Foreign Relations, and Nicolas Regaud, the assistant defense policy director at the French Ministry of Defense, addressed Europe's role in a 1997 publication. The authors stated that if a conflict occurred in the South China Sea, "European powers might independently decide to become engaged to uphold international norms and rules, such as freedom of passage on the high sea, or to protect their economic interests in the region."[58]

The British and the French, moreover, both possess capable navies that enable them to project power and deploy their own aircraft carriers.[59] France, in particular, has evidenced its global reach through the deployment of its *Jeanne d'Arc* group, a helicopter carrier–led fleet that passes through the South China Sea on its annual travels from the Mediterranean to the Pacific.[60] Additionally, France's aircraft carrier, the *Charles De Gaulle*, played a supporting role to the U.S. efforts in Afghanistan in 2001. Likewise, the *Charles de Gaulle* was instrumental in the 2011 Libya operation that ousted Muammar Gaddafi and in the 2015 engagement of the Islamic State in Iraq and Syria.[61]

French defense minister Jean-Yves Le Drian announced the desire of France to coordinate joint EU naval patrols in the South China Sea along with calling for a "regular and visible presence" in the region.[62] With a permanent military presence already stationed in the Indo-Pacific and several joint naval drills under its belt in the South China Sea, France is well placed to coordinate such an exercise. To be sure, France recognizes that it has a veritable role to address China's expansion in the region. It only needs to cast off.

The British navy, once considered the world's greatest maritime power, maintains only one aircraft carrier, the *Queen Elizabeth*, which was launched in 2014. While subject to defense budget constraints, construction of another British aircraft carrier, the *Prince of Wales*, should be completed by 2018.[63] Despite the United Kingdom's decision to leave the EU, defense secretary Michael Fallon did state that the United Kingdom could still take part in EU military exercises. This statement mainly was in reference to missions intended to tackle migrant smugglers and pirates. Nevertheless, the United Kingdom leaves open the door for it to join a French-led maritime patrol in the South China Sea under the EU flag.[64]

The United States maintains a more distinct capability than the EU to project military power into the South China Sea. One way the United States aims to deter Chinese misbehavior, including China's land reclamation efforts, is by operating a carrier strike group in the region. Each strike group is technically advanced and typically comprises an aircraft carrier, a guided missile cruiser, two guided missile destroyers, an attack submarine, and a support ship.[65] Following the ruling at The Hague, the U.S. Navy carried out a rare spectacle: a dual aircraft carrier strike group operation that featured the USS *John C. Stennis* (CVN 74) and the USS *Ronald Reagan* (CVN 76).[66] Although a significant gap exists between EU and U.S. naval capabilities, such member states as France and the United Kingdom possess competent navies and should join in a show of support for regional maritime security.

CONCLUSION

Although the EU promotes peace and stability in East Asia, the institution's lack of power projection capabilities in the area makes it difficult to support this goal. While the push by the French to lead EU naval patrols is promising, "The only way to stymie China's territorial claims is through a coordinated, tactical stance by the U.S., EU, and other partners."[67] The EU certainly cedes this military advantage to the United States. Diplomatically, the EU's position would benefit from developing a unified voice and a regional strategy that is unique from the United States but complementary to their joint goals. On a practical level, the geographical distance between the EU and China makes it difficult for Brussels to have an impact on the region. The EU's lack of security tension vis-à-vis China, theoretically, is an advantage. It opens the door for Brussels to increase its criticism of Beijing's reclamation practices.

Until now, the EU has not yet singled out China for land reclamation activities. Instead, Brussels has been keen to remain neutral and to promote broad measures of international maritime law to settle the South China Sea disputes. The EU can no longer tread water in the settlement process. Too much is at stake. That is because there are ramifications for casting aside UNCLOS as a means to resolve maritime disputes, thus leading to the potential for historical rights to become the new status quo. Consider the consequences of waterways surrounding Europe (for example, the Atlantic Ocean, Mediterranean Sea, and Arctic Ocean), and the possibility that a law of the sea dispute could arrive at Europe's doorstep. The EU needs a common thread to stitch its member states together and adopt a collective, censorious rhetoric against China's hawkish behavior. Such a unified role would serve two key purposes: It would solidify the EU's internal relationships at a time when several forces are working to dismantle the integrity of the union, and it would assert the EU's role as a global leader by defending maritime freedom and the international law of the sea.

The EU and United States could enact joint sanctions on China if it continues its controversial expansion and outpost building in the South China Sea. This option, however, would come at a great cost for Europe because China would likely retaliate with its own diplomatic and economic measures. Any confrontation in the South China Sea would have calamitous effects for the EU because of the economic stakes of the twenty-eight member states. Notwithstanding that sacrifice, remaining anchored off shore could yield more catastrophic consequences than navigating a rising tide.

Regarding shared economic foreign policy, the EU's economic ties with East Asia and Southeast Asia are substantial, and significant cooperation in both relationships has led to the emergence of global economic partnerships. Through the South China Sea, the European Union has established a gateway into vast markets and developed a role as a player in security and diplomacy issues, albeit a minimal role for the time being. Despite its current internal focus, the European Union cannot ignore strategic partnerships with China, Japan, and South Korea. It has a major role to play in the South China Sea.

Notes

1. European Commission Directorate General for Trade, "Client and Supplier Countries of the EU28 in Merchandise Trade," 2016, http://trade.ec.europa.eu/doclib/docs/2006/september/tradoc_122530.02.2017pdf.
2. European Commission Directorate General for Trade, "Association of South East Asian Nations (ASEAN)," 2016, http://ec.europa.eu/trade/policy/countries-and-regions/regions/asean/.
3. Ibid.; Association of Southeast Asian Nations, "Overview of ASEAN-EU Dialogue Relations," http://www.asean.org/news/item/overview-of-asean-eu-dialogue-relations.
4. World Bank, "European Union Data," http://data.worldbank.org/region/EUU, and "United States Data," http://data.worldbank.org/country/united-states.
5. European Commission Directorate General for Communication Publications, "The European Union Explained—How the European Union Works," June 1, 2013, http://eeas.europa.eu/archives/delegations/singapore/documents/more_info/eu_publications/how_the_european_union_works_en.pdf.
6. Ibid.
7. Ibid.

8. Council of the European Union, "Voting System—Unanimity," September 24, 2014, http://www.consilium.europa.eu/en/council-eu/voting-system/unanimity/.
9. Shi Zhiqin, "Understanding China-EU Relations," Carnegie-Tsinghua Center for Global Policy, October 15, 2012, http://carnegieeurope.eu/publications/?fa=49688.
10. European Commission, "A New Partnership with South East Asia," July 9, 2003, http://trade.ec.europa.eu/doclib/docs/2004/july/tradoc116277.pdf.
11. European Union, "Joint EU-U.S. Statement on the Asia-Pacific Region," July 12, 2012, http://www.consilium.europa.eu/uedocs/cms_data/docs/pressdata/EN/foraff/131709.pdf.
12. Ibid.
13. Ibid.
14. European Commission, "Joint Press Statement between the Socialist Republic of Vietnam and the European Union," August 25, 2014, http://europa.eu/rapid/press-release_STATEMENT-14-257_en.htm?locale=en.
15. Pia Lee-Brago, "China Ignores Global Outcry vs Reclamation," *Philippine Star*, April 19, 2015, http://www.philstar.com/headlines/2015/04/19/1445470/china-ignores-global-outcry-vs-reclamation.
16. David Brunnstrom and Idrees Ali, "U.S. Says Europeans Could Help More in South China Sea Dispute," Reuters, July 29, 2015, http://www.reuters.com/article/us-usa-eu-southchinasea-idUSKCN0Q401B20150730.
17. European Council and Council of the European Union, "Declaration by the High Representative on Behalf of the EU on the Award Rendered in the Arbitration between the Republic of the Philippines and the People's Republic of China," July 15, 2016, http://www.consilium.europa.eu/en/press/press-releases/2016/07/15-south-china-sea-arbitration/.
18. Robin Emmott, "EU's Statement on South China Sea Reflects Divisions," Reuters, July 15, 2016, http://www.reuters.com/article/us-southchinasea-ruling-eu-idUSKCN0ZV1TS.
19. Sven Milekic, "Major Chinese Business Summit Opens in Croatia," *Balkan Insight*, May 30, 2016, http://www.balkaninsight.com/en/article/biggest-chinese-business-summit-kicks-off-in-zagreb-05-27-2016.
20. Silvija Fister, "China and Slovenia—Building a Firm Foundation for Economic Cooperation," *Slovenia Times*, February 4, 2016, http://www.sloveniatimes.com/china-and-slovenia-building-a-firm-foundation-for-economic-cooperation.
21. Theresa Fallon, "The EU, the South China Sea, and China's Successful Wedge Strategy," Asia Maritime Transparency Initiative, October 13, 2016, https://amti.csis.org/eu-south-china-sea-chinas-successful-wedge-strategy/.
22. Lubold, Gordon, Adam Entous, and Jeremy Page. "U.S. Navy Tests China Over Sea Claims," *Wall Street Journal*, October 27, 2015, https://www.wsj.com/articles/china-says-it-warned-u-s-warship-in-south-china-sea-1445928223.
23. Ibid.
24. Franz-Stefan Gady, "U.S. Navy Destroyers Patrol Near China's Man-Made Islands in South China Sea," *The Diplomat*, July 8, 2016, http://thediplomat.com/2016/07/us-navy-destroyers-patrol-near-chinas-man-made-islands-in-south-china-sea/.

25. European Council on Foreign Relations, "European Policy Scorecard 2016," January 2016.
26. Ibid.; White House Office of the Press Secretary, "Remarks by President Obama and Prime Minister Abbott of Australia After Bilateral Meeting," November 10, 2014, https://www.whitehouse.gov/the-press-office/2014/11/10/remarks-president-obama-and-prime-minister-abbott-australia-after-bilate.
27. European Council on Foreign Relations, "European Policy Scorecard 2016."
28. Andreas Rinke, "Merkel Suggests China Resolve South China Sea Row in Courts," Reuters, October 29, 2015, http://www.reuters.com/article/southchinasea-china-germany-idUSL8N12T2WQ20151029.
29. Ibid.
30. Francesco Guarascio, "European Union Sides with United States on South China Sea Incident," Reuters, October 30, 2015, http://www.reuters.com/article/us-south chinasea-usa-eu-idUSKCN0SO22G20151031.
31. Ibid.
32. Angela Stanzel, "Merkel's Visit to China: A Balancing Act," *The Diplomat*, June 15, 2016, http://thediplomat.com/2016/06/merkels-visit-to-china-a-balancing-act/.
33. Press and Information Office of the Federal Government of German, "Speech by Federal Chancellor Angela Merkel on Receiving an Honorary Doctorate from Nanjing University on 12 June 2016 in Beijing," June 12, 2016, https://www.bundeskanzlerin.de/Content/EN/Reden/2016/2016-06-12-bkin-ehrendoktor-beijing_en.html.
34. Joshua P. Rowan, "The U.S.-Japan Security Alliance, ASEAN, and the South China Sea Dispute," *Asian Survey* 45, no. 3 (2005): pp. 414–36.
35. Ibid.
36. Frank Umbach, "Asian-European Relations," in *EU Through the Eyes of Asia*, vol. II, ed. Martin Holland et al. (Singapore: World Scientific Publishing, 2009).
37. European Commission Directorate General for Trade, "Client and Supplier Countries of the EU28 in Merchandise Trade."
38. Zhiqin, "Understanding China-EU Relations."
39. Ibid.
40. European External Action Service, "Shared Vision, Common Action: A Stronger Europe—A Global Strategy for the European Union's Foreign and Security Policy," June 2016.
41. European Council on Foreign Relations, "European Policy Scorecard 2016."
42. European External Action Service, "Shared Vision, Common Action."
43. World Bank, "Military Expenditure (% of GDP)," http://data.worldbank.org/indicator/MS.MIL.XPND.GD.ZS.
44. Anna Barcikowska, "EU Battlegroups—Ready to Go?" European Union Institute for Security Studies, November 2013, http://www.iss.europa.eu/uploads/media/Brief_40_EU_Battlegroups.pdf.
45. European Union External Action, "EU Battlegroups," April 2013, https://www.consilium.europa.eu/uedocs/cms_data/docs/pressdata/en/esdp/91624.pdf.

46. Martin Holland, "Assuming Superpower Status? Evolving Asian Perceptions of the EU as a Political and Economic Actor," in *EU Through the Eyes of Asia*.
47. James G. Neuger, "Europe Defense Cuts Imperil NATO Readiness, Group Says," Bloomberg, February 25, 2015, http://www.bloomberg.com/news/articles/2015-02-26/europe-defense-cuts-imperil-nato-readiness-group-says.
48. Ibid.
49. David Kerr, "Between Regionalism and World Order: Five Structural Factors in China-Europe Relations to 2025," in *The International Politics of EU-China Relations*, ed. David Kerr and Liu Fei (Oxford: Oxford University Press, 2007).
50. Ibid.
51. Olena Mykal, *The EU-Japan Security Dialogue: Invisible but Comprehensive* (Amsterdam: Amsterdam University Press, 2011).
52. Ibid.
53. M. Hachiya, "From an Issue-specific to a Global Partnership: Japan and the European Union," in *Europe-Asia Relations: Building Multilateralisms*, ed. Richard Balme and Brian Bridges (New York: Palgrave MacMillan, 2008).
54. Brian Bridges, "The European Union and the Korean Conundrum," in *Europe-Asia Relations: Building Multilateralisms*.
55. ASEAN Regional Forum, "Chairman's Statement of the 10th Meeting of the ASEAN Regional Forum, Phnom Penh, 18 June 2003," http://aseanregionalforum.asean.org/component/content/article/3-public-library/173-chairmans-statement-of-the-10th-meeting-of-the-asean-regional-forum-phnom-penh-18-june-2003.html.
56. European Commission Directorate General for Trade, "South Korea," April 20, 2015, http://ec.europa.eu/trade/policy/countries-and-regions/countries/south-korea/.
57. European External Action Service, "EU-South Korea Framework Agreement (FA)," June 1, 2014, http://eeas.europa.eu/korea_south/docs/framework_agreement_final_en.pdf.
58. Paul Stares and Nicolas Regaud, "Europe's Role in Asia-Pacific Security," *Survival* 39, no. 4 (1997): pp. 117–39.
59. Ibid.
60. Yo-Jung Chen, "South China Sea: The French Are Coming," *The Diplomat*, July 14, 2016, http://thediplomat.com/2016/07/south-china-sea-the-french-are-coming/.
61. Pierre Bienaimé, "Here's the Aircraft Carrier France Is Sending to Chase Down ISIS in Iraq," *Business Insider*, January 15, 2015, http://www.businessinsider.com/heres-the-aircraft-carrier-france-is-sending-to-chase-down-isis-in-iraq-2015-1.
62. Chen, "South China Sea."
63. Richard Norton-Taylor, "Prince of Wales Aircraft Carrier 'Makes Little Sense' Without Aircraft to Fly from It," *The Guardian*, March 23, 2015, http://www.theguardian.com/uk-news/2015/mar/24/prince-of-wales-aircraft-carrier-makes-little-sense-report.
64. Matt Dathan, "Britain Can Still Take Part in EU Military Missions Even after Brexit, Says Defence Secretary Michael Fallon," *Daily Mail*, July 20, 2016, http://www.dailymail.co.uk/news/article-3698972/Britain-EU-military-missions-Brexit-says-Defence-Secretary-Michael-Fallon.html.

65. U.S. Navy, "The Carrier Strike Group," http://www.navy.mil/navydata/ships/carriers/powerhouse/cvbg.asp.
66. Megan Eckstein, "Stennis, Reagan Conduct Dual-Carrier Operations in Philippine Sea," USNI News, June 20, 2016, https://news.usni.org/2016/06/20/stennis-reagan-dual-carrier-operations.
67. Peter Solomon, "China's One Horse Race in the South China Sea," *Journal of Political Risk*, June 28, 2016, http://www.jpolrisk.com/chinas-one-horse-race-in-the-south-china-sea/.

Conclusion

Bernard D. Cole

This book is both a product and a clarification of some of the disturbing events of the first decades of the twenty-first century in the relationship between China and major global powers, including the United States. These have featured maritime issues between the global powers, as well as between Beijing and claimants to various land features in the South China Sea. The South China Sea leads the list of dangerous scenarios in maritime Asia.

SOUTH CHINA SEA ENVIRONMENT

The South China Sea covers an area of some 4 million square kilometers. It contains vital trade arteries, with approximately one-third of the world's commerce passing through its waters, fisheries that account for as much as 12 percent of the global catch, and significant estimated reserves of oil and natural gas. It is approximately 1,400 nautical miles (nm) from north to south and 700 nm east to west, bordering the Southeast Asian mainland. It includes an area of approximately 1,423,000 square miles (3,685,000 square kilometers) and has a mean depth of 3,976 feet (1,212 meters).

Claims have been staked to parts of the South China Sea by Brunei, China, Malaysia, the Philippines, and Vietnam—and by Taiwan, which agrees almost entirely with Beijing's position. Indonesia is not a formal claimant, but the exclusive economic zone (EEZ) generated by its Natuna Islands overlaps with China's "U-shaped line," commonly referred to as the "nine-dash line."[1]

This line first appeared as eleven dashes on a Chinese map published by a government-sponsored committee of scholars in 1935. It reappeared in 1947 on a chart published by the Republic of China (ROC) government, then headquartered in Nanjing. The People's Republic of China (PRC) government removed two dashes from the Gulf of Tonkin in a 1953 chart. Finally, a tenth dash, east of Taiwan, appeared on a 2014 chart. No Chinese government, either the ROC (Taiwan) or the PRC, has ever delineated the coordinates of the "dash line" or clearly stated what it defines.

UNITED NATIONS CONVENTION ON THE LAW OF THE SEA

Maritime land features are categorized and described in the United Nations Convention on the Law of the Sea (UNCLOS), an international treaty concluded in 1982 after a decade of negotiations and effective as of 1994.[2] The treaty has been signed and ratified by 167 states and the European Union. Fourteen additional United Nations member states have signed but not ratified the convention. The United States is notable as a nonsignatory.

Understanding the dispute over the hundreds of land features in the South China Sea first requires an understanding of how UNCLOS defines land features, including an island, a rock, and a low-tide elevation (LTE).

UNCLOS implies that there are two requirements for a land feature to be classified as an island. First, it must be above water at all times, including during maximum high tide. Second, it must be capable of sustaining human life and/or economic life. If the land feature meets the first but not the second requirement, it is legally a rock, not an island. If it is not always above the ocean's surface, it is classified as an LTE, neither an island nor a rock.

UNCLOS grants an island several zones. First is the territorial sea, measured from the coastal baseline to a distance of twelve nautical miles (nm). The second UNCLOS zone is contiguous waters, measured to an additional distance of 12 nm (24 nm from the coastal baseline). Third is an exclusive economic zone, measured from the coastal baseline to a maximum distance of 200 nm. The last element is the continental shelf, a feature that is defined by the ocean bottom topography and that may be claimed to a maximum distance of 350 nm from the coastal baseline. Hence, given the dimensions of the South China Sea, the claimants to various land features will usually have to come to an agreement on where contiguous EEZs and claimed continental shelves divide.

While an island is entitled to all of these zones, a rock is entitled only to 12 nm of territorial waters. An LTE is not entitled to an UNCLOS zone at all but may claim a surrounding five-hundred-meter-wide security zone. This treaty recognizes that geography may not accommodate all such zones. For instance, if two coastal nations are less than 700 nm apart, both cannot effectively claim 350 nm continental shelves; if they are less than 400 nm apart, they both cannot effectively claim 200 nm EEZs. UNCLOS recommends ways of resolving such disputes, which are inherent in the South China Sea's relatively complex geography.

An associated and important issue of interest is that of claiming "historic rights." Here, too, China is not the only party to claim such rights, but they are of particular interest as Beijing claims such rights in areas of the South China Sea that are disputed by other claimants—some of whom, like Vietnam, also claim historic rights as justifying various claims, including sovereignty and fishing rights.[3]

The most frequent clashes over land features and maritime boundaries have occurred between China and Vietnam and China and the Philippines. During 2016, however, China apparently gratuitously engaged in a new contest over maritime territorial rights with Indonesia over possibly conflicting EEZs. Beijing has not disputed Jakarta's sovereignty over the Natuna Islands, which lie in the midst of especially rich energy and fishing waters north of Sumatra. Beijing seems responsible for needlessly increasing tensions and raising the risks of armed confrontations with Jakarta by emphasizing the theory of historic or traditional fishing rights. For instance, on June 19, 2016, Chinese ministry of foreign affairs spokesperson Hua Chunying described the most recent incident with Indonesia as occurring "in waters that are Chinese fishermen's traditional fishing grounds." The real danger of escalation is posed by the fact that these waters in Indonesia's EEZ also contain energy fields that are vital to Indonesia's economy.

More specifically, the following claims dominate the current crisis in the South China Sea:

- Brunei has implied a claim to Louisa Reef, which lies within its EEZ.
- China claims all land features "and associated waters" within the current ten-dash line, including features that never appear above the sea's surface.
- Indonesia's claimed EEZ overlaps China's (and Taiwan's) ten-dash line.
- Malaysia claims several Spratly Islands based on its continental shelf.
- The Philippines claims several Spratly Islands based on various UNCLOS principles.
- Taiwan's claims are basically the same as China's.
- Vietnam claims all the Paracel and Spratly Islands.

None of these nations have evinced any sense of flexibility in their claims; China is not maintaining a uniquely rigid negotiating position. However, one area of at least partially successful negotiation has occurred over the Gulf of Tonkin (called the Beibu Gulf by China), a semi-enclosed bay embraced by the mainland of China and Vietnam as well as by China's Hainan Island.

Beijing and Hanoi reached agreement on settling their land boundary in 1993; their maritime boundary dispute in the South China Sea remains unresolved, although Vietnam is recovering significant energy reserves from some of the disputed fields. The dispute has been marked by several violent clashes.

The other disputes in the South China Sea concern delimitation of maritime boundaries in the sea areas adjacent to the southern part of the South China Sea. As of 2015, Vietnam had occupied twenty-seven of the land features; the Philippines, eight; Malaysia, nine; China, seven; and Taiwan, one.

THE SPRATLY ISLANDS

Both Beijing and Hanoi cite extensive historical bases for their respective claims in the South China Sea. China's claims, in fact, approach the mystical as it cites unsubstantiated "historic rights" and pre–common era "evidence."

Since China seized all the Paracel Islands in the northern South China Sea after a brief naval battle with Republic of Vietnam forces in 1974, the most unresolved, contentious claims are those concerning the Spratlys, farther to the south.

China maintained occupation of several of these islands after a similar battle with Vietnamese naval units in 1988.[4] This group includes more than 400 land features—inhabited land, rocks, sand cays, and LTEs. Among them, only 33 rise above the sea, and only 7 have an area exceeding 0.3 square miles. They are scattered over an area that is 400 nm from east to west and 500 nm from north to south.

The area is rich in fish and may contain significant oil and other energy resources. Chinese surveys indicate that about 25 billion cubic meters of gas and 105 billion barrels of oil exist in the continental shelf around the Spratly Islands, but U.S. surveys are not nearly so optimistic. Reserves are uncertain and remain an issue of great contention between China and the other regional claimants.

The current state of tensions in the South China Sea may be dated to 2008–9, when China's coast guard and maritime militia (civilian fishing boats in the service of the government) harassed U.S. oceanographic survey vessels. The situation intensified in 2012, when a Sino-Philippine standoff began over Scarborough Shoal, located approximately 100 nm from the Luzon coast. Beijing used coast guard vessels to seize Scarborough, in contravention to a diplomatic agreement it had made with Manila.

Chinese tensions with Vietnam then increased significantly. In May 2014, Beijing began drilling operations with an oil rig owned by the state-owned China National Offshore Oil Corporation, 120 nm from the Vietnamese coast and 17 nm from Triton Island, part of the disputed Paracel Islands. Hanoi vehemently protested, and multiple collisions and water cannon exchanges then ensued between Vietnamese and Chinese fishing boats and coast guard vessels.[5]

South China Sea tensions since 2014 have further increased as a result of Chinese construction of artificial "islands" in the Spratlys built as military bases with runways capable of operating tactical aircraft, berthing facilities for warships, and weapons emplacements. Other claimants have engaged in similar construction, but China's efforts have been orders of magnitude greater.

Diplomatic efforts to resolve the South China Sea issues have included the 2002 Declaration on the Conduct of Parties in the South China Sea between China and the Association of Southeast Asian Nations (ASEAN) nations. This aspirational statement called for negotiating a peaceful resolution of all territorial claims, but very little has been achieved toward that goal. Beijing's insistence that any negotiations must be preceded by acknowledgment of Chinese sovereignty has vitiated possible diplomatic resolution of the disputes.

MILITARY ASPECTS

The Spratly Islands are also of strategic military significance because of their central position in the South China Sea amid vital sea lines of communication. These are the main transit routes from Southwest Asia and the Indian Ocean and Northeast Asia and the Pacific Ocean. The military installations China has built and, according to People's Liberation Army Navy (PLAN) commander Admiral Wu Shengli, will continue building, will eventually be able to monitor and perhaps dominate most of the South China Sea.

The South China Sea's most important military feature may be its possible use by China as a "bastion" for its developing seaborne nuclear deterrent. Beijing has constructed an impressive base for its *Jin*-class nuclear-powered ballistic missile submarines on Hainan Island, at the northern end of the sea. If these submarines are armed with intercontinental ballistic missiles (ICBMs) with sufficient range, they will likely restrict their operations to the South China Sea—significantly increasing the sea's strategic importance, especially to China and to the United States.

CHINA AND THE UNITED STATES

Beijing's primary national security concerns are in the domestic arena. China's leader, Xi Jinping, is the nation's president, chairman of the Central Military Commission, and leader of the Chinese Communist Party. He has established himself as a powerful national leader since assuming these three positions in 2012.

China continues to modernize and expand its navy as its economic and political maritime interests increase. However, domestic concerns will continue to take priority, and Xi will continue to treat foreign policy as a secondary concern, although one driven significantly by nationalism, popular pressure, and his "China Dream."[6]

Beijing is intent on changing the UNCLOS definitions and privileges of land features, both permanently and periodically submerged, to include LTEs, rocks, and islands. China believes it must take strong action to reassert its own sovereignty claims and presence.

Beijing is pursuing its South China Sea goals with "a fervent level of self-righteousness." This attitude contributes to the emerging maritime strategy China outlined in its 2015 Defense White Paper. Both soft and hard power policies are forwarded without any seeming sense of conflict between the two.

More recently, Wu Shicun, head of China's National Institute for South China Sea Studies, described Beijing's position as "a natural line of defense for Chinese national security, an important strategic waterway, and a strategic must-have for it to become a maritime power. For the United States, controlling the South China Sea and maintaining its presence there is indispensable for its dominance in the Asia-Pacific based on its bilateral alliances formulated in the post-war [World War II] era. In this sense, China-U.S. competition and rivalry in the South China Sea is structural, strategic, and irreconcilable."[7] In other words, China and the United States are in a position of opposing what each considers important, but not existential, geopolitical strategic positions.

Chinese analysts also deny that any of their country's actions or positions in the South China Sea "violate international law," that China "claims sovereignty over the whole" sea, "threatens freedom of navigation and over flight rights," "intends to change the 'status quo'," is "building 'artificial islands'," is "accelerating the militarization" of the sea, is damaging the environment, or is acting assertively. They also continue to defend the validity of the U-shaped line without specifying its precise meaning or location. These positions may lack validity in American and other foreign minds, but that does not negate the Chinese perceptions as factors that must be understood.[8]

THE INTERNATIONAL TRIBUNAL FOR THE LAW OF THE SEA

The United Nations created the International Tribunal for the Law of the Sea (ITLOS) to resolve disputes that arise under UNCLOS; the Republic of the Philippines appealed to the tribunal in 2013 in frustration at its inability to negotiate satisfactorily with China over disputed claims in the South China Sea, particularly over Scarborough Shoal. From the time it signed and ratified UNCLOS, China has disagreed with ITLOS jurisdiction and insisted from the case's onset that it would neither participate nor adhere to any of the court's proceedings and rulings.

ITLOS ruled almost entirely with Manila but did state in October 2015 that it would not rule on China's artificial island construction, since these were "military in nature" and hence not within its authority under UNCLOS.[9]

China's refusal to acknowledge the validity of the ITLOS ruling reflects its historic refusal to settle maritime sovereignty disputes, although it has settled many land disputes. In response to the ITLOS ruling, which was overwhelmingly in the Philippines' favor, China issued a white paper reaffirming its "territorial sovereignty and maritime rights and interests in the South China Sea." Beijing insisted that it held sovereignty over all the South China Sea "islands," citing various Chinese laws, "historic rights," and UNCLOS.[10]

The Philippines of course welcomed that decision "as an important contribution to ongoing efforts in addressing disputes in the South China Sea."

The ruling was issued in a 501-page document and contained the following primary "holdings":

- UNCLOS "comprehensively" governs the parties' respective rights to maritime areas in the South China Sea. Therefore, to the extent that China's nine-dash line is a claim of "historic rights" to the waters of the South China Sea, it is invalid.
- None of the features in the Spratly Islands generate an EEZ, nor can the Spratly Islands generate an EEZ collectively as a unit.
- China violated the Philippines' sovereign rights in its EEZ by interfering with Philippine fishing and hydrocarbon exploration, constructing artificial islands, and failing to prevent Chinese fishermen from fishing in the Philippines' EEZ.
- China has aggravated and extended the disputes through its dredging, artificial island building, and construction activities.

In fact, ITLOS ruled that none of the land features in the South China Sea are legally "islands" and hence cannot generate any geographic zone beyond a 12 nm territorial sea. The tribunal did note, however, "[W]e should not assume that these disputes are the product of *bad faith* on the part of the PRC; rather, they are the result of basic disagreements about respective rights and obligations and the applicability of UNCLOS." This statement implied Chinese blamelessness but did nothing to salve its resentment.

Beijing has not hesitated to employ nominally non-naval craft, coast guard, and maritime militia vessels to enforce its territorial and maritime claims in the South China Sea. The majority of these vessels do not display weapons above deck but use water cannon, bright lights, loud noisemakers, and ramming to attack other nations' fishermen and coast guards.

These clashes have occasionally resulted in the death of opposing personnel, as Beijing defines "freedom of navigation" in its own terms. Both civilian and military Chinese officials, as well as Chinese analysts and academics, doggedly protest that China has never posed and will never pose a threat to the freedom of navigation. They refer, however, to civilian vessels, not military vessels, which Beijing holds to a different standard, as expressed in one of the declarations it made when ratifying UNCLOS. This position is exacerbated by an extreme sensitivity to issues of sovereignty, due in part to the so-called hundred years of humiliation.

The U.S. interests in the South China Sea disputes are discussed in the essays by Sean Liedman and James Fanell. Washington's South China Sea policy is based on the historic issue of ensuring U.S. commercial, political, and military access to the maritime commons. This is not limited by UNCLOS but applies to all areas outside sovereign territorial waters, the 12 nm band measured from a coastal nation's shoreline. Guaranteeing access remains a primary U.S. naval mission, especially in the face of China's apparent goal of controlling the seas within the East Asian First and Second Island Chains.[11]

China's reaction to U.S. freedom of navigation cruises in the South China Sea has been vocal and threatening, including a recent statement by Admiral Sun Jianguo opposing "so-called military freedom of navigation" cruises and threatening that these "could even play out in a disastrous way." This highlights a key difference between China and the United States: the former believes that "freedom of navigation" under UNCLOS and international law applies only to civilian merchant vessels, while the United States (and the great majority of UNCLOS signatory states) believes that "freedom of navigation" applies universally, to all vessels.

In the first substantive chapter, Bill Hayton presents a well-constructed, historically based discussion of the validity of China's territorial claims in the South China Sea. He pays particular attention to Beijing's construction of "seven huge artificial islands." He addresses Beijing's possible reasons for this program but emphasizes the problematic nature of Chinese policymakers' legal and historical claims.

Hayton notes the "sense of national entitlement" that supports Beijing's claims on the land features in question and never misses the opportunity to note the weaknesses in China's attempts to substitute nationalism for facts or legal precedent. This results in large part from Beijing's priority on maintaining the communist regime in power, concerns about securing sea lines of communication, and proprietary feelings about maritime resources, even—or perhaps particularly—when those resources are disputed.[12]

These objectives are driving China to asserting claims to land features never previously ruled by China, to maritime claims that have never been part of a Chinese realm, and to rights over waters beyond the most common interpretations of UNCLOS. Beijing's inability or unwillingness to recognize other points of view in these issues seems to be a prime case of Edward Luttwak's "great power autism."

Hayton's most striking opinion may be that "China's sense of righteousness" and concerns about sovereignty issues unduly influence its policy choices, leading to continued military clashes. U.S. and other foreign policymakers must recognize this Chinese perspective to avoid misinterpreting possible Chinese actions, Hayton argues convincingly, including unexpected employment of military force. He further argues that solving the territorial disputes relies on "challenging the Chinese version of history and thereby undermining China's sense of righteousness." It does not criticize Hayton's view to point out how difficult this would be.

Ian Forsyth discusses China's maritime actions from the point of view of grand strategy—specifically, how Beijing's actions involve the elements of statecraft, including the diplomatic, military, economic, legal, and information instruments. His goal is to review past Chinese courses of action in the South China Sea as a baseline for addressing likely future actions by Beijing and the international tensions those might generate, particularly with respect to the July 2016 ruling by the Permanent Court of Arbitration and the policies and actions of the other South China Sea claimants.

Forsyth credits China with a coherent regional strategy, albeit one that originated in the 1990s and failed adequately to anticipate the reactions of the other regional disputants. This reflects, in Forsyth's view, Beijing's inaccurate analysis and shortsighted view of the Southeast Asian political environment.

Hence, increased anti-China sentiment has emerged, reflecting a strategic tone-deafness by Beijing. Few observers would disagree with Forsyth that China has achieved global power status and seeks to dominate East Asia. Indeed, he notes, Beijing appears to have discarded Deng Xiaoping's cautions about biding its time and now is pursuing militarily and politically active foreign policies.

Motivation for this more assertive policy position probably reflects China's global economic strength, increasing need for raw resources, and fervent belief that a global power of China's stature "deserves" to be a global military power. Along with this feeling is the widespread if generally unsubstantiated belief in China that the United States is actively trying to contain and surround it.

Ironically, perhaps, China's strategy concerning the South China Sea has achieved some material results but has resulted in widespread animosity among other Asian nations. This is a mismatch between strategic and regional goals that Beijing either does not understand or does not deem important.

Few observers of current Chinese military developments speak with more first-hand experience or authority than retired U.S. Navy captain James Fanell. He pulls no punches in addressing China's territorial expansion during the past half-decade or more that "has dramatically altered the geo-military balance of power in the Indo-Asia Pacific region."

He focuses on the new "islands" China has been constructing in the South China Sea but also notes Beijing's declaration of an air defense identification zone in the East China Sea and its dispute with Japan over the sovereignty of the Senkaku Islands. Fanell also examines China's increasing naval and air force operations throughout the Pacific and Indian Oceans and beyond, as Beijing expands its already formidable regional navy into a maritime force envisioned to operate globally.

This is all evidence, in Fanell's view, of the vacuity of Beijing's claim of a "peaceful rise." As a result, the United States and regional nations are attempting to increase their own military capabilities. The United States is relying largely on its security alliances and friendships but may still be underestimating China's duplicity and ultimate military and political goals.

Fanell describes a worst-case scenario in pointing out that

> Beijing is conducting ballistic missile submarine patrols in the Western Pacific and submarine operations in the Indian Ocean and Bay of Bengal, acquiring access to port facilities at Gwadar, Pakistan, and Piraeus, Greece, building a naval base in a foreign port (as is currently under

way in Djibouti), establishing air defense identification zones in the East China Sea (and likely in the South), and dispatching the PLAN into the "far seas" of the Mediterranean and Baltic Sea to support the Belt and Road Initiative. This flood of activity suggests that President Xi and the Communist Party of China are intent upon establishing China as a global power that seeks to control the international order for its advantage.

This scenario may be qualified by the still-delayed arming of China's *Jin*-class submarines with the JL-2 ICBM, the isolated and troubled location of Gwadar, and the fact that China's acquiring the use of Piraeus and construction of a logistics facility at Djibouti came about through an open commercial competition.

More important to the United States and indeed to the world community is Fanell's demonstration of China's desire to reorder international legal norms that it feels were imposed upon it before its late 1970s economic and military surge into modernity. China is certainly "reformist" if not "revisionist" in its desire to modify the post–World War II international status quo. Beijing's most important accomplishment in this area is not island building in the South China Sea or its self-proclaimed nine-dash line, but rather the effectiveness of its policy to split, buy off, and neuter ASEAN.

Fanell's dark view of China's strategy and possible future success is followed by Leszek Buszynski's terse description of ASEAN's attempts to emerge as more than just a "talk shop." This organization faces a tough environment, however, since the South China Sea has become a strategic issue for China, Japan, and the United States. Buszynski points out that the ASEAN states can do little in the face of such powers, with those who are nonclaimants in the South China Sea especially determined to downplay the issues in favor of a stronger economic relationship with Beijing. This means that Cambodia, Laos, and Thailand offer little or no support to international efforts to restrain China. This isolates Vietnam and the Philippines in their attempts to gain the support of the United States, Japan, and perhaps India for their claims in the South China Sea.

Buszynski correctly describes an unpromising future for ASEAN as a regionally influential force for peaceful resolution of regional disputes. He also notes that China's assertive positions have drawn increased U.S. and Japanese attention to the South China Sea, with an increased naval presence by both nations. In other words, Beijing is paying a cost for its rigid policies; that cost clearly is outweighed, however, by the gains China is accruing in the region.

The chapter by Sean Liedman begins with a brief historical review of U.S. foreign and security policies addressing China since 1945. He describes three strategic phases: "containment, cooperative engagement, and competition." These, in his view, were multifaceted, encompassing economic, diplomatic, and military interests.

Additionally, a fourth unstated strategic theme undergirds the above: prevailing in the event of conflict. This last "strategy" really just conditions the playing field; China's economic strength, increasingly sophisticated diplomatic efforts, and steadily modernizing military are driving it—perhaps inexorably—toward a state of equality with or even superiority to the United States.

Despite this "fight and win if necessary" foundation to the Sino-American relationship, the author perceptively describes the two elements of cooperation and competition that frame the strategic relationship between the United States and China in the South China Sea. The United States is cooperating by not taking a position on sovereignty issues while competing with Beijing to ensure that China does not establish dominance over the sea.

The author then summarizes possible U.S. responses to China's advances in the South China Sea. The first response would be conceding China's sovereignty of all the land features in the South China Sea, although some of these are occupied and administered by U.S. allies, such as the Philippines, and friends, such as Singapore and Malaysia. The second U.S. option, according to the author, is to "freeze the status quo," although he does not offer a realistic way to accomplish that. This is hardly a condemnation, given the unwillingness by any of the claimants to negotiate their sovereignty claims, not less that of the Chinese.

Liedman's third way forward for the United States is to "roll back" Beijing's claims, a path reminiscent of the Dwight D. Eisenhower administration's unattainable, dangerous, and ultimately embarrassing policy of rolling back Soviet territorial takeovers in central Europe following the end of World War II. This policy was championed by Secretary of State John Foster Dulles and came to grief with the 1956 Hungarian uprising.

There is little to criticize in Liedman's analysis, but his description of the 1949–50 period in U.S.-China relations is notable; he describes this all-too-brief period as one of "circumspect engagement." This title attests to the author's keen understanding of the history of the U.S. relationship with both sides in China's long civil war, won by the Communists with the October 1949 announcement of the establishment of the PRC.

Equally worthy of mention is Liedman's categorization of ways forward for the United States. None of the three delineated may be likely of success; indeed, they may well produce outcomes even less favorable to Washington's interests than those being endured during the current imbroglio. That said, the author is to be commended for his insightfulness of the complex economic and security relationship between the United States and China.

In his chapter, Tongfi Kim attempts to build on Liedman's essay by presenting a higher-level strategic analysis of the U.S.-China disagreements in the South China Sea. He describes the Barack Obama administration's rebalance to Asia as a "new U.S. grand strategy." This emphasizes the U.S. problem of not provoking China while maintaining a convincing role "as the protector of the status quo in the South China Sea."

Kim describes the Obama administration's announced policy of rebalancing to Asia as a "grand strategy," a debatable conclusion in view of the fragmented nature of the rebalance, which is still very much a work in progress. He echoes Liedman's concern about the conflicting goals of reassuring Asian allies while not provoking China.

Kim also argues that China's growing economy, with attractive opportunities for foreign direct investment, presents one side of a conundrum for other Asian nations, as it does to a lesser extent for the United States, and especially those regional states disputing South China Sea issues with Beijing. The other side of the problem nagging at the desire to invest in China's growing economy is the security umbrella provided by continued U.S. military superiority in Asia. The most important part of this superiority is the dominant U.S. Navy, which would be capable of determining the outcome of any armed struggle in the South China Sea.

China's navy is increasingly capable of conducting all the classic naval missions, from diplomatic presence to large-scale warfare, against all Asian navies and increasingly against the U.S. Navy. If and when Beijing believes its navy is capable of neutralizing and perhaps defeating U.S. naval forces, even in a limited scenario such as one centering on Taiwan, the Asian security environment will be dramatically changed.

Neither Liedman nor Kim is in a position to assess the future of the rebalance under a Donald Trump presidency. This is understandable, and while it weakens the usefulness of their analyses, they both emphasize significant points in the Sino-U.S. confrontation in Asia that will remain relevant for the immediate future.

Takashi Inoguchi and Ankit Panda also emphasize the economic and security keys to the current and future international dynamic in Asia. They offer an appreciation of Japan's policies and possible role in the South China Sea disputes. Their first point is that Tokyo is following a two-pronged policy of increasing its influence in Southeast Asia while maintaining the strongest possible security relationship with the United States. Second, China is viewed as the primary military threat to Japan.

Having acknowledged Tokyo's sustained interest in the South China Sea issue, the authors believe that Tokyo's strategic thinking with regard to the South China Sea will largely be determined by three critical dynamics and events. First, given the continued salience of the U.S.-Japan alliance, Tokyo will avoid making any public statements or taking any policy positions that contravene the United States' considered position on the South China Sea issue. The U.S. government's October 2015 initiation of regular freedom of navigation patrols in the South China Sea has been read by the Japanese government as a positive development that tested and revealed China's reaction to having its excessive maritime claims challenged. Second, as a long-term grand strategy, Tokyo will avoid putting undue pressure on China in the South China Sea to avoid a deterioration of the status quo in the East China Sea or in the general bilateral relationship. As China's 2010 decision to suspend commerce over the arrest of a Chinese fisherman demonstrates, Beijing is willing to impose costs on Tokyo for moves it perceives as threatening or worrisome. Third, Tokyo—like all stakeholders in the South China Sea, including the United States—will continue to take a particular interest in bilateral developments between the Philippines and China in the South China Sea. The tribunal's strong award in the Philippines' favor and nullification of China's U-shaped line claim will factor into Tokyo's calculus for its moves in the South China Sea leading into the 2020s.

Continuing the march through major Asian powers, the eighth chapter is an assessment of India's views of the South China Sea issues by Gordon Chang. A long-time forecaster of China's downfall, Chang argues that Beijing and New Delhi are engaged in "a competitive dynamic" that will drive India from nonalignment to a close relationship with the United States and its allies.

This conclusion is based in part on India's demonstrated if somewhat episodic policy of establishing a presence in the South China Sea. The Indian navy may be the foremost advocate of what Chang cites as "strategic," but that force continues to face severe budgetary and bureaucratic problems in fulfilling its extensive ambitions. The Indian navy's desire to dominate the Indian Ocean will have to take precedence over establishing a meaningful strategic presence east of Malacca but remains very short of accomplishment.

Chang rightly notes the increasingly close Indian relationship with Vietnam and some tentative moves with other Southeast Asia nations. The New Delhi–Hanoi relationship is defined by joint energy project development and agreements between the two nations' navies. These are meaningful steps, and ones that disturb Beijing, but the Indian-Vietnamese relationship is still at the nascent stage.

Furthermore, the primary Indian strategic priority remains at home, establishing the ability to control events in the Indian Ocean and bordering land space. This ambition is disturbed largely by China. First are the Chinese navy's operations in the Indian Ocean, ranging from building facilities in Myanmar, Bangladesh, Sri Lanka, Pakistan, and Djibouti, to the now-eight-year-long operations in the Gulf of Aden that are nominally dedicated to countering piracy.

On land, New Delhi is confronted by Beijing's "one belt–one road" (OBOR) program, which demonstrates a Chinese ambition to become the dominant economic power across the entire Eurasian land mass. Whether the subcontinent is included in, or bypassed by, the OBOR is a strategic question facing India. In turn, the Narendra Modi government seems to move consistently closer to engaging politically, militarily, and perhaps economically with the United States.

Stephen Blank then analyzes Russia's relationship with China, focusing on Moscow's hitherto largely unsuccessful attempt to increase its presence and influence in the Pacific, particularly in Southeast Asia. Here, Russia also confronts a dual challenge, balancing its continuing close defense relationship with Vietnam with its increasing dependence on China as its only significant diplomatic and economic partner.

Moscow's policy of increasing its influence in Southeast Asia is further hampered by the weak Russian economy and still "fundamental" orientation toward Europe. Blank is thus "spot on" with respect to Russian president Vladimir Putin's strategic vision. This is based on using a close relationship with China to counter the U.S.-led Western nations, whether operating under the North Atlantic Treaty Organization alliance or the European Union. Putin may not have written off the former Soviet state republics in Central Asia, but he seems to be treading softly, in view of Beijing's determination to solidify access to that region's very considerable energy reserves.

Blank underlines Moscow's vital interest in not alienating China and its assertive policies in Southeast Asia. That is countered to an extent by Russia's continuing support for Vietnam by selling it arms that could be employed against China and by engaging in joint venture-based energy exploration in the South China Sea. However, Moscow no doubt realizes Hanoi's clever stance with Beijing, recognizing the geographic and economic realities that dominate Southeast Asia, even in the face of the U.S. rebalance to the region.

Moscow may, in Blank's view, want to reestablish a naval and air force base in Cam Ranh Bay, a facility it used during the Cold War. Hanoi's friendly relationship with Washington, and the aforementioned Vietnamese caution dealing with its Chinese neighbor, makes this Russian ambition unlikely to occur.

Moscow's economic goals in Southeast Asia, in terms both of resource acquisition and marketing Russian goods, also seem unlikely, as Blank points out. He describes the hollowness of Putin's foreign policy as Russia's "determined and obsessive quest for status as it strives to make others see and accept it as Moscow wants to see itself and be seen." Hence, because of Russia's domestic problems and Moscow's priority on its relationship with Beijing, there seems little possibility that it will be able "to engage Asia or be recognized as a great Asian power."

The book's final chapter, written by Peter Solomon, looks at the European Union's (EU's) role and policies concerning the South China Sea. He criticizes the EU's failure to effectively contribute to regional stability, through either diplomatic or military efforts, but this seems a relatively minor failure for an organization whose very foundation is being threatened by Great Britain's decision to withdraw.

Another problematic factor in Solomon's argument is his assumption that the EU has "strategic partnerships" with the major Asian nations that make China's actions in the South China Sea a challenge that requires it to take action. More significant to his argument is that China's actions are threatening the integrity of UNCLOS and agreement important to EU member states' trade.

On a practical level, the geographical distance between the EU and China makes it difficult for Brussels to have an impact on the region. Indeed, the statement that the EU "has an important role to play in the South China Sea" is not convincing, and the author's work is more accurately a description of European aspirations than accomplishments now or in the near term. He concludes that "although the EU promotes peace and stability in East Asia, the institution's lack of power projection capabilities in the area makes it difficult to support this goal."

The United States does not wish to cause an incident that might escalate to armed conflict, but it does want to ensure that China is impressed with its determination to ensure freedom of navigation for both naval and civilian vessels throughout the South China Sea. Underlying China's actions in the South China

Sea and its reaction to the ITLOS ruling is the belief that the United States poses the primary threat to its national security interests, especially in view of the 1979 Taiwan Relations Act and the 1996 Taiwan Strait crisis, as well as the U.S. defense treaties with Japan, South Korea, the Philippines, and Australia. China is also wary of strengthening U.S. relations with Vietnam, Singapore, and India.[13] Washington is widely blamed for instigating the South China Sea actions of the Philippines and Vietnam. That also means that relations with the United States are at the top of China's foreign policy concerns and may temper future actions in the South China Sea.

China's future actions are not certain but could be escalatory. It might declare an air defense identification zone over the South China Sea; most dangerous would be turning Scarborough Shoal into an artificial island and military base, as it has done on seven other Spratly land features.

The United States could and should easily strengthen its position vis-à-vis the South China Sea by signing and ratifying UNCLOS. Other U.S. future actions are more certain: continuing to insist on the peaceful resolution of sovereignty disputes, and adherence to the alliance with the Philippines. This position would be strengthened by U.S. ratification of that treaty, but freedom of navigation cruises will continue.

The South China Sea issues are not just between China and the United States, of course. The U.S. stakes in that sea's disputes are less direct than those of China, Vietnam, Malaysia, Indonesia, Brunei, the Philippines, and even Taiwan. Washington cannot by itself resolve the issues at hand; final resolution remains in the capitals of the regional nations. The authors of this volume have expertly addressed the claims, interests, and regional sensibilities of those nations, as well as those of interested parties throughout Eurasia. It is hoped that this volume will add to the current discourse on the region.

Notes

1. The best source for past and current South China Sea activities is the Asia Maritime Transparency Initiative maintained by the Center for Strategic and International Studies at https://amti.csis.org.
2. The UNCLOS Treaty is available at http://www.un.org/depts/los/convention_agreements/texts/unclos/unclos_e.pdf.
3. China's claims are described in the five declarations it issued when it signed and ratified UNCLOS in 1992 and 1996, respectively. They are available at http://www.un.org/depts/los/convention_agreements/convention_declarations.htm. Also see China's 1992 Law on the Territorial Sea, http://www.npc.gov.cn/englishnpc/Law/2007-12/12/content_1383846.htm.

4. The Paracels battle is described in Toshi Yoshihara, "The 1974 Paracels Sea Battle," *Naval War College Review* 69, no. 2 (Spring 2016), https://www.usnwc.edu/getattachment/7b5ec8a0-cc48-4d9b-b558-a4f1cf92e7b8/The1974Paracels SeaBattle.aspx. The Spratlys battle is described in "The Day Vietnam Lost a Spratly Reef to China," *Asia Maritime Review* (March 14, 2017), http://asiamaritime.net/the-day-vietnam-lost-a-spratly-reef-to-china/.
5. See Lindsay Murdoch, "South China Sea: Vietnam Accuses China," *Sydney Morning Herald*, January 21, 2015, http://www.smh.com.au/world/south-china-sea-vietnam-accuses-china-of-dragging-oil-rig-into-its-waters-20160120-gmafr1.html.
6. Xi's "dream" and likely priorities are discussed in "Profile: Xi Jinping: Pursuing Dream for 1.3 Billion Chinese," english.news.cn, March 17, 2013, http:/news.xinhuanet.com/english/china/2013-03/17c_124467411.
7. Wu Shicun's argument is presented in "Why China is Right to Say No to the South China Sea Ruling," *China-U.S. Focus*, July 27, 2016, http://www.chinausfocus.com/author/111/Wu+Shicun.html.
8. Author conversations with senior Chinese PLA officers and civilian officials and analysts, October 2014, July 2016, in Shanghai and Beijing.
9. The Philippines vs. China case before the International Tribunal for the Law of the Sea (ITLOS) and the court's ruling are described at https://amti.csis.org/ArbitrationTL/.
10. "White Paper on the South China Sea," July 13, 2016, http://english.gov.cn/state_council/ministries/2016/07/13/content_281475392503075.htm.
11. Also see Sean R. Liedman, "U.S. Strategy in the South China Sea," *Journal of Political Risk* 4, no. 5 (May 19, 2016), http://www.jpolrisk.com/u-s-strategy-in-the-south-china-sea/; James Fanell's views are also presented in a podcast at http://cimsec.org/sea-control-114-china-capt-james-fannell/24028.
12. Also see Bill Hayton, *The South China Sea: The Struggle for Power in Asia* (New Haven: Yale University Press, 2014), 179.
13. The Taiwan Relations Act may be found at https://www.congress.gov/bill/96th-congress/house-bill/2479. The 1996 Taiwan Strait crisis is discussed in Bernard D. Cole, *Taiwan's Security: History and Prospects* (London: Routledge, 2006), 28–31.

Contributor Biographies

About the Editor

Anders Corr holds a PhD in government, with a focus on international relations, from Harvard University's Graduate School of Arts and Sciences. He spent five years working in military intelligence, including at U.S. Pacific Command Headquarters and Special Operations Command Pacific. His analysis of Asian security topics has appeared in the *New York Times, Nikkei Asian Review, Nonproliferation Review*, Reuters, Agence France-Presse, *Forbes, Foreign Policy*, and numerous other publications. He has spoken on the South China Sea to Bloomberg TV, Bloomberg Radio, and CNBC.

About the Contributors

Stephen Blank is an expert on Russian foreign and defense policies and international relations across the former Soviet Union. He is a leading expert on European and Asian security, including energy issues. Since 2013, he has been a senior fellow at the American Foreign Policy Council in Washington, D.C. From 1989 to 2013 he was a professor of Russian national security studies and national security affairs at the Strategic Studies Institute of the U.S. Army War College. Prior to his appointment at the Army War College, Dr. Blank was an associate professor for Soviet studies at the Center for Aerospace Doctrine, Research, and Education of Air University at Maxwell Air Force Base. He holds a PhD in Russian history from the University of Chicago. He is currently writing a book on Russian foreign policy in East Asia.

Leszek Buszynski is a visiting fellow with the National Security College in the Australian National University, Canberra, Australia. His writings on the South China Sea over the past twenty years include *The South China Sea Maritime Dispute: Political, Legal, and Regional Perspectives* (Routledge, 2014); "The South China Sea Maritime Dispute: Legality, Power, and Conflict Resolution" (*Asian Journal of Peacekeeping*, 2013); "The South China Sea: Oil, Maritime Claims, and U.S.-China Strategic Rivalry" (*Washington Quarterly*, 2012); "Chinese Naval Strategy, the United States, ASEAN and the South China Sea" (*Security Challenges*, 2012), and "Rising Tensions in the South China Sea: Prospects for a Resolution of the Issue" (*Security Challenges*, 2010).

Gordon G. Chang is the author of *The Coming Collapse of China* and *Nuclear Showdown: North Korea Takes On the World*, both from Random House. He lived and worked in China and Hong Kong for almost two decades, most recently in Shanghai, as counsel to the American law firm Paul Weiss and earlier in Hong Kong as partner in the international law firm Baker & McKenzie. He has spoken at the Council on Foreign Relations, the Heritage Foundation, the Brookings Institution, the Cato Institute, RAND, and the American Enterprise Institute. He has appeared before the House Committee on Foreign Affairs and the U.S.-China Economic and Security Review Commission. Chang has appeared on CNN, Fox News Channel, Fox Business Network, MSNBC, CNBC, PBS, and Bloomberg Television, and he is a frequent co-host and guest on the John Batchelor radio program/podcast. His writings have appeared in the *New York Times*, the *Wall Street Journal*, the *International Herald Tribune*, *Commentary*, *Barron's*, the *Weekly Standard*, the *National Interest*, and *National Review*.

Bernard D. Cole (Capt., USN, Ret.) served as a professor of maritime strategy at the National War College from 1995 to 2015, where he taught courses on Sino-American relations, Northeast Asian politics, Southeast Asian politics, joint operations, naval history, and maritime strategy. He currently works with the China team at the Center for Naval Analyses. He previously served thirty years in the Navy as a surface warfare officer, including tours as commanding officer, USS *Rathburne* (FF 1057), and commander, Destroyer Squadron 35. He also served as the Amphibious Ready Group's boat group commander during several amphibious operations in Vietnam in 1966–67 and as naval gunfire liaison officer with the Third Marine Division in Vietnam in 1967–68. He has written numerous articles, book chapters, and eight books: *Gunboats and Marines: The U.S. Navy in China, 1925–1928* (University of Delaware Press, 1982); *The Great Wall at Sea:*

China's Navy Enters the Twenty-First Century (Naval Institute Press, 2003); *Oil for the Lamps of China: Beijing's Twenty-First Century Search for Energy* (National Defense University Press, 2003); *Taiwan's Security: History and Prospects* (Routledge, 2006); *Sea Lanes and Pipelines: Energy Security in Asia* (Praeger, 2008); *Asian Maritime Strategies: Navigating Troubled Waters* (Naval Institute Press, 2013); and *China's Quest for Great Power: Ships, Oil, and Foreign Policy in China* (Naval Institute Press, 2016). He was named U.S. Naval Institute Press "Author of the Year" for 2014. He holds a PhD in history from Auburn University.

James E. Fanell (Capt., USN, Ret.) is a government fellow with the Geneva Centre for Security Policy. During his nearly thirty-year career as a naval intelligence officer, he focused on Indo-Asia Pacific security affairs, with an emphasis on the Chinese navy and its operations. He was most recently the director of intelligence and information operations for the U.S. Pacific Fleet. He served in a variety of afloat and ashore assignments across the Pacific region, highlighted by tours as the assistant chief of staff for intelligence for the U.S. Seventh Fleet aboard the USS *Blue Ridge*, the Office of Naval Intelligence China senior intelligence officer, and the senior intelligence officer for the USS *Kitty Hawk* aircraft carrier strike group. He was a national security affairs fellow at the Hoover Institution at Stanford University. He holds an MA in history from the University of Hawaii and is a distinguished graduate of the Air Command and Staff College, where he received a master of military operational art and science degree. He is also a public speaker, most notably at the AFCEA West/U.S. Naval Institute's panels on China in 2013 and 2014. He has been published in the *Wall Street Journal*, U.S. Naval Institute *Proceedings*, *Naval Intelligence Professionals Quarterly*, *Military Power Review*, and the *Hoover Digest*. He is the creator and manager of the Asia security forum Red Star Rising.

Ian Forsyth is an associate with a strategic consulting firm in Hawaii. He previously worked as an intelligence analyst focusing on China, Taiwan, and Japan with the Defense Intelligence Agency for fourteen years. Prior to that, he worked as an international lawyer with the firm of Arnberger, Kim, Buxbaum, and Choy in Ulaanbaatar, Mongolia. He holds a JD from Syracuse University College of Law and a PhD in international relations from the University of Southern California. He has written articles for *Contemporary Southeast Asia*, the Jamestown Foundation's *China Brief*, and for the S. Rajaratnam School of International Studies in Singapore, where he was a visiting fellow in 2014.

Bill Hayton is an associate fellow with the Asia Program at Chatham House. He also works for BBC World News TV in London. He has been with the BBC since 1998, including a posting as the BBC reporter in Vietnam from 2006 to 2007, and a secondment to the state broadcaster in Myanmar from 2013 to 2014 to assist with media reform. He is the author of *The South China Sea: The Struggle for Power in Asia* (Yale University Press, 2014), which *The Economist* nominated as one of its books of the year, and of *Vietnam: Rising Dragon* (Yale University Press, 2010). He has written for many publications, including the *South China Morning Post*, *National Interest*, and *The Diplomat*. He is a graduate of the University of Cambridge.

Takashi Inoguchi is professor emeritus at the University of Tokyo, former president of the University of Niigata Prefecture, and current university guest professor of J. F. Oberlin University in Tokyo. He received his PhD from the Massachusetts Institute of Technology. He taught political science and international relations for three decades at the University of Tokyo and was senior vice rector of the United Nations University at the rank of assistant secretary general. He has written on Japan, Asia, and international affairs and has co-edited several books, including *American Democracy Promotion* (Oxford University Press, 2000), *The Political Economy of Japan*, vol. 2 (Stanford University Press, 1988), and *The Troubled Triangle: Economic and Security Concerns for the United States, Japan, and China* (Palgrave Macmillan, 2013).

Tongfi Kim is an assistant professor of international affairs at Vesalius College in Brussels, Belgium. His research centers on security studies and the international relations of East Asia. He is the author of *The Supply Side of Security: A Market Theory of Military Alliances* (Stanford University Press, 2016), and his articles have appeared in *Asian Security*, *International Interactions*, *International Relations of the Asia-Pacific*, and *Security Studies*.

Sean R. Liedman (Capt., USN, Ret.) is the founder and president of Eagle Strategy, Inc., and an adjunct senior fellow at the Center for a New American Security. He was a naval flight officer for twenty-five years and commanded at the squadron and wing levels. He served two tours in the Air Warfare Division on the Chief of Naval Operations staff and a tour as the executive assistant to the Deputy Commander of U.S. Central Command. He was a federal executive fellow at the

Weatherhead Center for International Affairs at Harvard University and at the Council on Foreign Relations in New York. He is a distinguished graduate of the U.S. Naval Academy and the U.S. Naval War College.

Ankit Panda is a foreign affairs analyst, writer, and editor based in New York City. Panda is senior editor of *The Diplomat*, where he has written scores of analytical articles and commentaries tracking developments in Japanese foreign policy and disputes in the South China Sea, among other topics. He was a Carnegie Council New Leader in 2015–16 and is president of the New York chapter of the Center for International Maritime Security. Panda is a graduate of the Woodrow Wilson School of Public and International Affairs at Princeton University.

Peter M. Solomon works in government and regulatory affairs in the banking industry in New York. He holds an MA in international political economy from King's College, London, and a BA in English and political science from the University of Connecticut. The *Wall Street Daily* and the *Journal of Political Risk* have cited his research on the South China Sea, and the Center for International Maritime Security has published his writing on the subject.

Index

Abe, Shinzo, 17, 182, 202–6, 209, 210, 212, 214, 216, 234
active defense policy, 23, 53
Afghanistan, 4, 29, 152, 176–77
air defense identification zone (ADIZ), 20, 21, 26, 106, 116, 202, 229, 299, 305
Air Force, U.S., 11, 20, 79–80, 182, 202
anti-access/area denial strategy, 55–56, 65, 98, 163, 182
Arbitral Tribunal. *See* Permanent Court of Arbitration (PCA)
Arctic campaign, 248, 258–60, 265
artificial islands/land reclamation: ASEAN position on, 88, 128–30; brinksmanship strategy and, 25–27; bureaucratic interests and motivations for, 59–61; challenge to construction activities, 31, 94–95, 283–84; criticism over, 75; ecosystem damage from construction of, 74; global motivations for, 54–56; historic rights claims, 42; ITLOS ruling on, 61–62, 295–96; media coverage of construction of, 42; military facilities built on, concern about, 22; military opposition to expansion of activities, 26–27, 31, 78, 94–95, 283–84; motivation and reasons for construction of, 42, 53–61, 66–67, 297; national entitlement and claims on, 42–44, 297; pace, scale, and scope of reclamation activities, 50, 52–53, 74–75; pace and scope of reclamation activities, concern about, 22, 75; PCA ruling and legitimacy of as territory, 24; planning and preparations for, 52–53, 59–60; public diplomacy campaign to raise awareness of, 31; regional motivations for, 56–59; satellite imagery of construction of, 30–31, 41–42, 52, 63, 74, 111; strategic implications of, 62–95; timing of construction of, 61–62; tracking construction of, 171n57

Asia Infrastructure Investment Bank, 106, 215, 278
Asia Maritime Transparency Initiative, 63, 171n57, 305n1
Asia-Pacific Maritime Strategy, 93–94, 208
Asia-Pacific region: abandonment of by U.S., concern about, 20, 23, 31, 175–76; anti-China sentiments in, 98–99, 178, 213, 298; arms race in, 6; assertive moves and harassment tactics by China, 122–23, 136–37, 155–59, 178; buffer states, defense of, 31–32; China influence and power in, 8, 13, 31–32, 62–65, 180, 182–83, 195n55; China-India competition and rivalry, 226, 235–36, 238, 302; China-Japan competition in, 199; China-U.S. competition and rivalry in, 2, 12–13, 30, 94–99, 122, 152–54, 184, 294, 298; cooperation in, China disregard for, 116–17; economic importance of to U.S., 181; EU role in peace and stability in, 273–74, 276–77, 280–83, 304; EU strategic partnerships in, 273–74, 278–79, 284, 304; forward-deployed position of U.S. in, 4–5, 208; geo-military balance of power in, 106, 299; India interests in, 224–25, 238; instability in, sources of, 21–22, 23, 93–94, 95–96, 304–5; Japan

313

influence in, 189, 302; joint development in, 5–6, 10, 12, 27–29, 32–33n6, 39n117, 39n120; military spending by nations in, 4, 7; political environment of, 297; the Quad coalition in, 233–34; regional relationships, importance of, 96; regional strategy of China, 56–59, 75–77, 98–99, 185, 297; regional support for U.S. role in, 96; resolution of South China Sea disputes by nations in, 305; Russia interests in, 248–49, 265–66, 266n2, 303–4; Russia objectives in, 249–57; Russia role in security in, 248, 252, 254–58, 260, 265–66, 268n29; security in and strength of navies, 301; status quo protection without provoking China, 154, 174, 183, 190, 199, 207–8, 213, 216, 301, 302; suppression of democracy, human rights, and international law in by China, 5; untrustworthiness of China strategy, 115–17; U.S. commitment to alliances in, 175–77; U.S. defense spending for security in, 3–8; U.S. defense treaties with countries in, 9, 10, 175–76, 182, 186, 305; U.S. interests and alliances in, 8–13, 22–23, 30, 65, 91–94, 106, 140–41, 159, 162, 294, 299, 305; U.S. military withdrawal from, pressure for, 8, 140; U.S. position in, weakening of, 255–56; U.S. presence in, 43, 65, 75, 91–94, 98, 133–35, 177, 181–83, 207–8, 299, 301, 304–5

Association of Southeast Asian Nations (ASEAN): artificial islands construction and unity of, 128–30; autonomy and unity of, 96–98, 122–23, 130, 134, 136–37, 140–41; Cambodia as proxy for China in, 125–26, 189; centrifugal pressure within, 131–37; divisions in and support for China by some countries, 96–98, 99, 125–28, 133, 136–37, 140–41, 299; economic and trade relationships, 81, 90–91, 299; EU relations with, 274; impasse over China claims in South China Sea, 87; influence in South China Sea disputes, 2, 3, 201, 299; influence of China over, 122–23; joint development agreement and unity in, 28; land reclamation, call to halt, 88; peaceful and cooperative resolution of disputes, 116–17, 127, 155, 276–77, 293; Philippines claims, response to, 132–33; Plus Three meetings and trade framework, 80, 81; Russia engagement with, 257–60, 265–66; Russia security proposal for, 255–57; security of region and diplomacy responsibilities of, 22–23; sovereignty disputes, prevention of discussion and statement about, 87, 125–26, 133, 138, 180, 189; unity of and efforts to split and buy off members, 136–37, 299; U.S. influence over, 130; Vietnam claims, response to, 131–32

Australia: challenge to from militarized Spratly Islands facilities, 112; economic effects of sanctions against China, 97–98; India relations with, 233–34; Japan relations with, 198n87; joint patrols with, 30; military spending by, 7; PLAN facilities in, 120n50; rebalancing strategy, response to, 183; response to China expansionist territorial claims, 19–20; U.S. forces in, 30, 182, 194–95n49; U.S. relations and defense treaty with, 30, 175–76, 305

bastion strategy, 54, 56, 293
Beibu Gulf. See Tonkin, Gulf of (Beibu Gulf)
Belt and Road Initiative, 106, 116, 226–27, 239–40nn16–19, 240n22, 241nn25–26, 241–242n29, 299, 303
bilateral negotiations, 29, 77, 100n11, 124, 127–28, 138–39
Borneo, 63–64
brinksmanship, 2, 24, 25–27
Brunei: China relations with, 80, 97; continental shelf extension and sovereignty claims, 155; intimidation over resources claims, 5; joint development activities and relinquishing sovereignty by, 29; joint oil and gas development with China, 5–6, 27–28, 29, 32–33n6; media and social control in, 18; military spending by, 7; rebalancing strategy, response to, 187; South China Sea claims by, 1, 177–78, 289, 305; trade with China, 91; U.S. relations with, 187
Bush administration and George W. Bush, 19, 152, 176, 179, 191n3

Cambodia: China relations with, 97, 99, 125, 129, 137, 138, 189, 215, 299; development aid from China, 12; India relations with, 229; influence of China in, 87; Japan relations with, 214–15; proxy for China in ASEAN, 125–26, 189; Scarborough Shoal occupation, prevention of discussion of, 87, 125–26, 133, 138; trade with China, 91, 299
China (People's Republic of China, PRC): Arctic interests of, 258–60; arms embargo against, 150, 151; backing down from sovereignty claims by, 17–18; brinksmanship strategy of, 26–27; bureaucratic interests

and motivations for island construction, 59–61; centralization of power in, 14; challenging view of history held by, 297; core interests of, 19, 43, 76, 100nn10–11, 107; destabilizing activities confined to one area at a time, 203; disputes over land features and maritime boundaries by, 155–59, 291–92, 304–5; exploitation of peaceful countries and power and strength of, 4; hedging strategy against, 260; illicit technology acquisition by, 151; importance of China-U.S. relationship, 175–76; India land border dispute with, 190; influence and power of, 8, 13, 31–32, 62–65; internal control and expansion of external control by, 3; maritime strategy of, 294; media control in, 17–18; military modernization in, 8, 33n14, 294; military spending by, 3–8, 33n12, 82, 111, 280; national entitlement sense of, 13–14, 42–44, 54, 57, 297; national identity of, 76–77; national security and domestic policy in, 294; PCA ruling in favor of Philippines, response to, 2, 15–16, 18, 34–35n36, 89–90, 94–95, 111–12, 138–39, 157–59, 178, 302; Philippines development aid from, 12; power of, 3, 16, 94–99, 299; rebalancing strategy, response to, 183, 184–85, 196n61; sanctions against, 95, 97–98, 168, 284; suppression of democracy, human rights, and international law in, 5; tactics of, 77–82; Taiwan relations with, 10, 187, 197n78; U.S. defense spending to restrain power and influence of, 4–5; U.S.-China trade and economic relations, 12–13, 81, 151, 175–76, 180–81; weapons purchases from Russia by, 150–51; worldview of, 280–81
China Dream doctrine, 106, 107, 111, 112, 294
China National Offshore Oil Corporation (CNOOC), 58, 61, 85, 109, 119n19, 293
China Threat Theory, 111
circumspect cooperative engagement strategy, 148, 300
Clinton administration and Bill Clinton, 81–82, 151
code of conduct, 22, 25–26, 49, 50, 78, 81, 114, 123–28, 130, 136, 142n6, 201, 276, 293
Communist Party of China: global power–status of China, 116, 299; maintaining power of, 297; promotion of, 13; strength and power of, 16; victory narrative and end of century of humiliation, 45; Xi role in, 59, 294

containment strategy, 147, 148–49, 150, 154, 300
contiguous waters, 290–91
continental shelf: CLCS submissions and rulings, 78, 86, 89, 95, 102n43, 103n50, 155; delineation of, 290; extension of and sovereignty claims, 86, 89, 102n43, 103n50, 155; geography and South China Sea disputes, 290–91; land feature claims as delineated by, 290–91
cooperative engagement strategy, 147, 149–52, 300
coopetition strategy, 147, 152–54, 170n34, 300
Cuarteron, 48, 50, 51, 52, 74, 111, 156–57
cyber theft, 151

dash line. *See* U-shaped line/nine-dash line
Declaration on the Conduct of Parties in the South China Sea, 50, 78, 81, 86, 108, 114, 116–17, 124–25, 126–28, 142n6, 155, 201, 212, 293
democracy: global system of defense support for, 5; India alignment with mostly democratic states, 234–35, 245–46n82; suppression of by China, 5, 16; U.S. and allies support for, 4, 16
democratic security diamond, 234
diplomacy and diplomatic strategies: bilateral negotiations to resolve disputes, 29, 77, 100n11, 124, 127–28, 138–39; China actions and strategies, 27–29, 80–81, 86–88, 98–99; China disregard for law and efforts to resolve conflict, 2; China-Japan diplomatic relations, 202, 203; efforts to resolve South China Sea conflict, 3, 293; EU actions and strategies, 274, 276–80; India strategies, 231, 244n59; multilateral negotiations, 29, 78, 80, 127–28; negotiations, value of, 77–78; rebalancing strategy and, 174, 178–80; regional security and exclusion of U.S. defense activities, 80; rolling back sovereignty claims, 167; U.S. strategies and public diplomacy, 30–32
Duterte, Rodrigo, 12, 23, 28, 64, 85, 93, 96, 139–40, 157–58, 196n66, 211

East Asia Summit, 92, 154, 179, 180, 190–91, 212, 242n37, 242–43n40, 249, 255–58
East China Sea: ADIZ over, 20, 21, 106, 116, 202, 299; brinksmanship strategy in, 25; China control of resources in, 8; China sovereignty claims in, 17, 201–2; China-Japan disputes in, 182, 201–3; India interests in, 229; Japan strategy and policy in, 201–3,

302; Japan vessel clash with China fishing trawler in, 107; naval power to support claims in, 23; offensive territorial actions in, 5; restoration of good ties in, 203; status quo in, protection of, 216, 302

economics and economic strategies: ASEAN relations with China, 81, 90–91, 299; Asian financial crisis, 78, 81, 90; China disregard for law and efforts to resolve conflict, 2; China economic ambitions, 303; China economic growth and strength, 3, 78, 81, 175–77, 298, 301; China economic trend downward, 227, 240n22; China strategies, 81, 98–99; China-U.S. trade and economic relations, 12–13, 81, 151, 175–76, 180–81; efforts to resolve South China Sea conflict, 3; EU economy and regional relationships, 273–80, 284; foreign direct investment opportunities, 301; global economy, importance of China to, 175–77; global financial crisis, 19, 176–77; importance of Asia-Pacific region to U.S., 181; India economy, 235; Modernization Theory and spread of democracy, 3, 32n5; PLAN mission of economic stability, 53–54; rebalancing strategy and, 13, 30, 174, 180–81; regional trade and, 90–91; rolling back sovereignty claims, 167–68; Russia economy, 303; Russia investment and trade opportunities, 250, 253; sanctions against China, effects of, 97–98; SLOC and regional economies, 17, 54–55

eleven-dash line, 14, 290

encirclement game (wei qi), 226, 231, 239n13

energy/energy resources, 1, 23, 199–200, 291, 292. *See also* oil and natural gas

Enhanced Defense Cooperation Agreement (EDCA), 11, 85, 92–93, 96, 133, 139, 182, 195n50

EP-3 incident, 82, 151, 152

Europe: defense spending by nations in, 4; Russia orientation toward, 248, 303; U.S. defense spending for security in, 3–5

European Union (EU): ASEAN relations with, 274; China relations with, 278, 284; diplomacy in region, 274, 276–80; economy of and trade/economic relationships, 273–80, 284; euro as alternative to U.S. dollar, 279; global strategy of, 279–80; influence in South China Sea dispute, 2, 273–74; Japan relations and trade with, 273, 275, 278–79, 281–82, 284; military facilities and capabilities of, 280–83; military spending by, 280; peace and stability role of, 273–74, 276–77, 280–83, 304;

power projection by and geographical distance from region, 283, 304; South Korea relations with, 279, 281–82, 284; strategic partnerships in region, 273–74, 278–79, 284, 304; trade relationships in region, 273, 275, 277–80, 284; worldview of, 280–81

exclusive economic zone (EEZ): Brunei dispute, 291; China military activity within, 178; creation of concept of, 48; delineation of according to UNCLOS, 290–91; geography, contiguous EEZs, and South China Sea disputes, 290–91; Indonesia dispute, 110–11, 135–36, 291; Indonesia oil exploration and, 49; ITLOS ruling on Spratly Island EEZ claim, 295; Japan EEZ delimitation, 203; joint development activities and relinquishing sovereignty, 28–29; Malaysia dispute, 49, 57, 58, 66, 110, 134, 135; Mischief Reef and Philippines EEZ, 11, 19, 95; Natuna Island and Indonesian EEZ, 14, 18, 64, 110–11, 135–36, 289; oil rig incidents and Vietnam EEZ, 60, 63, 85, 109, 119n19, 131–32, 178, 203, 212, 213, 215, 293; PCA case and ruling on, 2, 15–16, 18, 34–35n36, 89–90, 111–12, 137–40, 156, 157–59, 210–11, 216, 302; Philippines dispute, 11, 19, 61–62, 89–90, 95, 108–9, 133, 137–40, 144n35, 155–56, 295–96; Russia Arctic campaign and EEZ claim, 258–60; Scarborough Shoal fishing dispute, 86–87, 95, 108, 155–56; U-shaped line and disputes over, 88–90, 102–3nn43–44, 111–12, 224, 302; Vietnam dispute, 18, 63, 85, 109, 119n19, 131–32, 224, 293

far seas operations, 116, 120n50, 226, 298–99

Fiery Cross Reef, 31, 49, 50, 51, 52, 63, 65, 74, 94, 111, 112, 156–57

First Island Chain, 16, 19, 53, 107, 296

fishing/fisheries: arrest of Chinese fishermen and China-Japan trade, 201–2, 216, 302; China control of and claim to resources, 8, 76–77, 88–90, 155; global catch in South China Sea, 289; historic or traditional fishing rights disputes, 291; historic rights claim over, 54, 57, 88–90; interference and intimidation over claims, 86–87; militarized fishing militia, 23; Natuna Island fishing dispute, 64, 86, 88, 110–11, 135–36; Natuna Island resources, 291; overseas interests of China, 23; Paracel Islands fishing dispute, 87; resources in South China Sea, 1, 16; Scarborough Shoal access for,

12; Scarborough Shoal fishing dispute, 86–87, 95, 108, 155–56; sovereignty claims and government support of fishing, 60–61; Spratly Islands disputes over, 81, 113–14; Spratly Islands resources, 292; Vietnam historic rights claim, 291

flag follows trade and trade follows flag, 19

foreign policy: India policy, 231–33; maritime and territorial rights claims as national priority, 42–43; militarily and politically active policies, 98–99, 298; misinterpretation of China actions, 297; noninterference policy, 150; Obama policy, 176–77, 178–80, 192n10; peaceful development, 75–76, 95, 107, 111, 115–17; peaceful rise, 75–76, 299; Russia policy, 304; U.S. relations as top concern of China, 305; Xi policy, 227, 294

France, 45–46, 47, 193–94n32, 204, 277, 278, 280, 282–83

freedom of navigation (FoN)/freedom of overflight: artificial islands construction and, 62–63, 65; ASEAN position on, 129–30; China control of South China Sea and regional trade, 17; cruises/patrols and operations to support, 31, 93–94, 95, 159, 160–61, 164, 165, 167, 183, 208, 216, 296, 302; definition of by China, 296; India support for operations to support, 228–29, 232, 242–43n40, 243n43; Japan interest in preservation of, 200, 302; Japan support for operations to support, 302; military freedom of navigation cruises, reaction to, 305; reaction to freedom of navigation cruises, 296; strategic importance of, 181, 279; Taiwan FoN importance in South China Sea, 10; UNCLOS and international law related to, applicability of, 296; U.S. activities to ensure for naval and civilian vessels, 296, 304–5; U.S. focus on, 18, 22; U.S. mission to maintain, 62, 277, 296; U.S. policy and strategy on, 159, 160–61; U-shaped line sovereignty claims and, 10; violent clashes with China over, 296

Freedom of Navigation Operations (FONOPs), 31, 93–94, 95, 159, 160–61, 164, 165, 167, 183, 208, 216, 296, 302

Gaven Reef, 48–49, 50, 51, 52, 74, 111, 156–57
Germany, 4, 277, 278, 280
global system of defense, 5
good neighbor policy, 75, 136–37, 140–41
grand strategy: anti-China sentiments and, 298; artificial islands construction and, 59–61; assessment of to optimize strategic choices, 1; China strategy, 77, 98–99, 122–23, 140–41, 226–27, 297–98; circumspect cooperative engagement, 148, 300; containment, 147, 148–49, 150, 154, 300; cooperative engagement, 147, 149–52, 300; coopetition, 147, 152–54, 170n34, 300; definition of, 2, 32n3; impact and significance of in South China Sea conflict, 1–2; India strategy, 225, 239n5; Japan strategy, 211, 216, 302; rebalancing to Asia as grand strategy, 301; South China Sea objectives of U.S., 159–62; untrustworthiness of China strategy, 115–17; U.S. as factor in China strategy, 77; U.S. future strategy and policy options, 163–68, 300–301; U.S. strategy and assessment of, 122, 147–59, 159–62, 300

great powers/power countries: China-U.S. competition and rivalry in Asia-Pacific region, 2, 12–13, 30, 94–99, 122, 152–54, 184, 294, 298; global nature of South China Sea conflict, 3; global power–status of China, 98–99, 115–17, 227, 240n19, 298, 299; great power autism, 67, 297; great power/global power–status of Russia, 251–54, 266, 267n23; great sea power ambitions of China, 227, 241n27, 241–42n29; impact and significance of in South China Sea conflict, 1–3; major power struggle as crux of conflict, 2; post–World War II international order, 3, 116–17, 199, 294, 299; powers with influence in South China Sea dispute, 2; rule-making by for smaller states, 253; U.S. global influence and failure to challenge China expansionist activities, 31

Greece, 116, 277, 299

Hainan Island, 56, 292, 293
Hong Kong, 5, 91, 273, 275
Hughes Reef, 48, 50, 51, 52, 74, 111, 156–57
human rights, 4, 5
humiliation, century of, 13, 42, 44, 45, 53, 76–77, 147, 150, 296

ideas and interests, fighting over, 236, 246n90
Impeccable, 65, 155, 178
incrementalism, 24
India: Act East Policy, 229–30; alignment with mostly democratic states, 234–35, 245–46n82; ambitions, motivations, and India's century, 230–36, 244n59; Asia-Pacific interests of, 224–25, 238; Australia relations with, 233–34; Cambodia relations with, 229; China land border dispute with, 190; China-India competition and

rivalry, 226, 235–36, 238, 302; coordination of Silk Road with initiatives in, 227, 241nn25–26; diplomatic strategies of, 231, 244n59; East China Sea interests of, 229; economy of, 235; encirclement strategy of China and, 226–27, 239–40nn16–17; FoN support from, 228–29, 232, 242–43n40, 243n43; foreign policy of, 231–33; grand strategy of, 225, 239n5; Himalayan region strategies of China, 5, 25; Indonesia relations with, 229; interference with hydrocarbon exploration and cutting seismic cables, 29; Japan relations with, 233–34; Look East, Link West policy, 230; Look East policy, 225, 229–30, 239n6; Malaysia relations with, 229; military spending by, 7, 111, 302; Myanmar military facilities for, 303; naval operations and ambitions of, 302–3; nonaligned policies of, 230, 234, 302; oil exploration with Vietnam, 224, 231, 232, 237–38, 238n3, 303; Pacific island nations relations with, 229–30; Philippines relations with, 229; rebalancing strategy, response to, 189–90; response to China expansionist territorial claims, 233; Singapore relations with, 229, 232–33; South China Sea interests and presence of, 228–30, 242n37, 242–43n40, 302; Thailand relations with, 229; trade routes of, 244n59; U.S. relations with, 175–76, 189–90, 230, 233–34, 302, 303, 305; Vietnam relations with, 185, 187, 189–90, 229, 236–38, 303; zero-sum contest against China, 225

Indian Ocean: China control of access to, 17; China influence in, 225; China military facilities and operations in, 225–26, 227, 241n27, 241–42n29; India naval operations and ambitions of, 302–3; maritime traffic management by China in, 225; naval operations in, 106, 115, 299; projects to connect ports in, 227; strategic encirclement strategy in, 226–27, 239–40nn16–17

Indonesia: autonomy of, 96–97, 188; China relations with, 80, 97, 188, 212, 222n82; EU trade with, 273, 275; as global maritime fulcrum, 212; India relations with, 229; Japan relations and defense agreement with, 189, 211–12; maritime security capabilities of, assistance in building, 183, 189; media and social control in, 18; military facilities and capabilities of, 63, 64, 66; military spending by, 7; nonaligned policies of, 133–34, 135–36, 137, 212; rebalancing strategy, response to, 183, 188;

security cooperation with U.S., 188; South China Sea claims by, 1, 305; sovereignty claims and support for PCA jurisdiction, 97; sovereignty claims, concern about, 177–78, 188; trade with China, 91; U.S. relations with, 97, 162, 175–76, 188. *See also* Natuna Island

intelligence and intelligence gathering, 1, 30–31, 41–42, 52, 63, 74, 111

International Tribunal for the Law of the Sea (ITLOS), 61–62, 90, 95, 295–96, 305

Iran, 3, 4, 34–35n36, 153, 163, 182, 204

Iraq, 4, 6, 29, 152, 176–77

islands: definition and recognition of by UNCLOS, 24, 290; development of by claimant countries, 49–50; ITLOS ruling on islands in South China Sea, 296; maps of, 46, 47; names of, 46; zones granted by UNCLOS for, 290–91. *See also* artificial islands/land reclamation

James Shoal, 46, 47, 54, 57, 58, 66, 87, 110, 134, 164

Japan: ADIZ over, 26; arrest of Chinese fishermen and trade with China, 201–2, 216, 302; ASEAN members relations with, 214–15; Australia relations with, 198n87; brinksmanship strategy against, 25; Cambodia relations with, 214–15; China as threat to, 216, 302; China relations with, 80, 201–2; China-Japan competition in region, 199; constitution of and engagement in war, 204–6; defense policies and reforms, 203–8, 215–16; defense policy and security interests of, 189, 199, 201–3; democratization of, 4; diplomatic relations with China, 202, 203; domestic politics and security policy of, 203–8; East China Sea policy and strategy, 201–3, 302; energy security of, 199–200; EU relations and trade with, 273, 275, 278–79, 281–82, 284; fossil fuels imports by, 200; grand strategy of, 211, 216, 302; India relations with, 233–34; Indonesia relations and defense agreement with, 189, 211–12; influence in Asia-Pacific region, 189, 302; joint U.S.-Japan patrols in South China Sea, 207–8; Laos relations with, 214–15; Malaysia partnership with, 189, 214; maritime security capabilities of Asia-Pacific countries, assistance in building, 189; military initiatives by, 9; military spending by, 7, 111; Myanmar relations with, 214–15; naval presence in region, 299; nuclear power use by and Tohoku earthquake and tsunami, 200; oil shipments through region, 278–79; pacifism and proactive pacifism of, 204, 205–6, 216; Philippines military assistance and training from, 11, 12, 189; Philippines relations with, 196n68, 209–11, 216; rebalancing strategy, response to, 183, 189–90; response to China expansionist territorial claims, 19–20; Russia relations with, 255; security partnerships in Asia-Pacific region, 198n87; SLOC and economy of, 17; SLOC importance to, 200, 302; South China Sea importance to, 199, 207, 215–16; South China Sea strategy and policy of, 200–201, 302; South China Sea–related activities, 208–15; South Korea relation with, 9; Thailand relations with, 214–15; TPP agreement, 180–81; trade relations with ASEAN countries, 90; trilateral process, U.S.-Japan-Vietnam, 213–14; U.S. alliance and relations with, 8–9, 30, 189–90, 198n87, 206–8, 216; U.S. military facilities and forces in, 8–9, 208; U.S. naval exercises with, 182, 189, 208; U.S. policy support and avoidance of statements against U.S. policy, 189, 198n87, 199, 216, 302; U.S. security relations and defense treaty with, 9, 10, 23, 175–76, 182, 186, 302, 305; Vietnam relations and security ties with, 132, 141, 185, 187, 212–15, 216. *See also* Senkaku Islands

Japan Self-Defense Forces, 9, 182, 189, 203, 208, 234

Jin-class ballistic missile submarines, 56, 293, 299

Johnson Reef, 48, 50, 51, 52, 74, 111, 133, 150, 156–57

land features: changes to definitions and privileges of, 294; definition and recognition of by UNCLOS, 24, 290, 294, 297; ITLOS ruling on islands in South China Sea, 296; Spratly Islands features and geography, 292; zones granted by UNCLOS for, 290–91, 294

land reclamation. *See* artificial islands/land reclamation

Laos: China relations with, 97, 99, 125, 129, 137, 138, 299; Japan relations with, 214–15; trade with China, 91, 299

law and international law: China disregard for, 2, 21, 22, 88–90, 94–95, 116–17, 162; China maritime court system, 90; compliance with, strategy to promote, 160, 162, 168; domestic law to legitimize territorial claims, 78–79, 80; global system of defense support for, 5; ITLOS ruling on islands in South China Sea, 61–62, 295–96, 305; jurisdiction of courts, questions about, 14, 15–16, 34–35n36, 36n54, 62, 117; reordering of legal norms, 299; resolution of maritime disputes under, 212, 283–84; sanctions for sovereignty interference by China, 95; South China Sea importance to, 1; suppression of by China, 5. *See also* Permanent Court of Arbitration (PCA); United Nations Convention on the Law of the Sea (UNCLOS)

Look East, Link West policy, 230

Look East policy, 225, 229–30, 239n6

low-tide elevation (LTE), 290, 291

Luconia Shoals, 57, 58, 110, 134, 135

major powers. *See* great powers/power countries

Malaysia: China relations with, 110, 125, 134, 187, 214; continental shelf extension and sovereignty claim, 86, 89, 102n43, 103n50, 155, 291; economic effects of sanctions against China, 97–98; EU trade with, 273, 275; FoN and trade access by, 17; India relations with, 229; intimidation over resources claims, 5; Japan partnership with, 189, 214; joint development activities and relinquishing sovereignty by, 29; joint oil and gas development with China, 5–6, 27–28, 29, 32–33n6; maritime security capabilities of, assistance in building, 183, 189; media and social control in, 18; military facilities and capabilities of, 63–64, 66; nonaligned policies of, 133–35, 137; rebalancing strategy, response to, 187; Russia relations with, 257; South China Sea claims by, 1, 14, 177–78, 289, 292, 305; sovereignty claims and support for PCA jurisdiction, 97; Spratly Islands claim and activity, 21, 41, 48, 49, 66, 75, 291; trade with China, 90–91; U.S. military exercises with, 134, 214; U.S. naval presence in, 75, 134–35; U.S. relations with, 162; U.S. security ties with, 133–34, 187

Marine Corps, U.S., 30, 134, 182, 194–95n49, 208

marine environment practices, 159, 162

maritime and territorial rights and sovereignty: all-stop order/freezing status quo on, 164–66, 300, 301; backing down from claims, 17–18; century/hundred years of humiliation and sensitivity toward, 13, 42, 44, 45, 53, 76–77, 147, 150, 296; China claim to South China Sea, 13–18, 42–44, 57, 102–3nn43–44, 200–201, 293, 294, 295–96;

continental shelf extension and sovereignty claims, 86, 89, 102n43, 103n50, 155; continued concessions to claims, 163–64, 300; countries staking claims to South China Sea, 1, 3, 32n2, 177–78, 289–90, 291–92, 305; disputes of claims and PCA jurisdiction, 97; domestic law to legitimize claims, 78–79, 80; escalation of disputes over claims, 155–59, 304–5; expansionist territorial claims of China, 18–23, 37n83, 106, 233, 299; historic rights claims, 13–18, 42, 47, 53, 66–67, 77, 78, 88–90, 103n50, 115–16, 178, 291, 295, 297, 305n3; Indonesian claim to Natuna Island, 291; joint development activities and relinquishing of, 29; land boundary dispute between Vietnam and China, 292; maritime sovereignty campaign, 107–11; military modernization to support claims, 8; military opposition to expansion of claims, 26–27, 78, 94–95, 283–84; national entitlement and claims by China, 13–14, 42–44, 54, 57, 297; national identity and, 76–77; new historic missions of PLA and claims of, 76–77, 83, 107–11; origins of China claim, 45–53; peaceful and cooperative resolution of claims, 100n11, 116–17, 127, 155, 158–59, 168, 216, 276–77, 283–84, 293, 305; rebalancing strategy and, 177–78; regional nations responsibility for resolution of, 3, 100n11, 305; righteousness of claims, 44, 297; rolling back claims, 166–68, 300; Russia position on China claims, 254–55; safeguarding rights against other countries, 23; Taiwan dispute with China, 10; U.S. access to maritime commons, 296; U.S. defense of South China Sea, lack of, 18–23; U.S. future strategy and policy on claims, 163–68, 300; U.S. position on claims, 91–92, 179–80, 181, 184, 300; U.S. presence as threat to, 43; U.S. response to China expansionist territorial claims, 18–23, 37n83, 77, 106; vessels for enforcement of claims, 296; Vietnam historic rights claim, 291; violent clashes with China over, 48, 60, 85, 109, 119n19, 150, 213, 292, 293, 296. *See also* freedom of navigation (FoN)/freedom of overflight

Maritime Silk Road initiative, 137, 239–40nn16–17, 240n22, 241nn25–26, 241–242n29

maritime strategy, 84–85, 294

Mekong Five, 214–15

military activity and strategies: acceptance of China military activities, 26–27, 94–95; artificial islands and power projection, 62–65, 76; brinksmanship, 2, 24, 25–27; China actions in South China Sea, 18–23, 37n83; China disregard for law and military brinkmanship, 2; China military capabilities, 18, 62–65, 77, 79–80, 82–85, 152–54; China strategies and objectives, 23–27, 53–61, 79–80, 94–99; conflict compared to dispute, 2; confrontation of U.S. military by China, 62; efforts to resolve South China Sea conflict, 3; escalation of actions by China, 305; eviction of U.S. from Philippines bases, 5; facilities built on artificial islands in Spratly Islands, 19, 22, 24, 52–53, 56, 63, 65, 78, 293, 305; global military power, entitlement to, 298; global system of defense, 5; incrementalism, 24; joint U.S.-Japan patrols in South China Sea, 207–8; military freedom of navigation cruises, 296; military freedom of navigation cruises, reaction to, 305; military modernization and preemptive, limited war between China and U.S., 8; military-to-military encounter agreement and procedures, 26, 81–82; nuclear deterrence and *Jin*-class submarines, 56, 293; preemptive actions, claim to not take, 23; reaction to freedom of navigation cruises, 296; rebalancing strategy and, 30, 174, 177, 181–83; rolling back sovereignty claims, 167; satellite imagery of artificial islands facilities, 30–31, 41–42, 52, 63, 74, 111; South China Sea importance to, 1; Spratly Islands importance related to, 55–56, 293; U.S. access to maritime commons, 296; U.S. global influence and failure to challenge China expansionist activities, 31; U.S. military advantage in and decline in, 18, 26, 83, 94, 95; U.S. response to China actions in South China Sea, 18–23, 37n83, 77; U.S. strategy for region, 93–94. *See also* war

military/defense spending: Australia, 7; Brunei, 7; China, 3–8, 33n12, 82, 111, 280; EU, 280; global defense spending compared to Asia region, 82; increase in by China, contributing factors to, 5–6; India, 7, 111, 302; Indonesia, 7; Japan, 7, 111; Philippines, 7, 82; Russia, 6, 7; South Korea, 7, 9, 111; Taiwan, 7, 111; U.S., 3–8, 176–77, 192n14, 207–8, 280; Vietnam, 7, 64

Mischief Reef: artificial island and military base construction on, 19, 49, 52, 60, 63, 65, 78, 111, 112, 156–57; ASEAN response to claim about, 132–33; challenge to construction activities in, 31; China occupation of, 11, 19, 49, 50, 78, 79, 133, 151–52; incident between naval vessels at, 79; natural state of, 50, 51; Philippines claim to and EEZ, 11, 19, 95; U.S. defense of, 11, 20, 23

missiles: antiaircraft missiles, 24; antiship missiles, 56, 64, 65, 82–83; surface-to-air missiles, 65, 74, 83; U.S. compared to China hardware, 18; U.S. missile defense in Asia, criticism of, 264

Modernization Theory and spread of democracy, 3, 32n5

Mongolia, 231, 234, 244n59

multilateral negotiations and relationships, 29, 78, 80, 123–24, 127–28, 140–41, 185

Myanmar, 91, 97, 138, 188–89, 214–15, 303

national security: active defense policy, 23, 53; China national security and domestic policy, 294; First Island Chain defense and naval blockades, 16; historic rights claim and, 53–54, 67; Japan defense policy, 189, 199; maritime security capabilities of Asia-Pacific countries, assistance in building, 182–83, 189; maritime security threats, 195n55; PLAN mission of, 53–54; U.S. as threat to China, 43, 77, 304–5

Natuna Island: EEZ dispute with China, 18, 110–11, 291; EEZ overlap with nine-dash line, 14, 64, 135–36, 289; energy and fishing resources in waters near, 291; fishing dispute with China, 64, 86, 88, 110–11, 135–36; Indonesian sovereignty over, 291; naval exercises with U.S. near, 188

naval power: military modernization to increase, 23; power projection by China, 8, 62–65, 76, 82–84, 114, 258; support of South China Sea and East China Sea claims with, 23

navigational freedom. *See* freedom of navigation (FoN)/freedom of overflight

Navy, U.S.: Asia-Pacific presence of, 43, 65, 75, 92–93, 98, 133–35, 177, 181–83, 299, 301, 304–5; brinksmanship strategy against, 25; challenges of U.S. fleet from PLAN, 113; dominance and superiority of, 301; exercises with Indonesia, 188; expansion of, 30; Japan exercises with, 182, 189, 208; joint U.S.-Japan patrols in South China Sea, 207–8; Malaysia exercise with, 214; Malaysia presence of, 134–35; mission to maintain freedom of navigation and overflight, 62, 277, 296; Singapore presence of, 30, 182; South China Sea facilities for, 56; stationing of in Japan, 208; strength and capabilities of, 79–80, 301; threats to from artificial islands facilities, 65

near-seas active defense, 53

New Security Concept, 80

nine-dash line. *See* U-shaped line/nine-dash line

North Korea, 3, 4, 9, 13, 153

nuclear weapons proliferation and deterrence, 18, 53, 56, 67, 153, 293

Obama administration and Barack Obama: China expansionist territorial claims activities during, 19, 20–23; continuance of policy of, 163–64; as "first Pacific President," 174; foreign policy of, 176–77, 178–80, 192n10; PCA ruling response by, 158–59; Philippines defense commitment of, 11, 12, 133; spheres of influence negotiations with, 264–65. *See also* Pivot to Asia policy/rebalancing strategy

ocean defense, building wall for, 42

oil and natural gas: China claim to and control of reserves, 57–59, 76–77; China consumption of, 59; China import of, 55, 77, 200; civilian vessels to enforce resource claims, 63, 293; development by countries adjacent to U-shaped line, 5–6, 32–33n6; intimidation over and interference with claims, 5, 29, 58, 86; Japan import of, 200; joint development activities, 5–6, 10, 12, 27–29, 32–33n6, 39n117, 39n120, 49; joint hydrocarbon exploration agreement, 28, 39n120, 58; oil rig incidents and Vietnam EEZ, 60, 63, 85, 109, 119n19, 131–32, 178, 203, 212, 213, 215, 293; reserves in South China Sea, 14–16, 58–59, 289; royalties and compensation for rights to develop in disputed areas, 5–6, 28, 32–33n6; sovereignty claims and government support of facilities, 61; Spratly Islands resources, 49, 292; strategic hydrocarbon reserve, 16; Triton Island drilling operations, 63, 85, 131–32, 178, 212, 293; Vietnam-India oil exploration, 224, 231, 232, 237–38, 238n3, 303; Vietnam-Russia oil exploration, 250, 258, 260–61, 262; violent clashes during exploration activities, 109, 119n19

One Belt, One Road project. *See* Belt and Road Initiative

Pacific Ocean: China control of access to, 17; India relations with island nations in, 229–30; naval operations in, 106, 299; Russia presence and influence in, 303

Paracel Islands: artificial islands and military base construction in, 24, 56, 74; China claim to, 14, 18, 45–46, 149–50, 178; China claim to with straight baseline around, 89, 102–3nn43–44; China seizure and occupation of, 149, 292; Chinese name for, 14; civilian vessels to enforce resource claims, 63, 293; dispute between Vietnam and China over, 292, 293; EEZ dispute with China, 18; fishing dispute with China, 87; FoN operations in, 94; interference and intimidation over claims, 87–88; landing on as refuge from storm, prevention of, 86; oil drilling near Triton Island, 63, 85, 131–32, 178, 212, 293; Taiwan claim to, 178; U-shaped line and claim to, 14; Vietnam claim to, 48, 49, 87, 149–50, 178, 291, 292

peaceful development/peaceful environment for development, 75–76, 95, 107, 111, 115–17

peaceful rise, 75–76, 299

peeling the cabbage, 24

People's Liberation Army (PLA): modernization of, 83–85, 111; national interests, mission of support in maintaining, 76–77, 83, 100nn10–11; new historic missions of, 76–77, 83, 101n23, 107–11; power projection by, 82–86, 101n23; strength and capabilities of, 82–86, 152–54; U.S. agreements with, 26; U.S. security agreement with, 81–82; world peace and development, role in, 83

People's Liberation Army Air Force (PLAAF): artificial islands facilities to support, 24, 41, 52, 62–65, 293; modernization of, 84; strength and capabilities of, 79–80, 101n16, 149

People's Liberation Army Navy (PLAN): active operations of and combat-ready posture of, 108; artificial islands facilities to support, 24, 41, 52, 62–65, 112, 157, 293; challenges of U.S. fleet from, 113; economic stability mission of, 53–54; expansion of, 60, 154, 299; foreign ports for, 116, 120n50, 298–99; as global navy, 154; great sea power ambitions of, 227, 241n27, 241–42n29; maritime security mission of, 83–84; maritime sovereignty campaign, 107–11; modernization of, 8, 23, 33n14, 60, 83–84, 294, 301; national security mission of, 53–54; piracy and anti-piracy operations, 8, 154; power projection by, 8, 62–65, 76, 82–84, 114, 258; strength and capabilities of, 80, 81–82, 83–84, 114, 149, 150, 154, 299, 301

People's Liberation Army Rocket Force (PLARF), 84

People's Republic of China. *See* China (People's Republic of China, PRC)

Permanent Court of Arbitration (PCA): artificial islands as territory, ruling on, 24; jurisdiction of, questions about, 15–16, 34–35n36, 117; Philippines case and ruling, 2, 15–16, 18, 34–35n36, 89–90, 111–12, 137–40, 156, 157–59, 210–11, 216, 302; response of China to ruling, 2, 15–16, 18, 34–35n36, 89–90, 94–95, 111–12, 138–39, 157–59, 178, 302; sovereignty claims and support for jurisdiction of, 97; tensions generated by filing claim and ruling, 108–9, 202, 297

Philippines: abandonment of by U.S., perception of, 20, 23, 31; ASEAN response to claims by, 132–33; assertive moves and harassment tactics against, 122–23, 155–56; central role in conflict, 3; China relations with, 23, 30, 79, 85, 93, 96, 139–40, 157, 185–86, 196nn65–66, 216, 302; continental shelf extension and sovereignty claims, 155; development aid from China, 12; dispute with China over land features and maritime boundaries, 291; EDCA with U.S., 11, 85, 92–93, 96, 133, 139, 182, 195n50; eviction of U.S. from bases in, 5; fishing claim disputes, 81, 113–14; India relations with, 229; interference with oil exploration activities, 29, 86; intimidation over resources claims, 5; island development and land reclamation by, 50; Japan relations with, 196n68, 209–11, 216; joint development activities and relinquishing sovereignty by, 29; joint hydrocarbon exploration agreement, 28, 39n120, 58; joint oil and gas development with China, 12, 27–29, 49; maritime reconnaissance operations of, 112–13; maritime security capabilities of, assistance in building, 183, 189; media and social control in, 18; military assistance and training from U.S. and Japan for, 11, 12, 183, 189; military facilities and capabilities of, 63, 64, 85, 112–13; military spending by, 7, 82; oil exploration and development by, 58, 86; PCA case and ruling in favor of, 2, 15–16, 18, 34–35n36, 89–90, 111–12, 137–40, 156, 157–59, 210–11, 216, 302; rebalancing strategy, response to, 183, 185–87; resupply of LST, interference with, 109, 156; ship purchases from U.S., 11; South China Sea claims by, 1, 14, 177–78, 289, 292, 305; sovereignty claims and support for PCA jurisdiction, 97; Spratly Islands claim and activity, 21, 41, 47–48, 49, 50, 66, 75, 157, 291, 292–93; Taiwan relations with, 10; threats to from artificial islands facilities, 65; trade with China, 91; U.S. alliance and relations with, 10–12, 23, 30, 93, 96, 123, 133, 137, 139, 141, 157, 185–87, 305; U.S. defense treaty with and defense of, 10–11, 20–21, 23, 175–76, 185, 186, 305; U.S. military facilities and forces in, 11, 30, 56, 75, 82, 85, 92–93, 96, 123, 133, 182, 186, 195n50; Vietnam security cooeration with, 88. *See also* Mischief Reef; Scarborough Shoal

piracy and anti-piracy operations, 8, 154

Pivot to Asia policy/rebalancing strategy: alliances and security in region, strengthening of, 13, 30, 92–93, 131, 154; announcement of, 13, 92, 154, 174; background to, 175–77; components and objectives of, 13, 29–30, 153–54, 174; criticism of name of, 191n3; diplomatic component, 174, 178–80; economic component, 13, 30, 174, 180–81; fragmented nature of, 174; future of, 190–91, 301; as grand strategy, 301; legacy of, 190–91; maritime and territorial disputes and, 177–78; military component, 30, 174, 175–76, 177, 181–83; military presence in region, 13, 30, 92–93, 98, 207–8; reactions to, 30, 183–90, 195–96n57, 196n61; status quo protection without provoking China, 154, 174, 183, 190, 199, 207–8, 301; success of, 190; Trans-Pacific Partnership, 13, 30, 177, 180–81, 187, 194n40, 266; weakness of, 30

policy relationship to strategy, 147

power countries. *See* great powers/power countries

Putin, Vladimir, 251, 252–53, 303

the Quad, 233–34

rebalancing strategy. *See* Pivot to Asia policy/rebalancing strategy

Reed Bank, 12, 29, 57, 58, 66, 86

reefs, 24

Republic of China. *See* Taiwan (Republic of China, ROC)

resources/natural resources: China claim to and control of, 5, 8, 47, 56–59, 67, 76–77, 88–90, 102–3nn43–44, 297; intimidation over and interference with claims, 5; national entitlement and claims on, 13–14, 54, 57, 297; South China Sea supplies, 16, 289; Spratly Islands resources, claims to, 47–48; Vietnam claim to, 5

Rim of the Pacific (RIMPAC) exercise, 26, 154, 168

rocks vs. islands, 290

Russel, Daniel R., 20–21, 24, 25

Russia: ambitions of and regional realities, 249, 265–66; Arctic interests and campaign of, 248, 258–60, 265; arms and military systems exports, 85–86, 110, 151, 250–51, 261–62; ASEAN engagement with, 257–60, 265–66; Asia-Pacific interests of, 248–49, 265–66, 266n2, 303–4; Asia-Pacific security role of, 248, 252, 254–58, 260, 265–66, 268n29; as benign oligarchy, 253; China relations with, 260, 262–66, 303–4; China territorial claims, position on, 254–55; Crimea annexation, U.S. response to, 23; economic goals in Asia-Pacific region, 304; economy of, 253; exploitation of peaceful countries and power and strength of, 4; foreign policy of, 304; great power/global power–status of, 251–54, 266, 267n23; hedging strategy against China, 260; importance of Asia-Pacific region to, 248–49; importance of, persuading other countries of, 249, 252–53; investment and trade opportunities with, 250, 253; Japan relations with, 255; joint position on Asia security, offer for, 260; Malaysia relations with, 257; military facilities in Vietnam, 304; military policy of, 251; military spending by, 6, 7; multipolarity and recognition by Southeast Asia states, 253–54; naval exercises in South China Sea, 262; objectives in Asia-Pacific region, 249–57; oil exploration with Vietnam, 250, 258, 260–61, 262; orientation of toward Europe, 248, 303; power projection by in South China Sea, 248–49; strategic interests of, 303–4; U.S. decline, speculation about and joy in, 254; U.S. defense spending to restrain power and influence of, 4–5; U.S.-Russia foreign aid competition, 12; Vietnam assistance from and relations with, 187, 260, 303–4; Vietnam military facilities for, 251, 260–61, 264–65, 304; Vietnam strategic partnership with, 260–62; weapons purchases by China from, 150–51

salami-slicing, 24, 94

Scarborough Shoal: artificial island and military base construction on, danger of, 56, 157, 305; ASEAN response to claim about,

133; bastion strategy and control of, 56; Cambodia role in preventing discussion of China occupation of, 87, 125–26, 133, 138; challenge to construction activities in, 31; China claim to, 14, 56, 87; China seizure and occupation of, 11, 19, 37n83, 108, 125, 133, 144n35, 293; dispute between Philippines and China over, 11, 61–62, 107–9, 178, 208, 292–93, 295–96; fishing access to, 12, 139–40; fishing dispute with China, 86–87, 95, 108, 155–56; interference and intimidation over claims, 87–88; ITLOS ruling on dispute over, 61–62, 295–96; joint oil and gas development and claims to, 12; name change of, 37n83, 118n6; Philippines claim to and EEZ, 11, 61–62, 133, 144n35, 292–93, 295–96; standoff between China and Philippines over, resolution of, 37n83; U.S. defense of, 20–21, 23; U.S. military response to activities in, 20; U.S. treaty for defense of, 11; U-shaped line and claim to, 14; war over U.S. and Philippines retaking of, 20
sea lines of communication (SLOC): China control of, 8, 17, 47, 53, 54, 67, 76, 297; economic importance to access to, 17, 54–55; importance of to Japan, 200, 207, 302; importance of to Taiwan, 10; overseas interests of China, 23; strategic importance of, 279. *See also* freedom of navigation (FoN)/freedom of overflight
Second Island Chain, 19, 296
Second Thomas Shoal, 21, 87, 95, 108–9, 152, 156, 164
Senkaku Islands: China claim to, 9, 10, 18, 54, 299; China military activity near, 21; Japan control of, 9, 10, 299; purchase of by Japan, 201; sovereignty dispute over, 106, 201–2, 203, 299; U.S.-Japan alliance and defense of, 186
Sierra Madre (Philippines), 108, 109, 152, 156
Silk Road Economic Belt, 226
Singapore: autonomy of, 96–97, 188; EU trade with, 273, 275; India relations with, 229, 232–33; rebalancing strategy, response to, 183, 188; sovereignty claims and support for PCA jurisdiction, 97; trade with China, 90–91; U.S. naval presence in, 30, 56, 75, 182; U.S. relations with, 305
South China Sea: ADIZ over, 116, 229, 299, 305; China control of and influence in, 5, 122–23, 182–83, 195n55, 294, 296; China control of seas within the island chains, 16, 296; China tactics in, 77–82; as core interest, 76, 100nn10–11; disputes with China over land features and maritime boundaries in, 291–93, 305; environmental and physical characteristics of, 289; escalation of disputes over land features and maritime boundaries in, 155–59, 304–5; global nature of conflict in, 3; historical narrative and imagined history of China claim to, 44–45, 53–54, 66–67, 115–16, 178; importance and symbolism of to claimant countries, 1; major power struggle as crux of conflict in, 2; maps of, 44, 46, 47, 290; names of islands and islets in, 46, 47; naval power to support claims in, 23; offensive territorial actions in, 5; peaceful and cooperative resolution of disputes, 100n11, 116–17, 127, 155, 158–59, 168, 216, 276–77, 283–84, 293, 305; spheres of influence in, 264–65; strategic value of, 181; tensions in over China sovereignty claims, 200–201, 208; U.S. control and presence in, importance of, 294; U.S. objectives in, 159–62; zero-sum contest in, 225. *See also* maritime and territorial rights and sovereignty
South Korea: China relations with, 80; China trade with, 9; EU relations with, 279, 281–82, 284; EU trade with, 273, 275, 279; gas shipments through region, 279; influence in South China Sea dispute, 9; Japan relations with, 9; military spending by, 7, 9, 111; North Korea relations with, 9; rebalancing strategy, response to, 183; response to China expansionist territorial claims, 19–20; SLOC and economy of, 17; U.S. defense treaty with, 175–76, 305; U.S. relations with, 8, 9, 30
Southeast Asia Maritime Security Initiative, 183
Southeast Asia Treaty Organization, 8
spheres of influence, 264–65
Spratly Islands: amount of land reclamation in, 24, 75, 94, 157; artificial islands construction in, 24, 41–42, 49–53, 74, 106, 156–57, 168, 171n57, 178, 293, 295; China claim to, 14, 18, 22, 44, 89, 150, 151–52, 292–93; China occupation and development of, 48–50, 66; dispute between Philippines and China over, 11; EEZ dispute with China, 18; fishing claim disputes, 81, 113–14; FoN operations in, 93–94, 183; French annexation and occupation of, 45–46, 47; impact of militarization of, 112–13; ITLOS ruling on EEZ claim, 295; Japan occupation of, 47; joint oil and gas development and claims to, 12; land features in and geography of, 292–93;

Malaysia claim to and activity on, 21, 41, 48, 49, 66, 75, 291; military aspects and importance of, 55–56, 293; military facilities built on artificial islands in, 19, 22, 24, 52–53, 56, 63, 65, 78, 111–14, 157, 168, 178, 293, 305; oil and gas resources and development, 49; Philippines claim to and activity on, 21, 41, 47–48, 49, 50, 66, 75, 157, 291, 292–93; resources in, claim of rights to, 47–48; satellite imagery of artificial islands in, 30–31, 41–42, 52, 63, 74, 111; Taiwan claim to and activity on, 21, 47, 50, 75; U.S. response to China expansion in, 159; U-shaped line and claim to, 14; Vietnam claim to and activity on, 21, 41, 48, 49, 50, 66, 75, 87, 150, 157, 291, 292–93; violent clashes with China in, 48

strategy: definition of, 147; EU global strategy, 279–80; policy relationship to, 147; regional strategy of China, 56–59, 75–77, 98–99, 185, 297; strategic encirclement strategy in Indian Ocean, 226–27, 239–40nn16–17; tactics-strategy mismatch, 77, 98–99; U.S. South China Sea strategy, 29–32. *See also* diplomacy and diplomatic strategies; grand strategy; military activity and strategies

Subi Reef, 49, 50, 51, 52, 63, 65, 88, 93–94, 111, 112, 156–57

submarines: ballistic missile submarines, 18, 54, 298–99; Indian Ocean operations, 299; *Jin*-class ballistic missile submarines, 56, 293, 299; modernization of China fleet, 84; Pacific Ocean operations, 299; Vietnam fleet, 85–86, 110, 261

Sunnylands Declaration, 88

Taiwan (Republic of China, ROC): abandonment of by U.S., perception of, 31; China claim to, 18, 53–54, 55–56; China relations with, 10, 187, 197n78; continental shelf extension and sovereignty claims, 155; as core interest, 19, 76, 107; dash line relationship to, 290; EU trade with, 273, 275; FoN and trade access by, 17; freedom of navigation of, 10; island development and land reclamation by, 50; joint oil and gas development with China, 27–28; military spending by, 7, 111; Philippines relations with, 10; rebalancing strategy, response to, 183, 187; reunification with mainland, 53, 107, 147; security in and strength of navies, 301; self-defense capabilities of, 10; SLOC and economy of, 17; South China Sea claims by, 1, 10, 32n2, 177–78, 289, 291, 292, 305; sovereignty and independent status of, 32n2; Spratly Islands claim and activity, 21, 47, 50, 75; suppression of democracy, human rights, and international law in by China, 5; suppression of independence movement in, 8; U.S. defense and support relations, 8, 10, 55–56, 148–49, 187

Taiwan Relations Act, 10, 162, 305
Taiwan Strait crisis, 10, 78, 305
Take and Talk strategy, 27
ten-dash line, 290, 291
territorial sea, delineation of according to UNCLOS, 290–91
terrorism, 3–5, 18
Thailand: autonomy of, 96–97; China aid to, 81; China relations with, 30, 97, 125, 129, 137, 138, 188, 215, 299; EU trade with, 273, 275; India relations with, 229; Japan relations with, 214–15; rebalancing strategy, response to, 183, 188; trade with China, 90–91, 299; U.S. alliance and relations with, 30, 175–76, 188
Third Island Chain, 19
Tiananmen Square massacre, 5, 12, 80, 150
Tibet, 19, 76, 100n10, 107
Tonkin, Gulf of (Beibu Gulf), 149, 290, 292
trade and commerce: arrest of Chinese fishermen and China-Japan trade, 201–2, 216, 302; ASEAN relations with China, 81, 90–91, 299; China imports and exports, 55, 90–91; China-U.S. trade and economic relations, 12–13, 81, 151, 175–76, 180–81; EU trade relationships, 273, 275, 277–80, 284; FoN and regional access to, 17; global commerce through South China Sea, 289; India dependence on sea trade, 231–32; Japan energy security and, 200; military modernization to support, 8; rebalancing strategy and, 13, 30, 177, 180–81, 194n40; regional economies and SLOC, 17, 54–55; regional trade relations, 90–91; Russia investment and trade opportunities, 250, 253; South China Sea strategic importance to, 1, 54–55, 199–200, 207; trade follows the flag and flag follows trade, 19; Trans-Pacific Partnership, 13, 30, 177, 180–81, 187, 194n40, 266; transportation-related value of South China Sea, 16–17. *See also* sea lines of communication (SLOC)
Trans-Pacific Partnership, 13, 30, 177, 180–81, 187, 194n40, 266
Treaty of Amity and Cooperation, 116–17, 123, 124–25, 179, 193–94n32
trilateral relationships, 213–14, 234

Triton Island drilling operations, 63, 85, 131–32, 178, 212, 293
Trump administration and Donald Trump: Asia-Pacific policy of, 13, 29, 174, 190–91, 191n4, 301; China relations with, 13; grand strategy of, 191n4; Navy expansion under, 30; Philippines relations with, 12; South China Sea policy of, 20, 168; TPP withdrawal by, 194n40

Ukraine, 31, 257
United Kingdom, 34–35n36, 204, 274, 277, 278, 280, 282–83, 304
United Nations Commission on the Limits of the Continental Shelf (CLCS), 78, 86, 89, 95, 102n43, 103n50, 155
United Nations Convention on the Law of the Sea (UNCLOS): ASEAN commitment to, 126; changes to definitions and privileges of land features, 294; China ratification and appended rights and exclusions, 78, 291, 305n3; definition and recognition of land features by, 24, 290, 294, 297; effective date for, 290; exceptions to boundary delimitations, bays, and titles, 34–35n36; geography and South China Sea disputes, 290–91; historic rights claims, 90, 291, 305n3; ITLOS ruling on islands in South China Sea, 61–62, 295–96, 305; Japan support for, 200–201; jurisdiction of, 137–38; jurisdiction of, questions about, 14, 36n54; navigation freedom under, applicability of, 296; negotiation of, 290; resolution of maritime disputes under, 61–62, 179–80, 200–201, 283–84, 295–96; signing and ratification of, 290, 296; U.S. as nonsignatory, 36n54, 194n33, 290, 305; U.S. signing and ratification of, benefits of, 305; zones for land features granted by, 290–91, 294
United States (U.S.): Asia-Pacific interests and alliances of, 8–13, 22–23, 30, 65, 91–94, 106, 140–41, 159, 162, 294, 299, 305; Asia-Pacific position, weakening of, 255–56; asymmetric threats against, 4; brinksmanship strategy against, 25; brinksmanship strategy of, 26–27; China-U.S. trade and economic relations, 12–13, 81, 151, 175–76, 180–81; decline of, speculation about and joy in, 254; defense treaties with Asia-Pacific countries, 9, 10, 175–76, 182, 186, 305; democratization and global human rights support by, 4; economic effects of sanctions against China, 97–98; forward-deployed position of, 4–5, 208;

global influence of and failure to challenge China expansionist activities, 31; military advantage of and decline in advantage, 18, 26, 83, 94, 95; military spending by, 3–8, 176–77, 192n14, 207–8, 280; response to China expansionist territorial claims, 18–23, 37n83, 77, 106; Russia-U.S. foreign aid competition, 12; South China Sea objectives of, 159–62; South China Sea policy of, 296; trade relations with ASEAN countries, 90; trilateral process, U.S.-Japan-Vietnam, 213–14; UNCLOS nonsignatory status of, 36n54, 290, 305; weakness of, global perception of, 23, 31. *See also* Pivot to Asia policy/rebalancing strategy
U-shaped line/nine-dash line: changes to over time, 44, 149, 289–90; coordinates/location of, 290, 294; EEZ disputes and, 88–90, 102–3nn43–44, 111–12, 224, 302; eleven-dash line, 14, 290; FoN and sovereignty claims of, 10; historic rights claims and, 13–14, 44, 47, 53–54, 57, 78, 89–90, 103n50, 137–40, 295; history of inclusion of on maps, 44, 47, 148, 290; illegality of, 89–90; incrementalism and control over area within, 24; joint development activities and relinquishing sovereignty, 29; maritime rights based on, 21, 88–90, 102–3nn43–44, 177–78, 179–80; meaning and purpose of, 47, 89, 290, 294; military facilities for defense of claim, 63; Natuna Island EEZ overlap with, 14, 64, 135–36, 289; oil and gas development by countries claims adjacent to, 5–6, 32–33n6; passport display of, 15, 135; PCA ruling on, 90, 216; sovereignty over all features within, 57; Taiwan South China Sea claim based on, 10; ten-dash line, 290, 291; U.S. position on, 179–80

Vanguard Bank, 57–58, 66
vessels: civilian vessels and navigational freedom, 296; civilian vessels to enforce resource claims, 63, 293; freedom of navigation for naval and civilian vessels, 304–5; navigation freedom, UNCLOS and international law related to, 296; Philippines ship purchases from U.S., 11
Vietnam: anti-China sentiments in, 178, 213; arms and military systems purchases from Russia, 85–86, 110, 250, 251, 261–62; arms embargo against, end to, 93, 132, 186, 213; ASEAN response to claims by, 131–32; assertive moves and harassment

tactics against, 122–23, 155; central role in conflict, 3; China relations with, 99, 185–87, 215, 303–4; comprehensive partnership with U.S., 186, 196–97n70; continental shelf extension and sovereignty claim, 86, 89, 102n43, 103n50, 155; dispute with China over land features and maritime boundaries, 291, 292; economic effects of sanctions against China, 97–98; EU trade with, 273, 275; FoN and trade access by, 17; historic rights claim by, 291; hydrocarbon exploration interference and cutting seismic cables, 29, 85, 86, 155; India relations with, 185, 187, 189–90, 229, 236–38, 303; intimidation over resources claims, 5; island development and land reclamation by, 50; Japan destroyer visit to port in, 189; Japan relations and security ties with, 132, 141, 185, 187, 212–15, 216; joint development activities and relinquishing sovereignty by, 29; joint hydrocarbon exploration agreement, 28, 39n120, 58; joint oil and gas development with China, 27–29; maritime security capabilities of, assistance in building, 183, 189; media and social control in, 18; military facilities and capabilities of, 63, 64, 66, 85–86, 93, 110; military spending by, 7, 64; oil exploration and development by, 49, 57–58, 86; oil exploration with India, 224, 231, 232, 237–38, 238n3, 303; oil exploration with Russia, 250, 258, 260–61, 262; oil rig incidents and EEZ of, 60, 63, 85, 109, 119n19, 131–32, 178, 203, 212, 213, 215, 293; Philippines security cooperation with, 88; rebalancing strategy, response to, 183, 185–87; resources claims of, 5; Russia assistance for and relations with, 187, 260, 303–4; Russia military facilities in, 251, 260–61, 264–65, 304; Russia strategic partnership with, 260–62; South China Sea claims by, 1, 14, 177–78, 289, 292, 305; sovereignty claims and support for PCA jurisdiction, 97; Spratly Islands claim and activity, 21, 41, 48, 50, 66, 75, 87, 157, 291, 292–93; trade with China, 90–91; trilateral process, U.S.-Japan-Vietnam, 213–14; U.S. relations and security ties with, 75, 93–94, 96, 123, 130–31, 132, 137, 141, 162, 185–87, 213–14, 264–65, 266, 305; violent clashes with China over claims, 48, 60, 85, 109, 119n19, 150, 213, 292, 293. *See also* Paracel Islands

war: armed conflict, incidents that might provoke, 304–5; artificial islands advantages during, 64–65; brinksmanship strategy, 2, 24, 25–27; global role for U.S.-Japan alliance, 206–7; regional countries, war with, 20; shooting war with U.S., last thing China wants, 20. *See also* military activity and strategies
wei qi (encirclement game), 226, 231, 239n13
win-win solutions, 5, 10, 27–29, 225
Woody Island, 24, 48, 74, 87, 148, 149, 157
World Trade Organization, 81, 151

Xi Jinping: artificial islands construction and policies of, 59–60, 158; centralization of power under, 14; China Dream doctrine, 106, 107, 111, 294; Communist Party role of, 59, 294; diplomatic meeting with Abe, 203; domestic concerns as priority of, 294; duplicity of, 97; foreign policy of, 227, 294; global power–status of China, 116, 299; historic rights claim over territory and resources, 57, 178; joint oil and gas development as win-win solution, 5, 10, 27; joint position on Asia security, offer to Russia for, 260; Maritime Silk Road initiative, 137, 226, 241–42n29; nationalism policies of, 13, 42–43; peaceful development and intentions of, 111, 115–17; power of, 294; sovereignty claims and U-shaped line, 15
Xinjiang, 19, 76, 107, 149, 240n17

The Naval Institute Press is the book-publishing arm of the U.S. Naval Institute, a private, nonprofit, membership society for sea service professionals and others who share an interest in naval and maritime affairs. Established in 1873 at the U.S. Naval Academy in Annapolis, Maryland, where its offices remain today, the Naval Institute has members worldwide.

Members of the Naval Institute support the education programs of the society and receive the influential monthly magazine *Proceedings* or the colorful bimonthly magazine *Naval History* and discounts on fine nautical prints and on ship and aircraft photos. They also have access to the transcripts of the Institute's Oral History Program and get discounted admission to any of the Institute-sponsored seminars offered around the country.

The Naval Institute's book-publishing program, begun in 1898 with basic guides to naval practices, has broadened its scope to include books of more general interest. Now the Naval Institute Press publishes about seventy titles each year, ranging from how-to books on boating and navigation to battle histories, biographies, ship and aircraft guides, and novels. Institute members receive significant discounts on the Press's more than eight hundred books in print.

Full-time students are eligible for special half-price membership rates. Life memberships are also available.

For a free catalog describing Naval Institute Press books currently available, and for further information about joining the U.S. Naval Institute, please write to:

> Member Services
> **U.S. NAVAL INSTITUTE**
> 291 Wood Road
> Annapolis, MD 21402-5034
> Telephone: (800) 233-8764
> Fax: (410) 571-1703
> Web address: www.usni.org